Medieval Europe

A SHORT HISTORY

About the
Author...

❧

¶ Warren Hollister is Professor of History at the University of California,
Santa Barbara. He is a Fellow of the Royal Historical Society, past Vice-
President for Teaching of the American Historical Association, former Presi-
dent of the Pacific Coast Conference on British Studies, and former Visiting
Research Fellow of Merton College, Oxford. The author of many books and
scholarly articles on medieval history, he has been honored with Guggenheim,
Fulbright, and N.E.H. Fellowships and has lectured at such universities as
Cambridge, Oxford, Ghent, Leyden, Utrecht, London, and Bologna. In 1970
he was the American Historical Association's representative in medieval
history to the Thirteenth International Congress of Historical Sciences,
Moscow, USSR. Among his other honors are the Triennial Book Prize of the
Conference on British Studies and the E. Harris Harbison Award for
Distinguished Teaching.

❧

Medieval Europe
A SHORT HISTORY

Fourth Edition

C. Warren Hollister

University of California
Santa Barbara

John Wiley & Sons

New York   Santa Barbara   Chichester
Brisbane   Toronto

Copyright © 1964, 1968, 1974, 1978, by John Wiley & Sons, Inc.

All rights reserved. Published simultaneously in Canada.

No part of this book may be reproduced by any means, nor transmitted, nor translated into a machine language without the written permission of the publisher.

Library of Congress Cataloging in Publication Data:

Hollister, Charles Warren.
  Medieval Europe.

  Includes bibliographies and index.
  1. Europe—History—476-1492.   I.   Title.
D117.H6   1978   940.1   77-19239
ISBN 0-471-01939-9

Printed in the United States of America

10 9 8 7 6 5 4 3 2 1

To My Parents

Preface

❡ The fourth edition of *Medieval Europe* retains the basic goals of the three earlier editions. It is designed to be used as a core book; it aspires to be lively, coherent, accurate, and relatively brief. The text has been reexamined word by word and revised throughout to incorporate new research and to achieve greater clarity.

New descriptive sections have been included on town life, the Jews, the landed noblemen and noblewomen, the peasantry, university life, and cathedral life. Recent research has prompted major revisions in my accounts of such topics as the Carolingian Empire, feudalism, English legal history, and the origins of Parliament—with minor revisions at countless other points. A section has been added on Italy in the centuries after Charlemagne. My treatments of St. Augustine and the south-Italian Normans have been largely rewritten, and sections throughout the book dealing with social and economic history have been expanded and revised to reflect recent scholarship. Finally, a number of added excerpts from original sources have been woven into the narrative at points where they seemed to me interesting and apt.

I am indebted to Professors Brian Tierney, Richard Dales, and Norman Cantor for their perceptive suggestions on various portions of the original edition and to more recent suggestions by teachers and students who have been using the book in their classes. I am also grateful to Sally Vaughn for reading the fourth edition typescript and spotting errors. In particular, I wish to thank Professor Donald W. Sutherland for his thorough and helpful critique of the third edition and for his generous comments about it.

C. Warren Hollister
Santa Barbara, California, 1978

Contents

Part 2
The High Middle Ages

Part 3
The Late Middle Ages

List of
Maps

༒

༒

Maps by Russell H. Lenz and John V. Morris

List of Illustrations

Medieval Europe
A SHORT HISTORY

INTRODUCTION

A centruy ago almost everyone deplored the Middle Ages. The era between A.D. 500 and 1500 was seen as a long, aimless detour in the march of human progress—a thousand years of poverty, superstition and gloom that divided the old golden age of the Roman Empire from the new golden age of the Italian Renaissance. During these thousand years, as a famous historian once said (in 1860), human consciousness "lay dreaming or half awake." Nothing much happened, nobody had an original idea, and ignorant priests controlled society. The Middle Ages were condemned as "a thousand years without a bath" by one well-scrubbed nineteenth-century writer, and to most others, they were simply "the Dark Ages." At length, sometime in the fifteenth century, the darkness is supposed to have lifted. Europe awakened, bathed, and began thinking and creating again. After a long medieval intermission, the march of progress resumed.

Historians today no longer believe in this Rip Van Winkle theory. Generations of research have shown that during the Middle Ages society was constantly changing, so much so that the Europe of 1300 was vastly different from the Europe of 600. Historians now realize that medieval Europe was tremendously creative. By the close of the Middle Ages—by about 1500—Europe's technology and political and economic organization had given her a decisive edge over all other civilizations of the earth. Columbus had discovered America; the Portugese had sailed around Africa to India; Europe had developed the cannon, the printing press, the mechanical clock, eyeglasses, distilled liquor, and numerous other ingredients of modern civilization.

During the "modern" centuries that followed, from about 1500 to 1945, European fleets, armies, and ideas spread across the globe and transformed it. Even today, independent non-European countries remain decisively committed to European ideas about science, medicine, economics, politics, and social justice. The legislative bodies that govern America, India, Japan, Israel, and many other non-European states are descendants of the parliaments and assemblies of medieval Europe. And the Communist systems of China, Russia, Cuba, and elsewhere are similarly based on Western European ideas, some of which can be traced back before the time of Karl Marx to the radical thought of various medieval writers. In 1381, for example, rebellious English peasants attacked the established social order with the slogan of a classless society: "When Adam delved and Eve span, who was then the gentleman?"

In short, anyone who wonders how Europe was able to transform the world, for good or ill, into the global civilization that envelops us today must look to the medieval centuries for an important part of the answer. For during the Middle Ages, Europe grew from an underdeveloped rural slum into a powerful, compelling civilization. It is this story that our book will tell.

Part 1

The Early Middle Ages

The genesis
of western
civilization

Chapter 1

ꝗ

Rome Becomes Christian

The "Golden Age" of Rome and its Transformation

❡ In the first and second centuries A.D., when Rome was at its height, its emperors ruled peacefully over an immense realm stretching from the Atlantic eastward to the Arabian Desert and from northern Britain southward to the Sahara. Not every emperor, of course, was a great statesman. Several were dull-witted and a couple were apparently mad. The first-century emperor Caligula used to have his favorite horse wined and dined at imperial banquets and made plans to raise the beast to the office of Roman consul. And the less said about the emperor Nero, the better. But many emperors were able and far-sighted, and even under the worst of them the imperial government continued to function effectively. Roman legions guarded the far-flung frontiers, paved roads tied the provinces to Rome, and Roman ships sailed the Mediterranean undisturbed by pirates or enemy fleets. Scattered across the empire were cities built in the classical Roman style with temples, public buildings, baths, schools, amphitheaters, and triumphal arches. Their ruins are still to be seen all around the Mediterranean and beyond—in Italy, France, Spain, England, North Africa, the Balkans, and the Near East—bearing witness even

ꝗ

now to the immense scope of Roman political authority and the tasteful uniformity of Roman architecture.

The culture of Rome's golden age, much of it derived from ancient Greece, captivated the historians of previous centuries. Never, they wrote, was the human race so happy as in the great days of the Empire.They viewed Rome's decline and fall as the supreme historical catastrophe—the triumph of barbarism and religion. But today historians are inclined to see the matter differently. Although Roman classical culture was impressive, it was also narrowly limited—shared only by the empire's upper-crust. And although all the inhabitants benefited from the Roman peace and reasonably efficient government, most of them remained impoverished. Women had no political rights; they were supposed to serve and obey their husbands at home. And a great many people of both sexes were enslaved. In all these respects, Roman civilization was neither worse nor significantly better than other civilizations of antiquity.

There came a time when the upper-crust culture of Roman classicism began giving way to styles and hopes that had long been percolating among the empire's masses. As these subterranean ideas rose to the surface, the elitist civilization of the first and second centuries was gradually transformed. Fundamental changes occurred in such areas as art, literature, imperial ceremonial, and political thought and organization. From the standpoint of future centuries, however, the most significant change of all was in religious attitudes.

The New Religious Mood

In the third and fourth centuries, while the empire was suffering from Germanic invasions and economic crises, the urban poor were turning more and more from the boisterous and unlikely gods of the traditional Olympic cult— Jupiter, Juno, Apollo, Minerva and the rest—to compelling new religions that offered release from individual guilt and the promise of personal salvation and eternal life. These new "mystery religions" were neither Roman nor Greek but came from the older, eastern cultures that Rome had absorbed into her empire. From Egypt came the cult of the goddess Isis, from Persia came the cult of the savior Mithras, from Asia Minor came the worship of the Great Earth Mother, and from Palestine came Christianity.

The gods and goddesses of Olympus survived for a time but in profoundly altered form. For during the third century, all that was vital in the pagan cults was incorporated into a new philosophical scheme called Neoplatonism (based loosely on the much earlier thought of the Greek philospher Plato). Neoplatonism was the creation of the third-century philosopher Plotinus, one of the most influential minds of the Roman imperial era. Plotinus taught the doctrine of one god, who was infinite, unknowable, and unapproachable, except through a mystical experience. This god was the ultimate source of all things, spiritual and physical. All existence was conceived of as a series of circles radiating outward from him, like concentric ripples in a pond, diminishing in excellence and significance as they grew more distant from their divine source. Human reason, which the Greeks had earlier exalted, was now reduced to impotence, for at the core of reality was a god that lay beyond reason's scope.

Despite their mystical doctrine of monotheism, Plotinus and his Neoplatonist followers allowed a place in their system for the countless deities of paganism. The pagan gods were interpreted as symbols of the true, Neoplatonic god—crude symbols, but useful nevertheless. The pagan cults, so radically unsuited to the deepening mood of otherworldliness, thus were given new life by the overarching structure of Neoplatonic philosophy. They were themselves brought into line with the trend toward mysticism and monotheism. The distinction between Jupiter and the new eastern deities was steadily blurring.

Christianity and the Empire

It was in this atmosphere of mysticism and the supernatural that Christianity won its final victories. It triumphed over its rivals partly because of the vivid, attractive character of Jesus himself (the rival "saviors" were altogether mythical), partly because of the potent concept of Hebrew monotheism on which Christianity was based, partly because it welcomed women and slaves, and partly because of Christianity's appealing ethical system of love, forgiveness, and service to others.

The Christians had suffered intermittent persecutions from the Roman authorities because of their refusal to honor the offical imperial deities. Their relationship to the empire changed dramatically in about A.D. 312 with the conversion of the emperor Constantine (306–337). Until then Christianity's chief appeal had been to the urban masses. They had found it easy to accept a savior who had worked as a carpenter, had surrounded himself with fishermen, ex-prostitutes, and similar riffraff, had been crucified by the Roman establishment, and had promised salvation to all who followed him—free or slave, man or woman. But in the years following Constantine's conversion, Christianity was taken up by the wealthy and powerful and was supported by a line of Christian Roman emperors.

The fourth century thus witnessed mass conversions to Christianity. From a vigorous, dedicated minority sect, it expanded into the dominant religion of the Mediterranean world. No longer persecuted and disreputable, it became offical, conventional, respectable. And, of course, it lost some of its former spiritual intensity in the process. Moreover, total victory was accompanied by a surge of internal dissention. Fourth-century Christianity was marked by bitter doctrinal struggles, and here, too, the Christian emperors played a commanding role. It was only through imperial suppression that the doctrine

Colossal Head of the Emperor Constantine.

known as Arianism—the most powerful of the fourth-century Christian heresies—lost its hold on the inhabitants of the empire. The Arians followed Christ's teachings but denied his full divinity. They constituted a potent force in the Church until the sternly orthodox emperor Theodosius I (378–395) condemned their teachings and broke their power, making orthodox Christianity the official religion of the Roman state. Indeed, Theodosius outlawed paganism as well, and the old gods of Rome, deprived of imperial sanction, gradually passed into memory.

By the close of the fourth century, orthodox Christianity dominated the empire, yet old heresies lingered on and vigorous new ones arose. And although Arianism was now prohibited in the empire, it survived among some of the Germanic tribes along the frontiers. These peoples had been converted by Arian missionaries around the middle of the fourth century, at a time when Arianism was still strong in the empire, and the persecutions of Emperor Theodosius I had no effect on the faith of Germanic tribes. Consequently, when in time these tribes poured into the Western Empire and established successor states upon its ruins, they found themselves divided from their Roman subjects not only by culture but by bitter religious antagonisms as well.

Christianity gained much from Constantine's conversion but also lost much. It was less fervent, less committed than before, and also less independent of imperial authority. The gratitude of Christians toward Constantine almost reached the point of adulation. He was regarded as a thirteenth Apostle, as the master of all churches, as a monarch whose office was commissioned by God. His regal presence dominated the great Ecumenical Council of Nicaea in 325, and it was at his bidding that the Council denounced Arianism. In the decades thereafter, the Arian-orthodox struggle swayed back and forth, following the shifting inclinations of the emperors. Sometimes the Arian leaders were forced into exile, sometimes the orthodox leaders were banished. When at last Arianism was condemned by Theodosius, good Catholics rejoiced. But they might well have been apprehensive of a situation in which such crucial matters of faith depended on the imperial will.

The Latin Doctors

Constantine's conversion was merely one event in the long, significant process of fusion between Christianity and Greco-Roman civilization. The process had been at work among early Christian writers who sought to present their faith in the intellectually respectable garb of Greek philosophy. These efforts culminated in the work of three Christian thinkers of the later fourth and early fifth centuries—St. Ambrose, St. Jerome, and St. Augustine—who came to be regarded as "Doctors of the Latin Church." Working at a time when the empire was swiftly becoming Christianized, yet before the intellectual vigor of classical antiquity had faded, they used their mastery of Greco-Roman thought to elucidate the Christian faith. Nearly seven centuries were to pass before Western Europe regained the intellectual level of late antiquity, and the writings of these three Latin Doctors, therefore, exerted a commanding influence on succeeding generations.

Although Ambrose, Jerome, and Augustine made their chief impact in the realm of thought, all three were immersed in the political and ecclesiastical affairs of their day. St. Ambrose (c. 340–397) was bishop of Milan, a great city of northern Italy that in the later fouth century replaced Rome as the imperial capital in the West. Ambrose was a superb administrator, a powerful orator, and a vigorous opponent of Arianism. Thoroughly grounded in the literary and philosophical traditions of Greco-Roman civilization, he enriched his Christian writings by drawing heavily from Plato, Cicero, Virgil, and other giants of the pagan past. And as one of the first champions of ecclesiastical independence from the authority of the empire, he stood at the source of the Church-state controversy that was to affect the medieval West so deeply in later generations. When Emperor Theodosius I massacred the rebellious inhabitants of Thessalonica, St. Ambrose excommunicated him from the church of Milan, forcing Theodosius to humble himself and beg forgiveness. The emperor's public repentance set a long-remembered precedent for the principle of ecclesiastical supremacy in matters of faith and morals.

St. Jerome (c. 340–420) was the most scholarly of the three Latin Doctors. A restless, troubled man, he wandered throughout the empire, living in Rome for a time, then fleeing the worldly city to found a monastery in Bethlehem. Jerome's monks devoted themselves to the copying of manuscripts, a task that was to be taken up by countless monks in centuries to come and which, in the long run, resulted in the preservation of important works of Greco-Roman antiquity that would otherwise have vanished. The modern world owes a great debt to Jerome and his successors for performing this essential labor.

St. Jerome himself was torn by doubts as to the propriety of a Christian immersing himself in the works of pagan literary giants such as Homer and Virgil, Horace and Cicero. He was terrified by a dream in which Jesus denied him salvation with the words, "You are a Ciceronian, not a Christian." For a time Jerome renounced all pagan writings, but he was much too devoted to the charms of classical literature to persevere. In the end he concluded that Greco-Roman letters might properly be used in the service of the Christian faith.

Jerome's supreme achievement lay in the field of scriptural commentary and translation. It was he who produced the definitive translation of the Bible from its original Hebrew and Greek into Latin—the language of the western Roman Empire and of medieval Western Europe. The result of Jerome's efforts was the Latin Vulgate Bible, which Catholics have used ever since. By preparing a trustworthy Latin version of the fundamental Christian text, he made a decisive contribution to Western Civilization.

St. Augustine of Hippo (354–430) was the towering intellect of his age. His achievements exceeded those of St. Ambrose, the ecclesiastical statesman, and St. Jerome, the scholar. For St. Augustine, too, was a statesman and a scholar, and he was a great philosopher as well. As bishop of Hippo, an important city in North Africa, he was deeply involved in the political-religious problems of his age, and his writings were produced in response to vital contemporary issues. In his *Confessions* he describes his own intellectual and moral journey along a twisting path from youthful hedonism to Christian orthodoxy. He writes in the hope that others, lost as he once was, might be led by God into the spiritual haven of the Church.

Augustine wrote voluminously against various pagan and heretical doctrines that threatened Christian orthodoxy in his age. In the course of these disputes he examined many of the central problems that have occupied theologians ever since—the nature of the Trinity, the existence of evil in a world created by a good and all-powerful God, the authority of the priesthood, the compatibility of free will and predestination. Out of his diverse writings there emerges a body of speculative thought that served as the intellectual foundation for medieval philosophy and theology.

Like so many of his contemporaries, Augustine worked toward the synthesis of classical and Christian thought, but more than any before him he succeeded in welding the two cultures into one. He was disturbed, as Jerome was, by the danger of pagan thought to the Christian soul. But, like Jerome, he concluded that although a good Christian ought not to *enjoy* pagan writings, he might properly *use* them for Christian ends. Accordingly, Augustine used the philosophy of Plato and the Neoplatonists as a basis for a new and thoroughly Christian philosophical scheme. It has been said that Augustine baptized Plato. As the thirteenth-century philosopher St. Thomas Aquinas observed, "Whenever Augustine, who was imbued with the philosophy of the Platonists, found in their teaching anything consistent with faith, he adopted it; those things which he found contrary to faith, he amended."

Plato's philosophy has been termed "idealism" because he taught that abstract ideas were more important than tangible things. He believed that we acquire true knowledge not by observing things and events in the world of nature but by reflecting on the fundamental ideas that underlie the physical universe, just as a mathematician operates in the abstract world of pure number. Elaborating on Plato, the Neoplatonists viewed God as the center and source of reality and saw the natural world as merely a dim reflection of its divine source—a faint outer ripple in the concentric circles of existence, scarcely worth considering.

Augustine used Christianity to reshape the insights of Plato and Plotinus. Like the Neoplatonists, he believed that the material world was less important—less real—than the spiritual world, but it was, nevertheless, the creation of a good and loving God who remained actively at work in it. God had created the first man and woman with the intention that they and all their descendants should attain salvation—should live forever in God's loving presence. But rather than creating mere human puppets, God gave humanity freedom to choose between good (accepting his love) and evil (rejecting it). As a consequence of Adam and Eve choosing wrongly, humanity fell from its original state of innocence, became incorrigibly self-centered, and thus severed its relationship with God. But God reknit the relationship by himself becoming man in the person of Jesus—suffering, dying, and rising again. The sin of the first man, Adam, was redeemed by the incarnation and crucifixion of the sinless God-man, Christ, and the possibility of human salvation was thereby restored.

Accordingly, the central goal of the Christian life is to attain the salvation that Christ has made possible. One can achieve this goal only by becoming a loving, unselfish person—loving God and loving others—and Augustine insisted that we are altogether powerless to overcome our self-centeredness, except through divine grace. He saw us as incapable of earning our own way into heaven, incapable of becoming loving persons, without God's help. This being so, nobody deserves salvation, yet some, nevertheless, achieve it because their moral characters are shaped and strengthened by God's grace.

The necessity of divine grace to human salvation is a central theme in the greatest of Augustine's works, the *City of God*. Here he set forth a comprehensive Christian philosophy of history that was both radically new and deeply influential. Rejecting the Greco-Roman notion that history repeats itself in endless meaningless cycles, he viewed it as a purposeful process of human-divine interaction beginning with the creation and continuing through Christ's incarnation to the end of the world. Augustine interpreted history not in economic or political terms but in moral terms. To him, the single determining force in history was human moral character; the single goal, human salvation. God was not interested in the fate of kingdoms or empires, except insofar as they affected the spiritual destiny of individuals. And individual salvation depended not on the victories of imperial legions but on the shaping of human moral character by divine grace. True history, therefore, had less to do with the struggles between states than with the war between good and evil that rages within each state and within each soul.

Augustine divided humanity into two oppposing groups: not Romans and barbarians as the pagan writers would have it, but those who live in God's grace and those who do not. The former are members of the "City of God," the latter belong to the "Earthly City." The two cities are hopelessly intertwined in this life, but their members will be separated at death by eternal salvation or damnation. Human history, therefore, has as its purpose the growth and welfare of the City of God.

The Romans had never excelled in the realm of speculative thought, but with St. Augustine, Latin philosophy came into its own at last. He was the western Empire's greatest philosopher and, indeed, one of the foremost minds in the history of Christianity. His theory of the two cities, although often simplified and reinterpreted in later generations, influenced western thought and politics for a thousand years. His Christian Platonism dominated medieval philosophy until the mid-twelfth century and remains a significant theme in religious thought to this day. His distinction between the ordained priesthood and the laity has always been basic to Catholic theology. And his emphasis on divine grace was to be a crucial source of inspiration to the Protestant leaders of the sixteenth century.

As a consequence of Augustine's work, together with that of his contemporaries, Ambrose and Jerome, Christian culture was firmly established on classical foundations. At Augustine's death in 430 the classical-Christian fusion was essentially complete. The strength of the Greco-Roman tradition that underlies medieval Christianity and Western Civilization owes much to the fact that these three Latin Doctors, and others like them, found it possible to be both Christians and Ciceronians.

Chapter 2

❧

The Waning of the Western Empire

"Decline and Fall"

In the year 330, a century before Augustine's death, Constantine founded a new, eastern imperial capital on a strategic waterway connecting the Black Sea with the Mediterranean. This city, a second Rome, was built in grand style on the site of a Greek town called Byzantium, which Constantine immodestly renamed Constantinople—"Constantine's City." When in later centuries the western half of the empire had fallen to Germanic invaders and the eastern half survived alone, Constantinople became Europe's greatest metropolis. The lands that its emperors ruled are commonly called the "Byzantine Empire," after old Byzantium.

Ever since the late third century, the Roman imperial office had been split from time to time between a western emperor and an eastern emperor, and by the end of the fourth century the split had become permanent. Thenceforth, although the Roman Empire continued to be regarded as a whole, one emperor ruled the eastern half from Constantinople, while another ruled the western half—no longer from Rome but from some more strategically situated capital, first Milan, then Ravenna.

This political split reflected a cultural and linguistic division of long stand-

❧

ing. The eastern half of the empire was predominantly Greek-speaking, the western half predominantly Latin-speaking. The eastern half—Greece, the Balkans, the eastern Mediterranean lands and Egypt—had been civilized far longer than the western lands of North Africa and Western Europe—far longer than Rome herself. And the eastern cities were larger, more numerous, and more commercially active than the newer cities of the West. Indeed, the western cities—including Rome—were chiefly military, administrative, and cultural centers rather than commercial hubs. Supported by taxes of the country folk, they were economic parasites, living off the labor and productivity of the agrarian regions around them. Thus, with the coming of large scale invasions by Germanic tribes in the fifth century, the Eastern Empire succeeded in weathering the storm, while the weaker Western Empire collapsed.

Many reasons have been proposed for Rome's decline and fall—reasons whose range encompasses sexual orgies, climatic changes, bad ecological habits, and Christianity. None of them make much sense. The Eastern Empire was more thoroughly Christianized than the Western, yet it survived for another thousand years. The most spectacular of the Roman orgies occurred in the pagan "golden age"; Christian conversion made them unstylish, and the invasions occurred long after the age of orgies had passed. More significant was the failure of the Roman economy to change or expand and the parasitical character of the western cities. Then, too, the fifth-century western emperors happened to be less competent, on the whole, than their eastern colleagues and more open to the hazardous policy of recruiting Germanic warriors into the Roman armies.

The riddle of Rome's "decline and fall" will probably never be completely solved, and even the question itself is misleading. For Rome did not literally fall. Instead, it underwent an immense strategic withdrawal from the newer, less productive West to the wealthy and long-civilized provinces of the eastern Mediterranean. The Roman tide receded and Western Europe was left high and dry.

Perhaps the fatal flaw in the western economy was its inability to compensate for the cessation of imperial expansion by more intensive internal development. There was no large-scale industry, no mass production; the majority of the population was far too poor to provide a mass market. Industrial production was inefficient and technology progressed at a snail's pace. The economy remained fundamentally agrarian, and farming techniques advanced very little during the centuries of the empire. The Roman plow was rudimentary; windmills were unknown and water mills rare. The horse could not be used as a draught animal because the Roman harness crossed the horse's windpipe and tended to strangle him under a heavy load. Consequently, Roman agriculture was based on the ox and on the muscles of slaves and peasants.

Economic exhaustion brought with it the twin evils of population decline and creeping poverty. And at the very time that the manpower shortage was becoming acute and impoverishment was paralyzing the middle classes, the army and bureaucracy were growing ever-larger and taxes were soaring. One result of these processes was the deurbanization of the West. By the fifth century the once vigorous cities were becoming ghosts of their former selves, drained of their wealth and much of their population. Only the small class of great landowners managed to prosper in the economic atmosphere of the late Western Empire, and these people now abandoned their town houses, withdrew from civic affairs, and retired to their estates where they often assembled sizeable private armies and defied the tax collector. The aristocracy, having now fled the city, would remain an agrarian class for the next thousand years. The rural elite of the Middle Ages had come into being.

The decline of the city was fatal to the urbanized administrative structure of the Western Empire. More than that, it brought an end to the urban-oriented culture of Greco-Roman antiquity. The civilization of Athens, Alexandria, and Rome could not survive in the fields. It is in the decay of urban society that we find the crucial connecting link between political collapse and cultural transformation. In a very real sense Greco-Roman culture was dead long before the final demise of the Western Empire; the deposition of the last Western emperor in 476 was merely the faint postscript to a process that had been completed long before. By then the cities were dying. The rational, humanist outlook had altogether collapsed. The army and even the civil government had become barbarized as the desperate emperors, faced with a growing shortage of manpower and resources, turned more and more to Germanic peoples to defend their frontiers and keep order in their state. In the end, Germans abounded in the army, entire tribes were hired to defend the frontiers, and Germanic military leaders came to hold positions of high authority in the Western Empire. Survival had actually come to depend on the success of Germanic defenders against Germanic invaders.

In another sense, however, Greco-Roman culture never died in the West. It exerted a profound influence, as we have seen, on the Doctors of the Latin Church and, through them, on the mind of the Middle Ages. It was the basis of repeated cultural revivals, great and small, down through the centuries—in the era of Charlemagne, in the High Middle Ages, in the Italian Renaissance, and in the neoclassical movements of the eighteenth and nineteenth centuries. And if in one sense the Roman state was dead long before the line of western emperors ended in 476, in another it survived long thereafter—in the ecclesiastical organization of the Roman Catholic Church and in the medieval Holy Roman Empire. Roman law endured to inspire western jurisprudence; the Latin tongue remained the language of educated Europeans for a thousand years and more, while evolving in the lower levels of society into the Romance languages: Italian, French, Spanish, Portuguese, and Rumanian. In countless forms, the rich legacy of classical antiquity was passed on to the Middle Ages. Europeans for centuries to come would be nourished by Greek thought and haunted by the memory of Rome.

The Germanic Peoples

The civilization of medieval Europe built creatively upon a synthesis of three cultures: Classical, Christian, and Germanic. The age of Ambrose, Jerome, and Augustine witnessed the virtual completion of the Classical-Christian synthesis, but the impact of Germanic culture had only begun to be felt. It was not until the eighth century or thereabouts that a fusion of Classical-Christian culture with Germanic culture was achieved, and only then can it be said that Western Civilization was born. The intervening era—the sixth and seventh centuries—provides a fascinating view of a new civilization in the process of formation. Throughout these turbulent years the Classical-Christian tradition was preserved and fostered by the Church while the Germanic tradition governed the political and social organization of the successor states that rose on the carcass of the Western Empire. The Germanic invaders soon became at least nominal Christians, but for centuries a cultural gulf remained between the Church with its Greco-Roman-Christian heritage, and the Germanic kingdoms with their primitive, war-oriented culture. The Church of the early Middle Ages was able to preserve ancient culture only in a debased form, for as time went on ecclesiastical leaders and aristocratic laymen came more and more to be drawn from the same social milieu. Still, it remained the great task of the early medieval Church to civilize and Christianize the Germanic peoples.

Most of the tribes that invaded the Western Empire seem to have come originally from the Scandinavian area, the homeland of the later Vikings. Gradually they migrated into central and southeastern Europe and began to press against the imperial frontiers. It is hazardous to make broad generalizations regarding their culture and institutions, for customs varied considerably from tribe to tribe. The Franks, the Angles, and the Saxons, for example, were agrarian peoples whose movements were slow, but who, once settled, were difficult to displace. Little influenced by Roman civilization they came into the empire as non-Christians. The Visigoths, Ostrogoths, and Vandals, on the other hand, were far more mobile. All three had absorbed Roman culture to some degree before they crossed the frontiers, and all had been converted in the fourth century to Arian Christianity. But such differences notwithstanding, the political and social structures of the various Germanic tribes disclose significant similarities.

A good contemporary account of early Germanic institutions is to be found in a short book entitled *Germania*, written by the Roman historian Tacitus in A.D. 98. This work is not altogether trustworthy; it is a morality piece written with the intention of criticizing the "degeneracy" of the Romans by comparing them unfavorably with the simple, upright Germans. Nevertheless, it is an invaluable source of information on early Germanic customs and institutions. We can accept Tacitus' description of the Germans as large, blue-eyed people with reddish-blond hair, living in simple villages. And he correctly points out that Germanic women enjoyed considerable independence and respect, at least by Roman standards. But Tacitus exaggerates when he praises the Germans for their chastity and generally virtuous behavior. For on the whole their vices seem to have been no less numerous than those of the Romans, but simply cruder. Their standards of personal hygiene are suggested by the observation of a fifth-century Roman gentleman: "Happy the nose that cannot smell a barbarian."*

Although the Germans used iron tools and weapons, their social and economic organization was in many ways reminiscent of late stone-age cultures. Their chief activities were tending crops or herds and fighting wars. Violence was common, not only between tribes but within them as well. When a man was killed, his kinsmen were bound to avenge his death by conducting a feud—declaring war, as it were—against the killer and his kinsmen. In the boisterous milieu of the tribe, killings were all too common, and in order to keep the social fabric from being torn apart by blood feuds, it became customary for the tribe to establish a *wergeld*, a sum of money that the killer might pay to the relatives of his victim to appease their vengeance. Wergelds varied in size depending on the victim's social status. And smaller payments were established for lesser injuries such as the cutting off of a victim's arm, leg, thumb, or finger, until in time every imaginable injury was covered, down to the little toe. There was no guarantee, however, that the man who did the killing or maiming would agree to make the payment, or that the victim or his kinsmen would agree to accept it. Despite all efforts to control them, blood feuds continued far into the Middle Ages.

Ties of kinship were strong among the early Germans, but they were rivaled by those of the war band or *comitatus*. Kinship played no part in this institution; it consisted rather of a group of warriors bound together by their loyalty to a chief or king. The comitatus was a kind of military brotherhood based on honor, fidelity, courage, and mutual respect between the leader and his men. In warfare the leader was expected to excel his men in courage and prowess, and should the leader be killed, his men were honor-bound to fight to the death even if their cause should appear hopeless. The heroic virtues of the comitatus persisted throughout the early Middle Ages as the characteristic ideology of the European warrior nobility.

The comitatus was a subdivision of a larger unit, the tribe, whose members were bound together by their allegiance to a chieftain or king and by their recognition of a common body of customary law. The laws of the Germanic tribes were primitive compared with those of the Roman Empire. Legal decisions often depended on whether the parties were able to adhere precisely to complex procedural formalities. Innocence or guilt was determined by requiring the accused to submit to a process known as the "ordeal." He might, for example, be required to grasp a bar of red-hot iron and carry it some specified distance, or take a stone from a boiling cauldron. If, after several days, his

* The author, some of whose best friends are Anglo-Saxon, disclaims any ethnic bias. The crudeness of the Germanic peoples was due to their lack of social and educational opportunities.

hand was healing properly, he was judged innocent. If his hand was infected, he was guilty. Similarly, he might be lowered by rope into a lake or pond. If he sank he was innocent; if he floated he was guilty; the pure waters would not "accept" a guilty man. Throughout the early Middle Ages it was chiefly these Germanic customs rather than the sophisticated concepts of Roman law that governed jurisprudence in Western Europe. Roman law persisted in fragmentary or bastardized form, but not until the twelfth century did it undergo a fundamental revival in the West. And even then its victory over Germanic law was gradual and incomplete.

Germanic law, crude though it was, made one crucial contribution to Western thought: implicit in the Germanic system was the concept that law arose from the immemorial customs of the people rather than from the will of the ruler. Since law transcended the royal authority, no king could be absolute. The rulers of the early Middle Ages often put the customs of their people into writing, but changed them only with great caution and in consultation with a council of nobles. The constitutional principle of government under the law did not emerge clearly for centuries to come, but when it did appear at last, in the High Middle Ages, it was rooted in the traditions of Europe's Germanic past.

The centuries just preceding the invasions witnessed the development of relatively stable royal dynasties among many of the Germanic tribes. Perhaps an unusually gifted warrior with a particularly large comitatus might start such a dynasty, but before many generations had gone by, the kings were claiming descent from some divine ancestor. When a king died, the assembly of the tribe chose as his successor the ablest member of his family. This might or might not be his eldest son, for the tribal assembly was given considerable latitude in its power to elect. The custom of election persisted in most Germanic kingdoms far into the Middle Ages. Its chief consequence during the fifth-century invasions was to ensure that the tribes were normally led by clever, battle-worthy kings or chieftains at a time when the Western Empire was ruled by weaklings and nincompoops.

Nineteenth-century historians made much of the fact that certain Germanic institutions seemed to contain the seeds of constitutionalism and popular sovereignty. Democracy, so it was said, had its genesis in the forests of Germany. It should be obvious, however, that the veneration of a customary "law of the folk" or the political prominence of a tribal assembly is not uniquely Germanic but is common to many primitive peoples. The significant fact is not that early Germanic kings were limited by customary law, but that the institution of limited monarchy endured and developed over the centuries of the Middle Ages.

The Invasions

The Germanic peoples had long been a threat to the empire. They had defeated a Roman army in the first century; they had probed deeply into the empire in the second century and again in the mid-third. But until the late fourth century, the Romans had always managed eventually to drive the invaders out. Beginning in the mid-370s, however, an exhausted empire was confronted by renewed Germanic pressures of an unprecedented magnitude. Lured by the relative wealth, the good soil, and the sunny climate of the Mediterranean world, the Germanic tribes tended to regard the empire not as something to destroy but as something to enjoy. Their age-long yearning for the fair lands across the Roman frontier was suddenly transformed into an urgent need by the westward thrust of a tribe of Asiatic nomads known as the Huns. These fierce horsemen conquered one Germanic tribe after another and turned them into satellites. They subdued the Ostrogoths and made them a subject people. The other Gothic tribe, the Visigoths, sought to preserve their independence by appealing for sanctuary behind the Roman Empire's Danube frontier. The eastern emperor Valens, a fervent Arian, sympathized with the Arian Visigoths, and in 376 the entire tribe crossed peacefully into the empire.

There was trouble almost immediately. Corrupt imperial officials cheated and abused the Visigoths, who retaliated by going on a rampage. At length Emperor Valens himself took the field against them, but the emperor's military incapacity cost him his army and his life at the battle of Adrianople in 378. Adrianople was a military debacle of the first order. Valens' successor, Theodosius I, managed to pacify the Visigoths, but he could not expel them. When Theodosius died in 395, imperial authority was split between his two sons, one of them ruling the eastern half of the empire, the other ruling in the West. As it happened, the two halves were never again rejoined under a single ruler. Not long after Theodosius' death, a vigorous new Visigothic leader named Alaric led his people on a second campaign of pillage and destruction that threatened Italy itself. In 406 the desperate Western Empire recalled most of its troops from the Rhine frontier to block Alaric's advance, with the disastrous result that the Vandals and a number of other tribes crossed the unguarded Rhine into Gaul. Shortly thereafter the Roman legions abandoned distant Britain, and the defenseless island was gradually overrun by Angles, Saxons, and other Germanic war bands. In 408 the only able general in the West was executed by the frantic, incompetent Emperor Honorius, who then abandoned Rome and took refuge behind the marshes of Ravenna. The Visigoths entered Rome unopposed in 410 and Alaric permitted them to plunder the city for three days.

The sack of Rome had a devastating impact on imperial morale. "My tongue sticks to the roof of my mouth," wrote St. Jerome on hearing of the catastrophe, "and sobs choke my speech." But in historical perspective, the event was merely one incident in the disintegration of the Western Empire. The Visigoths soon left the city to its feeble emperor and turned northward into southern Gaul and Spain. There they established a kingdom that endured until the Muslim conquests of the eighth century. Meanwhile other tribes were carving out kingdoms of their own. The Vandals swept through Gaul and Spain and across the Straits of Gibraltar into Africa. In 430, the very year of St.

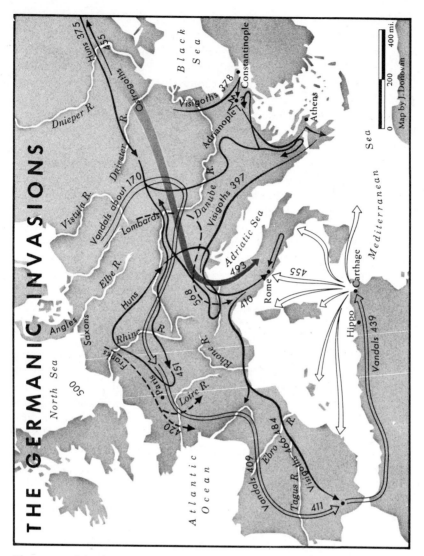

The routes of the Germanic invaders.

Augustine's death, they took his city of Hippo. A Vandal kingdom was now established in North Africa, centering on ancient Carthage. Almost immediately the Vandals began taking to the sea as buccaneers, devastating Mediterranean shipping and sacking one coastal city after another. Vandal piracy shattered the long peace of the Mediterranean and dealt a crippling blow to the waning commerce of the Western Empire.

Midway through the fifth century the Huns themselves moved against the West, led by their pitiless leader Attila, the "Scourge of God." Defeated by a Roman-Visigothic army in Gaul in 451, they returned the following year, hurling themselves toward Rome and leaving a path of devastation behind them. The western emperor abandoned Rome to Attila's mercies, but the Roman bishop, Pope Leo I, traveled northward from the city to negotiate with the Huns on the chance that they might be persuaded to turn back. Surprisingly, Pope Leo succeeded in his mission. Perhaps because the health of the Hunnish army was adversely affected by the Italian climate, perhaps because the majestic Pope Leo was able to overawe Attila, the Huns retired from Italy. Shortly afterward Attila died, the Hunnish empire collapsed, and the Huns themselves vanished from history. They were not mourned.

In its final years the Western Empire, whose jurisdiction now scarcely extended beyond Italy, fell under the control of hard-bitten military adventurers of Germanic birth. The emperors continued to reign for a time, but their Germanic generals were the powers behind the throne. In 476 the general Odovacar, who saw no point in perpetuating the farce, deposed the last emperor, sent the imperial trappings to Constantinople, and asserted his sovereignty over Italy by confiscating farmlands for the use of his Germanic troops. Odovacar claimed to rule as an agent of the Eastern Empire, but in fact he was on his own. A few years later the Ostrogoths, now free of Hunnish control and led by an astute king named Theodoric, advanced into Italy, conquered Odovacar, and established a strong state of their own.

Theodoric ruled Italy from 493 to 526. More than any other Germanic king he appreciated and respected Roman culture, and in his kingdom the Arian Ostrogoths and the orthodox Romans lived and worked together in relative harmony, repairing aqueducts, erecting impressive new buildings, and bringing a degree of prosperity to the long-troubled peninsula. The improving political and economic climate gave rise to a minor intellectual revival that contributed to the transmission of Greco-Roman culture into the Middle Ages. The philosopher Boethius, a high official in Theodoric's regime, produced philosophical works and translations which served as fundamental texts in western schools for the next five hundred years. His masterpiece, *The Consolation of Philosophy*, was written at the end of his life, when he had fallen from official favor and been imprisoned. The book's central theme is that earthly misfortunes cannot affect the inner life of a virtuous man. Although such a notion is consistent with Christianity, Boethius drew his ideas primarily from the thought of Plato and other pagan philosophers. Boethius was himself an orthodox Christian, yet Christianity is never mentioned explicitly in his *Consolation of Philosophy*. Nevertheless, this work remained immensely popular throughout the Middle Ages.

Theodoric's own secretary, Cassiodorus, was another scholar of considerable distinction, though incorrigibly long-winded. A wealthy Roman aristocrat, Cassiodorus spent his later years as abbot of a monastery that he had erected on his own lands in southern Italy. Like Jerome, he set his monks to the task of copying and preserving the literary works of antiquity, both Christian and pagan. His example was not lost on a younger contemporary, St. Benedict, who stressed manuscript copying in the immensely influential monastic order which he founded, thus prompting countless generations of western monks to carry on the good work.*

During the years of Theodoric's rule in Ostrogothic Italy, another Germanic king, Clovis (481–511), was creating a Frankish kingdom in the former Roman province of Gaul. Clovis was far less Romanized than Theodoric, and far crueler. He mastered the political technique of inviting potential rivals to dinner and having them murdered. But Clovis's kingdom proved to be the most enduring of all the Germanic successor states. The Franks were good farmers as well as good soldiers, and they established deep roots in the soil of Gaul. Moreover, the Frankish regime was buttressed by the enthusiastic support of the Catholic Church, for Clovis, who had been untouched by Arianism, was converted directly from Germanic paganism to Catholic Christianity. The conversion of Clovis doomed Arianism and foreshadowed the rise of Catholic France. Clovis himself remained a savage to the end, yet the Church came to regard him as another Constantine, a defender of orthodoxy in a sea of Arianism. As the centuries went by, the royal name "Clovis" was softened to "Louis" and the "Franks" became the "French." And the friendship between the Frankish monarchy and the Church developed into one of the determining elements in European politics.

Europe in A.D. 500

As the sixth century dawned, the Western Empire was only a memory. In its place was a group of Germanic successor states that vaguely prefigured the nations of modern Western Europe. Theodoric headed a tolerant and relatively enlightened Ostrogothic-Arian regime in Italy. The barbaric but orthodox Clovis was completing the Frankish conquest of Gaul. The Vandal monarchy, Arian in religion and increasingly corrupt and brutal, lorded it over the restive orthodox population of North Africa. The Arian Visigoths were being driven out of southern Gaul by the Franks, but their regime continued to dominate Spain for the next two centuries. And the Angles and Saxons were in the process of establishing a group of small, non-Christian kingdoms in Britain that would one day coalesce into "Angle-land" or England.

At the very time that the Germanic kingdoms were establishing themselves in the West, the Roman papacy was beginning to play an important independent role in European society. We have seen how the mid-fifth-century pope, Leo I (440–461), assumed the task of protecting the city of Rome from the Huns, thereby winning for himself the moral leadership of Italy. Leo and his successors declared that the bishops of Rome—the popes—constituted the highest authority in the Church, and following the example of St. Ambrose, they insisted on the supremacy of Church over state in spiritual matters. In proclaiming its doctrines of papal supremacy in the Church and ec-

*See pp. 45–46.

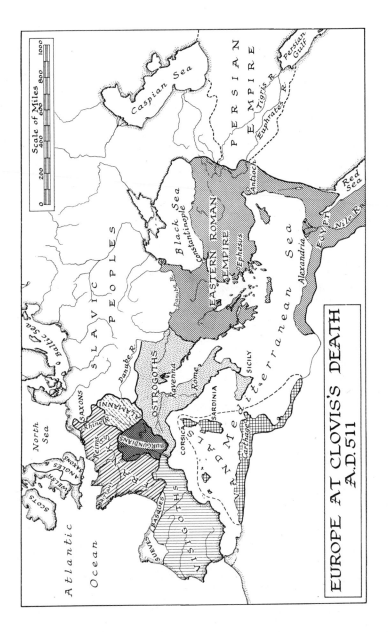

EUROPE AT CLOVIS'S DEATH
A.D. 511

clesiastical independence from state control, the papacy was wisely disengaging itself from the faltering western emperors. In the fifth century these papal doctrines remained little more than words, but they were to result in an ever-widening gulf between the Eastern and Western Church. More than that, they constituted the opening phase of the prolonged medieval struggle between the rival claims of Church and state. The mighty papacy of the High Middle Ages was yet many centuries away, but it was already foreshadowed in the bold independence of Leo I. The Western Empire was dead, but eternal Rome still claimed the allegiance of the world.

All Dates A.D.

96-180:	The age of the great second-century emperors
205-270:	Plotinus
235-284:	Height of the third-century anarchy
306-337:	Reign of Constantine
325:	Council of Nicaea
330:	Founding of Constantinople
354-430:	St. Augustine of Hippo
376:	Visigoths cross Danube
378:	Battle of Adrianople
378-395:	Reign of Theodosius I
395:	Final division of Eastern and Western Empires
410:	Alaric sacks Rome
430:	Vandals capture Hippo
451-452:	Huns invade Western Europe
440-461:	Pontificate of Leo I
476:	Last western emperor deposed by Odovacar
481-511:	Clovis rules Franks, conquers Gaul
493-526:	Theodoric the Ostrogoth rules Italy

Chapter 3

ℰ

Byzantium Endures

The Survival of the East Roman Empire

By the opening of the sixth century, the Western Empire had dissolved into a group of Germanic successor states. But the eastern emperors, with their capital at Constantinople, retained control of an immense, crescent-shaped realm girdling the eastern Mediterranean from the Balkans through Asia Minor, Syria, and Palestine, to Egypt. As we have seen, the East had always been more populous than the West. Its civilization was far older and more deeply rooted; its cities were larger and more numerous. The East had remained the commercial and industrial center of the empire even in the great days of Rome, and when disaster struck it proved to be far more resilient then the West.

Moreover, the Eastern Empire enjoyed important strategic and geopolitical advantages. The province of Asia Minor, protected from Germanic incursions by invulnerable Constantinople, was the Eastern Empire's great reservoir of manpower and revenues. For centuries it was to remain the chief recruiting ground for the Byzantine army and the most dependable source of imperial taxes. During the cataclysmic fifth century, while Germanic tribes were conquering the western provinces, Asia Minor was a bulwark of

ℰ

the empire. Its tough, loyal troops provided the eastern emperors with an invaluable alternative to the hazardous policy of complete dependence on hired Germanic armies.

With the rich material and human resources of Asia Minor behind it, the eastern capital at Constantinople held fast against the Germanic onslaught. This great city, the New Rome, dominated the passage between the Black Sea and the Mediterranean. Secure behind its massive landward and seaward walls, it became the economic and political heart of the Eastern Empire, and so long as Constantinople remained inviolate, the empire endured. Over the centuries Constantinople's walls repelled the attacks of Germanic and Asiatic tribes, Persians and Muslims. Under the circumstances, it is understandable that the Germanic tribes should have preferred to carve out their states in the feebler, more vulnerable west.

The Eastern Empire had the further advantage, during the crucial fifth century, of being better governed than the Western Empire. A series of able eastern emperors carefully husbanded their resources, fattened their treasury, and strengthened the fortifications of Constantinople while the Western Empire was collapsing. Superior leadership undoubtedly helped the East weather the storm, but its emperors could have accomplished little had it not been for the superb strategic location of their capital and the enduring commercial and human resources of the lands they ruled.

Byzantine Government

The civilization of the Byzantine Empire was a synthesis of three elements: Roman government, Christian religion, and Greco-Oriental culture. From Rome the Eastern Empire drew its legal system, its bureaucracy, and its principles of administration. Indeed, Byzantine government was a direct offspring of the third- and fourth-century Roman political system. Byzantine autocracy had its roots in the glorification of late-Roman emperors such as Constantine; tight imperial control of the Byzantine Church harked back to the policies of Constantine and Theodosius I. The heavy taxation of the late Roman emperors continued, and life in the Byzantine Empire remained burdensome and insecure.

The prevailing Byzantine mood, like the mood of the late Roman Empire, was one of defense and self-preservation. To the Byzantines, their state was the ark of civilization in an ocean of barbarism—the political embodiment of the Christian faith—and as such it had to be preserved at all costs. The appropriate virtues in such a state were entrenchment, not expansion; caution, not daring.

This defensive, conservative mood is evident in both the Byzantine bureaucracy and the Byzantine army. The bureaucracy, huge and precedent-bound, abhorred change and seldom took risks. Resisting the policies of Byzantium's vigorous and imaginative emperors, it gave cohesion to the state during the reigns of incompetents, thereby contributing to the endurance of the empire. The army, small and highly trained, also clung to a policy of few risks. Its generals, often men of remarkable skill, usually pursued policies of cunning and caution. They knew only too well that the preservation of their empire might depend on the survival of their armies.

Byzantine Christianity

The Byzantine emperors drew invaluable strength from the loyalty of their tax-ridden but fervent Christian subjects. The orthodox Christians within the empire regarded their ruler as more than a mere secular sovereign: he was God's vice-regent, the protector of the Holy Church, and as such he merited their unquestioned allegiance. Thus, Byzantine armies fought not merely for the empire but for God. The Byzantine warrior was no mere soldier, he was a crusader. Christianity was a potent stimulus to patriotism, and the Byzantine emperors enjoyed popular support to a degree unknown in the pagan Rome of old.

But the emperor's central position in Byzantine Christianity was a source of weakness as well as of strength. Religious controversy was a matter of imperial concern, and heresy became a grave threat to the state. The fifth and sixth centuries were singularly rich in doctrinal disputes, and in the end these religious conflicts cost the empire dearly. The most widespread heresy of the age was Monophysitism, a doctrine that arose in Egypt and spread quickly into Syria and Palestine, creating a mood of hostility toward the orthodox emperors. The controversy between the orthodox and the Monophysites turned on the question of whether Christ's humanity and divinity constituted two separate natures (as the orthodox said) or were fused together into one nature (Monophysitism). The Monophysite Christ possessed a single nature in which divinity tended to supersede humanity. Monophysitism has thus been seen as a return to the spiritualism of the ancient Near East, which tended to regard the physical world as evil. The dualism of evil-matter *versus* good-spirit conflicted with the orthodox Christian doctrine of God-made-flesh.

Monophysitism also can be viewed as a protest doctrine, upheld in districts that had been civilized long before the days of Roman rule, by people whose commitment to Greco-Roman culture was compromised by their own far older cultures. Even without Monophysitism, the inhabitants of Egypt and Syria might well have been expected to show separatist tendencies against embattled Byzantium, and Monophysitism, although far more than a mere excuse for rebellion, was nevertheless an appropriate vehicle for the antagonisms of Near Eastern peoples against a millennium of Greco-Roman domination.

The orthodox-Monophysite quarrel raged long and bitterly and constituted a dangerous threat to the unity of the Byzantine Empire. The emperors, convinced that doctrinal unity was essential to the preservation of their state, followed first one policy, then another; sometimes they persecuted the Monophysites, sometimes they favored them, and sometimes they worked out compromise doctrinal formulas that were intended to satisfy both sides but, in fact, satisfied neither. Whatever policy the emperors might follow, the controversy remained an open wound in the body politic until the seventh century, when the rich but disaffected Monophysite provinces were swallowed by the expanding Islamic world. Only then, at the Ecumenical Council of Constantinople in 680, did Byzantine orthodoxy win its definitive victory within the empire.

Byzantine Culture

Roman government, Christian religion, Greco-Oriental culture—these were the three pillars of Byzantine civilization. And all three were shaped— and to a degree transformed—by the experience of the fourth-century Christian Empire. As a consequence of that experience, Byzantium inherited Roman government in its late, authoritarian form. Byzantine Christianity was a direct outgrowth of the Christianity of the later Roman Empire—its theology tightened and defined by the reaction to Arianism, its priestly hierarchy overshadowed by the power of the emperors. Just as Constantine had dominated the clergy at the Council of Nicaea in 325, so likewise did the Byzantine emperors, over the centuries, tend to dominate the patriarchs of Constantinople.

Byzantium's Greco-Oriental culture, too, was molded by the intellectual and cultural currents of the third, fourth, and fifth centuries. The Greek culture that Byzantium inherited was by no means the culture of Periclean Athens—with its superbly proportioned classical architecture, its deeply human drama, its bold advances into uncharted regions of speculative thought, and its controlled, tensely muscular sculpture. That tradition had undergone successive modifications in the ages that followed, and above all, during the third- and fourth-century empire. The mood of otherworldliness that gradually seized Roman culture resulted in a momentous transformation of the classical spirit. There had always been a potent spiritual-mystical element in Greco-Roman culture, coexisting with the traditional classical concern with the earthly and the concrete. Now the mystical element grew far stronger. More and more of the better minds turned to theology, scriptural study, and the quest for individual salvation. Artists were less interested in portraying physical perfection and more interested in portraying sanctity. The new Christian art depicted slender, heavily robed figures with solemn faces and deep eyes—windows into the soul. Techniques of perspective, which the artists of the classical era had developed to a fine degree, mattered less to the artists of the new age. De-emphasizing physical realism, the artists of the late empire adorned their works with rich, dazzling colors that stimulated in the beholder a sense of heavenly radiance and religious solemnity.

Such was the artistic tradition which Byzantium inherited. It conformed so perfectly to the Byzantine spirit that the artists of the Eastern Empire were

Mosaic of female martyrs; Sant' Apollinare Nuovo, Ravenna (6th century).

able to produce enduring masterpieces without ever departing far from its basic aesthetic canons. Majestic churches arose in the Byzantine style— churches such as Sancta Sophia in Constantinople, St. Vitale in Ravenna, and St. Mark's in Venice—whose interiors shone with glistening mosaics portraying saints and statesmen, Christ and the Virgin, on backgrounds of gold. Here was an art vastly different from that of Greek antiquity, with different techniques and different goals, yet in its own way just as valid, just as successful, as the art of the Athenian golden age.

In this new, transcendental environment, Greek culture was significantly altered, yet Byzantine civilization remained Greek nonetheless. Greek was the language of most of its inhabitants, and despite their deep commitment to the Christian faith, they never forgot their Greek heritage. Indeed, the transition from late Roman to Byzantine civilization is marked by an increasing dissociation from the Latin-Roman past and a heightened emphasis on the legacy of Hellenism. As time went on, Byzantine scholars forgot their Latin; Greek became the language of the imperial court. The Byzantine Church, under the patriarch of Constantinople, all but lost contact with the Roman pope. Greek philosophy and letters were studied with undying diligence by scholars who cherished their ties with the Hellenic past.

The Age of Justinian

The first great creative surge of Byzantine civilization occurred during the reign of Justinian (527–565). In many respects Justinian stands as the last of the Roman emperors; in others, he was a Byzantine through and through. He spoke in the Latin tongue and was haunted by the dream of reconquering the west and so reviving the Roman Empire of old. It was under his direction that the vast heritage of Roman law was assembled into one coherent body. In these respects he was a ruler in the Roman tradition. On the other hand, his reign witnessed a golden age of Byzantine art and the climax of imperial autocracy that typified Byzantine culture over the centuries that followed.

The spectacular achievements of Justinian's reign were a product not only of the genius of the emperor but also the wise and cautious rule of his predecessors who endured the worst of the Germanic invasions, nurtured the financial resources of the empire, and gradually accumulated a sizeable surplus in the treasury. Justinian was also fortunate in that the Germanic kingdoms of the west, which he had determined to conquer, were losing much of their early vigor. Theodoric, the great Ostrogothic king, died in 526, a year before Justinian ascended the Byzantine throne, and the Vandal monarchy of North Africa, once a cruel oppressor of its subject people, was now merely corrupt.

Justinian, a man of determination and boundless ambition, was prepared to seize these opportunities. He was aided immeasurably by his wife and co-ruler, Empress Theodora, a woman no less ambitious than he, and even more resolute. Formerly a public entertainer and courtesan, Theodora was gifted with extraordinary practical intelligence. Together, she and Justinian brought new energy and boldness to the old, conservative regime. The plans to rebuild Constantinople, reform Roman law, and reconquer the West are usually ascribed to Justinian himself, but since he consulted Theodora on all matters of policy, it is often impossible to distinguish her ideas from his. In any event, without Theodora's iron will none of these policies could have been carried out. For early in the reign a great urban riot resulted in the burning of much of Constantinople. With the city in flames and rioters advancing on the imperial palace, Justinian was on the point of abandoning his imperial office and fleeing

San Vitale, Ravenna (526–547): Exterior (below), Interior (opposite).

in panic when Theodora restored his courage. Refusing to depart, she announced that she intended to die an empress. As a result of her determination, the riots were quelled and the regime survived.

Justinian's audacious policies, though reasonably successful in his own time, left the empire exhausted and unstable. He applied his considerable knowledge of theology to the tangled problem of reconciling the orthodox and the Monophysities (he himself was orthodox, whereas Theodora had Monophysite leanings), but his complex compromise satisfied neither group. After the riot and conflagration, he devoted immense funds to the rebuilding of Constantinople on an unprecedented scale. The most notable product of his rebuilding program was the church of Sancta Sophia—one of Byzantium's foremost works of art. Gold, silver, ivory, and dazzling mosaics adorned its interior, and a vast dome seemed almost to float on air above it. The total ef-

San Vitale, Ravenna: Mosaic of Theodora and her Court.

fect was such as to stun even Justinian: he is said to have exclaimed on its completion, "Glory to God who has judged me worthy of accomplishing such a
work as this! O Solomon, I have outdone thee!"

It was at Justinian's bidding that a talented group of lawyers set about to
assemble the immense mass of legal precedents, juridical opinions, and imperial edicts that constituted the legacy of Roman law. These materials were
arranged into a vast, systematic collection known as the *Corpus Juris Civilis*—
the "body of civil law." Justinian's *Corpus* not only became the keystone of
future Byzantine jurisprudence but also served as the vehicle in which Roman
law returned to Western Europe in the twelfth century to challenge the age-
long domination of Germanic legal custom. The appearance of the *Corpus
Juris Civilis* in the twelfth-century West was of incalculable importance to the
development of sophisticated and rational legal systems in the European
states. Indeed, its effect is still very much apparent in the legal codes of modern
nations. But the importance of the *Corpus Juris Civilis* extended even beyond
this. Roman law had formerly contained strong elements of popular sovereignty, but in Justinian's hand it acquired some of the autocratic flavor of the
Byzantine state. Thus, in the late-medieval and early-modern west it tended to
support the rise of royal absolutism, acting as a counterpoise to the limited-
monarchy notions of Germanic legal tradition. The monarchs of late-medieval

Sancta Sophia, Constantinople: full interior.

and early-modern Europe found much to admire in Justinian's precept that the emperor's decree is law.

Historians are prone to criticize Justinian for lavishing the limited resources of his empire on the chimerical policy of reconquering the West. In one sense they are correct: the reconquest did drain the treasury and prostrate the empire, and the victories of Justinian's western armies proved in time to be largely ephemeral. Yet Justinian, keenly sensitive to the Roman imperial tradition, could not rest until he had made one all-out attempt to recover the lost western provinces and to re-establish imperial authority in the city of Rome. His armies, small but led by brilliant generals, conquered the worm-eaten Vandal kingdom of North Africa with ease in 533–534 and succeeded in wresting a long strip of the Spanish Mediterranean coast from the Visigoths. For twenty years his troops struggled against the Ostrogoths in Italy, crushing them at length in 555 but only after enormous effort and expense. The campaigns in Italy, known as the "Gothic Wars," devastated the Italian peninsula and left Rome itself in ruins. The Visigothic sack of 410 was nothing compared with the havoc wrought by Justinian's armies.

During the final years of his reign Justinian ruled almost the entire Mediterranean coastline, but his vastly expanded empire was impoverished and bankrupt. Theodora died in 548, and Justinian, deprived of his astute co-ruler, became demoralized and irresolute. Moreover, a devastating outbreak of plague swept across Byzantium and Western Europe in 541–543 and recurred sporadically over the succeeding decades, taking a fearful toll of human lives and crippling the Byzantine economy. But even without the plague, Byzantium would have found it difficult to hold its newly conquered territories. With his military attention focused westward, Justinian was powerless to prevent a great flood of Slavic peoples and Bulgars from ravaging the Balkans. In 561, the Avars, warlike nomads from the Asiatic steppes, settled on the Danube shore and proceeded to subjugate the Slavs and Bulgars. Byzantium now found itself living in the shadow of a hostile Avar state, far more threatening than Vandal North Africa or Ostrogothic Italy. This new danger pointed up Justinian's great shortcoming—his inability to match ambitions to resources. The huge empire that he bequeathed to his successors was dangerously vulnerable.

Retrenchment and Revival

The Byzantine Empire aspired to be Roman yet was destined by the realities of geopolitics to be Balkan and Near-Eastern. Justinian's western conquests were not enduring. In 568, three years after his death, a savage Germanic tribe known as the Lombards (Langobards or Long Beards) burst into Italy, further devastating that troubled land and carving out an extensive kingdom in northern Italy centering on the Po Valley. Byzantium retained much of southern Italy and clung to Ravenna and other cities along the Adriatic coast, but its hold on Italy was badly shaken. Shortly afterward, the Visigoths reconquered the Byzantine territories in southern Spain, and eventually, in the 690s, Byzantine North Africa—the former Vandal state—fell to the Muslims. In 751 the Lombards took Ravenna, and Byzantine power in Italy was reduced still further.

Justinian's successors were forced to abandon his ambitious policies and face the hard necessities of survival, turning their back on the West to face more immediate threats from hostile people to the north and east. The Persian Empire pressed dangerously against Byzantium's eastern frontier, and the Avars with their Bulgar and Slavic subjects won control of most of the Balkans.

The great crisis occurred during the reign of Emperor Heraclius (610–641), when Persian armies occupied Syria, Palestine, and Egypt, and when, in 626, Constantinople just barely withstood a furious combined siege of Persians and Avars. Heraclius crushed the Persian army at last in 628 and recovered the lands that had been lost to Persia. He succeeded also in re-establishing imperial suzerainty over the Balkans. But no sooner had the Persians been defeated than the Muslim armies exploded out of Arabia to wrest Syria, Palestine, and Egypt from the empire and put Constantinople once again in grave danger. The Muslims besieged the city on several occasions, most determinedly in

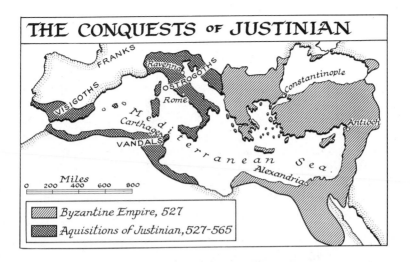

THE CONQUESTS OF JUSTINIAN

FRANKS
Ravenna
OSTROGOTHS
VISIGOTHS
Constantinople
Rome
Carthage
VANDALS
Mediterranean Sea
Antioch
Alexandria

Miles
0 200 400 600 800

▨ Byzantine Empire, 527
▦ Aquisitions of Justinian, 527-565

717–718, at which time the dogged Byzantine defense may have prevented not only the empire but much of eastern and central Europe from being absorbed into the Arab world. The empire withstood the powerful northward thrust of Islam, retaining Constantinople, Asia Minor, and an unsteady overlordship in the Balkan peninsula, thereby preserving the division of medieval western Eurasia into the three great cultures of Byzantium, Islam, and Western Christendom. The Christian kingdoms of the West were able to develop behind the shield of Constantinople's walls.

The Macedonian Emperors and the Conversion of the Slavs

Byzantium had won the time necessary for the gradual conquest and conversion of southeastern Europe. In the course of the seventh century it had lost to Islam such great urban centers as Damascus, Alexandria, Antioch, and Carthage, with the result that the empire became far smaller and poorer, yet more homogeneous, more unified in religion and culture, and more completely centered on the one great city remaining: Constantinople.

After several generations of retrenchment, Byzantium began to expand once again under the dynasty of "Macedonian" emperors (867–1056). A rich literary and artistic revival was accompanied by a series of important territorial conquests and by a surge in missionary activity that resulted in the conversion of countless Slavic peoples to Eastern Orthodox Christianity. Byzantium's political and religious expansion under the Macedonian emperors shaped the cultural development of Eastern Europe for the next millennium.

The Macedonians reconquered northern Syria for a time and pushed their frontiers in Asia Minor northeastward. But their most significant military accomplishment, in the long run, was the establishment of firm Byzantine rule over the Balkan Slavs and Bulgars. The greatest ruler of the dynasty, Basil II, "the Bulgar-Slayer" (976–1025) campaigned year after year in the Balkans, demolishing a Bulgarian army in 1014 and eventually crushing all resistance to Byzantine imperial authority.

In the meantime, beginning in the middle years of the ninth century, the process of Byzantine religious conversion and acculturation among the peoples of southeastern Europe began in earnest. Missionaries such as Cyril and Methodius, "the Apostles to the Slavs," evangelized tirelessly among the south Slavs and Russians, drawing them into the orbit of Byzantine Christianity and culture. Cyril and Methodius, in the second half of the ninth century, invented the first Slavonic alphabet and employed it in the creation of a Slavic vernacular Bible and liturgy. Thus the Slavonic written language and the Slavonic Christian Church came into being side by side. Ultimately, the evangelism of the Macedonian age brought the Balkans and Russia into the Orthodox Church and into the sphere of Byzantine culture.

The Conversion of Russia

The age of the Macedonian emperors was concurrent with the rise of Russia—far beyond the political boundaries of the empire. Byzantium had always had economic and political interests on the northern shore of the Black Sea. In the ninth and tenth centuries, trade flourished between the Black Sea and the Baltic and linked the Byzantine Empire with the vigorous commerce of the Viking world. Numerous Byzantine coin hoards dating from this era have been unearthed in Scandinavia, and Norsemen were widely employed as Byzantine mercenaries. Swedish Vikings probed deep into Russia in the ninth century and established a dynasty in the Russian trading center of Novgorod, ruling over the native Slavic population and later intermarrying with it. In the tenth century a ruler of Novgorod captured the strategic Russian commercial town of Kiev, which became the nucleus of the first important Russian state.

The Macedonian emperors at Constantinople took great pains to maintain warm diplomatic relations with Kievan Russia. Basil II, the Bulgar-Slayer, received crucial military aid from Prince Vladimir of Kiev and promised in return to give his own sister to Vladimir in marriage. The result of this marriage was nothing less than the conversion of Kievan Russia. For Vladimir, on marrying his Byzantine princess, agreed to adopt Christianity. Kiev never submitted politically to the Byzantine emperors, but its people became spiritual subjects of the patriarch of Constantinople.

In the course of the eleventh century, Kievan Russia disintegrated politically, and in the thirteenth century it was brought under the yoke of Mongol invaders, but its Christian-Byzantine culture survived these political disasters. In the sixteenth century, after the Byzantine Empire itself was demolished, the Christian princes of Moscow assumed the imperial title (Caesar—Czar). As Constantinople had been the "Second Rome," they intended Moscow to become the "Third Rome," and they asserted their dominion over both church and state much as their imperial "predecessors" at Constantinople had done. Some scholars have even suggested that the present rulers of Russia, with their control of both the state and the Communist ideological apparatus, are perpetuating in secular form the Byzantine tradition of imperial control over church and state.

Military Disaster and Cultural Survival

The dynamism and grandeur of the Macedonian age came to an end in the eleventh century with the passing of the Macedonian dynasty (1056) and the coming of a powerful new Asian tribe, the Seljuk Turks, into the Middle East. Recently converted to Islam, the Seljuks had made a puppet of the Islamic caliph at Baghdad. In 1065 they wrested Armenia from the Byzantines, and when an imperial army attempted to drive them from Asia Minor, it was annihilated at the epochal Battle of Manzikert in 1071.

Manzikert is one of the great turning points in Byzantine history. Even though the Seljuk Turks did not adequately follow up their great triumph, the disaster emasculated the empire by breaking the age-long Byzantine hold on Asia Minor. In the same fatal year of 1071, the Normans in southern Italy conquered the vital Byzantine Adriatic port of Bari, marking the virtual end of Byzantium's presence in the West. By now, Western Christendom was acquiring the wealth and power of a great civilization, and prostrate Byzantium was forced to beg aid from the papacy and the Franks. The century of Manzikert ended with the First Crusade and the fall of Jerusalem (1099), not to Byzantine warriors but to French crusaders. Byzantium tottered on until the mid-fifteenth century, but it was never again the same. Its years of expansion were over, and its energies were thenceforth consumed in its struggle to endure.

Yet Byzantine culture survived the blow of Manzikert. Art and learning continued, and even at the very close of its long history, in 1453, Byzantium was in the midst of an impressive classical-humanist revival that made a significant impact on the Italian Renaissance.

To the end, Byzantium revered its classical heritage. As a custodian of Greco-Roman culture, the Eastern Empire provided an invaluable service to the emerging civilization of Western Europe. Roman law and Greek philosophy and literature were studied in Constantinople at a time when they were all but unknown in the West. The influence of Byzantine art on medieval Western Christendom was, in the words of a modern historian, "far-flung and everywhere beneficial: and whatever else the West disliked and despised about the East, its mosaics and enamels, its textiles and ivories, its pearl and onyx, its painting and its gold work were eagerly coveted and jealously guarded in western treasuries."*

Yet Byzantium's government was never able to transcend the stifling

*Romily Jenkins, *Byzantium, The Imperial Centuries*, Vintage Books, New York, 1969, p. 385.

autocracy of the late Roman Empire or the fundamentally defensive mood that it implied. Byzantium's creative impulses were dimmed by its remorseless conservatism; creative originality was less valued than the preservation of a priceless heritage.

Byzantium's lasting contribution to European history lies above all in its conversion of Russia and the Balkans. Eastern Orthodox Christianity is similar in basic doctrine to the traditional religions of Western Europe, yet it differs in numerous important ways. The culture of Orthodox Eastern Europe, deriving as it does from Byzantium, is more open to Westernizing influences than, say, the culture of the Islamic or Hindu or Buddhist peoples. Eastern Europe today is Westernized, yet not fully Western. Its culture is similar, yet different; industrialized but not fully at ease with parliamentary democracy on the Western pattern. Its historic traditions are varied and complex, but the tradition of Byzantium is not the least among them.

BYZANTINE CHRONOLOGY

330:	Constantine founds Constantinople
395:	Final division of Eastern and Western Empire
527–565:	Reign of Justinian
533–534:	Conquest of Vandal North Africa
535–555:	Gothic Wars; conquest of Italy
541–543:	Great plague
548:	Death of Empress Theodora
568:	Lombards invade Italy
610–641:	Reign of Heraclius; Islamic conquests of Syria, Palestine, and Egypt
680:	Ecumenical Council of Constantinople: orthodoxy triumphs over Monophysitism
690s:	Muslims conquer Byzantine North Africa
717–718:	Great Muslim siege of Constantinople
867–1056:	Macedonian dynasty: reconquest of Balkans; conversion of south Slavs
976–1025:	Reign of Basil the Bulgar-Slayer
c.980–1015:	Reign of Prince Vladimir of Kiev, who converts to Byzantine Christianity
1071:	Seljuk Turks rout Byzantines at Manzikert; loss of Asia Minor
1453:	Fall of Constantinople to Ottoman Turks

Chapter 4

❦

Early Western Christendom

❦ The ignorance and poverty of the early medieval West stand in sharp contrast to the urbanity of Byzantium. Yet Western Europe had the inestimable advantage of a fresh start. It was inspired and enriched by the classical heritage, but not shackled by it.

In the aftermath of the Germanic invasions, Western Europe found itself cut adrift from the government of the Roman Empire. The Church survived to carry on much of the old classical legacy. But Germanic kings and nobles were generally incapable of preserving the political and economic institutions of the Roman past. Towns had been declining in Western Europe ever since the third century; by A.D. 600 they were shrunken phantoms of what they once had been. North of the Alps the municipal governments of antiquity had disappeared without a trace. But many of the towns themselves managed to endure, after a fashion, as centers of ecclesiastical administration. They remained the headquarters of episcopal government and the sites of the bishops' cathedral churches. Many towns became important pilgrimage centers, for the more important cathedral churches possessed relics—portions of the bodies or clothing of departed saints—which were regarded as agents of spiritual and physical

❦

healing. The cathedral at Tours, for example, possessed the bones of the noted miracle-worker, St. Martin, which were said to have healed many who touched them.

These episcopal centers played only a minor role in the culture and economy of the successor states. Far more important were the monastery, the peasant village, and the great farm or villa owned by a Roman or Germanic aristocrat and cultivated by slaves or by semi-free tenant farmers. A small-scale luxury trade persisted, but by and large the economy of the sixth and seventh centuries was local and self-contained. Small agrarian communities produced most of their own needs, for their life was meager and their needs were few.

Moreover, there is some reason to believe that huge areas of western European farmland were abandoned altogether and resettled only much later. Aerial photographs of the southern French countryside disclose typically medieval patterns of fields that radiate outward from a central village; but often these radiating fields appear superimposed on earlier Roman patterns of square and rectangular fields, systematically laid out. Since no governmental authority in the early Middle Ages had either the power or will to effect such a fundamental change in field patterns, one can only conclude that the Roman fields had reverted to wilderness and generations thereafter had been resettled and reshaped. Aerial photographs do not permit absolute dating, but the silent catastrophe they record may well be associated with the violence and depopulation resulting from Rome's collapse in the west.

There can be little doubt that Western Europe's population declined sharply in this period. Its ethnic character was similarly transformed, as multitudes of Germanic peoples moved into the old western provinces. Except in Britain and northeastern Gaul, the Germanic settlers gradually fused with the older, indigenous population. In the process, free Germanic farmers often descended into the ranks of the semi-servile peasantry that had survived from Roman times. But at the aristocratic level the pattern of life was set by the Germanic warrior nobility, and consequently the civility of the Roman villa gradually disappeared. The Roman and Germanic landed aristocracies blended through intermarriage into one class—hard-bitten and warlike—far more Germanic than Roman.

Government; Intellectual Life

With the exception of Theodoric, the Germanic kings proved incapable of perpetuating the Roman administrative traditions which they inherited. They allowed the Roman tax system to break down; they permitted the privilege of minting coins to fall into private hands. The power and wealth of the state declined, not because the kings were generous but because they were ignorant. They lacked the slightest conception of responsible government and regarded their kingdoms as private estates to be exploited or alienated according to their whims. They made reckless gifts of land and public authority to nobles and churchmen and regarded what remained as their personal property, to be exploited for their own enrichment. In brief, they succeeded in combining the worst features of anarchy and tyranny.

During the late Roman Empire, Western Europe had been overtaxed and overgoverned; now it was radically undergoverned. The Germanic monarchs did precisely nothing to enliven the economy or ameliorate the general impoverishment. The Church strove to fill the vacuum by dispensing charity and glamorizing the virtue of resignation, but it was ill-equipped to cope with the chaos of the post-Roman West. Its organization was confined largely to the defunct towns and walled monasteries. Only gradually were rural parishes organized to meet the needs of the countryside. Not until after the eighth century did the country parish become a characteristic feature of the western Church. In the meantime a peasant was fortunate if he saw a priest once a year. The monarchy and the Church, the two greatest landholders, were better known among the peasantry as acquisitive landlords than as fountains of justice and divine grace. Rural life was harsh, brutish, and short, and the countryside was politically and spiritually adrift.

The intellectual life of the West was almost as backward as its political and economic life. The culture of old Rome was rotting, and the new civilization of Western Europe had scarcely begun to develop. The intellectual level of the sixth and seventh centuries can best be appreciated by looking at a few leading scholars of the period. Bishop Gregory of Tours (d. 594), whose *History of the Franks* is our best source for the reigns of Clovis and his successors, must be counted one of the leading historians of his age. Yet Gregory's *History* is written in ungrammatical Latin and is filled with outrageous and silly miracles. The world portrayed by Gregory of Tours was dominated by savage cruelty and beclouded by superstitious fantasy. Both the story that he presents and the way in which he presents it attest to the decline of civilization in sixth-century Gaul.

Pope Gregory the Great (d. 604) was awarded a place alongside Ambrose, Jerome, and Augustine as one of the four Doctors of the Latin Church. But Pope Gregory's writings, although marked by profound practical wisdom and psychological insight, suffer from the cultural decadence of his age. They do not approach the level of the fourth-century doctors in philosophical depth and scholarly sophistication. Pope Gregory watered down Augustinian theology for the benefit of his own naive contemporaries. The lofty theological issues with which Augustine grappled are overshadowed in Gregory's thought by a concentration on such secondary matters as demons and relics.

Bishop Isidore of Seville (d. 636) was known as the foremost scholar of his generation. His most impressive work, the *Etymologies*, was intended to be an encyclopedia of all knowledge. It was a valuable work for its time and was studied by many generations thereafter. But its value was diminished by Isidore's lack of critical powers. He included every scrap of information that he could find, whether likely or unlikely, profound or absurd. It can perhaps be said that he was victimized by the credulity of the ancient writers on whom he depended and was left adrift by the weakness of the Roman scientific tradition. Nevertheless, as the greatest mind of his age he was naive. On the subject of monsters he writes as follows:

❝ The Cynocephali are so called because they have dogs' heads and their very barking betrays them as beasts rather than men. These are born in India. The Cyclopses, too, hail from India, and they are so named because they have a single eye in the midst of the forehead. . . The Blemmyes, born in Libya, are believed to be headless trunks, having mouth and eyes in the breast; others are born without necks, with eyes in the shoulders . . . . They say the Panotii in Scythia have ears so huge that they cover the whole body with them. . . . The race of the Sciopodes is said to live in Ethiopia. They have one leg apiece, and are of a marvelous swiftness, and . . . in summertime they lie on the ground on their backs and are shaded by the greatness of their feet. **❞**

Finally, with a touch of skepticism, Isidore concludes:

❝ Other fabulous monstrosities of the human race are said to exist, but they do not; they are imaginary. **❞**

In fairness to Isidore it should be said that his treatment of monsters fails to show him to best advantage, and that it was drawn from earlier materials dating from the ancient world. But he combined and synthesized these materials with an intellectual abandon typical of his age.

The Germanic Kingdoms

The century between A.D. 500 and 600 witnessed important changes in the political structure of Western Christendom. In A.D. 500 Theodoric's Ostrogothic regime dominated Italy, the Vandals ruled North Africa, the Visigoths governed Spain, Clovis and his Franks were conquering Gaul, and the Anglo-Saxons were beginning their settlements in Britain. A century later, two of these states had been destroyed by Justinian's armies: North Africa was now Byzantine rather than Vandal, and the Ostrogothic kingdom of Italy had collapsed.

By 600 the Anglo-Saxon tribes had occupied much of Britain, enslaving many of the indigenous Celtic inhabitants and driving others into the western mountains of Wales, or across the English Channel to Brittany. Anglo-Saxon Britain was now a confused medley of small, independent kingdoms in which the process of Christian conversion was just beginning.

Gaul in 600 was thoroughly dominated by the Franks under the cruel and incompetent successors of Clovis, founder of the *Merovingian* dynasty.* This dynasty followed the Frankish custom of dividing the kingdom among the sons of a deceased ruler. Often the sons would engage in bitter civil war until, as it sometimes happened, one of them emerged as sole monarch of the Franks. At his death, the kingdom would be divided among his own sons, and the bitter comedy would be repeated. Merovingian government became more and more predatory, and the Frankish Church became increasingly disorganized and corrupt.

Corruption also was paralyzing Church and state in Visigothic Spain. The monarchy, which shed its Arianism and embraced Catholicism in 589, was able at length to reconquer its Mediterranean shore from feeble Byzantium (*c.* 624). But the Visigothic kings allowed their power to slip little by little into the hands of a greedy and oppressive landed aristocracy. The regime was an easy prey for the conquering Muslims in the early 700s.

The century since Theodoric's reign had been a disastrous one for Italy. The horrors of Justinian's Gothic wars were followed by the invasion of the Lombards. By 600 the decimated peninsula was divided between the Byzantines in Ravenna and the south, and the Arian Lombards in the north. The papacy, under nominal Byzantine jurisdiction, dominated the lands around Rome and sought to preserve its fragile independence by playing Lombard against Byzantine. At critical moments, however, it looked to the Byzantines as its defenders.

Creative Forces

Such was the condition of Western Europe in 600. At first glance one can see little to hope for in the all-prevailing gloom. Yet this was the society out of which Western Civilization was born. This was the formative epoch—the age of genesis—in which apparently minor trends would one day broaden into traditions that would govern the course of European history. Even in 600 there were glimmerings of light in the darkness. Classical culture still survived, if only in a sadly vulgarized form. Isidore of Seville was no Augustine, but he was far more than a mere barbarian. The Church, although tainted by the ignorance and corruption of its environment, still retained something of its power to inspire, enlighten, and civilize.

Far to the north, Ireland had been won for Christianity by St. Patrick in the fifth century; by 600 it had developed an astonishingly creative Celtic-Christian culture. Irish scholars were familiar with both Greek and Latin literature at a time when Greek was unknown elsewhere in the West. By the later seventh century, Irish artists were producing magnificent illuminated manuscripts in a flowing, curvilinear Celtic style. Irish Christianity, isolated

---

* Named after Clovis' half-mythical ancestor, Merovech.

EUROPE AROUND 600

from the continental Church by the pagan Anglo-Saxon kingdoms, developed distinctive customs. It was organized around the monastery rather than the diocese, and its leaders were abbots rather than bishops. Irish monks were famous for their learning, the austere holiness of their lives, and the vast geographical scope of their missionary activities. They converted large portions of Scotland to their own form of Christianity and by the early 600s were conducting missionary activities on the Continent itself.

Monasticism

Monasticism was the most dynamic and significant institution in the early Middle Ages. The impulse toward monastic life is not peculiar to Christianity but is found in many religions—Buddhism and Judaism, to name but two. The Essenes, for example, whose cult may have produced the famous Dead Sea scrolls, constituted a kind of Jewish monastic order. There have always been religious people who long to withdraw from the world and devote their lives to uninterrupted communion with God, but among Christians this impulse was particularly strong. Monasticism came to be regarded as the most perfect form of the Christian life—the consummate embodiment of Christ's own words: "Anyone who has forsaken home, or brothers, or sisters, or father, or mother, or wife, or children, or lands for my name's sake, shall receive his reward a hundred times over and obtain everlasting life" (Matt., XIX, xxix).

This impulse toward withdrawal and renunciation first affected Christianity in the later third century when the Egyptian St. Anthony retired to the desert to live the ascetic life of a godly hermit. In time the fame of his sanctity spread, and a colony of ascetics gathered around him to draw inspiration from his holiness. Anthony thereupon organized a community of hermits who lived together but had no communication with one another—like apartment dwellers in an American city. Similar hermit communities soon arose throughout Egypt and spread into other regions of the empire. Hermit saints abounded in the fourth and fifth centuries. One of them, St. Simeon Stylites, achieved the necessary isolation by living atop a sixty-foot pillar for thirty years, evoking widespread admiration and imitation.

In the meantime a more down-to-earth type of monasticism was developing. Beginning in early fourth-century Egypt and then expanding quickly throughout the Roman Empire, monastic communities, based on a cooperative rather than a hermit life, were attracting numerous fervent Christians who found insufficient challenge in the increasingly complacent post-Constantine Church. The holy individualism of the desert and pillar saints thus gave way to a more ordered monastic life. Yet the early communities remained loosely organized and continued to emphasize ascetic practices of severe fasting and purifying lashings, which had been pioneered by the ancient hermits and which still fascinate modern psychologists.

St. Benedict and his Rule

St. Benedict of Nursia (c. 480–544) changed the course of western monasticism, tempering its flamboyant holiness with common sense and realistic principles of organization. As a youth, Benedict fled corrupt Rome and took up the hermit life in a cave near the ruins of Nero's country palace. In time word of his saintliness circulated and disciples gathered around him. As it turned out, Benedict was more than a mere ascetic; he was a man of keen psychological insight—a superb organizer who slowly learned from the varied experiences of his youth how the monastic life might best be lived. Born of a Roman aristocratic family, he brought to his task a practical genius and a sense of order and discipline that were characteristically Roman. He founded a number of monasteries that drew not only prospective saints but ordinary people as well—even the sons of wealthy Roman families. At length he established his great monastery of Monte Cassino atop a mountain midway between Rome and Naples. For centuries thereafter Monte Cassino was one of the chief centers of religious life in Western Europe. It became a model monastery, governed by a comprehensive, compassionate rule. In the midst of Justinian's

Gothic Wars, St. Benedict died, but his rule survived to inspire and transform Western Europe.

Pope Gregory the Great described the Rule of St. Benedict as "conspicuous for its discretion." Modern scholars have discovered that it was derived from an earlier, anonymous monastic rule, but St. Benedict gave it a novel quality of humane practicality. It provided for a busy, closely regulated life, simple but not ruthlessly ascetic. Benedictine monks were decently clothed, adequately fed, and seldom left to their own devices. Theirs was a life dedicated to God and the attainment of personal sanctity, yet it was also a life that could be led by any dedicated Christian. It was rendered all the more attractive by the increasing brutality of the outside world. The monastic day was filled with carefully arranged activities: communal prayer, devotional reading, and work—field work, household work, manuscript copying—according to the needs of the monastery and the ability of the monk. The fundamental obligations were chastity, poverty, and obedience: the monk must be celibate; he must discard all personal possessions; he must obey his abbot. The abbot, elected by the monks for life, was the unquestioned master of the monastery, but he was to consult the monks in all his decisions. He was strictly responsible to God and was instructed to govern justly in accordance with the Rule. He was cautioned not to sadden or "overdrive" his monks or give them cause for "just murmuring." Here especially is the quality of discretion to which Pope Gregory alludes and that doubtless has been a major factor in the Rule's-success.

Contributions of the Benedictines

Within two centuries of Benedict's death, the Rule had spread throughout Western Christendom. The result was not a vast hierarchical monastic organization but rather a host of individual, autonomous monasteries sharing a single Rule and way of life, yet administratively unrelated. Benedict had visualized his monasteries as spiritual sanctuaries into which pious men might withdraw from the world. But the chaotic and illiterate society of early Western Christendom, desperately in need of the discipline and learning of the Benedictines, could not permit them to abdicate from secular affairs.

In reality, therefore, the Benedictines had an enormous impact on the world they renounced. Their schools produced the vast majority of literate Europeans during the early Middle Ages. They served as a cultural bridge, transcribing and preserving the writings of Latin antiquity. They spearheaded the penetration of Christianity into the forests of Germany and later into Scandinavia, Poland, and Hungary. They served as scribes and advisers to kings and were drafted into high ecclesiastical offices. As recipients of gifts of land from pious donors over many generations, they held and managed large estates that became models of intelligent agricultural organization and technological innovation. With the coming of feudalism, Benedictine abbots became great vassals responsible for political and legal administration and military recruitment over the large areas under their control. Above all, as islands of security and learning in an ocean of political chaos, the Benedictine monasteries were the spiritual and intellectual centers of the developing classical-Christian-Germanic synthesis that underlay European civilization. In short, Benedictine monasticism became the supreme civilizing influence in the early Christian west.

Pope Gregory the Great

The Benedictines carried out their civilizing mission with the enthusiastic and invaluable support of the papacy. The alliance between these two institutions was consummated by the first Benedictine pope, Gregory the Great, who recognized how effective the Benedictines might be in spreading the Catholic faith and extending papal leadership far and wide across Christendom.

We have already encountered Pope Gregory as a scholar—a popularizer of Augustinian thought. His theology, although highly influential in subsequent centuries, failed to rise much above the intellectual level of his age. His real genius lay in his keen understanding of human nature and his ability as an administrator and organizer. He wrote an extraordinarily popular biography of St. Benedict, which drew widespread attention and support to the Benedictine movement. And his *Pastoral Care*, a treatise on the duties and obligations of a bishop, is a masterpiece of practical wisdom and common sense. It answered a great need of the times and became one of the most widely read books in the Middle Ages.

Gregory loved the monastic life and ascended the papal throne with genuine regret. On hearing of his election he went into hiding and had to be dragged into the Roman basilica of St. Peter's to be consecrated. But once resigned to his new responsibilities, Gregory bent every energy to the extension of papal authority. He believed fervently that the pope, as successor of St. Peter, was the rightful ruler of the Church. He reorganized the financial structure of the papal estates and used the increased revenues for charitable works to ameliorate the wretched poverty of his age. His integrity, wisdom, and administrative ability won for him an almost regal position in Rome and central Italy, towering over the contemporary Lombards and Byzantines who were struggling for control of the peninsula. The reform of the Frankish Church was beyond his immediate powers. But he set in motion a process that would one day bring both France and Germany into the papal fold when he dispatched a group of Benedictine monks to convert the pagan Anglo-Saxons.

The Conversion of England

The mission to England was led by the Benedictine St. Augustine (not to be confused with the great theologian of an earlier day, St. Augustine of Hippo).

In 597, Augustine and his followers arrived in the English kingdom of Kent and began their momentous work. England was then divided into a number of independent Germanic kingdoms of which Kent was momentarily the most powerful, and Augustine was assured a friendly reception by the fact that King Ethelbert of Kent had a Christian wife. The conversion progressed speedily, and on Whitsunday, 597, King Ethelbert and thousands of his subjects were baptized. The chief town of the realm, "Kent City" or Canterbury, became the headquarters of the new Church, and Augustine himself became Canterbury's first archbishop. Under his influence Ethelbert issued the first written laws in the Anglo-Saxon language.

During the decades that followed, the fortunes of English Benedictine Christianity rose and fell with the varying fortunes of the Anglo-Saxon kingdoms. Kent declined after King Ethelbert's death, and by the mid-600s political power had shifted to the northernmost of the Anglo-Saxon states, Northumbria. This remote outpost became the scene of a deeply significant encounter between the two great creative forces of the age: Irish-Celtic Christianity moving southward from its monasteries in Scotland, and Roman-Benedictine Christianity moving northward from Kent.

Although the two movements shared a common faith, they had different cultural backgrounds, different notions of monastic life and ecclesiastical organization, and even different systems for calculating the date of Easter. At stake was England's future relationship with the Continent and the papacy; a Celtic victory might well have resulted in the isolation of England from the main course of Western Christian development. But at the Synod of Whitby in 664, King Oswy of Northumbria decided in favor of Roman-Benedictine Christianity, and papal influence in England was assured. Five years later, in 669, the papacy sent the scholarly Theodore of Tarsus to assume the archbishopric of Canterbury and reorganize the English Church into a coherent hierarchical system. As a consequence of Northumbria's conversion and Archbishop Theodore's tireless efforts, England, only a century out of paganism, became Europe's most vigorous and creative Christian society.

The Irish-Benedictine encounter in seventh-century Northumbria produced a significant cultural surge known as the Northumbrian Renaissance. The two traditions influenced and energized one another to such an extent that the evolving civilization of the Christian West reached its pinnacle in this remote land. Boldly executed illuminated manuscripts in the Celtic curvilinear style, a new script, a vigorous vernacular epic poetry, an impressive architecture—all contributed to the luster of Northumbrian civilization in the late 600s and early 700s. The Northumbrian Renaissance centered in the monasteries founded by Irish and Benedictine missionaries, particularly in the Benedictine monastery of Jarrow. Here the supreme scholar of the age, St.Bede the Venerable, spent his life.

Bede entered Jarrow as a child and remained there until his death in 735. The greatest of his many works, the *Ecclesiastical History of England*, displays a critical sense far superior to that of Bede's medieval predecessors and con-

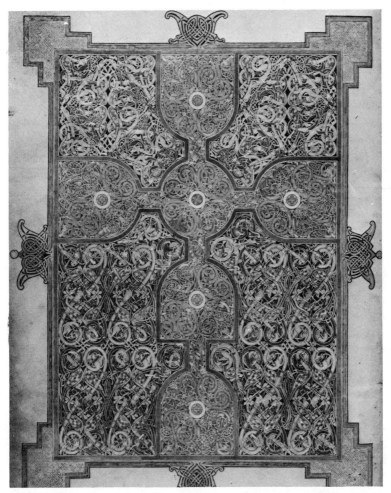

Cross Page from the *Lindisfarne Gospels* (*c.* A.D. 700), illustrating the artistic illuminations typical of the Northumbrian Renaissance.

temporaries. The *Ecclesiastical History,* our chief source for early English history, is the first major historical work to employ the modern chronological framework based on the Christian era (A.D.—Anno Domini—the year of the Lord). And Bede's chronological innovation reflects his deep sense of historical unity and purpose: the transformation of the world—and particularly of England—through the spread of the Christian gospel and the monastic life. The *Ecclesiastical History* reflects a remarkable cultural breadth and a penetrating mind; it establishes Bede as the foremost Christian intellect since Augustine of Hippo.

By Bede's death in 735, the Northumbrian kings had lost their political hegemony, and Northumbrian culture was beginning to fade. But the tradition of learning was carried from England back to the Continent during the eighth century by a group of Anglo-Saxon Benedictine missionaries. In the 740s the English monk St. Boniface reformed the Church of Frankland, infusing it with Benedictine idealism, systematizing its organization, and binding it more closely to the papacy. Pope Gregory had now been in his grave for 140 years, but his spirit was still at work. St. Boniface and other English missionaries founded new Benedictine monasteries among the Germans east of the Rhine and began the long, difficult task of Christianizing and civilizing Germany, just as Augustine and his monks had once Christianized Kent. By the later 700s the cultural center of Christendom had shifted southward again from England to the rising empire of the Frankish leader, Charlemagne.* Significantly, the leading scholar in Charlemagne's kingdom was Alcuin, a Benedictine monk from Northumbria, a student of one of Bede's own pupils.

The Church and Western Civilization

The West differed from the Byzantine East in innumerable ways, the most obvious being its far lower level of civilization. But just as important is the fact that the Western Church was able to develop more or less independently of the state. Church and state often worked hand in hand in the Christian west, but religion and secular politics were never merged to the degree that they were in Constantinople and, indeed, in most ancient civilizations. Early western Christendom was marked by a separation between cultural leadership that was ecclesiastical and monastic, and political power that was in the hands of the Germanic kings. This split contributed much to the fluidity and dynamism of western culture. It produced a creative tension that tended toward change rather than crystallization, toward an uninterrupted series of cultural climaxes, and toward ever-new intellectual and spiritual configurations. Like St. Augustine's two cities, the warrior culture of the Germanic states and the classical-Christian culture of Church and monastery remained always in the process of fusion, yet never completely fused. The interplay between these two worlds governed the development of medieval civilization.

*See below, pp. 72, ff.

Chapter 5

ℭ

The Explosion of Islam

Background and Origins

❡ Islam, Byzantium, and Western Christendom were the three major
civilizations of medieval western Eurasia, and of the three, Western Christendom remained for many centuries the most primitive and underdeveloped.
It had much to learn from Islam and Byzantium, and its developing synthesis
of classical, Christian, and Germanic traditions was shaped in many ways by
its two neighboring civilizations. The influence of these neighbors was imped-
ed, however, by Europe's hostility toward the "infidel" Muslims and the "ef-
fete, treacherous" Byzantines. In the eighth and ninth centuries Western
Europe's contacts with Islam were limited largely to the battlefield. Only after
the turn of the millennium did the west begin to draw upon the rich legacy of
Muslim thought and culture.

Islam today is a distinctive culture and a living religion extending across
an immense stretch of South Asia, the Middle East, and North Africa—from,
Indonesia to Pakistan to the Arab world of southwest Asia and Mediterranean
Africa. This vast Islamic belt was created by a militant, compelling religion
that burst into the world in seventh-century Arabia and spread outward with
remarkable speed. In the first hundred years of its existence, Islam shattered

ℭ

the Christian domination of the Mediterranean basin, destroyed the Persian Empire, seized Byzantium's richest provinces, absorbed Spain, pressed into the heart of France, and expanded far into southern Asia.

Muhammad

For countless centuries prior to the time of the prophet Muhammad (c. 571–632), nomadic tribes from the Arabian Peninsula (the modern Saudi Arabia) had repeatedly invaded the rich civilized districts of Palestine, Syria, and Mesopotamia to the north. Many Semitic invaders and empire builders of the ancient Near East had come originally from the Arabian Desert—the Amorites, the Chaldeans, the Canaanites, even the Hebrews. These peoples had quickly assimilated the ancient civilization of the Fertile Crescent and developed it in new, creative ways. But their kinsmen who stayed in Arabia remained primitive and disorganized.

In Muhammad's time most Arabians still clung to their nomadic ways and to their crude, polytheistic religion, but by then new civilizing influences were beginning to make themselves felt. A great caravan route running northward from southern Arabia served as an important link in a far-flung commercial network between the Far East and the Byzantine and Persian Empires. Along this route cities developed to serve the caravans, and with city life came a modicum of civilization. Indeed, the greatest of these trading cities, Mecca, became a bustling commercial center that sent its own caravans northward and southward and grew wealthy on its middleman profits. As the tribal life of Mecca and other caravan cities began to give way to commercial life, new foreign ideas challenged old ways and old viewpoints. It was in Mecca, around the year 571, that the prophet Muhammad was born.

At Muhammad's birth the Emperor Justinian had been dead for six years. Muhammad's contemporaries include such men as Pope Gregory the Great and Bishop Isidore of Seville. When the Benedictine mission from Rome landed in Kent in 597 to begin the conversion of England, Muhammad was in his twenties, as yet unknown outside his own immediate circle.

The future architect of one of the world's great religions was born of a poor branch of Mecca's leading clan. With little formal education behind him he became a caravan trader, and his travels brought him into close contact with Judaism, Christianity, and Persian Zoroastrianism. A sensitive man with a powerful, winning personality, he underwent a mystical experience while in his late thirties and began to set forth his new faith by preaching and writing. He won little support in Mecca apart from his wife and relatives and a few converts from the underprivileged classes. The ruling businessmen of Mecca were immune to the teaching of this "low-born upstart." They seem to have feared that his new religion would discredit the chief Meccan temple, the *Kaaba*, which housed a sacred meteoritic stone and was a profitable center of pilgrimages. Their belief that Muhammad's faith would ruin Mecca's pilgrim business was a staggering miscalculation, but their hostility to the new teaching forced Muhammad to flee Mecca in 622 and settle in the town of Medina, 280 miles northward on the caravan route.

The flight to Medina, known among the Muslims as the Hegira (He-ji'-ra) was a momentous turning point in the development of Islam and marks the beginning date of the Muslim calendar. Muhammad quickly won the inhabitants of Medina to his faith and became the city's political chief as well as its religious leader. Indeed, under Muhammad's direction religious and civil authority were fused; the sacred community was at once a state and a church. In this respect Muhammad's community at Medina foreshadowed the great Islamic state of later years.

The Medinans made war on Mecca, raiding its caravans and blockading its trade. In 630 Medina conquered Mecca and incorporated it into the sacred community. During the two remaining years of his life Muhammad, now an almost legendary figure in Arabia, received the voluntary submission of many tribes in the peninsula. By the time of his death in 632 he had united the Arabians as never before into a coherent political-religious group, well-organized, well-armed, and inspired by a powerful new monotheistic religion. The energies of these desert people were now channeled toward a single goal: the conquest and conversion of the world.

The Islamic Religion

Faith was the cement with which Muhammad unified Arabia. The new faith was called *Islam*, the Arabic word for "surrender." Muhammad taught that his followers must surrender to the will of Allah, the single, almighty God of the universe. Muhammad did not regard himself as divine but rather as the last and greatest of a long line of prophets of whom he was the "seal." Among his predecessors were Moses, the Old Testament prophets, and Jesus.

Islam respected the Old and New Testaments and was relatively tolerant toward Jews and Christians—the "people of the book." But the Muslims had a book of their own, the *Koran*, which superseded its predecessors and was believed to contain the pure essence of divine revelation. The *Koran* is the comprehensive body of Muhammad's writings, the bedrock of the Islamic faith: "All men and jinn in collaboration," so it was said , "could not produce its like." Muslims regard it as the word of Allah, *dictated* to Muhammad by the angel Gabriel from an original "uncreated" book located in heaven. Accordingly, its divine inspiration and authority extend not only to its precepts but also to its every letter (of which there are 323,621), making any translation a species of heresy. Every good Muslim must read the *Koran* in Arabic, and as Islam spread, the Arabic language necessarily spread with it.

The *Koran* is perhaps the most widely read book ever written. More than a manual of worship, it was the text from which the non-Arabian Muslim learned his Arabic. And since it was the supreme authority not only in religion but also in law, science, and the humanities, it became the standard text in Muslim schools for every imaginable subject. Muhammad's genius is vividly illustrated by his success in adapting a primitive language such as seventh- century Arabic to the sophisticated religious, legal, and ethical concepts that one encounters in his sacred book.

Muhammad offered his followers the assurance of eternal salvation if they led upright, sober lives and followed the precepts of Islam. Above all, they were bound to a simple confession of faith: "There is no god but Allah, and Muhammad is his prophet." The Muslim also was obliged to engage in ritual prayers and fasting, to journey as a pilgrim to Mecca at least once in his lifetime, and to work devoutly toward the welfare and expansion of the sacred community. Holy war was the supremely meritorious activity, for service to the faith was identical with service to the state. Public law in Islamic lands had a religious sanction, and the fusion of religion and politics, which Muhammad created at Medina, remained a fundamental characteristic of Islamic society. There was no Muslim priesthood, no Muslim "church" apart from the state: Muhammad's political successors, the caliphs, were defenders of the faith and guardians of the faithful. The tension between Church and state that proved such a stimulus to medieval Europe was thus unknown in the Muslim world.

The Early Conquests: 632–655

In the year immediately after Muhammad's death the explosive energy of the Arabs, harnessed at last by the teachings of the Prophet, broke upon the world. The spectacular conquests resulted in part from the youthful vigor of Islam, in part from the weakness and exhaustion of its enemies. The Emperor Heraclius had just defeated the Persians, and both Byzantium and Persia were spent and enfeebled by their long, desperate conflict. And the Monophysites of Syria and Egypt remained deeply hostile to their orthodox Byzantine masters.

The Arabs entered these tired, embittered lands afire with religious zeal, lured by the wealth and luxuries of the civilized world. They had no master plan of conquest—most of their campaigns began as plundering expeditions— but their momentum grew with each unexpected victory. Moving into Byzantine Syria they annihilated a huge Byzantine army in 636, captured Damascus and Jerusalem, and by 640 had occupied the entire land, detaching it more or less permanently from Byzantine control. In 637 they inflicted an overwhelming defeat on the Persian army and entered the Persian capital of Ctesiphon, gazing in bewilderment at its opulence and wealth. Within another decade they had subdued all Persia and arrived at the borders of India. In later years they penetrated deeply into the Indian subcontinent and laid the foundations of the modern Muslim states of Pakistan and Bangladesh. The Persians gradually adopted the Islamic faith, exchanging Zoroaster for Muhammad and thus preparing themselves for the great role that they would later play in Islamic politics and culture.

Meanwhile Muslims were pushing westward into Egypt. They captured Alexandria in the 640s, absorbing into their cultural sphere the great metropolis that had for centuries been a center of Greek science and, later, Hebrew and Christian theology. With Egypt and Syria in their hands they took to the sea, challenging the long-established Byzantine domination of the eastern Mediterranean. They took the island of Cyprus, raided ancient Rhodes, and in 655 won a major victory over the Byzantine fleet in the "Battle of the Masts."

The Civil War: 655–661

In 655 Islamic expansion ceased momentarily as the new empire became locked in a savage dynastic struggle. The succession to the caliphate was contested between the Umayyads, a leading family in the old Meccan commercial oligarchy, and Ali, the son-in-law of Muhammad himself. Ali headed a faction that was to become exceedingly powerful in later centuries. His followers insisted that the caliph must be a direct descendant of the Prophet. As it happened, Muhammad had left no surviving sons and only one daughter, Fatima, who married the Prophet's cousin, Ali.

In 661 the Umayyad forces defeated Ali in battle and initiated an Umayyad dynasty of caliphs that moved the Islamic capital to Damascus in Syria and ruled there for nearly a century. But the legitimist faction that had once supported Ali persisted as a troublesome, dedicated minority, throwing its support behind various of the numerous descendants of Ali and Fatima. In time the political movement evolved into a heresy known as *Shi'ism* which held that the *true* caliphs—the descendants of Muhammad through Fatima and Ali—were sinless, infallible, and possessed of a body of secret knowledge not contained in the *Koran. Shi'ism* became an occult underground doctrine, which occasionally rose to the surface in the form of civil insurrection. In the tenth century the Shi'ists gained control of Egypt and established a "Fatimid" dynasty of caliphs in Cairo. Shi'ism inspired a band of Muslim desperadoes know as the "Assassins" who used hashish as a means of divine illumination. In various forms, the Shi'ite movement survives to this day.

The Umayyad Dynasty: 661–750

The intermission in the Muslim expansion ended with the Umayyad victory over Ali in 661. And even though the Islamic capital was now Damascus rather than Medina, the old Arabian aristocracy remained in firm control. Constantinople was now the chief military goal, but the great city repulsed a series of powerful Muslim attacks between 670 and 680. The Byzantine defense was aided by a secret weapon known as "Greek Fire"—a liquid that ignited on exposure to air and could not be extinguished by water, but only by vinegar or sand. In 717–718 a great Arab fleet and army assaulted Constantinople in vain, and having expended all their energies and resources without success the Muslims abandoned their effort to take the city. Byzantium survived for another seven centuries, effectively barring Muslim inroads into southeastern Europe until the late Middle Ages.

In the meantime, however, Muslim armies were enjoying spectacular success in the west. From Egypt they moved along the North African coast into the old Vandal kingdom, now ruled by distant Byzantium. In 698 the Muslims took Carthage. In 711 they crossed the Straits of Gibraltar into Spain and crushed the tottering Visigothic kingdom at a blow, bringing the Spanish Christians under their dominion and driving the Christian princes into mountain hideaways in the Pyrenees. Next the Muslims moved into southern Gaul and threatened the kingdom of the Merovingian Franks. In 732, a century after the Prophet's death, the Muslims were halted at last on a battlefield between Tours and Poitiers by a Christian army led by the able Frankish warrior, Charles Martel.

The Christians at Tours were not the white-clad defenders of the Gospel that former generations imagined them. They were long-haired Franks, clad in wolfskins. But they managed to halt the momentum of militant Islam in Western Europe, just as the Byzantines had stopped it in the east.

The Muslim army at Tours was small and makeshift in comparison with the great force that had besieged Constantinople in 717–718, but together these two battles brought an end to the era of major Islamic encroachments against the territories of the two Christian civilizations. The remainder of the Middle Ages witnessed a continuance of Christian-Islamic warfare and some territorial change—most of Spain, for example, had reverted to Christian control by the middle of the thirteenth century. But by and large, Islam, Byzantium, and Western Christendom had achieved equilibrium by the mid-700s and remained in balance for centuries to come.

Throughout the rest of the Middle Ages, the three civilizations tended to expand not at one another's expense but away from each other—Byzantium into the Balkans and Russia, Islam into South Asia, Western Christendom into Germany, Scandinavia, Hungary, and Poland. The Crusades were, ultimately, only a minor exception to this generalization; the Christian reconquest of Spain and the victory of the Seljuk Turks over the Byzantines in Asia Minor were much more important exceptions. But it was not until the fourteenth century, when the Islamic Ottoman Turks swept into the Balkans, that the balance of the three powers was upset altogether.

The Golden Age of the Abbasids

In 750, eighteen years after the battle of Tours, the Umayyads were overthrown. Their successors, the Abbasids, were Arabians—as caliphs had always been. But the Abbasids, unlike their Umayyad predecessors, encour-

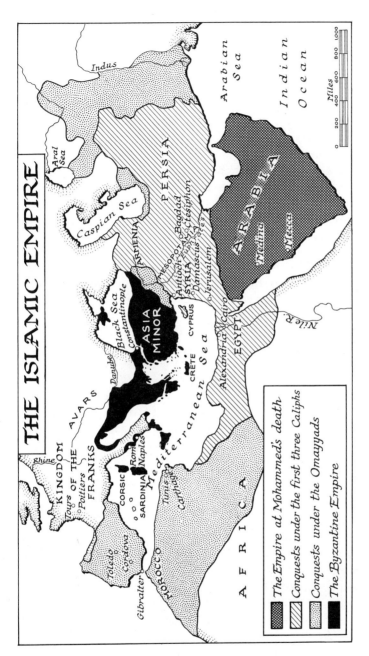

THE ISLAMIC EMPIRE

Indus

Aral Sea

Caspian Sea

PERSIA

ARMENIA

MESOPOTAMIA
Antioch
Bagdad
Ctesiphon
SYRIA
Damascus
Jerusalem

Arabian Sea

Indian Ocean

Miles
0 200 400 600 800 1000

ARABIA

Medina

Mecca

Black Sea
Constantinople

ASIA MINOR

CYPRUS

Alexandria
Cairo
EGYPT

Nile R.

Danube

CRETE

Mediterranean Sea

AVARS

FRANKS

KINGDOM

Tours of the
Poitiers

Rhine

Rome
Naples

CORSICA

SARDINIA

Tunis
Carthage

Toledo
Cordova

Gibraltar

MOROCCO

A F R I C A

The Empire at Mohammed's death

Conquests under the first three Caliphs

Conquests under the Omayyads

The Byzantine Empire

aged the political participation of the highly civilized conquered peoples, now converting in large numbers to Islam. It was above all the Islamized Persian aristocracy whom the Abbasids favored, and shortly after the victory of the new dynasty, the Islamic capital was moved from Damascus to Baghdad on the Tigris River, deep within the old Persian Empire. This move was accompanied by an eastward shift in Islam's political interests, which relieved some of the pressure against Constantinople and the West.

The rise of the Abbasids thus marks the end of the Arabian aristocracy's monopoly on political power. The new government at Baghdad was run by a medley of races and peoples, and men of humble origin could rise high in the service of the caliph. As one disgruntled aristocrat observed, "Sons of concubines have become too numerous among us; O God, lead me to a land where I shall see no bastards."

Baghdad, under the early Abbasid caliphs, became one of the world's great cities. It was the center of a vast commercial network spreading across the Islamic world and far beyond. Silks, spices, and fragrant woods flowed into its wharves from India, China, and the islands of Indonesia; furs, honey, and slaves were imported from Scandinavia; and gold, slaves, and ivory from tropical Africa. Baghdad was the nexus of a far-flung banking system with branches in other cities across the Islamic world. A check could be drawn in Baghdad and cashed in Morocco, 4000 miles to the west. The Abbasid imperial palace, occupying fully a third of the city, contained innumerable apartments and public rooms, quarters for eunuchs, harems, and government officals, and a remarkable reception room known as the "hall of the tree", which contained an artificial tree of gold and silver on whose branches mechanical birds chirped and sang.

The wealth and culture of Baghdad reached their height under the Abbasid caliph, Harun-al-Rashid (786–809), whose opulence and power became legendary. Harun was accustomed to receiving tribute from the Byzantine Empire itself. When on one occasion the tribute was discontinued he sent the following peremptory note to the emperor at Constantinople:

In the name of God, the merciful, the compassionate.
From Harun, the commander of the faithful,
* to Nicephorus, the dog of a Roman.*
Verily I have read thy letter, O son of an infidel mother.
* As for the answer, it shall be for thine eye to see,*
* not for thine ear to hear. Salaam.*

The letter was followed by a successful military campaign which forced the unlucky Byzantines to resume their tribute.

The era of Harun-al-Rashid was notable, too, for its vigorous intellectual life. Islamic scholars studied and synthesized the learned traditions of Greece, Rome, Persia, and India. In Baghdad, Harun's son and successor founded the House of Wisdom—a great intellectual institute that was at once a library, a university, and a translation center. Here and elsewhere Islamic scholars pushed their learning far beyond the point it had reached under the Umayyads. Drawing from various older traditions, Islamic culture had come of age with remarkable speed. At a time when Charlemagne was struggling to civilize his rustic, illiterate Franks, Harun reigned over glittering Baghdad.

The Abbasid government drew heavily from the administrative techniques of Byzantium and Persia. A sophisticated, complex bureaucracy ran the affairs of state from the capital at Baghdad and kept in touch with the provinces through a multitude of tax-gatherers, judges, couriers, and spies. The government was enlightened up to a point, although no more sensitive to the demands of social justice than other governments of its day. The Abbasid regime undertook extensive irrigation works, drained swamps, and thereby increased the amount of land under cultivation. But the status of the peasant and unskilled laborer was kept low by the competition of multitudes of slaves. The brilliance of Abbasid culture had little effect on the impoverished masses who, aside from their fervent Islamic faith, retained much of the same primitive way of life that they had known for the last two thousand years.

The Decline of Abbasid Power

The Abbasids were unable to maintain their power throughout the vast reaches of the Islamic empire. Communications were limited by the speed of sailing vessels and camels, and governors of remote provinces required sufficient independence and military strength to defend themselves from infidel attacks. Such local independence and power could easily ripen into full autonomy. The Abbasid revolution of 750 was followed by a long process of political disintegration as one province after another broke free of the control of the caliphs at Baghdad. Even in the palmy days of Harun-al-Rashid, the extreme western provinces—Spain, Morocco, and Tunisia—were ruled by independent local dynasties. Spain, indeed, had never passed under Abbasid control but remained under the domination of Umayyad rulers. And by the later ninth century the trend toward disintegration was gaining momentum as Egypt, Syria, and eastern Persia (Iran) broke free.

By then the Abbasid caliphs were slowly losing their grip on their own government in Baghdad. Ambitious army commanders gradually usurped power, establishing control over the tax machinery and the other organs of government. In the later tenth and eleventh centuries the Fatimid caliphate of Cairo rose to great power, extending its authority to Syria and briefly occupying Baghdad itself. Since about the mid-tenth century, the Abbasid caliphs of Baghdad had been controlled by members of a local Persian aristocratic dynasty who took the title of "sultan" and ruled what was left of the Abbasid state. A century later, in 1055, the chief of the Seljuk Turks conquered Baghdad, assumed the title of "Grand Sultan," and then turned his forces against Byzantium with the devastating effects that we have already seen. Seljuk power declined in the twelfth century, to be followed by a period of further Islamic political disintegration concurrent with the Crusades. By the later twelfth century Islam recovered itself in Syria and Egypt, and in the course of the thirteenth century the crusaders were driven out. In that same century the emasculated Abbasid caliphate was destroyed. The Mongols took Baghdad in

1258, massacred a good part of its population (allegedly, 800,000 people were murdered), and brought to an end the dynasty and the office that had ruled Baghdad, in fact or in name, for five centuries.

Economic and Religious Change

The political troubles that the Abbasids endured from about 950–1258 were accompanied by a serious economic decline. Trade dried up, money became scarce, and Islamic rulers, whether in Baghdad, Cairo, or Damascus, were forced to reward their political underlings with land or revenue rights rather than wages. Thus, imperialism gave way to localism, and wealth tended increasingly to be identified with land rather than with commerce.

The general unrest of the period encouraged waves of popular protest, both socio-economic and religious. Bands of Shi'ite desperadoes embarked on widespread terrorism and revolution. At the same time a quasi-heretical, mystical movement known as Sufism became immensely popular throughout the Islamic world. For centuries the Sufi movement, although never tightly coordinated, had provided the chief impetus to missionary work among the infidel. These Sufi mystics, often illiterate, always fervent, had achieved the conversion of millions of people in Africa, India, Indonesia, Central Asia, and China. And it was they, rather than the orthodox religious scholars and lawyers, who could bring hope to the Muslim masses in times of trouble. Drawing from the Neoplatonic notion that reality rests in God alone, the Sufis sought mystical union with the divine and stressed God's love over the orthodox emphasis on God's authority. The orthodox Islamic scholars contended vigorously against this mystical trend, but by the tenth century Sufism was the most powerful religious force among the people of Islam. It affects Islamic personal devotion to this day.

Islamic Culture: Conversion and Diffusion

Throughout the epoch of political disintegration, the Muslim world remained united by a common tongue, a common culture, and a common faith. It continued to struggle vigorously with Byzantium for control of the Mediterranean and managed, at various times between the ninth and eleventh centuries, to occupy the key islands of Crete, Sicily, Sardinia, and Corsica. As early as the reign of Harun-al-Rashid, most of the inhabitants of Syria, Egypt, and North Africa had converted to Islam, even though these lands had once supported enthusiastic and well-organized Christian churches. The Muslims did not ordinarily persecute the Christians; they merely taxed them. And the prolonged tax burden was probably a more effective instrument of conversion than ruthless persecution would have been.

The intellectual awakening of Harun-al-Rashid's day continued unabated for another four centuries. The untutored Arab from the desert became the cultural heir of Greece, Rome, Persia, and India, and within less than two centuries of the Prophet's death, Islamic culture had reached the level of a mature, sophisticated civilization. Its mercurial rise was a consequence of the Arabs' success in absorbing the great civilized traditions of their conquered people and employing these traditions in a cultural synthesis both new and unique. Islam borrowed, but never without digesting. What it drew from other civilizations it transmuted and made its own.

The political disintegration of the ninth and tenth centuries was accompanied by a diffusion of cultural activity throughout the Muslim world. During the tenth century, for example, Cordova, the capital of Umayyad Spain, acquired prodigious wealth and became the center of a brilliant cultural flowering. With a population of half a million or more, Cordova was another Baghdad. No other city in Western Europe could remotely approach it in population, wealth, or municipal organization. It was the wonder of the age — with its magnificent mansions, mosques, aqueducts, and baths, its bustling markets and shops, its efficient police force and sanitation service, its street lights, and its splendid, sprawling palace, flashing with brightly colored tiles and surrounded by graceful minarets and sparkling fountains.

All across the Islamic world, from Cordova to Baghdad and far to the east, Muslim scholars and artists were developing the legacies of past civilizations. Architects were molding Greco-Roman forms into a graceful and distinctive new style. Philosophers were studying and elaborating the writings of Plato and Aristotle, despite the hostility of narrowly orthodox Islamic theologians. Physicians were expanding the ancient medical doctrines of Galen and his Greek predecessors, describing new symptoms and identifying new curative drugs. Astronomers and astrologers were tightening the geocentric system of Ptolemy, preparing accurate tables of planetary motions, and giving the stars Arabic names that are used to this day—names such as Altair, Deneb, Aldebaran, and (regretfully) Zubenelgenubi. The renowned astronomer-poet of eleventh-century Persia, Omar Khayyam, devised a calendar of singular accuracy. Muslim mathematicians borrowed creatively from both Greece and India. From the Greeks they learned geometry and trigonometry. And from the Hindus they developed algebra (Arabic: *al Jabr*) and appropriated the so-called Arabic numerals—the set of nine number symbols plus the zero—which were ultimately passed on to the west to revolutionize European mathematics.

Islamic literature produced no long, systematic masterpieces but excelled in short works of poetry and prose. The individual anecdote took precedence over the extended narrative. Muslim poets endeavored to perfect individual verses rather than to create long, coherent poems. The quatrains of Omar Khayyam's *Rubaiyat* seem to have been arranged in alphabetical order rather than conforming to any overall plan. The chapters of the Koran itself, which had been left completely unorganized by Muhammad, were assembled shortly

Interior of the mosque at Cordova (tenth century).

after his death in order of decreasing length, with no attempt at structural unity. The enduring value of these works lies in the power and beauty of their individual chapters and verses.

The Arab conquests during the century after Muhammad changed the historical course of North Africa and Southwest Asia decisively and permanently. The Arabs conquered their vast territories thrice over: with their armies, their faith, and their language. In the end, the term "Arab" applied to every Muslim from Morocco to Iraq, regardless of his ethnic background. Within its all-encompassing religious and linguistic framework, Arab culture provided a new stimulus and a new orientation to the long-civilized peoples of former empires. With its manifold ingredients, the rich Islamic heritage would one day provide invaluable nourishment to the mind of the twelfth-and thirteenth-century West. Later, Islamic armies would bring Byzantium to an end and make Constantinople a Muslim city. Later still, in the sixteenth and seventeenth centuries, they would be at the gates of Vienna. Only in the nineteenth century did Islam become clearly subordinate to the West militarily and politically. And today there are clear signs that this subordination is at an end.

MUSLIM CHRONOLOGY

---

c.571–632: Muhammad
    622: The Hegira
632–655: The first conquests: Syria, Persian Empire, Egypt
655–661: Civil war: Umayyads *versus* Ali
661–750: Umayyad Dynasty; new conquests: North Africa, Spain
717–718: Arabs besiege Constantinople
    732: Arabs defeated at Tours
750–1258: Abbasid dynasty at Baghdad
786–809: Harun-al-Rashid; zenith of Abbasid power

Chapter 6

❧

Carolingian Europe

The Significance of the Carolingian Age

❡ In the course of the eighth century Western Christendom began to emerge
as a coherent civilization. It did so under the aegis of the Carolingian
Empire—a vast constellation of territories welded together by the Frankish
king Charlemagne and his talented predecessors. Here for the first time the
various cultural ingredients—classical, Christian, and Germanic—that went
into the making of European civilization achieved a degree of synthesis.
Charlemagne was a Germanic king who surrounded himself with Germanic
warrior-aristocrats. But he also drew churchmen and classical scholars around
him and took very seriously his role as protector and sustainer of the western
Church. Although his empire was fundamentally Germanic, its intellectual
life, limited though it was, drew heavily from the classical-Christian tradition.
The fusion of these cultural ingredients was evident in the life of the Carolingian court, in the rising vigor of the Carolingian Church, and in the person
of Charlemagne himself.

Charlemagne's Frankland stood in sharp contrast to contemporary
Byzantium and the Abbasid Empire of Islam. Baghdad and Constantinople
were the centers of brilliant, opulent, mercantile civilizations. Charlemagne's

❧

Franks were half-civilized rustics. But eighth-century western Europeans were steadily moving toward a life of larger meaning for themselves and for those who came after them. For the first time it began to dawn on a few of them that they were a people apart, that they were *Europeans*—agents of a new, distinctive civilization with its roots in Athens and Jerusalem, Germany and Rome, bound together—much as the Byzantines and Muslims were—by a common faith, a common scholarly language, and a common heritage.

The new Europe was spiritually and intellectually enlivened by the wide-ranging Benedictines, who disseminated a cultural tradition based on the Bible, the writings of the Latin Doctors and their contemporaries, and the surviving masterpieces of Latin literature. This evolving culture was bound together politically by a new dynasty of Frankish monarchs, the Carolingians.*

Carolingian Europe differed profoundly from the western Roman Empire of old. It was a land without large cities, thoroughly agrarian in its economic organization, with its culture centered on the monastery, the cathedral, and the perambulatory royal court rather than the urban marketplace. And although Charlemagne extended his authority into Italy, the center of his activities and his interests remained northern Frankland. In a word, the new Europe no longer faced the Mediterranean; its axis had shifted northward.

Agricultural Technology

The relative brightness of the age of Charlemagne was the product of creative processes that had been at work during the preceding centuries. Benedictine evangelism and Northumbrian culture contributed much to the Carolingian revival. So, too, did the gradual development of a new agrarian technology that increased the productivity of north European farmlands.

By the opening of the eighth century, the light scratch plow of the ancient Mediterranean world had been superseded throughout much of northwestern Europe by a heavy compound plow. This new device—with wheels, colter, plowshare and moldboard—cut deeply into the soil, pulverized it, and turned it aside, so creating a drainage system of ridges and furrows. Well suited to the heavy lowland soils and rainy climate of northern Europe, the new plow may perhaps have been brought into the west by the Slavs in the sixth or seventh centuries. Its introduction opened up vast areas of rich soil in which the earlier scratch plow was ineffective and fostered the tendency toward dividing fields into long strips cultivated by teams of four to eight oxen, which the heavy plow required. Peasants pooled their oxen and their labor in order to exploit the new plow; in so doing they laid the foundation for the cooperative agricultural communities of medieval Europe with strong village councils to

*They were so named by later historians after their most illustrious representative, Charles the Great or Charlemagne (Latin: *Carolus Magnus*).

Illuminations from the Flemish *Hours of the Virgin* (*c.* 1515): on the left, the month of July; on the right, the month of September. Note two examples of medieval technological achievement: the windmill and the compound plow with moldboard.

regulate the division of labor and resources. In these village communities the medieval peasantry learned the attitude of responsible, voluntary co-operation—an attitude that may have influenced the rise of capitalist enter-prise many centuries later.

The newly opened farmlands were often fertile enough to permit more fre-quent crop rotation than had previously been feasible. By the Carolingian age, parts of northern Europe were just beginning to adopt a three-field system of cultivation in place of the two-field system typical of Roman times. Formerly, a typical farm had been divided into two fields, one of which was planted each year and allowed to lie fallow the second year. But it was found that the rich northern soils, opened by the heavy plow, did not require a full year's rest be-tween crops. Instead, they were sometimes divided into three fields, each of which underwent a three-year cycle of autumn planting, spring planting, and fallow. Three-field agriculture developed slowly and irregularly. In time, however, it had an important impact on the European economy, for it in-creased food production and brought a degree of prosperity to northern Europe. It is possible that the heavy plow and the three-field system, which could not be employed efficiently in the light, dry soils of the Mediterranean south, contributed to the northward shift in medieval Europe's economic and cultural orientation.

The early Middle Ages also profited from a trend toward mechanization.

The water mill, which was used occasionally in antiquity for grinding grain, had now come into more widespread use and was often to be seen on Carolingian farms. During the centuries following Charlemagne's death, the water mill was put to new uses—to power the rising textile industry of the eleventh century and to drive triphammers in forges. Thus, the technological progress of Merovingian and Carolingian times continued into the centuries that followed. By 1000 the development of the horseshoe and a new, efficient horse collar, both apparently imported from Siberia or central Asia, made possible the very gradual replacement of the ox by the more energetic horse as the chief draught animal on the farms of northwestern Europe. And in the twelfth century the windmill made its debut in the European countryside. These new advances resulted in the increased productivity that underlay the prosperous civilization of the High Middle Ages (c. 1050–1300). Slowly the custom of human slavery declined as human power gave way more and more to animal and machine power.

Carolingian Europe gained from the earlier phase of this drawn-out revolution in agrarian technology, but its chief impact was yet to come. Carolingian peasants remained near the level of subsistence, owing in part to the rise of population along with productivity. During a great famine of 791, for example, peasants were driven to cannibalism and were even reported to have eaten members of their own families. Conditions may have been improving, but only very gradually, and a single bad year could be disastrous.

The Rise of the Carolingians

The Merovingian dynasty, founded by Clovis, had weakened over the centuries. Their primary problem was the necessity of giving away portions of their crown lands, generation after generation, in order to attract loyal followers. By the later 600s, the Merovingians were impoverished, and all real power had passed to the aristocracy. Meanwhile, as a consequence of the Merovingian policy of dividing royal authority and crown lands among the sons of a deceased king, Frankland had split into several distinct districts, the most important of which were Neustria (Paris and northwestern France), Austrasia (the heavily Germanized northeast including the Rhinelands), and Burgundy in the southeast (see map, p. 76).

During the seventh century a great landholding family, known to historians as the Carolingians, rose to power in Austrasia. The Carolingians became "mayors" of the itinerant royal household; that is, they held the chief administrative post in the Austrasian government (such as it was) and made their office hereditary. As the Merovingians grew increasingly powerless, the Carolingians became the real masters of Austrasia. The Carolingian mayor built up his power by gathering around him a considerable number of trained warriors somewhat in the tradition of the old Germanic comitatus. These men became his vassals, placing themselves under his protection and maintenance and swearing their loyalty to him. Other nobles also had their private vassalic armies. But the Carolingians, with far the greatest number of followers, dominated the scene.

In 687 a Carolingian mayor named Pepin of Heristal led his Austrasian army to a decisive victory over the Neustrians at Tertry, and the Carolingians thenceforth were the dominant family in Frankland. With Neustria under their control they were able to dominate Burgundy, and when the Muslims moved into Gaul in the early 730s, the Franks were able to unite against them under the able leadership of Pepin of Heristal's son, the vigorous Carolingian mayor, Charles Martel.

Charles Martel ("The Hammer"): 714–741

This able, ruthless warrior not only turned back the Muslims at the battle of Tours (732); he also won victory after victory over Muslims and Christians alike, consolidating his power over the Franks and extending the boundaries of the Frankish state. Like the Adams family in American history, the Carolingians of the seventh and eighth centuries had the good fortune to produce exceedingly able men over several generations. Martel's father, Pepin of Heristal, had conquered Neustria. Martel himself defeated the Muslims and, indeed, almost everybody he faced. His son, Pepin the Short, gained the Frankish crown, and his grandson, Charlemagne, won an empire.

The Carolingians followed the same policy of divided succession among male heirs that had so weakened the Merovingians. But here, too, Carolingian luck played a crucial role in history. For as it happened, the Carolingian mayors and later kings, over several generations, had only one long-surviving heir. Frankish unity was maintained not by policy, but in spite of it. When Charles Martel died in 741 his lands and authority were divided among his two sons, Carloman and Pepin the Short. But Carloman ruled only six years, retiring to a Benedictine monastery in 747—leaving the field to his brother Pepin. Carloman represented a new kind of Germanic ruler, deeply affected by the spiritual currents of his age, whose piety foreshadowed that of numerous saint-kings of later centuries. Christian culture and Germanic political leadership were beginning to draw together.

Missions from Northumbria

The fusion of these two worlds was carried still further by Pepin the Short (741–768). Pepin supported a Benedictine Christian revival in Frankland and consummated an alliance of far-reaching consequences between the Frankish monarchy and the papacy. At the time of Charles Martel's death in 741, English Benedictine monks had long been engaged in evangelical work among the Germanic peoples east of the Rhine. The earliest of these missions were directed at the Frisians, a maritime people who were settled along the coast of the Netherlands. The first of the Benedictine evangelists were monks from Northumbria who brought to the Continent not only the strict organizational discipline and devotion to the papacy that had been characteristic of the Northumbrian Benedictines but also the venturesome missionary fervor which the Celtic monks had contributed to the Northumbrian revival. So it was that Benedictine monks such as Wilfrid of Ripon and Willibrord left their Northumbrian homeland during the later 600s to evangelize the Frisians. The course of Western Civilization was deeply affected by the transference to Frankland and Germany of the vital force of Northumbrian Christianity with its vibrant culture, its Roman-Benedictine discipline, and its spiritual commitment. Wilfrid of Ripon, Willibrord, and their devoted followers represent the first wave of a movement that was ultimately to infuse the Frankish empire of Charlemagne with the spiritual life that had developed in Anglo-Saxon England during the century following St. Augustine's mission. The dynamic thrust of Roman-Benedictine Christianity, having leapt from Rome to Kent and then to remote Northumbria, was returning to the Continent.

St. Boniface in Germany

The key figure in this cultural movement was St. Boniface, an English Benedictine from Wessex. Reared in monasteries of southern England, Boniface left Wessex in 716 to do missionary work among the Frisians. From then until his death in 754 he devoted himself above all other tasks to Christianizing the Germanic peoples. Boniface was a man of boundless energy and considerable learning, a wise, magnetic leader. And he worked in close cooperation with both the papacy and the Anglo-Saxon church. A great number of his letters survive, many of which request support from his compatriots in Wessex and advice from Rome. On three occasions he visited Rome to confer with the pope, and from the beginning his work among the Germans was performed under papal commission. In 732 the papacy appointed him archbishop in Germany. Some years later he was given the episcopal see at Mainz as his headquarters. Throughout his career he was a devoted representative of the Anglo-Saxon church, the Benedictine Rule, and the papacy. As he put it, he strove "to hold fast the Catholic faith and unity, and to yield submission to the Church of Rome as long as life shall last for us."

Boniface also worked with the backing of the Frankish mayors—Charles Martel, Carloman, and Pepin the Short. Armed with the Christian faith and the Benedictine rule, and supported by England, Frankland, and Rome, Boniface labored among the Germanic tribes in Frisia, Thuringia, Hesse, and Bavaria. There he won converts, founded new Benedictine monasteries in the German wilderness, and erected the organizational framework of a disciplined German church. He suffered moments of discouragement, as when he wrote to an English abbot, "Have pity upon an old man tried and tossed on all sides by the waves of a German sea." Yet Boniface accomplished much, and the monasteries which he established—particularly the great house of Fulda in Hesse—were to become centers of learning and evangelism that played a great role in converting and civilizing the peoples of Germany.

Reform of the Frankish Church

During the decade following Charles Martel's death in 741, Boniface devoted much of his energy to Frankland itself, for the Frankish church of the early eighth century stood in desperate need of reform. On the whole it was corrupt, disorganized, and ignorant—the product of several centuries of Merovingian misrule. Many areas of Frankland had no priests at all; numerous peasants were scarcely removed from paganism, and priests themselves are reported to have hedged their bets by sacrificing animals to the pagan Germanic gods. Charles Martel, although willing enough to support Boniface's missionary endeavors among the Germanic pagans, had no taste for ecclesiastical reforms within his own Frankish church. Indeed, he weakened the church by confiscating a considerable amount of ecclesiastical property and granting it to his military vassals. Carloman and Pepin, however, encouraged Boniface to work toward the reform of the Frankish church, and beginning in 742 he held a series of synods for that purpose. Working in close collaboration with the papacy, Boniface remodeled the Frankish ecclesiastical organization on the disciplined pattern of Anglo-Saxon England and papal Rome. He reformed Frankish monasteries along the lines of the Benedictine Rule, saw to the establishment of monastic schools, encouraged the appointment of dedicated prelates, and worked toward the development of an adequate parish system to bring the Gospel to the countryside. Thus Boniface laid the groundwork for both the new Church in Germany and the reformed Church in Frankland. In doing so, he served as one of the chief architects of the Carolingian cultural revival.

The Franco-Papal Alliance

Boniface's introduction of Roman discipline and organization into the Frankish church was followed almost immediately by the consummation of a political alliance between Rome and Frankland. It may well have been at Boniface's prompting that the Carolingian mayor, Pepin the Short, sought papal support for his seizure of the Frankish crown. Although the Merovingian monarchs retained the enormous prestige always enjoyed by a Germanic royal dynasty, they had long been impoverished puppet-kings. Even so, if the Carolingians hoped to replace the Merovingians on the Frankish throne, they would have to call upon the most potent spiritual sanction available to their age: papal consecration. In supporting Boniface and his fellow Benedictines, the Carolingian mayors had fostered papal influence in the Frankish church. Now, seeking papal support for a dynastic revolution, Pepin the Short could reasonably expect a favorable response in Rome.

For their part, the popes had been seeking a strong, loyal ally against the Byzantines and Lombards who had long been contending for political supremacy in Italy. The Carolingians, with their policy of aid to the Benedictine missionaries and their support of Boniface's reform measures, must have seemed strong candidates for the role of papal champion. And by the mid-eighth century a champion was badly needed. Traditionally the papacy had followed the policy of turning to Byzantium for protection against the Lombards who, although they had by now converted from Arianism to Catholic Christianity, remained an ominous threat to papal independence. By 750 the popes could no longer depend on Byzantine protection for two reasons: (1) the Byzantine emperors had recently embraced a doctrine known as *iconoclasm,*which the papacy regarded as heretical, and (2) Lombard aggression was rapidly becoming so effective that the Byzantine army could no longer be counted on to defend the papacy.

The iconoclastic controversy was the chief religious dispute of the Christian world in the eighth century. It was a conflict over the use in Christian worship of statues and pictures of Christ and the saints. These icons had gradually come to assume an important role in Christian worship. Strictly speaking, Christians might venerate them as symbols of the holy persons whom they represented, but in fact there was a strong tendency among the uneducated to worship the objects themselves. A line of reform emperors in Constantinople, beginning with Leo the Isaurian (717–741), sought to end the superstitious practice of worshiping images—vigorously fostered by the numerous monks of the Eastern Empire—by banning icons altogether. This sweeping decree served the interests of the Byzantine emperors by weakening the power of the eastern monasteries, which controlled far too much land and wealth for the empire's good. But the decree offended a great many Byzantines, image worshipers and intelligent traditionalists alike. In the West little or no support was to be found for the policy of iconoclasm; the papacy in particular opposed it as heretical and contrary to the Christian tradition. Although it ultimately failed in the Byzantine Church, iconoclasm in the 750s was a vital issue and a storm center of controversy that aroused intense enmity between Rome and Constantinople. The papacy was deeply apprehensive of depending on the troops of a heretical emperor for its defense.

Even without the iconoclastic controversy it was becoming increasingly doubtful that the papacy could count on the military power of Byzantium in Italy. For by 750 the Lombards were on the march once again, threatening not only Byzantine holdings but also the territories of the pope himself. In 751 the Lombards captured Ravenna, which had long served as the Byzantines' Italian capital, and the papal position in Italy became more precarious than ever. If Pepin the Short needed the support of the papacy, the papacy needed Pepin's support even more.

Accordingly the alliance was struck. Pepin sent messengers to Rome with the far from theoretical query, "Is it right that a powerless ruler should continue to bear the title of king?" The pope answered that by the authority of the Apostle Peter, Pepin was henceforth to be king of the Franks, and ordered that he should be anointed into his royal office by a papal representative. The anointing ceremony was duly performed at Soissons in 751. It had the purpose of buttressing the new Carolingian dynasty with the strongest of spiritual sanctions. Not by force alone, but by the supernatural potency of the royal anointing was the new dynasty established on the Frankish throne. Appropriately, this ceremony—the symbolic junction of the power of Rome and Frankland—was performed by the aged Boniface.

With Pepin's coronation the last of the Merovingians were shorn of their long hair (a symbol of their royalty) and packed off to a monastery. Three years thereafter Boniface, now nearing eighty, returned to his missionary work in Frisia and met a martyr's death. In the same year, 754, the pope himself traveled northward to Frankland where he personally anointed Pepin and his two sons at the royal monastery of St. Denis, thereby conferring every spiritual sanction at his disposal on the upstart Carolingian monarchy. At the same time he sought Pepin's military support against the Lombards.

Pepin obliged, leading his armies into Italy, defeating the Lombards, and granting a large portion of central Italy to the papacy. This "Donation of Pepin" was of lasting historical significance. It had the immediate effect of relieving the popes of the ominous Lombard pressure. In the long run, it became the nucleus of the Papal States, which were to remain a characteristic feature of Italian politics until the later nineteenth century. For the moment, the papacy had been rescued from its peril. It remained to be seen whether the popes could prevent their new champion from becoming their master.

Pepin the Short, like all successful monarchs of the early Middle Ages, was an able general. As the first Carolingian king he followed in the warlike tradition of his father. Besides defeating the Lombards in Italy, he drove the Muslims from Aquitaine and maintained domestic peace. He died in 768, leaving Frankland larger, more powerful, and better organized than he had found it.

Charlemagne (768–814)

Pepin was a remarkably successful monarch, but he was overshadowed by his even more successful son. Charlemagne was a talented military commander, a statesman of rare ability, a friend of learning. And he exhibited a strong sense of responsibility for the welfare of the society over which he ruled. In this last respect he represents a distinct advance over his Merovingian predecessors, whose relationship to their state was that of a leech to its host.

Charlemagne towered over his contemporaries both figuratively and literally. He was 6′3½″ tall, thick-necked, and pot-bellied, yet imposing in

Statue of Charlemagne: from Church of St. Johann, Mustair in Grison (9th century).

appearance for all that. Thanks to his able biographer, Einhard, whose *Life of Charlemagne* was written a few years after the emperor's death, Charlemagne has come down to posterity as a three-dimensional figure. Einhard, who was dwarfish in stature, wrote enthusiastically of his oversized hero. The Roman historian Suetonius was Einhard's model, and he lifted whole passages from Suetonius's *Lives of the Twelve Caesars,* adapting many other phrases from the work to his own purposes. Yet there is much in Einhard's *Life* that represents his own appraisal of Charlemagne's deeds and character. Reared at the monastery of Fulda, Einhard served for many years in Charlemagne's court and so gained an intimate knowledge of the emperor. Einhard's warm admiration for Charlemagne emerges clearly from the biography, yet the author was able to see Charlemagne's faults as well as his virtues:

❝ Temperate in both eating and drinking, he hated drunkenness in anybody, particularly in himself and those of his household. But he found it difficult to abstain from food and often complained that fasts injured his health. . . His meals usually consisted of four courses, not counting the roast, which his huntsmen used to bring in on the spit. He was fonder of this than of any other dish. While at the table he listened to reading or music. The readings were stories and deeds of olden times; he was also fond of St. Augustine's books, especially of the one entitled *The City of God.* So moderate was he in the use of wine and all sorts of drink that he rarely allowed himself more than three cups in the course of a meal.* **"**

Einhard provides a full account of Charlemagne's military and political career; but the most fascinating passages in the biography deal with the emperor's way of life and personal idiosyncrasies that disclose him as a human being rather than as a shadowy hero of legend:

" While he was dressing and putting on his shoes, he not only gave audience to his friends, but if the Count of the Household told him of any lawsuit in which his judgment was necessary, he had the parties brought before him forthwith, considered the case, and gave his decision, just as if he were sitting on the judgment seat. **"**

Einhard also was at pains to show Charlemagne's thirst for learning. He portrays the emperor as a fluent master of Latin, a student of Greek, a speaker of such skill that he might have passed for a teacher of rhetoric, a devotee of the liberal arts, and in particular a student of astronomy who learned to calculate the motions of the heavenly bodies. Einhard concludes this impressive discussion of Charlemagne's scholarship with a final tribute which unwittingly discloses the emperor's severe limitations:

" He also tried to write, and used to keep tablets and blank pages in bed under his pillow so that in his leisure hours he might accustom his hand to form the letters; but as he did not begin his efforts at an early age but late in life, they met with poor success. **"**

Charlemagne could be warm and talkative, but he could also be hard, cruel, and violent, and his subjects came to regard him with both admiration and fear. He was possessed of a strong, if superficial, piety that prompted him to build churches, collect relics, and struggle for a Christian cultural revival in Frankland. But it did not prevent him from filling his court with concubines and other disreputable characters. In short, Charlemagne, despite his military and political genius, was a man of his age, in tune with its most progressive forces yet by no means removed from its past.

*The size of the cup is not provided.

The Expansion of the Empire

Above all else Charlemagne was a warrior-king. He led his armies on yearly campaigns as a matter of course. When his magnates and their retainers assembled around him annually on the May Field the question was not whether to go to war but whom to fight. It was only gradually, however, that Charlemagne developed a coherent scheme of conquest built on a notion of Christian mission and addressed to the goal of unifying and systematically expanding the Christian west. At the behest of the papacy, he followed his father's footsteps into Italy. There he conquered the Lombards completely in 774, incorporated them into his growing state, and assumed for himself the Lombard crown. Thenceforth he employed the title, "king of the Franks and the Lombards."

Between 778 and 801 Charlemagne conducted a series of campaigns against the Spanish Muslims which met with little success. He did manage to establish a frontier district, the "Spanish March," on the Spanish side of the Pyrenees. In later generations the southern portion of Charlemagne's Spanish March evolved into the county of Barcelona, which remained more receptive to the influence of French institutions and customs than any other district in Spain. A relatively minor military episode in Charlemagne's Spanish campaign of 778—an attack by a band of Christian Basques against the rearguard of Charlemagne's army as it was withdrawing across the Pyrenees into Frankland—became the inspiration for one of the great epic poems of the eleventh and twelfth centuries: the *Song of Roland*. The unknown author or authors of the poem transformed the Basques into Muslims and made the battle a heroic struggle between the rival faiths. Charlemagne was portrayed as a godlike conqueror, phenomenally aged, and Roland, the warden of the Breton March and commander of the rearguard, acquired a fame in literature far out of proportion to his actual historical importance.

Charlemagne devoted much of his strength to the expansion of his eastern frontier. In 787 he conquered and absorbed Bavaria, organizing its easternmost district into a forward defensive barrier against the Slavs. The East March or *Ostmark* became the nucleus of a new state later to be called Austria. In the 790s Charlemagne pushed still farther to the southeast, destroying the rich and predatory Avar state, which had long tormented eastern Europe. For many generations the Avars had been enriching themselves on the plunder of their victims and on heavy tribute payments from Byzantium and elsewhere. Charlemagne had the good fortune to seize a substantial portion of the Avar treasure; it is reported that fifteen four-ox wagons were required to transport the hoard of gold, silver and precious garments back to Frankland. The loot of the Avars contributed significantly to the resources of Charlemagne's treasury and broadened the scope of his subsequent building program and patronage to scholars and churches.

Charlemagne's most prolonged military effort was directed against the pagan Saxons of northern Germany. With the twin goals of protecting the

THE CAROLINGIAN EMPIRE

PICTS

SCOTS

North

Sea

SWEDES

DANISH KINGDOM

ANGLO-SAXON KINGDOMS

FRISIA

SAXONY

SLAVS

Rhine R.

Elbe R.

Cologne

Aachen

Fulda

BRITTANY

NEUSTRIA

Rouen

Rheims

Paris

AUSTRASIA

Angers

Loire R.

Orleans

Tours

Poitiers

Danube R.

BAVARIA

St. Gall

AVARS

AQUITAINE

Rhône R.

BURGUNDY

LOMBARDY

Pavia

Po R.

Venice

SLAVS

Ravenna

PYRENEES MTS.

SPANISH MARCH

Ebro R.

CORSICA

Rome

Monte Cassino

BALEARIC IS.

SARDINIA

MILES
0   100   200   300   400

Byzantine Empire

Frankish Rhinelands and bringing new souls into the Church, he campaigned for some thirty-two years, conquering the Saxons repeatedly and baptizing them by force, only to have them rebel when his armies withdrew. In a fit of savage exasperation he ordered the execution of 4500 unfaithful Saxons in a single bloody day in 782. At length Saxony submitted to the remorseless pressure of Charlemagne's soldiers and the Benedictine monks who followed in their wake. By about 804 Frankish control of Saxony was well established, and in subsequent decades Christianity seeped gradually into the Saxon soul. A century and a half later, Christian Saxons were governing the most powerful state in Europe and were fostering a significant artistic and intellectual revival that was to enrich the culture of tenth-century Christendom.

The Imperial Coronation of A.D. 800

Charlemagne's armies, by incorporating central Germany into the new civilization, had succeeded where the legions of ancient Rome had failed. No longer a mere Frankish king, Charlemagne, by 800, was the master of the west. A few small Christian states remained outside his jurisdiction—the principalities of southern Italy, the kingdoms of Anglo-Saxon England. But with a handful of exceptions such as these, Charlemagne's political sway extended throughout Western Christendom. He was, in truth, an emperor, and on Christmas Day 800, his immense accomplishment was given formal recognition when Pope Leo III placed the imperial crown on his head and acclaimed him "Emperor of the Romans." From the standpoint of legal theory, this dramatic act reconstituted the Roman Empire in the west after a 324-year intermission. In another sense it was the ultimate consummation of the Franco-papal alliance of 751.

Charlemagne's imperial coronation has evoked heated controversy among historians. According to Einhard, Pope Leo III took Charlemagne by surprise and bestowed on him an unwanted dignity. Charlemagne had such an aversion to the titles of Emperor and Augustus, so Einhard reports, "that he declared he would not have set foot in the Church the day that they were conferred, although it was a great feast day, if he could have forseen the design of the pope."

Many modern historians have tended to be skeptical of this assertion. It has been argued that Charlemagne was too powerful—too firmly in control of events—to permit a coronation that he did not wish. It has been pointed out that scholars in Charlemagne's court, beguiled by the dream of empire, may well have urged their emperor on. Some historians have stressed the fact that Byzantium lacked an emperor in 800 and that Charlemagne disclosed his interest in the Roman imperial crown by engaging unsuccessfully in marriage negotiations with the Byzantine empress Irene. Conversely, it has been suggested that the coronation was largely a product of internal Roman politics during the years 799–800. In any event, the acclamation that Charlemagne received from the people of Rome immediately after his coronation had obviously been well rehearsed, and it is hard to believe that Charlemagne did not know what was afoot.

Most likely Charlemagne's imperial coronation of 800, like the royal coronation of Pepin the Short in 751, represents a coalescence of papal and Carolingian interests. For some years Charlemagne had been attempting to attain a status comparable to that of the Byzantine emperors. In 794 he had abandoned the practice, traditional among Germanic kings, of traveling constantly with his court from estate to estate, and had established his permanent capital at Aachen in Austrasia. Here he sought, though vainly, to create a Constantinople of his own. Aachen was called "New Rome," and an impressive palace church was built in the Byzantine style—almost literally a poor man's Sancta Sophia. Even though Charlemagne's "Mary Church" at Aachen was a far cry from Justinian's masterpiece, it was a marvel for its time and place and made a deep impression on contemporaries. Einhard describes it as a beautiful basilica adorned with gold and silver lamps, with rails and doors of solid brass, and with columns and marbles from Rome and Ravenna. It was evidently the product of a major effort on Charlemagne's part—an effort not only to create a beautiful church but also to ape the Byzantines. The coronation of 800 may well have been an expression of this same imitative policy.

The papacy, on the other hand, may well have regarded the coronation as an opportunity to regain some of the initiative it had lost to the all-powerful Charlemagne. To be sure, the Carolingians had been promoted from kings to emperors; but their empire thenceforth bore the stamp, "Made in Rome." In later years the popes would insist that what they gave they could also take away. If the papacy could make emperors it could also depose them. Indeed, it was only shortly before that the papal chancery had produced a famous forged document called the "Donation of Constantine"* in which the first Christian emperor allegedly gave to the pope the imperial diadem and governance over Rome, Italy, and all the west. The pope is alleged to have returned the diadem but kept the power of governance. Later popes, drawing on the "Donation of Constantine," regarded Charlemagne's imperial successors as stewards exercising political authority by delegation from the papacy, wielding their power in the interests of the Roman Church.

So convincing was this theory of papal supremacy in the eyes of the popes that it justified the use of a forgery to support the case. The "Donation of Constantine," therefore, was not an effort to rewrite history but an attempt to buttress the papal position by manufacturing evidence for an event that had actually occurred, so the papacy imagined, but for which the documentation had unfortunately vanished.

Though Charlemagne always respected the papacy, he was unwilling to cast himself in the subordinate role which papal theory demanded of him. He was careful to retain the title, "king of the Franks and the Lombards" alongside his new title of "emperor." When the time came to crown his son emperor, Charlemagne excluded the pope from the ceremony and did the honors himself. In these maneuvers we are witnessing the prologue to a long, bitter struggle over the correct relationship between empire and papacy—a struggle that reached its crescendo in the eleventh, twelfth, and thirteenth centuries.

*Probably sometime in the 740s.

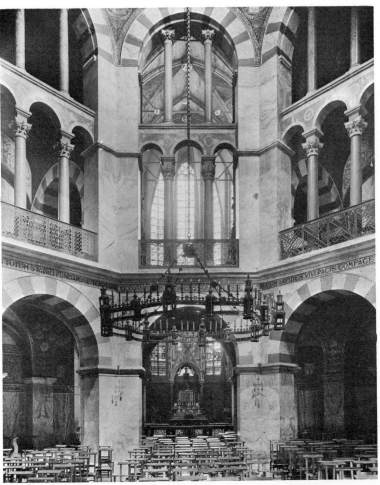

Interior of the "Mary Church" in Aachen (796–804). The Byzantine arches and the structural formation are very similar to Justinian's basilica of San Vitale in Ravenna.

But during the reign of Charlemagne the struggle remained latent. Charlemagne's power was unrivaled, and the popes were much too weak to oppose him seriously. Indeed, the warm Carolingian-papal relations of Pepin's day continued, and the papacy was nearly smothered in Charlemagne's affectionate embrace.

Carolingian Theocracy

At no time since has Europe been so nearly united as under Charlemagne. And never again would Western Christendom flirt so seriously with theocracy. The papal anointing of Pepin and Charlemagne gave the Carolingian monarchy a sacred, almost priestly quality. Charlemagne used his immense authority to govern not only the body politic but the imperial Church as well. The laws and regulations of his reign, known as *capitularies*, dealt with both ecclesiastical and secular matters. At his Synod of Frankfurt in 796, he issued legislation on Christian doctrine. Driven by a sense of responsibility for purifying and systematizing ecclesiastical discipline, he was a far greater force in the Carolingian Church than was the pope. Indeed, the significant intellectual revival known as the "Carolingian Renaissance" grew out of Charlemagne's concern for the welfare of the Church and the perpetuation of ecclesiastical culture as essential buttresses of the Carolingian state.

The Carolingian Renaissance

The term "Carolingian Renaissance" can be misleading. Charlemagne's age produced no serious abstract thought, no original philosophical or theological system, no Thomas Aquinas or Leonardo da Vinci. If we look for a "renaissance" in the ordinary sense of the word, we are bound to be disappointed. The intellectual task of the Carolingian age was far less exalted, far more rudimentary: to rescue continental culture from the pit of ignorance into which it was sinking.

As with so many other aspects of the era, the Carolingian Renaissance bears the stamp of Charlemagne's will and initiative. It was he who saw the desperate need for schools in his kingdom and sought to provide them. There could be no question of establishing institutions of higher learning. None existed north of the Alps, and none would emerge until the High Middle Ages. All that the Carolingians could do was to promote primary and secondary education, and this itself was an immensely difficult task. Frankland had no professional class of teachers either lay or clerical. The only hope for pedagogical reform lay with the Church, which had an almost complete monopoly on literacy. So Charlemagne tried to force the cathedrals and monasteries of his realm to operate schools that would preserve and disseminate the rudiments of classical-Christian culture. A capitulary of 789 commands that

❝In every episcopal see and in every monastery, instruction shall be given in the psalms, musical notation, chant, the computation of years and seasons, and grammar, and all books used shall be carefully corrected.**❞**

A curriculum of the sort proposed in this capitulary can hardly be described as intellectually sophisticated or demanding, yet many Carolingian monasteries and cathedrals fell considerably short of the modest standards that it sought to establish. Still, Charlemagne succeeded in improving vastly the quantity and quality of schooling in his empire. There was even an attempt to make village priests provide free instruction in reading and writing. Only a minute fraction of Charlemagne's subjects acquired literacy. But those few provided an all-important learned nucleus that kept knowledge alive and transmitted it to future generations. It was above all in the monastic schools that learning flourished—in houses such as Fulda, Tours, and Reichenau. During the turbulent generations following Charlemagne's death many of these monastic schools survived to become seedbeds of the far greater intellectual awakening of the eleventh and twelfth centuries. In sum, Charlemagne's pedagogical reforms ensured that learning in continental Europe would never again descend to its pre-Carolingian level.

As an integral part of his effort to raise the intellectual standards of his realm and sustain Christian culture, Charlemagne assembled scholars at his court from all over Europe. One such scholar was the emperor's biographer, Einhard, from eastern Frankland. Another was the poet-historian Paul the Deacon, of the great Italian Benedictine house of Monte Cassino. Paul the Deacon's *History of the Lombards* provides an invaluable account of that Germanic tribe and its settlement in Italy. From Spain came Theodulf, later bishop of Orléans and abbot of Fleury, a tireless supporter of Charlemagne's pedagogical reforms and a poet of considerable talent. The most important of these Carolingian scholars was the Northumbrian, Alcuin of York, the last significant mind to be produced by the Northumbrian Renaissance. Alcuin, along with his countrymen of an earlier generation—Wilfrid of Ripon, Willibrord, and Boniface—represents the vital connecting link between the Christian cultural life of seventh- and eighth-century England and the intellectual upsurge of Carolingian Frankland.

Alcuin performed the essential task of preparing an accurate new edition of the Bible, purged of the scribal errors which had crept into it over the centuries, thereby saving Christian culture from the confusion arising from the corruption of its most fundamental text. For many years the chief scholar in Charlemagne's court school, Alcuin spent his final years as abbot of St. Martin of Tours. He was extraordinarily well-educated for his period, and his approach to learning typified the whole philosophy of the Carolingian Renaissance: to produce accurate copies of important traditional texts, to encourage the establishment of schools, and in every way possible to cherish and transmit the classical-Christian cultural tradition (without, however, adding to it in any significant way). Alcuin and his fellow scholars were neither intellectual innovators nor men of conspicuous holiness. Drawn by Charlemagne's wealth and power and enriched by his patronage, they struggled to improve the scholarly level of the Carolingian Church; but they showed little concern for deepening its spiritual life or exploring uncharted regions of speculative thought. They had the talents and inclinations—and the limitations—of a schoolmaster. At best they were scholars and humanists; in no sense could they be described as philosophers or mystics.

Accordingly, Alcuin, Theodulf, Einhard, Paul the Deacon, and others like them purified and regularized the liturgy of the Church and encouraged the preaching of sermons. They carrried on some of the monastic reforms begun by Boniface and saw to it that every important monastery had a school. It was a question not of producing new Platos and Augustines but of preserving literacy itself. A new, standardized script was developed—the Carolingian minuscule—which derived in part from the Irish and Northumbrian scripts of the previous century. Thenceforth the Carolingian minuscule superseded the often illegible scripts earlier employed on the Continent. Throughout the realm monks set about copying manuscripts on an unprecedented scale. If classical-Christian culture was advanced very little by these activities it was at least preserved. Above all, its base was broadened. In the task they set themselves, the Carolingian scholars were eminently successful.

The Renaissance after Charlemagne

It was characteristic of the powerful theocratic tendencies of the age that this significant pedagogical achievement was accomplished through royal rather than papal initiative. Germanic monarchy and classical-Christian culture had joined hands at last. With the breakdown of European unity after Charlemagne's death, the momentary fusion of political and cultural energies dissolved, yet the intellectual revival continued. A deeply spiritual movement of monastic reform and moral regeneration began in Aquitaine under the leadership of the ardent and saintly Benedict of Aniane. Soon the influence of this movement took hold at the court of Charlemagne's son and successor, Louis the Pious. Louis gave St. Benedict of Aniane the privilege of visiting any monastery in the empire and tightening its discipline in whatever way he chose, to the chagrin of numerous abbots and monks. And in 817 a significantly expanded version of the Benedictine Rule, based on the strict monastic regulations of Benedict of Aniane, was promulgated for all the monasteries of the empire and given the weight of imperial law. Benedict of Aniane's reform represents a marked shift from the spiritually superficial monastic regulations of Charlemagne's day to a deep concern for the Christ-centered life. The elaborated Benedictine Rule of 817 lost its status as imperial law in 840, with the death of Louis the Pious, but it remained an inspiration to subsequent monastic reform movements in the centuries that followed. Thenceforth the Benedictine life par excellence was based on Benedict of Aniane's modification of the original Rule.

While Carolingian spiritual life was deepening in the years after Charlemagne's death, Carolingian scholarship continued to flourish in the cathedral and monastic schools. A vigorous controversy over the question of free will and predestination testifies to the vitality of Carolingian thought in the early and middle decades of the ninth century. And in keeping with the Carolingian intellectual program of preserving the classical-Christian tradition, learned churchmen of the Carolingian Renaissance's "second generation" devoted themselves to the preparation of encyclopedic compilations of received knowledge. None of these works were very original, but they were important, nonetheless, in the process of cultural transmission. For example, Raban Maur (d. 856), abbot of the great monastery of Fulda, provided an elaborate encyclopedia on the pattern of Isidore of Seville's *Etymologies*, entitled *De Universo*. Raban also carried forward the Carolingian pedagogical tradition by writing a handbook on the instruction of the clergy—*De Clericorum Institutione*—which had a significant influence on the operation of monastic schools.

John Scotus

The most interesting scholar in this "second generation" was the Irishman, John Scotus Erigena, who stands as the one original thinker of the whole Carolingian age. John Scotus, or John the Scot (the "Scots" in his day were inhabitants of Ireland rather than Scotland), served for years in the court of Charlemagne's grandson, Charles the Bald. Not only a brilliant speculative thinker, he was also a precocious wit, at least if we can give credence to the later legend of a dinner table conversation between John the Scot and King Charles the Bald. The king, intending to needle his court scholar, asked the rhetorical question, "What is there that separates a Scot from a sot," to which John is alleged to have replied, "Only the dinner table."

John Scotus was a student of Neoplatonism and the only western European scholar of his age to master the Greek tongue. He translated into Latin an important Greek philosophical treatise, *On the Celestial Hierarchy*, written by an anonymous late-fifth-century Christian Neoplatonist known as the Pseudo-Dionysius. This author was incorrectly identified in the Middle Ages as Dionysius the Areopagite, a first-century Athenian philosopher who is described in the *Acts of the Apostles* as being converted to Christianity by St. Paul. He was further misidentified as St. Denis, evangelist of the Gauls and first bishop of Paris, who was decapitated by the pagans and in whose honor the great royal monastery of St. Denis was built. Accordingly, the writings of the Pseudo-Dionysius, even though tinged with pantheism, passed into the Middle Ages with the commanding credentials of an early Christian author, a Pauline convert, and a martyred missionary who brought Christianity to Gaul. In reality, the importance of the Pseudo-Dionysius lay in his providing a Christian dimension to the philosophical scheme of Plotinus and other pagan Neoplatonists. The unknowable and indescribable Neoplatonic god—the center and source of the concentric circles of reality—was identified with the God of the Christians. Such a god could not be approached intellectually but only by means of a mystical experience; hence, the Pseudo-Dionysius became an important source of inspiration to later Christian mystics.

Stimulated by the work of the Pseudo-Dionysius, which he translated from Greek into Latin, John Scotus went on to write a highly original Neoplatonic treatise of his own, *On the Divisions of Nature*. In its blurred distinction between God and the created world, the treatise reflected the Neoplatonic tendency toward pantheism. It was condemned as heretical in the thirteenth century but made little impact on contemporaries, who lacked both the interest and the background to understand it. John Scotus is a lonely figure in intellectual history, without any immediate predecessors or successors. He founded no schools of thought and carried on no real philosophical dialogue with his contemporaries, who were poets and pedants rather than abstract thinkers. He figures as the supreme intellect in the West between St. Augustine and the philosophers of the High Middle Ages, yet being neither the direct product of earlier intellectual currents nor the cause of subsequent ones, he played a minor role in the evolution of thought. He remains, nevertheless, the one interesting philosopher of the Carolingian epoch.

The intellectual revival instigated by Charlemagne echoed through subsequent generations. John Scotus' Neoplatonism may have been generally ignored and quickly forgotten. Yet in the monasteries and cathedrals of the ninth and tenth centuries, particularly in the German districts of Charlemagne's old empire, documents continued to be copied, schools continued to operate, and commentaries and epitomes of ancient texts continued to appear. By the eleventh century, Europe was ready to build on her sturdy Carolingian foundations.

The Dynamics of Carolingian Expansion and Decline

The Carolingian Empire was ephemeral. Rising out of a chaotic past, it disintegrated in the turbulent era that followed. The Carolingians had achieved their early successes, under Pepin of Heristal and Charles Martel, not only because of strong leadership but also because of the sizeable landed resources that the family came to control, and the loyal, well-armed vassals whom these resources could attract. Carolingian armies were better organized and better disciplined than those of most neighboring powers. And once Carolingian expansion was underway it fed on its own momentum. Conquests brought plunder and new lands with which the Carolingians could enrich themselves and reward their vassals. Indeed, it became Carolingian policy to install loyal Austrasian Franks as counts and dukes of the conquered provinces. Accordingly, the interests of the Frankish aristocrats became ever more closely tied to the political and military success of their Carolingian leaders. As long as the Carolingians could bring in profits from military campaigns, they commanded the enthusiastic obedience of disciplined followers. A Frank would gladly obey Charlemagne if it meant a cut of the Avar treasure or a lordship in Italy or Saxony. In short, Carolingian expansion was like a snowball, growing as it rolled, rolling as it grew.

Even at the height of Charlemagne's power, his empire remained, by Byzantine and Islamic standards, economically primitive and undergoverned. Despite the plunder of conquests, Charlemagne had nowhere near the funds sufficient to support a salaried bureaucracy.Like his predecessors, he had to depend on the competence and loyalty of the Frankish counts, dukes, and margraves who administered his provinces. The power of these officials was great, for in place of salaries they were given extensive lands from which they could not easily be dislodged. Moreover, most of them were separated from their king by hundreds of miles of wretched roads. Charlemagne kept some control over his provincial administrators by sending out pairs of inspectors known as *missi dominici* (envoys of the lord) to assure the implementation of his will. The *missi dominici*, consisting usually of one churchman and one layman, typified the theocratic trend of Charlemagne's reign. They were moderately effective, but only because they represented a monarch who had the power to punish and reward. A count who owed his office to Charlemagne and whose authority over potentially troublesome provincials depended on Charlemagne's continued backing, would receive the *missi dominici* with respect. Provincial officials obeyed royal commands and capitularies not out of patriotic allegiance to the Carolingian state but because of their devotion to Charlemagne's person—a devotion based on the bonds of common interest that linked the conquering monarch and his highly favored aristocracy.

These bonds had always been fragile; and when the Carolingian Empire ceased expanding, as it did after the final submission of Saxony in 804, they began to loosen. As the flow of lands and plunder dried up, aristocratic loyalty diminished and the empire started disintegrating. Disaffection and rebellion clouded the final decade of Charlemagne's life and brought political chaos to the reign of his son and heir, Louis the Pious. Once the snowball stopped rolling it began to melt.

Carolingian Europe: An Overview

The Carolingian Empire, impressive though it was, lacked a high culture, a vigorous commercial life, and other necessary ingredients of a flourishing civilization. Its revenues were small and its administrative institutions grossly inadequate to the needs of a great state. Beneath the military and cultural veneer, Carolingian Europe was still only half-civilized.

But even though Charlemagne's "Roman Empire" was merely a faint shadow of its ancient namesake, one cannot help but respect its founder for doing so much with so little, for making such an effort to transcend his own primitive past, for struggling to master the art of writing and the subtleties of Augustine's *City of God.*The historian Christopher Dawson caught the spirit of Charlemagne's achievement perfectly when he wrote, "The unwieldy empire of Charles the Great did not long survive the death of its founder, and it never really attained the economic and social organization of a civilized state. But, for all that, it marks the first emergence of the European culture from the twilight of prenatal existence into the consciousness of active life."

Chapter 7

ঙ্গ

The New Invasions

Tentative though it was, the Carolingian economic and cultural revival might conceivably have evolved much further had it not been for a series of new invasions that began afflicting Western Christendom around A.D. 800. Until then Charlemagne's realm had enjoyed relative internal peace. Intellectual life, although still rudimentary, was in the process of reawakening, and with the stimulus of the silver coinage that Charlemagne issued, commerce quickened. There are some indications that towns may have been starting to grow and flourish once again under the bracing influence of Charlemagne's economic policies and in the encouraging environment of domestic peace. But these hopeful signs proved to be a false dawn. During the ninth and tenth centuries Europe was hammered by the attacks of three separate peoples: the semi-nomadic Hungarians (Magyars) from the east, the Saracens (Muslims) from the south, and the seafaring Vikings from the north. The advent of a higher civilization was delayed for another two centuries. And Europe emerged from its ordeal with a political organization radically different from that of the Carolingian Empire.

ঙ্গ

Louis the Pious (814–840)

One cannot ascribe the political fragmentation of Carolingian Europe entirely to these outside forces. Charlemagne himself, in keeping with Frankish tradition, planned to divide his state among his several sons. As it happened, however, Charlemagne outlived all but one of them. The luck of the Carolingians was still running, and when the great conqueror died in 814 his realm passed intact to his remaining heir, Louis the Pious.

Although Louis was by no means incompetent, his military and political talents were less impressive than those of his father Charlemagne, his grandfather Pepin the Short, and his great-grandfather Charles Martel. And with the cessation of Carolingian expansion a few years prior to his accession, Louis could not reward his vassals and officials on the scale to which they had long been accustomed. The result was widespread disaffection and repeated challenges to imperial authority. Carolingian unity continued, but Carolingian leadership began to falter.

Louis the Pious was well named. He ran Charlemagne's minstrels and concubines out of the imperial court and replaced them with priests and monks. He gave his wholehearted support to the monastic reforms of Benedict of Aniane. And far more than his hardheaded father, Louis committed himself to the dream of a unified Christian Empire—a City of God brought down to earth. But empires cannot be sustained on dreams alone, and Louis lacked the resources necessary to maintain unity and cohesion in the immense, heterogeneous empire that the Carolingians had won. He was the first of his line to conceive the notion of bequeathing supreme political authority to his eldest son, thereby making the unity of the kingdom a matter of policy rather than luck. But ironically, he turned out to be the last Carolingian to rule an undivided Frankish realm. His bold plan for a single succession was foiled by the ambitions of his younger sons, who rebelled openly against him, vied with him for aristocratic support, and plunged the empire into civil war.

The Treaty of Verdun

When Louis the Pious's unhappy reign ended in 840, his three surviving sons struggled bitterly for the spoils. The eldest of the three, Lothar, claimed the indivisible imperial title and supreme power over the entire realm. The other two sons, Louis the German and Charles the Bald, fought to win independent royal authority in East and West Frankland respectively. In the end Lothar had to yield to the combined might of his younger brothers. The controversy was settled by the Treaty of Verdun in 843, which permanently divided the empire and foreshadowed the political structure of modern Europe. Lothar was permitted to keep the imperial title but was denied any superior jurisdiction over the realms of Louis the German and Charles the Bald. Louis ruled East

Frankland, which became the nucleus of the modern German state. In a sense, he was Germany's first king. Charles the Bald became king of West Frankland, which evolved into modern France. Lothar retained a long, narrow strip of territory that stretched for some thousand miles northward from Italy through

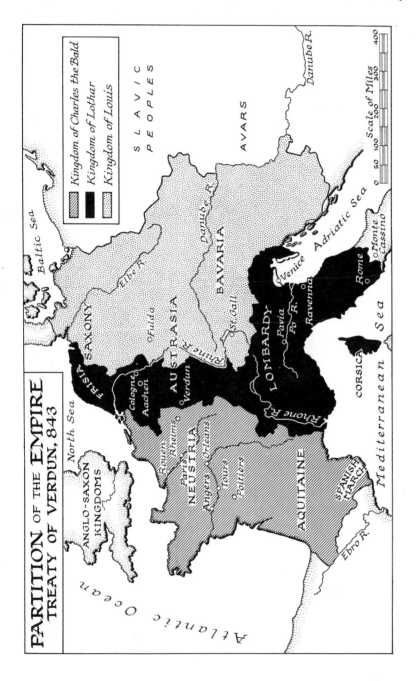

PARTITION OF THE EMPIRE
TREATY OF VERDUN, 843

Kingdom of Charles the Bald
Kingdom of Lothar
Kingdom of Louis

Burgundy, Alsace, Lorraine, and the Netherlands, embracing considerable portions of western Germany and eastern France. This Middle Kingdom included the two "imperial capitals"—Rome and Aachen—but its frontiers were difficult to defend, and it lacked unity. At Lothar's death in 855 it was subdivided among his three sons, one of whom inherited Carolingian Italy and the increasingly insignificant imperial title. From the ninth century to the twentieth, fragments of Lothar's middle kingdom have been the source of endless bitter territorial disputes between Germany and France.

The struggles among Charlemagne's grandsons occurred against a background of Viking, Hungarian, and Saracen invasions, which accelerated the tendency toward political fragmentation brought about by internal weaknesses. But even without the invasions, and without the Frankish tradition of divided succession, Charlemagne's huge, unwieldy empire could not have long remained intact once the conquests ceased. As it turned out, even the more modest political units arising from the Treaty of Verdun were too large—too far removed from the desperate realities of the countryside—to cope successfully with the lightning raids of Viking shipmen or Hungarian horsemen. During the ninth and tenth centuries Carolingian leadership was visibly failing. The ineffectiveness of the later Carolingians is graphically illustrated in their names: Charles the Fat, Charles the Simple, Louis the Child, Louis the Blind, Louis the Stammerer.

CAROLINGIAN CHRONOLOGY

687:	Pepin of Heristal, Carolingian mayor of Austrasia, defeats Neustria; Carolingian hegemony established
714–741:	Rule of Charles Martel
732:	Arabs defeated at Tours
741–768:	Rule of Pepin the Short
751:	Pepin crowned king of the Franks; Merovingian Dynasty ends
754:	Death of St. Boniface
768–814:	Reign of Charlemagne
772–804:	Charlemagne's Saxon Wars
800:	Charlemagne crowned Roman Emperor
814–840:	Reign of Louis the Pious
843:	Treaty of Verdun

The Impact of the Invasions

The Saracens, Hungarians, and Vikings who plundered the declining Carolingian state were in part drawn by its growing political instability and in part impelled by forces operating in their own homelands. Europe suffered much from their marauding, yet it was strong enough in the end to survive and absorb the invaders. And these invasions were the last that Western Christendom was destined to endure. From about A.D. 1000 to the present, the West has had the'unique opportunity of developing on its own, sheltered from alien attacks that have so disrupted other civilizations over the past thousand years. As the historian Marc Bloch said, "It is surely not unreasonable to think that this extraordinary immunity, of which we have shared the privilege with scarcely any people but the Japanese, was one of the fundamental factors of European civilization . . . "

Yet in the ninth and tenth centuries Europe's hard-pressed peoples had no way of knowing that the invasions would one day end. A Frankish writer of the mid-ninth century bemoaned the Viking attacks in these melodramatic words: "The number of ships grows larger and larger; the great host of Northmen continually increases; on every hand Christians are the victims of massacres, looting, and arson—clear proof of which will remain as long as the world itself endures. The Northmen capture every city they pass through, and none can withstand them" In southern Gaul people prayed for divine protection against the Saracens: "Eternal Trinity . . . deliver thy Christian people from the oppression of the pagans." To the north they prayed, "From the savage nation of the Northmen, which lays waste our realms, deliver us, O God." And in northern Italy: "Against the arrows of the Hungarians be thou our protector."

Saracens and Hungarians

The Saracens of the ninth and tenth centuries, unlike their Muslim predecessors in the seventh and early eighth, came as brigands rather than conquerors and settlers. From their pirate nests in Africa, Spain, and the Mediterranean islands they preyed on shipping, plundered coastal cities, and sailed up rivers to carry their devastation far inland. Saracen bandit lairs were established on the southern coast of Gaul, from which the marauders conducted raids far and wide through the countryside and kidnapped pilgrims crossing the Alpine passes. Charlemagne had never possessed much of a navy, and his successors found themselves helpless to defend their coasts. In 846 Saracen brigands raided Rome itself, profaning its churches and stealing its treasures. As late as 982 a German king was severely defeated by Saracens in southern Italy; but by then the raids were tapering off. Southern Europe, now bristling with fortifications, had learned to defend itself and was even beginning to challenge Saracen domination of the western Mediterranean.

The Hungarians or Magyars—fierce nomadic horsemen from the Asiatic steppes—settled in the land now known as Hungary. From the late 800s to 955 they terrorized Germany, northern Italy, and eastern and central France. Hungarian raiding parties ranged across the land, seeking defenseless settlements to plunder, avoiding fortified towns, outriding and outmaneuvering the armies sent against them. In time, however, they became more sedentary, gave more attention to their farms, and lost much of their nomadic aggressiveness. In 955 King Otto the Great of Germany crushed a large Hungarian army at the battle of the Lechfeld and brought the raids to an end at last. Within another half-century, the Hungarians had adopted Christianity and were becoming integrated into the community of Christian Europe.

Vikings

The Vikings, or Norsemen, were the most fearsome invaders of all. These redoubtable warrior-seafarers came from Scandinavia, the very land that had, centuries before, disgorged many of the Germanic tribes into Europe. Thus the ninth century Vikings and the Germanic invaders of Roman times had similar ethnic backgrounds. But to the ninth-century European—the product of countless Germanic-Celtic-Roman intermarriages, tamed by the Church and by centuries of settled life—the pagan Vikings seemed a hostile and alien people.

Then, as now, the Scandinavians were divided roughly into three groups: Danes, Swedes, and Norwegians. During the great age of Viking expansion in the ninth and tenth centuries the Danes, who were brought cheek to jowl with the Carolingian Empire by Charlemagne's conquest of Saxony, focused their attention on Frankland and England. The Norwegians raided and settled in Scotland, Ireland, and the North Atlantic. The Swedes concentrated on the East—the Baltic shores, Russia, and the Byzantine Empire. Yet the three Norse peoples had much in common, and the distinctions among them were by no means sharp. It is, therefore, proper to regard their raids, their astonishing explorations, and their far-flung commercial enterprises as a single great international movement.

Though the breakdown of Carolingian unity doubtless acted as a magnet to Viking marauders, their raids on the West began as early as Charlemagne's age. The basic causes for their outward thrust must be sought in Scandinavia itself. Since pre-tenth-century Scandinavia is almost a closed book to historians, our explanations for the Viking outburst are little more than educated guesses. It is likely, however, that the Scandinavian population, once sharply reduced by the outward migrations of Roman times, had increased by the later 700s to a level that the primitive Norse agriculture was unable to support. The pressure of overpopulation was probably aggravated by the growth of centralized royal power, which cramped the more restless spirits and drove them to seek adventures and opportunities abroad. A third factor was the development of improved Viking ships, eminently seaworthy, propelled by both sail and oars, and capable of carrying crews of forty to a hundred warriors at speeds up to ten knots. In these longships the tall, reddish-haired Viking warriors struck the ports of northern Europe. They sailed up rivers far into the interior, plundering the towns and monasteries of Frankland and England, sometimes stealing horses and riding across the countryside to spread their devastation still further.

The people of Europe were accustomed enough to warfare among their own nominally Christian warrior-aristocracy. But Christian warriors tended to respect the sanctity of the monasteries, which with their wealth enticed the acquisitive Vikings and with their near monopoly on literacy produced almost all our information about the Viking raids. The monastic chroniclers of the time, accustomed to peace within their walls, doubtless exaggerated the violence of the Viking age and the ferocity of the Viking armies. Yet the Viking impact on northern France, England, and Russia was real, and it was lasting.

Attacks against England

England was the first to suffer from Viking attacks. About 789 three longships touched the Channel coast in Dorset and Vikings poured out of them to loot and sack a nearby town. Thenceforth the Anglo-Saxon kingdoms were tormented by incessant Viking raids. In 794 Norse brigands annihilated the Northumbrian monastery of Jarrow, where Bede had lived and died. And the other major abbeys of Northumbria suffered a similar devastation.

In 842 the Danes plundered London. A few years thereafter they began to establish permanent winter bases in England, which freed them from the necessity of returning to Scandinavia after the raiding season. By the later 800s they had turned from piracy to large-scale occupation and permanent settlement. One after another the Anglo-Saxon kingdoms were overrun until at length, in the 870s, only the southern kingdom of Wessex remained free of Danish control. And even Wessex came within a hair's breadth of falling to the Danes.

Attacks against the Continent

To mariners such as the Vikings, the English Channel was a boulevard rather than a barrier, and their raiding parties attacked the English and Frankish shores indiscriminately. They established permanent bases at the mouths of large rivers and sailed up them to plunder defenseless monasteries and sack towns. Antwerp was ravaged in 837, Rouen in 841, Hamburg and Paris in 845, Charlemagne's old capital at Aachen in 881.

But if some Europeans were driven to helpless resignation, others fought doggedly to protect their lands. King Alfred the Great of Wessex saved his kingdom from Danish conquest in the late 870s and began the task of rolling back the Danish armies in England. King Arnulf of East Frankland won a decisive victory over the Norsemen in 891 at the battle of the Dyle and thereby decreased the Viking pressure on Germany—although it was at this very time that the Hungarian raids began. West Frankland continued to suffer for awhile, but in about 911 King Charles the Simple created a friendly Viking buffer state in northern France by concluding a treaty with a Norse chieftain

THE VIKING, HUNGARIAN
AND MUSLIM INVASIONS

ICELAND

Ocean

VIKINGS

Atlantic

NORWAY

SWEDEN

Dnieper R.

SCOT LAND

DENMARK

Kiev R.

IRELAND

ENGLAND

Aachen

Rouen

Rhine R.

Paris

Seine

Danube R.

Loire R.

Tours

HUNGARIANS

Danube R.

Black Sea

LOMBARDY

PROVENCE

Marseilles

Constantinople

CORSICA

Rome

Monte Cassino

Naples

SARDINIA

BALEARIC IS.

SICILY

MUSLIMS

Mediterranean Sea

→ Vikings

--→ Muslims

→ Hungarians

MILES

0   200   400   600   800

named Rolf. The Vikings in Rolf's band had been conducting raids from their settlement at the mouth of the River Seine. Charles, less simple than his name would imply, reasoned that if he could make Rolf his ally the Seine settlement might prove an effective barrier against further raids. Rolf became a Christian, married Charles the Simple's daughter, and recognized at least in some sense the superiority of the West Frankish monarchy. Thus his state acquired a degree of legitimacy in the eyes of Western Christendom. Expanding gradually under Rolf and his successors, it became known as the land of the Northmen, or "Normandy." Over the next century and a half the Normans became as good Christians as the Franks. They adopted French culture and the French language, yet retained much of their former adventurousness and wanderlust. In the eleventh century Normandy was producing some of Europe's most vigorous warriors, Crusaders, administrators, and monks.

Ireland, Greenland, North America

France, England, and Germany formed only a part of the vast Viking world of the ninth and tenth centuries. By the mid-800s Norwegians and Danes had conquered the greater part of Ireland, and between 875 and 930 they settled remote Iceland. There a distinctive Norse culture arose which for several centuries remained only slightly affected by the main currents of Western Civilization. In Iceland the magnificent oral tradition of the Norse saga flourished and was eventually committed to writing. The Icelandic Norsemen were perhaps the greatest sailors of all. They settled on the coast of Greenland in the late 900s, and in the eleventh century they established temporary settlements on the northern coasts of North America itself, anticipating Columbus by half a millennium.

Russia

To the east, Swedish Vikings overran Finland and penetrated far southward across European Russia to trade with Constantinople and Baghdad. The Byzantine emperors took pride in the tall Norse mercenaries who served in their imperial guard. In Russia a Swedish dynasty established itself at Novgorod in the later ninth century, ruling over the indigenous Slavic population. In the tenth century a Norse prince of Novgorod captured the south-Russian city of Kiev, which became the capital of the powerful, well-organized state of Kievan Russia. Deeply influenced by the culture of its subjects, the dynasty at Kiev became more Slavic than Scandinavian. Around the turn of the millennium, as we have already seen, Prince Vladimir of Kiev adopted Byzantine Christianity. Submitting himself and his subjects to the spiritual authority of the patriarch of Constantinople, Vladimir opened Russia to the influence of Byzantine culture (see pp. 36–37).

Twilight of the Viking Age

The development of centralized monarchies in Denmark, Norway, and Sweden, which may well have been a factor in driving enterprising Norse seamen to seek their fortunes elsewhere, ultimately resulted in taming the Viking spirit. As Scandinavia became increasingly civilized its kings discouraged the activities of roaming warrior bands, and its social environment gave rise to a more humdrum, sedentary life. Far into the eleventh century, England continued to face the attacks of Norsemen, but these invaders were no longer pirate bands; instead, they were royal armies led by Scandinavian kings. The nature of the Scandinavian threat had changed, and by the late eleventh century the threat had ceased altogether. Around the year 1000 Christianity was winning converts all across the Scandinavian world. In Iceland, in Russia— even in the kingdoms of Scandinavia itself—the Norsemen were adopting the religion of the monks whom they had formerly terrorized. Scandinavia was becoming a part of western European culture.

Even at the height of the invasions, the Norsemen excelled at commerce as well as piracy. They were the greatest seafarers of the age. They introduced Europe to the art of ocean navigation and enlarged the horizons of Western Christendom, injecting a spirit of enterprise and cosmopolitanism into the conservative, landbound outlook of Carolingian civilization.

Chapter 8

ℭ

Europe
Survives
the Siege

Response to the Invasions: England

❡ The invasions of the ninth and tenth centuries wrought significant changes in the political and social organization of Western Europe. In France political authority tended to crumble into small local units as unwieldly royal armies failed to cope with the lightning raids. But elsewhere, the invasions had the effect of augmenting royal power. The German monarchy, after a period of relative weakness, underwent a spectacular recovery in the tenth century, while in England the hammerblows of the Danes had the ultimate result of unifying the several Anglo-Saxon states into a single kingdom. In general, Europeans rallied behind whatever leadership could provide an effective defense—whether kings, local magnates, or, as in northern Italy, urban bishops.

In the later eighth century, on the eve of the Viking invasions, England was politically fragmented, as it had been ever since the Anglo-Saxon conquests. But over the centuries the several smaller kingdoms had gradually passed under the control of three larger ones: Northumbria in the north, Mercia in the Midlands, and Wessex in the south. The Danish attacks of the ninth century, by destroying the power of Wessex's rivals, cleared the field for the

ℭ

Wessex monarchy and thereby hastened the trend toward consolidation that was already underway. But if the Danes were doing the Wessex monarchy a favor, neither side was aware of it during the troubled years of the later ninth century. For a time it appeared that the Danes might conquer Wessex itself.

King Alfred (871–899)

At the moment of crisis a remarkable leader, Alfred the Great, rose to the throne of Wessex. Alfred did everything in his power to save his kingdom from the Vikings. He fought ferocious battles against them. He even resorted to bribing them. In the winter of 878 the Danes, in a surprise attack, invaded Wessex and forced Alfred to take refuge, with a handful of companions, on the isle of Athelney in a remote swamp. Athelney was England's Valley Forge. In the following spring Alfred rallied his forces and smashed a Danish army at the battle of Edington. This victory turned the tide of the war; the Danish leader agreed to take up Christianity, to withdraw from the land, and to accept a "permanent" peace. Wessex was never again seriously threatened.

But other Danes under other leaders refused to honor the peace, and Alfred in his later campaigns extended his authority to the north and east. In 886 he captured London—even then England's chief city—and shortly thereafter a new peace treaty gave Wessex most of southern and southwestern England. The remainder of England—the "Danelaw"—remained hostile, but virtually all of non-Danish England was now united under King Alfred.

Like all successful leaders of the age, Alfred was an able warrior. But more than that, he was an imaginative organizer who systematized military recruitment and built a navy, seeing clearly that Christian Europe could not hope to drive back the Vikings without challenging them on the seas. He dotted his kingdom with fortresses that served both as defensive strongholds and as places of sanctuary for the agrarian population in time of war. And gradually, as the Danish tide was rolled back, more fortresses were built to secure the territories newly reconquered. Alfred clarified and rationalized the laws of his people, enforced them strictly, and ruled with an authority such as no Anglo-Saxon king had exercised before his time.

King Alfred was also a scholar and a patron of learning. His intellectual environment was even less promising than Charlemagne's. The great days of Bede, Boniface, and Alcuin were far in the past and by Alfred's time, Latin—the key to classical-Christian culture—was almost unknown in England. Like Charlemagne, Alfred gathered scholars from far and wide—England, Wales, the Continent—and set them to work teaching Latin and translating Latin classics into the Anglo-Saxon language. Alfred himself participated in the work of translation, helping to render such works as Boethius's *Consolation of Philosophy,* Pope Gregory's *Pastoral Care,* and Bede's *Ecclesiastical History* into the native tongue. In his translation of Boethius, Alfred added a regretful comment of his own: "In those days one never heard of ships armed for war."

ENGLAND ABOUT 885

Scale of Miles
0 20 40 60 80 100

And in his preface to the *Pastoral Care* he alluded with nostalgia to the days "before everything was ravaged and burned, when England's churches overflowed with treasures and books." Alfred's intellectual revival, even more than Charlemagne's, was a salvage operation rather than an outburst of originality. He was both modest and accurate when he described himself as one who wandered through a great forest collecting timber with which others could build.

Alfred's task of reconquest was carried on by his able successors in the first half of the tenth century. By the mid-900s all England was in their hands, and the kings of Wessex had become the kings of England. Great numbers of Danish settlers still remained in northern and eastern England—the amalgamation of Danish and English customs required many generations. But the creative response of the Wessex kings to the Danish threat had brought political unity to the Anglo-Saxon world. Out of the agony of the invasions the English monarchy was born.

The Renewal of the Danish Attacks

For a generation after the Anglo-Saxon conquest of the Danelaw, from about 955 to 980, England enjoyed relative peace and prosperity. English fleets patrolled the shores, the old fortresses began to evolve into commercial centers, and churchmen addressed themselves to the task of monastic reform. But the Danish inhabitants of northern and eastern England remained only half committed to the new English monarchy, and with the accession of a bumbling child-king, Ethelred "the Unready" (978–1016), the Danish invasions resumed.

The new invasions evolved into a campaign of conquest directed by the Danish monarchy. The English defense was plagued by incompetence, treason, and panic. In 991 Ethelred began paying a tribute to the Danes, known thereafter as "danegeld." In later years the danegeld evolved into a land tax that was exceedingly profitable to the English monarchy, but at the time it was a symbol of weakness. In 1016 Ethelred died, and in the following year King Canute of Denmark became the monarch of England.

Canute (1017–1035)

King Canute was known to later generations as "Canute the Great," and appropriately so. He conquered Norway as well as England, and joining these two lands to his kingdom of Denmark, he became the master of a huge empire centering on the North Sea. A product of the new civilizing forces at work in eleventh-century Scandinavia, Canute was no footloose Viking. He issued law codes, practiced Christianity, and kept the peace. Devoting much of his time to England, he cast himself as an Anglo-Saxon king in the old Wessex tradition. He respected and upheld the ancient customs of the land and gave generously to monasteries. Despite his Danish background, he was a far more effective English monarch than Ethelred. His reign was a continuation of the past, and he added luster to the crown that Alfred's dynasty had forged.

English religion and culture prospered as before: "Merry sang the monks of Ely as Canute the king rowed by."

But Canute's Danish-Norwegian-English empire was hopelessly disunited and failed to survive his death in 1035. When the last of his sons died in 1042 the English realm fell peacefully to Edward the Confessor, a member of the old Wessex dynasty who had grown up in exile in Normandy.

The Aftermath

Though a poor general and mediocre administrator, Edward the Confessor ruled England in relative peace. But his childless marriage ensured a disputed succession upon his death in 1066 and set the stage for the Norman Conquest. When William the Conqueror, duke of Normandy, invaded England and won its crown in 1066, he inherited a prosperous kingdom with strong, well-established political and legal traditions—a kingdom still divided by differences in custom but with a deep-seated respect for royal authority. Ethelred the Unready notwithstanding, the Wessex dynasty had done its work well. With the timber that Alfred collected, his successors had built an ample and sturdy edifice.

Response to the Invasions: French Feudalism

In England the invasions stimulated the trend toward royal unification; in France they encouraged a shattering of political authority into small local units. This paradox can be explained in part by the fact that France, unlike England, was far too large for the Vikings to conquer. Although many of them settled in Normandy, the chief Norse threat to France came in the form of plundering expeditions rather than large conquering armies. Distances were too great, communications too primitive, the aristocracy too independent, and the national territorial army too unwieldy for the king to take the lead in defending his realm. Military responsibility descended to such local lords as were able to protect the countryside from the swift Viking assaults. The French Carolingians became increasingly powerless until at length, in 987, the crown passed to a new dynasty—the Capetians. During the twelfth and thirteenth centuries the Capetian family produced some of France's most illustrious kings, but for the time being, the new dynasty was nearly as impoverished and powerless as the old one. After 987, as before, the aristocracy overshadowed the king. About all one can say of the French monarchy in these dark years is that it survived.

The Viking Age witnessed the emergence of feudalism in France. In a very real sense feudalism was a product of France's response to the invasions. Yet in another sense the Franks had long been drifting in a feudal direction. The roots of feudalism ran deep: one root was the honorable bond of fidelity and service of a warrior to his lord that characterized the lord-vassal relationship of late-Merovingian and early-Carolingian times, and the still earlier comitatus of the Germanic tribes. Another root was the late-Roman and early-medieval concept of land-holding in return for certain services to the person who granted the land. An estate granted to a tenant in return for service was known as a *benefice.*

The early Carolingians took an important step toward feudalism by joining the institutions of benefice and vassalage. Charles Martel confiscated Church property on a large scale and granted the appropriated estates to his military vassals. One reason for this step was the shortage of money in the early Middle Ages; it was almost impossible for a ruler to support his soldiers with wages. Often the vassals of an important Frankish lord were fed and sheltered in his household. Indeed, the "household knight" persisted throughout the feudal age. But as their military importance grew these warrior-vassals exhibited an ever-increasing hunger for land. Their lords were therefore under considerable pressure to grant them estates—benefices—in return for their loyalty and service.

This tendency was associated with a shift in Frankish military tactics. The Franks had originally been infantrymen or light cavalrymen, but gradually heavy cavalry became increasingly important. The Frankish warrior *par excellence* became the armored, mounted knight, more effective than before, but also far more expensive to support. The knight needed a fine mount, heavy armor and weapons, several attendants, and years of training. Hence, the tendency for a lord to support his knightly vassals by granting them estates in return for their service. The knight did not, of course, labor on his own fields; instead, he administered them and collected dues, chiefly in kind, from his peasants.

The Carolingian military vassal was typically a knight. As knightly tactics came more and more to dominate warfare, the custom of vassalage spread widely. Frankish magnates of Charlemagne's time had pledged their allegiance to their emperor and had thereby recognized that they were his vassals and he their lord. Moreover, these royal vassals had vassals of their own who owed primary allegiance to their immediate lords rather than to the emperor. Charlemagne himself approved of this practice of private lordship and encouraged the free men of his realm to become vassals of his magnates. In time of war these vassals of vassals (or subvassals) were expected to join their lords' contingents in the royal army. The disintegrative tendencies implicit in such an arrangement are obvious. Yet Charlemagne, lacking a coherent civil service or adequate funds to hire a professional army of his own, was obliged to depend on this potentially unstable hierarchy of authority and allegiance.

With the drying up of the spoils of conquest and under the pressure of the invasions, the rickety hierarchy began to collapse into its component parts. Charlemagne's old territorial officials, the dukes, counts, and margraves, backed by their own vassals, tended increasingly to usurp royal rights. They administered justice and collected taxes without regard for the royal will. In time they built castles and assumed all responsibility for the defense of their districts. They evolved from royal officials into independent territorial princes, too powerful to be coerced by the crown. Their authority was limited chiefly by the independence of their vassals, who began to create subvassals or sub-subvassals of their own. At the height of the feudal age the lord-vassal relationship might run down through some ten or twenty levels; there was scarcely a vassal to be found who was not the lord of some still lower vassal.

The ultimate consequences of these developments have been described as "feudal anarchy." In a sense the term is apt, but it should not mislead us into thinking of feudalism simply as a "bad thing." Given the instability of the Carolingian Empire and the vulnerability of France in the Viking era, feudalism emerges as a successful accommodation to the realities of the age. Roman Europe succumbed to Germanic invasions; feudal Europe survived its invaders and ultimately absorbed them.

French feudalism reached its height in the tenth and eleventh centuries. Its key institution was the military benefice, the estate granted by a lord to his vassal in return for allegiance and service—primarily knightly military service. This military benefice was commonly known as a *fief* (rhyming with beef). It was a practical response to the requirements of local defense, the breakdown of central authority, and the scarcity of money that necessitated the paying for service in land rather than wages. A great lord would grant an estate—a fief—to his vassal. The vassal might then grant a part of the estate—another fief—to a vassal of his own. And so on and on, down and down, the process of enfeoffment went. The result was a hierarchically-organized landed, knightly aristocracy. Each knight gave homage and fealty—that is, pledged his personal allegiance—to his immediate lord; each lived off the labor and dues of a dependent peasantry which tilled the fields that his fief embraced; each administered a court and dispensed justice to those below him.

Such were the essential ingredients of feudalism. The term is extremely difficult to define and has often been abused and misunderstood. The great French scholar Marc Bloch described feudalism in these words:

❝A subject peasantry; widespread use of the service tenement (that is, the fief) instead of a salary, which was out of the question; the supremacy of a class of specialized warriors; ties of obedience and protection which bind man to man and, within the warrior class, assume the distinctive form called vassalage; fragmentation of authority—leading inevitably to disorder; and in the midst of all this, the survival of other forms of association, family and state . . . —such then seem to be the fundamental features of European feudalism.**❞**

With this description in mind, it may be helpful to emphasize some of the things that feudalism was not. It was not, for one thing, a universal and symmetrical system. Born in northern France in the Viking age, it took on many different forms as it spread into other areas. In northern France itself it varied widely from one region to another. It by no means encompassed all the land, for even at its height many landowners owed no feudal obligations and had no feudal ties. And even where feudalism had become well-entrenched, bonds of kinship usually proved more compelling than bonds of vassalage. Moreover, the feudal "hierarchy" was riddled with ambiguities: a single vassal might hold several fiefs from several lords; a lord might receive a fief from his own vassal. The degree of confusion possible in feudalism is well illustrated by this twelfth-century act of enfeoffment:

❝ I, John of Toul, affirm that I am the vassal of the Lady Beatrice, countess of Troyes, and of her son Theobald, count of Champagne, against every creature living or dead, excepting my allegiance to Lord Enjourand of Coucy, Lord John of Arcis, and the count of Grandpré. If it should happen that the count of Grandpré should be at war with the countress and count of Champagne in his own quarrel, I will aid the count of Grandpré in my own person, and will aid the count and countess of Champagne by sending them the knights whose services I owe them from the fief which I hold of them. **❞**

Feudalism was not, in its heyday, associated with the romantic knight errant, the many-turreted castle, or the lady fair. The knight of the ninth, tenth, and eleventh centuries was a rough-hewn warrior. His armor was simple, his horse was tough, his castle was a crude wooden tower atop an earthen mound, and his lady fair was any available wench. Chivalry developed after a time, but not until the foundations of the old feudal order were being eroded by the revival of commerce, royal government, and infantry tactics. Only then did the knight compensate for his declining usefulness by turning to elaborate armor, courtly phrases, and fairy-tale castles.

Feudalism was not exclusively a military institution. The vassal owed his lord not only military service but a variety of additional obligations as well. Among these were the duty to join his lord's retinue on tours of the countryside; to serve in his lord's court of justice; to feed, house, and entertain his lord and his lord's retinue on their all-too-frequent visits; to give money to his lord on a variety of specified occasions; to contribute to his lord's ransom should he be captured in battle. Early in its history the fief became hereditary. The lord, however, retained the right to confiscate it should his vassal die without heirs, to supervise and exploit it during a minority, and to exercise a power of veto over the marriage of a female fief-holder. In return for such rights as these, the lord was obliged to protect and uphold the interests of his vassals. The very essence of feudalism was the notion of reciprocal rights and obligations, and the feudal outlook played an important role in steering medieval Europe away from autocracy.

Feudalism was both a military and a political system. With military responsibility went political power. As the central government of West Frankland demonstrated an ever-increasing incapacity to cope with the invasions or keep peace in the countryside, sovereignty tended to sink to the level of the greater feudal lords. Although originally vassals of the Carolingian kings, these magnates became powers unto themselves, ruling their own territories without royal interference and maintaining their own courts and administrative systems as well as their own armies. In the days of the Viking raids many of these magnates had extreme difficulty in controlling their own turbulent vassals; feudal tenants several steps down in the pyramid were often able to behave as though they had no real superiors. Subvassals with their own courts and armies were frequently in a position to defy their lords. Accordingly, it is hard to identify the real locus of political power in early feudal France. Sovereignty was spread up and down the aristocratic hierarchy, and a lord's real power depended on his military prowess, his castles, his ruthlessness, and his luck.

Specialists in medieval history are inclined to limit "feudalism" to the network of rights and obligations existing among members of the knightly aristocracy—the holders of fiefs. Although resting on the labor of peasants, the feudal structure itself encompassed only the warrior class of lords and vassals. There was, in other words, a world of difference between a vassal and a serf. Beneath the level of the feudal warrior class, eighty or ninety percent of the population continued to labor on the land, producing the food that sustained society. Yet the peasants were scorned by the nobility as boors and louts and were largely ignored by the chroniclers of the age.

The feudal chaos of ninth and tenth century France, with its fragmentation of sovereign power and its incessant private wars, gradually gave way to a somewhat more orderly regime. Great territorial magnates such as the counts of Anjou and Flanders and the duke of Normandy extended their frontiers at the expense of weaker neighbors and tightened their control over their own vassals and subvassals. France became a patchwork quilt of tough and increasingly well-organized territorial principalities. But not until the twelfth and thirteenth centuries did the French monarchs begin to rise above the level of their greater magnates and assert real authority over the realm. The high noon of feudalism was a period of virtual eclipse for the French crown.

Response to the Invasions: Germany

In England the invasions brought royal unification, in France, feudal particularism. The response of Germany differed from those of both England and France, owing to the special character of the invasions that Germany faced and the unique conditions prevailing in Germany itself. Although East Frankland (Germany) was subject to Viking attacks, the real threat came from the Hungarian horsemen of the east. When the late-Carolingian kings of Germany proved incapable of coping with the Hungarian raids, authority descended, as in France, to the great magnates of the realm. But these magnates were not the dukes and counts of Carolingian officialdom. Most of Germany had remained outside Frankish control until the Carolingian conquests of the eighth century, and the Frankish system of local administration was not deeply rooted. The ancient tribal allegiances of Saxons, Bavarians, and Swabians were still strong. In the critical decades of the late ninth and early tenth centuries, ambitious aristocrats exploited this tribal patriotism by grasping leadership over the old tribal districts. These men of the hour assumed the title of duke, and the regions that they ruled came to be known as tribal duchies. The "tribal" dukes sought to dominate the local ecclesiastical organizations, to seize the royal Carolingian estates in their duchies, and to usurp royal powers. It was they who stood up to the Hungarian thrust.

In the early tenth century Germany was dominated by five tribal duchies: Saxony, Swabia, Bavaria, Franconia, and Lorraine. The first three had been incorporated only superficially into the Carolingian state, whereas the western duchies of Franconia and Lorraine were much more strongly Frankish in outlook and organization. The five "tribal" dukes might well have become the masters of Germany. Their ambitions were frustrated by two closely related factors: (1) their failure to curb the Hungarians, and (2) the reinvigoration of the German monarchy under an able, new dynasty. The Carolingian line came to an end in Germany in 911 with the death of King Louis the Child. He was succeeded first by the duke of Franconia and then, in 919, by the duke of Saxony—the first of an illustrious line of kings whose power was based on their domination of the powerful Saxon duchy.

Otto I

The Saxon kings struggled vigorously to assert their authority over the tribal duchies. With the duchy of Saxony under the authority of the monarchy, the Saxon kings quickly won direct control over Franconia as well. But the semi-independent dukes of the two southern duchies, Swabia and Bavaria, presented problems. The real victory of the Saxon monarchy occurred in the reign of the second and ablest of the Saxon kings, Otto I (936–973).

Otto I, or "Otto the Great," directed his considerable talents toward three goals: (1) the defense of Germany against the Hungarian invasions; (2) the establishment of royal power over the remaining tribal duchies; and (3) the extension of German royal control to the crumbling, unstable Middle Kingdom that the Treaty of Verdun had assigned to Emperor Lothar back in 843. We have already seen how this Middle Kingdom began to fall to pieces after Lothar's death. By the mid-tenth century it had become a political shambles. Parts of it had been taken over by Germany and France, but its southern districts—Burgundy and Italy—retained a chaotic independence. The dukes of Swabia and Bavaria both had notions of seizing these territories. Otto the Great, in order to forestall the development of an unmanageable rival power to his south, led his armies into Italy in 951 and assumed the title "King of Italy."

From 951 onwards events developed rapidly. Otto the Great had to leave

Italy in haste to put down a major uprising in Germany. His victory over the rebels enabled him to establish his power there more strongly than ever. In 955 he won the crucial victory of his age when he crushed a large Hungarian army at the battle of the Lechfeld, bringing the Hungarian raids to an end at last. Otto's triumph at the Lechfeld served as a vivid demonstration of royal power—a vindication of the monarch's claim that he, not the "tribal" dukes, was the true defender of Germany. With the Hungarians defeated, Germany's eastern frontier now lay open to the gradual penetration of German-Christian culture. The day of the tribal duchies was over; the monarchy was supreme. Otto the Great now towered over his contemporaries as the greatest monarch of the West and the most powerful ruler since Charlemagne. The invasions of Germany, which had begun by uplifting the tribal duchies, ended with the revival of royal authority.

Not long after his victory over the Hungarians, Otto I turned his attention to still another crisis. Since his departure from Italy, a Lombard magnate had seized the Italian throne and was harassing the pope. In response to a papal appeal—which dovetailed with his own interests—Otto returned to Italy in force and recovered the Italian throne. In 962 the pope hailed Otto as Roman Emperor and placed the imperial crown on his head. It is this momentous event, rather than the coronation of Charlemagne in 800, that marks the true genesis of the medieval Holy Roman Empire.

Although the events of 962 are reminiscent of 800, Otto's empire was vastly different from Charlemagne's. Above all, Otto and his imperial successors exercised no jurisdiction over France or the remainder of Western Christendom. The medieval Holy Roman Empire had its roots deep in the soil of Germany, and most of the emperors subordinated imperial interests to those of the German monarchy. From its advent in 962 to its long-delayed demise in the early nineteenth century, the Holy Roman Empire remained fundamentally a German phenomenon. *

The German orientation of Otto's empire is illustrated by the fact that neither he nor the majority of his successors over the next two centuries made any real effort to establish tight control in Italy. Only when they marched south of the Alps could they count on the obedience of the Italians; when they returned to Germany they left behind them no real administrative structure but depended almost solely on the fickle allegiance of certain Italian magnates and bishops. The German emperors were never successful in straddling the Alps.

In Germany conditions were quite different. There the coming of feudalism was delayed for more than a century after Otto's imperial coronation. The great magnates became vassals of the king but normally had no vassals of their own. The chief tool that Otto and his successors used in

*The term "Holy Roman Empire" was not actually employed until the twelfth century. It is used here for convenience and with apologies to the purist. A later cynic, in an outburst of ponderous wit, observed that the Holy Roman Empire was neither holy nor Roman nor an Empire.

The Holy Roman Emperor with orb and scepter: manuscript illumination from the Gospel Book of Otto III, A.D. 1000.

governing their state was the Church. In an era of a weak papacy the German kings dominated the churchmen within their realm and kept close control over important ecclesiastical appointments. Otto had successfully wrested control of the Church in the various tribal duchies from the defunct dukes, and the great bishops and abbots of Germany were the king's men. They made ideal royal lieutenants. They could not pass on their estates to heirs, and when a bishop or abbot died his successor was handpicked by the king. Thus the loyalty and political capacity of the king's administrator-churchmen were assured. After 962 the German monarchy was, on occasion, successful even in appointing popes. There would come a time when churchmen would rebel at such treatment, but in Otto's reign the time was still far off.

Otto's claims to proprietorship of the imperial Church were supported by both tradition and theory. Otto was regarded as more than a mere secular monarch. He was *rex et sacerdos*, king and priest, sanctified by the holy

THE HOLY ROMAN EMPIRE IN 962

North Sea

Baltic Sea

K. OF DEN.

SLAVS

FRISIA

SAXONY

Rhine R.

Elbe R.

LORRAINE

FRANCONIA

BOHEMIA

FRANCE

SWABIA

Lechfeld

BAVARIA

Danube R.

CARINTHIA

HUNGARIANS

Rhone R.

KINGDOM OF BURGUNDY

KDM. OF ITALY

Venice

KDM. OF CROATIA

SERVIA

CORSICA

Rome

BENEVENTO

APULIA

SARDINIA

| 0 | 100 | 200 | 300 MILES |

████ *The Holy Roman Empire*

▒▒▒▒ *The Five Stem Duchies*

CALABRIA

SICILY

anointing ceremony which accompanied his coronation. He was the vicar of God—the living symbol of Christ the King—the "natural" leader of the Church in his empire. And in the closing years of his reign his actual political powers over church and state came close to matching his exalted pretensions.

The Ottonian Renaissance

Otto's reign provided the impulse for an impressive intellectual revival that reached its culmination under his two successors, Otto II (973–83) and Otto III (983–1002). This "Ottonian Renaissance" produced a series of able administrators and scholars, the greatest of whom was the churchman Gerbert of Aurillac—later Pope Sylvester II (d. 1003). Gerbert visited Spain and returned with a comprehensive knowledge of Islamic science. With this event the infiltration of Arab thought into Western Christendom began.

Gerbert had an encyclopedic though unoriginal mind. A master of classical literature, logic, mathematics, and science, he astonished his contemporaries by teaching the Greco-Arab doctrine that the earth was spherical. It was widely rumored that he was a wizard in league with the Devil—but the rumors were dampened by his elevation to the papacy. Gerbert was no wizard but an advance agent of the intellectual awakening that Europe was about to undergo.

Although successors of Otto the Great were no longer troubled by the tribal duchies or the Hungarians, they were obliged to cope with new problems and devise new solutions. In 1024 the Saxon dynasty died out and was replaced by a Franconian line known as the Salian dynasty (1024–1125). The "tribal" dukes gave way to a new, particularistic aristocracy whose impulse toward independence taxed the ingenuity of the emperors. Still, the early Salian kings were generally successful in maintaining their power. Working hand in glove with the German church, the Salians improved and expanded the royal administration and ultimately came to exercise even greater authority than Otto I. In the mid-eleventh century the strongest of the Salian emperors, Henry III (1039–56), ruled unrivaled over Germany and appointed popes as freely as he selected his own bishops. In 1050, at a time when France was still a checkerboard of feudal principalities and England, under Edward the Confessor, was relatively small and more-or-less isolated, the German emperor Henry III dominated central Europe and held the papacy in his palm.

Italy: The Rise of Cities

When Charlemagne conquered Lombard Italy in 774 he was faced with the problem of reorganizing a kingdom much different from his own. For one thing, urban life had retained far more vitality in Italy than elsewhere in Western Christendom. For another, the Lombard royal administration that Charlemagne inherited differed sharply from the administration of Carolingian Frankland. The Lombard kings had managed to exercise strong authority only in a region of northern Italy which came to be known as the Lombard Plain, or simply Lombardy. They ruled only loosely over the Lombard dukes of Friuli to the northeast (near Venice) and Spoleto to the south. Still further south, below Rome, Lombard royal authority was nonexistent. Here a con-

England	France	Germany
c.787: First Danish raid	814–840: Louis the Pious	814–840: Louis the Pious
	840–877: Charles the Bald	840–876: Louis the German
871–899: Reign of Alfred	843: Treaty of Verdun	843: Treaty of Verdun
878: Battle of Edington	c.911: Normandy recognized	891: Vikings defeated by Arnulf
c.954: Reconquest of Danelaw completed		936–973: Reign of Otto the Great
		955: Otto defeats Hungarians at the Lechfeld
978–1016: Reign of Ethelred	987: Capetians replace Carolingians	962: Otto crowned Roman Emperor
1017–1035: Reign of Canute		973–983: Reign of Otto II
1042–1066: Reign of Edward the Confessor		983–1002: Reign of Otto III
1066: Norman Conquest of England		1003: Gerbert of Aurillac dies
		1039–1056: Reign of Henry III

gregation of small powers waged incessant war with one another: independent duchies, coastal towns (Amalfi, Naples, Salerno), Saracen bandits' nests, and Byzantine enclaves left from Justinian's conquests.

Characteristically, Charlemagne installed Frankish counts on the Lombard Plain in the places of Lombard royal officials, and in Friuli and Spoleto Lombard dukes gave way to new dukes drawn from Carolingian officialdom. Charlemagne never established his authority south of Rome, and even in Lombardy the new Carolingian order did not have time to jell. Within a generation or two, Carolingian royal authority was faltering. And by the late 800s the north Italian crown had become the object of a brutal and confused power struggle involving the dukes of Spoleto and Friuli and other ambitious families.

None of these contending dynasties could hope to hold the crown for long without establishing control over the Lombard Plain. Consequently, as one family after another seized the throne, it would place its own supporters in the controlling positions as counts in Lombardy. As a result of these policies, the old Carolingian aristocracy was replaced throughout the Lombard Plain by a

ITALY
ABOUT 1000

FRIULI

LOMBARDY

VENICE

Controlled by
Holy Roman Empire

CROATIA

ROMAGNA

TUSCANY

Adriatic Sea

SPOLETO

CORSICA

PAPAL STATES

BENEVENTO

CAPUA

APULIA

NAPLES

SALERNO

SARDINIA

CALABRIA

Mediterranean Sea

Scale of Miles
0   50   100   150   200

SICILY

Italy, C.1000

new aristocracy dependent on one or another of the short-lived royal dynasties. Thus Lombardy, unlike France, experienced a nearly complete break with the Carolingian past. Whereas most of the principalities of feudal France were ruled by descendants of Carolingian counts, the counties of Lombardy were not. And whereas in France the power of the counts was growing, in Lombardy it was diminishing for want of dynastic continuity.

As the position of the Lombard counts weakened, the cities that they governed grew more and more independent. And with the coming of the Hungarian and Saracen invasions, it was the Italian cities, under the leadership of their bishops, that became the chief centers of resistance. The contending Italian kings depended increasingly on their cities to repel the invaders and had no choice but to grant the urban bishops extensive powers and privileges—the right to build walls and fortified towers, and the right to collect tolls and public revenues with which the defensive works might be financed. By the early 900s the cities had won full exemption from the counts' jurisdiction. The bishops acquired control not only of the cities' defenses but of their revenues and courts of justice as well.

Generations thereafter, Lombard townspeople would seize these privileges from their bishops and would subject the surrounding countryside to the authority of their cities. These processes occurred only with the economic revival of the eleventh century and amidst the concurrent struggle between pope and emperor. But even in the early tenth century, forces were clearly at work that would one day transform northern Italy into a land of self-governing city-states.

Throughout the 900s, however, the bishops remained firmly in power. Ruling and defending their cities, they became the decisive force in northern Italian politics. The royal dynasties required their support, and more than once, the opposition of bishops cost a monarch his crown. Indeed, it was at the urging of a group of important Lombard bishops that Otto the Great intervened in the mid-900s, bringing an end to the royal dynastic squabbles by incorporating northern Italy into his empire.

Otto the Great and his imperial successors ruled northern Italy from a distance. Except on the rare occasions when they led their armies southward across the Alps, they based their authority on the support of the urban bishops, whose powers endured and grew under German rule. In this respect, Otto's conquest changed nothing, but it did furnish Italy the vitally important benefits of relative peace and stability after a century of anarchy. The emperors helped relieve Italy of the Muslim menace, both by leading armies against Muslim enclaves and by providing a settled environment that encouraged urban growth and commercial revival. By the late 900s the north Italian ports of Genoa and Pisa were developing a vigorous and widespread Mediterranean trade and a growing merchant class. In the course of the next century, Genoa and Pisa seized the offensive from the Muslims, expelling them from the important Mediterranean islands of Sardinia and Corsica and launching raids against Muslim ports in Spain and North Africa. Other Italian coastal cities, beyond the lands ruled by the German emperor, were taking to the sea as well: Amalfi, Salerno, and Naples in southern Italy and, above all, the republic of Venice on the northern shore of the Adriatic Sea.

Long a Byzantine dependency, Venice had achieved virtual independence by the ninth century and yet continued to send fleets to assist Byzantium in its wars. By carefully cultivating her relations with both Constantinople and Islamic North Africa, Venice developed a flourishing triangular trade. And during the 900s she evolved into the foremost commercial center in Western Christendom. In a Europe that was overwhelmingly agrarian, the Venetians developed the first state to live by trade alone. Enriched by the exporting of salt from their lagoons and glass from their furnaces, and by the profits of commerce, they grew no foodstuffs but purchased them instead in the markets of northern Italian towns. A Lombard writer remarked with astonishment that "These people neither plow nor sow nor gather grapes," but "buy grain and wine in every market place."

In this respect Venice was unique, but other Italian ports—Genoa, Pisa, Amalfi—were following her into the lucrative Mediterranean trade. And their burgeoning commercial life stimulated the growth of inland cities such as Milan, Bologna, and Florence. Tenth century Milan was not only the largest city in Lombardy but one of the most populous in all Western Christendom. Although not yet a tenth as large as Constantinople, it was more than ten times the size of Paris. With the closing of the age of invasions, Italy had thus achieved the reversal of two age-long historical trends: its cities were growing once more, and its well-armed fleets were challenging, at last, the Byzantine and Muslim domination of Mediterranean commerce.

The Organization of Agriculture

During the tenth and eleventh centuries the commercial city remained a rarity in Western Christendom. Almost everywhere wealth and power were associated with the holding of land. And beneath the social layer of princes and nobles, the great majority of Europeans labored on the soil.

To discuss the typical medieval farm is as difficult as to discuss the typical American business. Medieval agrarian institutions were almost infinitely diverse; medieval agriculture exhibited countless variations. Nevertheless some features of agrarian life recur throughout much of the more fertile and heavily populated portions of northern Europe. Certain generalizations can be made about medieval agrarian institutions, if we bear in mind that numerous exceptions to any of them can be found.

Any discussion of medieval husbandry must begin by distinguishing between two fundamental institutions: the village and the manor. The village, the basic unit of the agrarian economy, consisted of a population nucleus ranging from about a dozen to several hundred peasant families living in a cluster. In regions where the soil was poor, peasant families lived in separate farms or hamlets; but throughout the fertile lowlands of northern France, England, and Germany village life was the norm.

The manor, on the other hand, was an artificial unit—a unit of jurisdiction and economic exploitation controlled by a single lord. The lord might be a king or great baron with numerous manors under his control. Or he might be a simple knight with only one or two manors at his disposal. The manor—the unit of jurisdiction—was often geographically identical with the village; but some manors embraced two or more villages, and an occasional large village might be divided into two or more manors. In any case the agrarian routine of plowing, planting, and harvesting was based on the village organization, whereas the peasants' dues, obligations, and legal and political subordination were based on the manor.

The Village

The ordinary village consisted of a grouping of peasants' huts surrounded by large fields. There would normally be either two or three such fields. Two had been the traditional number and remained so throughout southern Europe. But, as we have seen, the agrarian economy had been shifting in some districts of northern Europe from a two-field to a three-field system of rotation. The peasants of a three-field village would plant one field in the spring for fall harvesting, plant the second field in the fall for early summer harvesting, and let the third field lie fallow throughout the year. The next year the fields would be rotated and the process repeated. Although three-field agriculture was becoming common in northern Europe, many villages continued to function with only two fields, while others might have four, five, or even more, all subject to complex rotation arrangements.

The arable lands surrounding the village were known as *open fields* and were normally divided into unfenced strips, each about 220 yards long. Typically, a single peasant family possessed several strips scattered throughout the fields, but the peasant community labored collectively, pooling their plows, their draught animals, and their toil. Collective husbandry was necessary because plows were scarce and had to be shared and because no one peasant owned sufficient oxen to make up the team of four to eight beasts necessary to draw the heavy plow. The details of this collective process were ususally worked out in the village council and were guided by immemorial custom.

The shape, contour, and method of cultivation of the open fields varied enormously from place to place, depending as they did on the topography of the region and the fertility of the soil. The strips themselves were products of the heavy plow and the necessity of reversing the ox team as seldom as possible. The length of the strips was determined by the distance a team could draw the plow without rest. A group of four strips, which constituted the normal day's work of a plow team, became the basis of our modern acre.

The open fields were fundamental to the village economy and, indeed, to the entire agrarian system of northern Europe. But there was more to the village community than the cluster of peasants' huts and the encircling fields. Besides his scattered strips in the fields, a peasant ordinarily had a small garden adjacent to his hut where vegetables and fruits could be raised and fowl kept to provide variety to his diet. The village also included a pasture where the plow animals might graze, and a meadow from which hay was cut to sustain the precious beasts over the winter. Some village communities kept sheep on their pasture as a source of cheese, milk, and wool. Certain districts, particularly in Flanders and northern England, took up sheep raising on a scale so large as almost to exclude the growing of grains.

Attached to most village communities was a wooded area from which fuel and building materials could be gathered. It also served as a forage for pigs, which provided most of the meat in the peasants' diet. There was commonly a stream or pond nearby that supplied the community with fish, a water mill for grinding grain, and a large oven that the community used for baking bread. By the eleventh century most village communities were organized as parishes. Each parish possessed a village church supervised by a priest, usually of peasant birth, who had land of his own scattered among the strips of the open fields.

The village community tended to be a closed system, economically self-sufficient, capable of sustaining the material and spiritual needs of the villagers without much contact with the outside world. The economy of the early Middle Ages, lacking a vigorous commercial life and a significant urban population, failed to provide villages with much incentive to produce beyond their immediate needs. There was only the most limited market for surplus grain. Accordingly, village life was uneventful, tradition-bound, and circumscribed by the narrowest of horizons. On the other hand, gradual but profound changes were occurring in medieval civilization that eventually made a deep impact upon the village. The early-medieval innovations in agrarian technology significantly increased agricultural efficiency and productivity. Moreover, the commercial and urban revival of the High Middle Ages provided an expanding market for surplus grain. These developments in turn eroded village parochialism, freed the village economy from its self-sufficiency by incorporating it into a regional economic system, and provided enterprising peasants with a means of acquiring considerable money. They also encouraged the expansion of villages and fields through the clearing of forests and wilderness and the draining of marshes. Timeless though it might have seemed, the village economy was changing.

The Manor

Superimposed on the economic structure of the village was the political-juridical structure of the manor. In the eleventh century the manorial regime was only incompletely established in England and was scarcely evident at all in Scandinavia, Italy, and parts of northern Germany and southern France. But throughout much of northern France and, later, southern England, the average peasant villager was bound to a manorial lord. Some agrarian laborers were outright slaves, but slavery was declining during the early Middle Ages and had become uncommon by the end of the eleventh century. Some peasants were of free status, owing rents to their lord but little or nothing more. A few were landless laborers working for a wage. But the great middle stratum of the peasantry consisted of serfs—people of unfree status, bound to their lords and usually bound also to their land, like the peasantry of late-Roman times. In return for his strips in the open fields, the serf owed various dues to his manorial lord, chiefly in kind, and was normally expected to labor for a certain number of days per week—often three—on the lord's fields.

The lord drew his sustenance from the dues of his peasants and from the produce of his own fields. The lord's fields were strips scattered among the strips of the peasants and were known collectively as his demesne. Theoretically, then, the fields of the manor were divided into two categories: the lord's demesne (perhaps one-fourth to one-third of the total area) and the peasants' holdings. But in fact the demesne strips and the peasants' strips were intermixed. The demesne was worked by the peasants who also paid their lord a percentage of the produce of their own fields and rendered him fees for the use of the pasture, the woods, and the lord's mill and oven. These were some of the more common peasant obligations on many manors. But such obligations were exceedingly diverse.

The lord also enjoyed significant political authority over his peasants—authority that flourished and grew in rhythm with the disintegration of sovereign power which occurred in late Carolingian times. The administrative center of the manor was the manorial court, usually held in the lord's castle or manor house. Here a rough, custom-based justice was meted out, disputes settled, misdeeds punished, and obligations enforced. Since most lords possessed more than one manor, authority over individual manors was commonly exercised by an agent of the lord known as a bailiff or steward. It was he who supervised the manorial court, oversaw the farming of the demesne, and collected the peasants' dues. In addition to the peasants' agrarian obligations, the lord also was entitled to certain payments deriving from his political and personal authority over his tenants. He might levy a *tallage*—an arbitrary manorial tax that was theoretically unlimited in frequency and amount but was usually circumscribed by custom. He was normally entitled to payments when a peasant's son inherited the holdings of his father and when a peasant's daughter married outside the manor.

In general, the serfs had no standing before the law. Their lords were restrained from exploiting them arbitrarily only by the force of custom. Some ruthless lords ignored this restraint and abused their serfs pitilessly. But custom was strong in the Middle Ages and could protect the serf in many ways. He was by no means a chattel slave. He could not be sold away from his family or be deprived of his own hereditary lands. After paying his manorial dues, he was entitled to the remaining produce of his fields. The serf's condition was hardly enviable, but it was better than the slavery of ancient times.

The Post-Carolingian Church

The existence of parish churches in eleventh-century villages illustrates the deeply significant fact that the long process of Christianizing Europe was by now far advanced. Whatever were the intellectual and moral shortcomings of the village priests, they were at least representatives of the international Church operating at the most immediate local levels throughout the European countryside. At a rather more elevated level was the work and influence of the Benedictines. They offered prayers to God, copied manuscripts, taught in their schools, supplied knights from their estates to secular armies, and served as counselors to counts, dukes, and kings. While continuing their traditional spiritual activities they played, even more than in Carolingian times, a major role in political life.

The greatest Benedictine house of the eleventh century was Cluny in Burgundy. Founded in 910 by the duke of Aquitaine, Cluny was free of local episcopal jurisdiction, subject to the pope alone, and blessed with a series of remarkably able and long-lived abbots. Cluny followed Benedict of Aniane's modifications of the original Benedictine Rule. Its monks, shunning field work, devoted themselves to an elaborate sequence of daily prayers and liturgical services and a strict, godly life. This strictness was relative, falling short of the austere regimes of several of the more ascetic orders of the High Middle Ages. Yet the Cluniacs were successful in avoiding the abuses and corruption that flourished in many monasteries of their day.

Richly endowed, holy, and seemingly incorruptible, Cluny was widely admired. Gradually it began to acquire daughter houses until, in time, it became the nucleus of a great congregation of reform monasteries extending across Europe—all of them obedient to the abbot of Cluny. In the mid-eleventh century the Congregation of Cluny was both powerful and wealthy, and its new abbey church, completed in the early twelfth century, was the most splendid building of its time in all Western Europe. Cluny's high ideals were tempered by a sense of dignity—and perhaps also by a comfortable feeling of spiritual success and social acceptance. Enriched and supported by the lay aristocracy, it was by no means in radical opposition to secular society; instead, it tended on the whole to uphold the social system of its day and to worship the Lord God without disparaging the lords of men.

Cluny's attitude typified that of the entire Church in the earlier eleventh century. As the lay world became more and more exposed to Christianity, as kings such as Edward the Confessor in England and Henry III in Germany

Model of the Abbey Church at Cluny showing Romanesque apse.

demonstrated their concern for the welfare of their churches, the Church itself tended increasingly to come to terms with lay society. Through the ceremony of anointing, kings became virtual priest-kings. Indeed, contemporary political theory taught that the Church and the world were one—a single, God-oriented organism in which churchmen and lay lords each had appropriate roles to play.

Apart from Cluny, the monasteries and bishoprics of eleventh-century Europe were largely under lay control. They were dependent on lay patronage and were often entangled in the feudal system. Their prelates were appointed by lay lords in much the same way that village priests were chosen and controlled by manorial lords. Although not independent, the Church was wealthy, respected, and comfortable, and few churchmen were inclined to challenge the situation. Those few, however, were to undertake in the later eleventh century a political-spiritual revolution that severely undermined the long-established church-state entente.

Europe on the Eve of the High Middle Ages

During the centuries between the fall of the Roman Empire in the West and the great economic and cultural revival of the later eleventh century, the foundations were built on which Western Civilization rose. Kingdoms were forming, distinctive customs and institutions were developing, and a classical-Christian intellectual tradition was gradually being absorbed, adapted, and broadened. At the bottom of the social scale, the peasant had become firmly attached to the soil and his productivity was rising.

By 1050 both England and Germany were comparatively stable, well-organized kingdoms. The Church was poised for a great movement of reform and centralization. The French monarchy was still weak, but by the end of the following century it would be on its way toward dominating France. Meanwhile, feudal principalities such as Normandy, Champagne, Flanders, and Anjou were well on the road to political coherence. Warfare was still endemic, but it was beginning to lessen as Europe moved toward political stability. Above all, the invasions were over—the siege had ended. Hungary and the Scandinavian world were being absorbed into Western Christendom, and Islam was by now on the defensive. The return of prosperity, the increase in food production, the rise in population, the quickening of commerce, the intensification of intellectual activity—all betokened the coming of a new era. Western Civilization was on the threshold of an immense creative surge.

SUGGESTED READINGS

The asterisk indicates a paperback edition.

GENERAL WORKS

*CHRISTOPHER DAWSON, *The Making of Europe* (1946). A thoughtful, sympathetic analysis of early medieval culture, stressing the role of the Catholic faith.

*M.L.W. LAISTNER, *Thought and Letters in Western Europe: A.D. 500–900* (rev. ed., 1936). Still the best intellectual history of the period.

*ROBERT LATOUCHE, *The Birth of Western Economy* (1966). A provocative account of early medieval economic trends, emphasizing the importance of the small farm.

*ROBERT S. LOPEZ, *The Birth of Europe* (1967). A treatment of the entire medieval period that stresses social and economic history and emphasizes southern Europe.

*J.M. WALLACE-HADRILL, *The Barbarian West: 400–1000 (1962).* A skillful popularization by England's foremost authority on early-medieval Frankland.

CHRISTIANITY

*PETER BROWN, *Augustine of Hippo: A Biography* (1969). An extraordinarily sensitive study of Augustine's life and times.

*C.N. COCHRANE, *Christianity and Classical Culture* (1944). A penetrating study, sympathetic to the mystical viewpoint.

*JEAN DANIÉLOU and HENRI MARROU, *The Christian Centuries*, Vol. I. *The First Six Hundred Years* (1964). Comprehensive and written with clarity.

*NOREEN HUNT, *Cluny under St. Hugh: 1049–1109* (1968). A study of Cluny in its greatest years, showing that its political role was a byproduct of its central commitment to the reformed monastic life.

*JEFFREY B. RUSSELL, *A History of Medieval Christianity* (1968). A short, lucid work examining the Church's response to the opposing forces of prophecy and order.

THE LATER EMPIRE AND THE GERMANIC INVASIONS

*PETER BROWN, *The World of Late Antiquity: A.D. 150–750* (1971). A sympathetic study of social and cultural change in Eastern and Western Europe and the Near East.

*J.B. BURY, *History of the Later Roman Empire* (2 vols. 1957). A reprint of a classic older work.

*FERDINAND LOT, *The End of the Ancient World and the Beginnings of the Middle Ages* (1961). A reprint of a masterful study stressing economic factors in Rome's decline.

LUCIEN MUSSET, *The Germanic Invasions: The Making of Europe, A.D. 400-600* (1975). Discusses the state of scholarly investigations and controversies; not for beginners.

BYZANTIUM

DENO J. GEANAKOPLOS, *Interaction of the "Sibling" Byzantine and Western Cultures in the Middle Ages and Italian Renaissance* (1976). A lucid discussion of Byzantine-Western interaction across thirteen centuries.

*J.M. HUSSEY, *The Byzantine World* (1961). A brief, skillful summary.

*ROMILY JENKINS, *Byzantium: The Imperial Centuries* (1969). A fine account of the period from Heraclius to the battle of Manzikert, particularly valuable on the age of the Macedonian emperors.

*GEORGE OSTROGORSKY, *History of the Byzantine State* (rev. ed., 1969). The most comprehensive single-volume history of Byzantium.

*SPEROS VRYONIS, *Byzantium and Europe* (1969). A short, well-illustrated interpretive survey picturing Byzantium as "a society and culture midway between those of Islam and the Latin west."

THE WEST BEFORE THE CAROLINGIANS

*ELEANOR DUCKETT, *The Wandering Saints of the Early Middle Ages* (1964). Perceptive biographical portraits of Patrick, Boniface, and other missionaries.

*PETER LASKO, *The Kingdom of the Franks* (1971). A splendidly illustrated account of the Merovingian Franks, emphasizing Frankish art.

*BRYCE LYON, *The Origins of the Middle Ages: Pirenne's Challenge to Gibbon* (1972). A study on conflicting historical interpretations of the early-medieval West.

*HENRI PIRENNE, *Mohammed and Charlemagne* (1955, reprint). The firmest statement by the great Belgian scholar of his controversial thesis that Roman civilization endured in the West until the eighth century. This book should be read in connection with Lyon (above).

*J.M. WALLACE-HADRILL, *Early Germanic Kingship in England and on the Continent* (1971). Authoritative studies of kingship from the early Germanic tribes through Charlemagne and Alfred.

*J.M. WALLACE-HADRILL, *The Long-Haired Kings and Other Studies in Frankish History* (1962). Illuminating essays on the Merovingian era.

ISLAM

*G.E. VON GRUNEBAUM, *Medieval Islam* (2nd ed., 1963). A learned and original work; the best on the subject.

*P.K. HITTI, *History of the Arabs* (6th ed., 1958). Broad, yet full; a monumental work. For a short survey by the same author, see *The Arabs: A Short History* (1956).

*ARCHIBALD LEWIS, *The Islamic World and the West: A.D. 642–1492* (1970). A thoughtful collection of essays by modern historians and original sources in English translation.

*W.M. WATT and PIERRE CACHIA, *A History of Islamic Spain* (1967). A good, short survey from the fall of the Visigoths to the fall of Granada, particularly full on the tenth-century golden age of Cordova.

CAROLINGIAN AND POST-CAROLINGIAN EUROPE

*FRANK BARLOW, *Edward the Confessor* (1970). Barlow shows that Edward's sanctity was largely a matter of posthumous reputation.

*GEOFFREY BARRACLOUGH, *The Crucible of Europe* (1976). A well-written political analysis of Western Europe *c.* 800–1050 with new interpretations.

*GEOFFREY BARRACLOUGH, *The Origins of Modern Germany* (1963). A general account of German constitutional history that places particular emphasis on the medieval period.

*MARC BLOCH, *Feudal Society* (2 vols. 1961; originally published 1940). A masterly work, challengingly written and boldly original in its conclusions. Bloch treats feudalism in a broad sociological sense.

*MARC BLOCH, *French Rural History* (1966). Originally published in French in 1931, this book has changed our ways of looking at medieval agrarian life and institutions.

*JACQUES BOUSSARD, *The Civilization of Charlemagne* (1968). This important French work, which was immediately translated, is now the best single book in English on the age of Charlemagne.

*GEORGES DUBY, *The Early Growth of the European Economy: Warriors and Peasants from the Seventh to the Twelfth Century* (1974). An impressive work of synthesis by the most innovative and influential living historian of the medieval French economy.

*ELEANOR DUCKETT, *Alfred the Great* (1956). "This is a very simple book," the author states. It is also short, sound, and well-written.

*ELEANOR DUCKETT, *Carolingian Portraits* (1969). Sensitive biographical sketches of ninth-century figures.

*F.L. GANSHOF, *Feudalism* (2nd ed., 1961). A short, somewhat technical, survey of medieval feudal institutions by a great Belgian scholar.

*F.L. GANSHOF, *Frankish Institutions under Charlemagne* (1968). A masterful work of institutional history.

*GWYN JONES, *A History of the Vikings* (1973). An impressive work of scholarly synthesis, stylishly written.

*SIDNEY PAINTER, *French Chivalry* (1957). Short, witty, and perceptive.

*SIR FRANK STENTON, *Anglo-Saxon England* (3rd ed., 1971). A massive masterpiece.

*CARL STEPHENSON, *Medieval Feudalism* (1956). Brief, semipopular, and lucid; a well-organized account, though dated; broader than Ganshof's and less detailed.

*LYNN WHITE, JR., *Medieval Technology and Social Change* (1962). This important pioneering work covers the whole of the Middle Ages.

SOURCES

*ST. AUGUSTINE'S *Confessions* has been published in several paperback editions. For *The City of God*, see the good paperback abridgment by Vernon I. Bourke.

*BEDE, *A History of the English Church and People*, tr. Leo Shirley-Price.

*EINHARD, *Life of Charlemagne*, tr. S.E. Turner.

*EUSEBIUS, *The History of the Church*, tr. G.A. Williamson.

*GREGORY OF TOURS, *History of the Franks*, tr. Ernest Brehaut.

*GREGORY THE GREAT, *Dialogues, Book II: St. Benedict*, tr. Myra L. Uhlfelder. Pope Gregory I's biography of St. Benedict of Nursia.

*BOYD HILL, ed., *The Rise of the First Reich: Germany in the Tenth Century* (1969). Original sources and modern historians' interpretations in English translation.

There are a number of general collections of medieval sources in translation. Among the best (all paperbacks) are: ROBERT BRENTANO, ed., *The Early Middle Ages: 500–1000*; CAROLLY ERICKSON, ed., *The Records of Medieval Europe*; and DAVID HERLIHY, ed., *Medieval Culture and Society*.

Part II

The High Middle Ages

The first
flowering of
european culture

Chapter 9

ℭ

Town, Countryside, and Frontier

The High Middle Ages: *c.* 1050–1300

❡ The term *High Middle Ages* is commonly used to describe the economic and cultural flowering of the later eleventh, twelfth, and thirteenth centuries. No spectacular event occurred in 1050 to signal the advent of the new era; no cataclysm occurred in 1300 to mark its end. The transition from early Middle Ages to High Middle Ages was gradual and uneven. It might be argued that the High Middle Ages came to Italy and Germany as early as the tenth century. Ever since the waning of the Viking, Hungarian, and Saracen invasions, many decades before 1050, Europe had been pulsing with new creative energy. Broadly speaking, though, the scope and intensity of the revival did not become evident until the later eleventh century. By the century's end, Europe's lively commerce and bustling towns, its intellectual vigor and political inventiveness, its military expansion, and its heightened religious enthusiasm left no doubt that vital new forces were at work—that Western Christendom had at last become a major civilization.

The causes of Europe's cultural awakening are far too complex to be identified precisely or listed in order of importance. One essential element was the ending of the invasions and the increasing political stability that followed. We

ℭ

know that in the eleventh century Europe's population was beginning to increase significantly and that its food production was rising. Whether increased productivity led to increased population or vice versa is difficult to say. But productivity could not have risen as it did without the revolutionary developments in agricultural technology: the three-field system, which was spreading across much of northern Europe; the windmill; the water mill (by 1086 there were over five thousand water mills in England alone); the heavy, wheeled plow; the horseshoe and improved horse collar that transformed horses into efficient draught animals; and the tandem harness that made it possible to employ horses and oxen in large teams to draw plows or to pull heavy wagons. These and numerous related inventions came to the West gradually over the centuries, but they had a powerful cumulative influence on the economic boom of the High Middle Ages.

Towns and Commerce

The rise in productivity and population was accompanied by a commercial revival and a general reawakening of urban life. In turn, the new towns became the foci of a reinvigorated culture. The intimate human contacts arising from town life stimulated European thought and art. The cathedral and the university, perhaps the two greatest monuments of high medieval culture, were both urban phenomena. The Franciscan order, possibly the most dynamic monastic institution of the new age, devoted itself chiefly to evangelical work among the new urban population, and its founder was the son of an urban merchant. The towns were also, and above all, centers of commercial and industrial enterprise. The European economy in the High Middle Ages remained fundamentally agrarian, but the towns were the economic and cultural catalysts.

There had been towns in Europe ever since antiquity. The administrative-military town of the Roman Empire gave way in time to the far humbler cathedral town of the early Middle Ages. But both had one crucial thing in common: both were economic parasites living off the blood, labor, and taxes of the countryside; like modern government-cities such as Washington, D.C. and Sacramento, California, they consumed more than they produced. The towns of the High Middle Ages, on the other hand, represented something new to Western Europe. With few exceptions, they were true commercial entities that earned their own way, living off the fruits of their merchant and industrial activities. Small, foul, disease-ridden, and often torn by internal conflict, they were nevertheless western Europe's first cities in the modern sense.

The commercial towns arose in rhythm with the upsurge of international commerce and the development of vigorous markets for local agrarian products. Often they began as suburbs of older cathedral towns or as humble settlements outside the walls of some of the many fortresses that had risen in ninth- and tenth-century Europe. These fortresses were generally known by some form of the Germanic word *burgh*, and in time the term came to apply to the town itself rather than the fortress that spawned it. By the twelfth century a burgh, or *borough*, was an urban commercial center, inhabited by *burghers* or *burgesses*, who constituted a new class known later as the *bourgeoisie*.

In the later eleventh century, towns were developing rapidly all over Europe. They were thickest in northern Italy where the immense opportunities of international commerce were first exploited. In Italy, as we have seen, Venetian merchants had long been trading with Constantinople and Islam, while other Italian ports—Genoa, Pisa and Amalfi—soon followed Venice into the profitable markets of the eastern Mediterranean. We have seen too how the ramifications of their far-flung trade brought vigorous new life to towns of interior Italy, such as Milan and Florence. During the High Middle Ages the Muslims were virtually driven from the seas and Italian merchants dominated the Mediterranean.

Meanwhile the towns of Flanders were growing wealthy from the commerce of the north—from trade with northern France and the British Isles, the Rhineland and the shores of the Baltic Sea. Flanders itself was a great sheep-growing district, and its towns became centers of woolen textile production. In time, the towns were processing more wool than Flemish sheep could supply, so that from the twelfth century onward Flemish merchants began to import wool on a large scale from England. By then Flanders was the industrial center of northern Europe, and its textile industry the supreme manufacturing enterprise of the age.

The new urban class emerged from a society that had heretofore been almost exclusively agrarian. The burgher class was drawn from vagabonds, runaway serfs, avaricious minor noblemen and, in general, the surplus of a mushrooming population. At an early date ambitious traders began to form themselves into merchant guilds in order to protect themselves against exorbitant tolls and other exactions levied by a greedy landed aristocracy. A town was almost always situated on the territories of some lord—baron, count, duke, or king. And the merchants found that only by collective action could they win the privileges essential to their calling: personal freedom from servile status, freedom of movement, freedom from inordinate tolls at every bridge or feudal boundary, and the rights to own town property, to be judged by the town court, to execute commercial contracts, and to buy and sell freely. By the twelfth century, a number of lords, recognizing the economic advantages of having flourishing commercial centers on their lands, were issuing town charters that guaranteed many of these rights. Indeed, some farsighted lords began founding and chartering new towns on their own initiative.

At first the urban charters differed greatly from one another, but in time it became customary to pattern them after certain well-known models. The charter granted by King Henry I of England to Newcastle-on-Tyne, and that of the French king Louis VI to the community of Lorris, were copied repeatedly throughout England and France. In effect these charters created semi-autonomous political and legal entities, each with its own local government, its own court, its own tax-collecting agencies, and its own customs. These urban communes paid well for their charters and continued to render regular taxes to their lord. But—and this is all-important—they did so as political units. Individual merchants were freed from the harassments of their lords' agents. These townspeople enforced their own law in their own courts, collected their own taxes, and paid their dues to their lord in a lump sum. In short, they had won the invaluable privilege of handling their own affairs.

One should not conclude, however, that the medieval towns were even remotely democratic. It was the prosperous merchants and master craftsmen who profited chiefly from the charters, and it was they who came to control the town governments, ruling as narrow oligarchies over the towns' less exalted inhabitants. Some towns witnessed the beginnings of a significant split between large-scale producers and wage-earning workers. Indeed, the medieval town was the birthplace of European capitalism. For as time progressed towns tended to become centers of industry as well as commerce. Manufacturing followed in the footsteps of trade. And although most industrial production took place in small shops rather than large factories, some enterprising businessmen employed considerable numbers of workers to produce goods, usually textiles, on a large scale. Normally, these workers did not labor in a factory but instead worked in their own shops or homes. Since the entrepreneur sent his raw materials out to his workers, rather than bringing the workers to the materials, this mode of production has been called the "putting-out system." As a direct antecedent of the factory system, it was a crucial phase in the early history of capitalism.

The more typical medieval manufacturer worked for himself in his own shop, producing his own goods and selling them directly to the public. As early as the eleventh century, these craftsmen were organizing themselves into craft guilds, as distinct from merchant guilds. In an effort to limit competition and protect their market, the craft guilds established strict admission requirements and stringent rules on prices, wages, standards of quality, and operating procedures. A young craftsman would learn his trade as an apprentice in the shop of a master craftsman. After a specified period, sometimes as long as seven years, he ended his apprenticeship. With good luck and rich parents he might then become a master himself. But normally he had to work for some years as a day laborer—a journeyman—improving his skills and saving his money, until he was able to demonstrate sufficient craftsmanship to win guild membership and accumulate enough money to establish a shop of his own. Toward the end of the High Middle Ages, as prosperity waned and urban society crystallized, it became increasingly common for journeymen to spend their whole lives as wage earners, never becoming masters at all. Accordingly, the town became the scene of bitter class antagonisms that erupted from time to time into open conflict.

There were many who made their fortunes in commerce and manufacturing. Europe was astir with new life, and for a clever, enterprising person the possibilities were vast. In the twelfth and thirteenth centuries, merchants were moving continuously along the roads and rivers of Europe. Italians crossed the Alps bringing spices and luxury goods from the Near East and the Orient to the aristocracy of France and Germany. French, Flemish, and German merchants carried goods far and wide across the continent, "buying cheap and selling dear."

A series of annual fairs along the overland trade routes provided the long-distance merchants with excellent opportunities to sell their goods. As commerce grew, credit and banking grew with it, and by the thirteenth century several Italian banking families had amassed huge fortunes. So it was that the period which is often regarded as an "age of faith" witnessed the rise of large-scale commerce. Indeed, Christian culture and the commercial awakening were interconnected. It was money that built the Gothic cathedrals, supported the Crusades, financed the pious charities of St. Louis, and gave substance to the magnificent religious culture of the thirteenth century—money and, of course, an ardent faith. For townspeople, by and large, exhibited a piety that was more vibrant and intense than that of the peasantry and aristocracy. The surge of urban piety became a crucial factor in the evolution of medieval Christianity—spawning cathedrals and hospitals, saints and heretics. In the electric atmosphere of the new cities, Christianity acquired an emotional content unknown to the farms and villages.

Twelfth-Century London

We can gain some impression of life in a medieval city by looking at London as it existed toward the end of the twelfth century. With a population of about 30,000, London was by far the largest city of its time in the British Isles and one of the leading commercial centers of northwestern Europe. Many of England's bishops, abbots, and barons maintained townhouses there, and the king himself conducted much of his business at a palace (which stands to this day) in London's western suburb of Westminster. The Londoners were served by 139 churches, whose bells pealed across the city and its suburbs to mark the hours of the day.

London's narrow streets were lined with houses and shops, most of them built of wood. The streets were mostly unpaved and during the day were crowded with people, dogs, horses, and pigs. (Half a century earlier a crown prince of France was killed when his horse tripped over a pig in the streets of Paris.) But by twelfth-century standards, London was a great, progressive metropolis. The old wooden bridge across the River Thames was being replaced by a new London Bridge made entirely of stone. Sanitation workers were employed by the city to clear the streets of garbage. There was a sewer system—the only one in England—consisting of open drains down the centers of streets. There was even a public lavatory.

By today's standards, the city was a small, filthy, odoriferous firetrap. But twelfth-century Londoners were proud of it. One of them, William fitz Stephen, writing around 1175, describes it in these glowing words:

❝ Among the noble and celebrated cities of the world, London, the capital of the kingdom of the English, extends its glory farther than all others and sends its wealth and merchandise more widely into far distant lands. It holds its head higher than all the rest. It is fortunate in the healthiness of its air, in its observance of Christian practice, in the strength of its fortifications, in its natural setting, in the honor of its citizens, and in the modest behavior of its wives. It is cheerful in its sports and the fruitful mother of noble men . . . . * **❞**

All medieval cities were fortified, and London more strongly than most:

❝ It has on the east the Tower of London, very great and strong . . . . On the west there are two powerful castles, and from there runs a high and massive wall with seven double gates and with towers along the north at regular intervals . . . . **❞**

Within these walls, London was a hive of commercial activity:

❝ Those engaged in businesses of various kinds—sellers of merchandise, hirers of labor—go off every morning into their various districts according to their trade. Besides, there is a public cook shop in London, located on the riverbank in the district where wines are offered for sale in ships and in the cellars of the wine merchants. Each day, at this cook shop, you will find food according to the season—dishes of meat, roasted, fried, and boiled; large and small fish; coarser meats for the poor and more delicate for the rich, such as venison and large and small birds . . . . **❞**

The delicacies offered by this medieval Colonel Sanders could be enjoyed not only by Londoners but also by visitors from afar:

❝ To this city merchants delight to bring their trade by sea from every nation under heaven. The Arabian sends gold; the Sabaean spice and incense. The Scythian brings arms, and from the rich, fat lands of Babylon comes palm oil. The Nile sends precious stones; the Norwegians and Russians send furs and sables; nor is China absent with her purple silk. The French come with their wines. **❞**

William fitz Stephen goes on and on. He describes London's entertainments and sports: the miracle plays, the annual Carnival Day with its

---

*Among the noble "men" born in twelfth-century London, William fitz Stephen proudly includes the Empress Matilda.

rooster fights and athletic contests when ball teams from various London guilds and schools competed in the fields outside the city's walls. "On feast days throughout the summer, the young men engage in the sports of archery, running, jumping, wrestling, slinging stones, hurling javelins beyond a certain mark, and fighting with sword and buckler." And in winter,

" Swarms of young men come out to play games on the ice. Some, gaining speed in their run, slide sideways over a vast expanse of ice, their feet set well apart. Others make seats out of a large lump of ice, and while one person sits on it, the others, with linked hands, run in front and drag him along behind them. So swift is their sliding motion that sometimes their feet slip, and they all fall on their faces. Others, more skilled at winter sports, put on their feet the shin bones of animals, binding them firmly around their ankles, and then, gripping iron-shod poles, which they strike from time to time against the ice, they are propelled as swiftly as a bird in flight. **"**

William fitz Stephen is prone to exaggeration. He speaks of the healthiness of London's air, and yet we know that London had a smog problem even in the twelfth century. The author's chamber-of-commerce viewpoint contrasts sharply with the testimony of a twelfth-century Jewish merchant from France, who gives this warning to a friend about to leave for England:

" If you go to London pass through it quickly . . . . Every evil or malicious thing that can be found anywhere on earth you will find in that one city. Steer clear of the crowds of pimps; don't mingle with the throngs in eating houses; avoid dice and gambling, the theater and the tavern. You will meet with more braggarts there than in all of France. The number of parasites is infinite. Actors, jesters, smooth-skinned lads, Moors, flatterers, pretty boys, effeminates, degenerates, singing girls and dancing girls, quacks, belly dancers, sorceresses, extortioners, night wanderers, magicians, mimes, beggars, buffoons: all this tribe fill all the houses. So if you don't want to deal with evildoers, don't go to London. **"**

The same Jewish merchant gives equally bad news about other English towns. In Exeter both men and beasts are provided the same food. Bath, lying amidst "exceedingly heavy air and sulphurous fumes, is at the gates of hell." At Bristol, "there is nobody who is not or has not been a soap maker." Ely stinks perpetually from the surrounding marshes. And York is "full of Scotsmen—filthy and treacherous creatures, scarcely men."*

If we are to get a balanced view of twelfth-century English urban life, we must obviously steer a middle course between the biases of the French merchant and the rhapsodic civic pride of William fitz Stephen.

*These views are ascribed to the merchant by the English chronicler Richard of Devizes, who may himself have invented the whole business.

The Jews of Medieval Europe

Well might a twelfth-century Jewish merchant be unenthusiastic about urban life in England—or, for that matter, throughout most of Western Christendom. For in a civilization that was almost unanimously Christian, members of a minority faith were apt to suffer. The Jews of Christian Europe had always been subjected to legal disabilities and popular bias. And their condition worsened in the High Middle Ages with the growth of Christian self-awareness, militancy, and popular devotion to the suffering Christ. Good Christian theology insists that Christ died for the sins of all humanity, but popular sentiment often held that he was murdered by the Jews. And there were those who arrived at the grotesque conclusion that the "murder" should be avenged. The persecution of Jews—and of other dissenting groups such as heretics, witches, and magicians—represents the wormy underside of high-medieval Christian piety.

Jews had played a vital part in the earlier phases of medieval urban growth. They were active in the commercial life of Italian cities throughout the early Middle Ages, and in 875 King Charles the Bald brought a community of Jews home with him from a visit to Italy and settled them in his kingdom. Soon they spread into numerous cities of France and Germany and finally into England in the wake of the Norman Conquest of 1066. Wherever they settled, they stimulated commerce through their mercantile expertise. In the tenth century and into the eleventh, they were the leading merchants—almost the only merchants—of northern Christendom. And they contributed much to the north's commercial revival through their commercial links with Jewish merchants in Italy and throughout the Islamic Mediterranean world, where Jewish communities had long flourished. Only in the course of the eleventh century did north-European Christians move into commerce on a large scale.

Ever since the Christian conversion of the Roman Empire, however, Jews had been at best second-class citizens. A Church council of 451 had prohibited Christians from marrying Jews, having dinner with them, or even going to Jewish physicians. Jews were not to hold Christian slaves, to take Christian oaths of fealty, or to be lords over Christians. Such rules were not strictly enforced in the early Middle Ages, but by the later twelfth century, Jews were required to wear special badges or hats so that Christians might be warned to keep their appropriate social distance. The papacy was never a great friend of Jews, but it did endeavor to protect them from the violence of popular prejudice. An eleventh-century pope wrote to the bishops of Spain,

ℓℓ We are pleased with the account we have recently heard concerning the way you have protected the Jews who live among you from destruction by those who are setting out to fight the Saracens. For these warriors, moved by stupidity or perhaps blinded by avarice, wished to behave like savages, destroying those whom divine, fatherly love may well have intended for salvation . . . . Indeed, the cases of the Jews and Saracens are altogether distinct:

warfare is rightful against the Saracens, who persecute Christians and drive them from their own towns and lands; but the Jews are everywhere ready to do service. **"**

As this passage suggests, crusades against Islam could escalate Christian anti-Semitism to the point of bloodthirsty violence. Such was the effect of the First Crusade to the Holy Land in 1096. It dawned on some crusaders that their mission to extend Christian power over infidels abroad might be prefaced by slaughtering the "infidel" minority in Christendom itself. According to one Christian writer,

" They should have traveled their road for Christ, recalling the divine commands and holding to the discipline of the Gospel, while instead they turned to madness and shamefully, wantonly, cruelly cut down the Jewish people in the cities and towns through which they passed. **"**

Massacres of Jews did not begin with the Crusades, but they became more frequent thereafter. Most were products of prejudice among common Christian town dwellers, whipped to a frenzy by popular rumors that Jews desecrated the transfigured bread of the Holy Sacrament or that they murdered Christian infants (as they had allegedly murdered Christ). A pope decreed in 1272 "that Jews arrested on such an absurd pretext be freed from captivity."

Here again the papacy was assuming responsibility for protecting Jews from mindless grassroots savagery, and the responsibility was shared by kings and emperors. But these enthroned guardians demanded much of the Jews in return for protection. They borrowed heavily from Jewish burghers, milked them through arbitrary taxes, seized the property and loan accounts of Jews who had died without heirs, and charged enormous sums for the rights to travel freely, enjoy a fair trial, and pass their property on to their heirs. As the High Middle Ages closed, Jews were being expelled *en masse* from one kingdom after another by monarchs who coveted their wealth. By then their services as moneylenders were no longer essential; Italian bankers were providing an alternative source of credit. Many Jews subsequently filtered back or were invited to return when royal policy shifted. But by the fourteenth and fifteenth centuries they were being segregated into ghettos. And persecution continued unabated throughout most of Europe for centuries thereafter.

The Jews of the High Middle Ages have usually been associated almost exclusively with such activities as moneylending and commerce. But while it is true that Jews were excluded from Christian guilds and forbidden to be lords of Christian peasants, recent scholarship suggests that many Jews, particularly in southern Europe, blended almost invisibly into the general urban society. Their activities were less strictly limited in the south than in the north, and it is certain that, throughout Christendom, moneylending and commerce occupied only a small, highly visible minority of medieval Jews. Still, they differed from

Christians in ways other than faith alone: they achieved a much higher literacy rate than their Christian contemporaries (every substantial Jewish community had its own school), and their contribution to medieval medicine, biblical scholarship, and philosophy was all out of proportion to their numbers. The Spanish Jew, Moses Maimonides (1135-1204), in his highly creative use of Aristotle, did much to shape Christian philosophy in the thirteenth century. And in the areas of medicine and commerce, too, the contacts of European Jews with their Jewish counterparts in other cultures contributed much to the ending of Europe's isolation.

The Landholding Aristocracy

The commercial revival had a substantial impact on medieval aristocratic life in the north-European countryside. For one thing, the much-increased circulation of money gradually eroded the tenure-service relationship of early medieval feudalism. Rulers came to depend less on the military and administrative services that vassals performed in return for their fiefs, and resorted increasingly to the use of mercenary troops and paid officials—first in England, and later on the continent. Beginning in the twelfth century, English knights were often asked to pay a tax called *scutage* ("shield money") in lieu of personal service in a royal campaign, and in time this practice spread to France and elsewhere.

Moreover, money and commerce made new luxuries available to the landed aristocracy: pepper, ginger, and cinnamon for baronial kitchens, finer and more colorful clothing, jewelry, fur coats for the cold winters (and to impress the less fortunate), and—for the castle—carpets, wall hangings, and more elaborate furniture. These amenities, in turn, drove many nobles deeply into debt, thus increasing the business (and unpopularity) of Jewish lenders. The high-medieval aristocracy regarded overspending as a virtue—the mark of a generous spirit. A monk gives us this disapproving picture of the late-eleventh-century magnate, Hugh, earl of Chester, whose life-style was grander than most, yet not atypical:

❝ He was a great lover of the world and its pomp, which he regarded as the greatest blessing of the human lot. He was always in the vanguard in battle, lavish to the point of prodigality, a lover of games and luxuries, entertainers, horses, dogs, and similar vanities. He was always surrounded by a huge following, noisy with swarms of boys both low-born and high-born. Many honorable men, clerics and knights, were also in his entourage, and he cheerfully shared his wealth and labors with them . . . . He kept no check on what he gave or received. His hunting was a daily devastation of his lands, for he thought more highly of hawkers and hunters than of peasants or monks. A slave to gluttony, he staggered under a mountain of fat, scarcely able to move.

He was given over to carnal lusts and sired a multitude of bastards by his concubines. **"**

Along with their improvidence, many aristocrats displayed an almost childish lack of emotional control. Always quick to take offense, a baron could be carried away by a fit of rage. An act of savage violence—a murderous assault or a pillaging campaign—might be followed by remorse so overwhelming that the baron would lavish wealth on the Church or embark on a pilgrimage or Crusade.

The medieval aristocracy was, above all, a military class, trained from early youth in the practice of mounted combat. Whatever romantic images may surround our conception of the knight, he was, essentially, a warrior. Mounted and clad in helmet and chain mail, he might even be regarded as a military "machine"—the medieval equivalent of the modern tank. The analogy becomes even closer when, in the fourteenth century, chain mail gave way to plate in response to the development of the longbow.

Warfare was all too common in the High Middle Ages, not only among kings and great princes, but also between neighboring barons and minor castellans. In time the growing authority of monarchs and princes curtailed private wars, particularly in England. But it was a slow process and did not seriously affect the French countryside until well into the thirteenth century. Fighting was what aristocrats has been trained for; indeed, it was the chief justification for their existence. They were viewed (ideally) as the protectors of Church and society, but most of them were interested primarily in defending and extending their own estates. And to some, nothing was more fulfilling than to do battle with the enemy—any enemy. As a twelfth-century French writer puts it:

" I tell you that I never eat or sleep or drink so well as when I hear the cry, "Up and at 'em!" from both sides, and when I hear the neighing of riderless horses in the brush and hear shouts of "Help! Help!" and see men fall . . . and the dead pierced in the side by gaily-pennoned spears. **"**

War could ravage the land, destroying farms and churches, but it was less dangerous to the aristocracy than might be imagined. Great battles were rare, and even when they occurred, the knight was well protected by his armor. Most medieval warfare consisted of castle sieges and the harrying of an enemy's possessions (including his peasants). The great risk was to be taken captive in battle, which obliged the victim to raise a large ransom in return for his release. On the other hand, a skillful and lucky knight might take many captives in the course of his campaigning and enrich himself from their ransoms.

In peacetime, tournaments took the place of battles. The Church legislated against tournaments, fruitlessly but with good reason. For they often involved day-long mock battles among groups of as many as a hundred knights, in the course of which a participant might be wounded, killed, or taken for ransom. The aristocracy relished these melees as opportunities to train for war or to collect ransoms—or simply for the fun of fighting.

Magnates had more sober tasks to perform as well: presiding at the castle court, giving counsel to their lords, and managing their revenues and estates—a responsibility that they took more and more seriously as the High Middle Ages progressed. And for recreation they went hunting or hawking in their private forests. Besides the sheer enjoyment of it, hunting rid the forests of dangerous beasts—wolves and wild boars—and provided tasty venison for the lord's table. Lords and ladies alike engaged in falconry, a sport which consisted of releasing a trained falcon to soar upward, kill a wild bird in flight, and return it to earth uneaten. Both hunting and falconry were refined during the High Middle Ages into complex arts.

Indeed, the process of gradual refinement characterized high-medieval aristocratic life as a whole, and was much needed. Most baronial castles of the eleventh and early twelfth centuries were nothing more than square wooden towers of two or three stories. They were usually set atop hills or artificial mounds and surrounded by barracks, storehouses, stables, workshops, kitchen gardens, manure heaps, and perhaps a chapel—all enclosed, along with assorted livestock, within a large stockade. The tower (or "keep") was apt to be stuffy, leaky, gloomy, and badly heated. Since it was built for defense rather than comfort, its windows were narrow slits for outgoing arrows, and its few rooms had to accommodate not only the lord and lady and their family but servants, retainers, and guests as well. It was a world of enforced togetherness in which only the wealthiest of aristocratic couples could enjoy the luxury of a private bedchamber.

By the late thirteenth century, however, rich aristocrats were living in much more commodious dwellings, usually built of stone and mortar. Privacy remained rare, for great lords now commanded larger retinues than before. But the sweaty, swashbuckling life of the eleventh-century baron had evolved by 1300 into a new, courtly life-style of good manners, troubadour songs, and gentlemanly and ladylike behavior. In much of Christendom war had become less incessant, and the barracks atmosphere was softening. The old military aristocracy was becoming a "high society," increasingly conscious of itself as a separate class—distinguished from others by its good breeding and good taste. And since only the greatest landholders could afford this way of life, the aristocracy became more exclusive and rigidly defined than in its earlier, less stylish days.

Aristocratic Women

In an aristocracy of warriors, women were relegated to supporting roles. They could assert themselves at times, as when some Norman wives summoned home their husbands who had left them for the conquest of England in 1066:

❝ At this time certain Norman women, consumed by raging lust, sent message after message to their husbands urging them to return at once, and adding that, unless they did so with all speed, they would get other husbands for themselves . . . . Many men left England heavy-hearted and reluctant, because they were abandoning their king while he struggled in a foreign land. They returned to Normandy to oblige their wanton wives. **❞**

The monk who relates this story objects to the women's initiative, for in medieval society wives were expected to be submissive. Indeed, the subordination of women characterizes most premodern cultures; it was less pronounced in Western Christendom than, for example, in Islamic civilization where the harem flourished. The notion of female inferiority was rooted in all three major cultural traditions underlying medieval European civilization—the classical, the Christian, and the Germanic. The classical viewpoint was summarized by the Greek philosopher Aristotle, who "proved" the natural inferiority of women and slaves. St. Paul, who was a Roman citizen, injected a typically Roman antifeminine bias into the mainstream of Christianity. St. Paul conceded that, at least in God's eyes, there was no distinction between men and women or between slave and nonslave. But this heavenly egalitarianism did not, in St. Paul's opinion, extend to earthly affairs: "Let your women keep silent in the churches," he wrote, "for it is not permitted to them to speak . . . . And if they wish to learn anything, let them ask their husbands at home." The attitude of the early Germanic tribes was somewhat better, but not enormously so. The Germanic laws permitted wife-beating and treated wives, in some sense, as their husbands' property: "If a free man lies with another free man's wife, he shall pay the husband a [sum of money] and shall buy the husband another wife."

High-medieval Christianity echoed some of these earlier attitudes. Women could not be priests; they could hold no office in the Church hierarchy, except abbess or prioress of a nunnery. Holy men often regarded women as threats to male purity, and thus as objects—like a tempting beefsteak to a wavering vegetarian. The canons of a thirteenth-century priory expelled the nuns from their community on these grounds:

❝ Recognizing that the wickedness of women is greater than all the other wickedness of the world, and that there is no anger like that of women, and that the poison of asps and dragons is easier to cure and less hazardous to men than associating with women, we and our whole community of canons have unanimously decreed, for the preservation of our souls no less than of our bodies and property, that we will on no account receive any more nuns, to the increase of our damnation, but will avoid them as we would avoid poisonous beasts. **❞**

But alongside the notion of woman as harlot, high-medieval Christianity evolved a concept of idealized womanhood from its emphasis on Mary, the virgin mother of Jesus. As the great symbol of maternal compassion, Mary became the subject of countless miracle stories. Sinners who trembled at the prospect of God's judgment would turn their prayers to Mary, confident that she could persuade Christ to forgive them—for what son could refuse his mother? Many of Europe's greatest cathedrals were dedicated to Mary under the name of "Notre Dame"—our Lady.

The high-medieval troubadour songs and the rise of stylized courtesy in noble households resulted in still another kind of idealization. As romanticized ladies-fair, women were placed on pedestals, from which they are only now descending. This idealization of women was itself a kind of dehumanizing process: for high atop their pedestals, women remained objects still. But the pedestals tended to raise women from their former inferior status as threats to male purity, or objects of casual knightly seduction and rape, or victims of boorish, wife-beating husbands. The courtly lady remained an object, but a more revered and idealized object than before.

Such at least was the condition of noblewomen in courtly theory. But one must always recall the gulf that separated social and literary convention from real life. Medieval lords and ladies did not always behave like characters in some courtly romance. Eleanor of Aquitaine was one of the great women of twelfth-century Europe and a patroness of troubadours. But she was imprisoned by her husband, King Henry II of England, for urging their sons to rebel, and so spent many years in confinement. Only at her husband's death was she released to live out her final years as a valued adviser to her royal sons and as a wealthy and independent *grande dame* of the realm.

Other medieval queens and noblewomen often served as regents, ruling the dominions in their husbands' absences. In the thirteenth century Blanche of Castile, mother of King Louis IX (St. Louis), ruled France for eight years in her son's name until he came of age and again when he was off crusading. A woman of strong personality and heroic size, Blanche of Castile put down a major baronial rebellion at the beginning of St. Louis' reign through an adroit blend of warfare and diplomacy. "To all intents and purposes," writes a modern French historian, "she may be counted among the kings of France."

Blanche and Eleanor were of course exceptional. In general, feudal society was a warrior's world, and women were not expected to fight in battle. Still, the convention could occasionally be defied: Isabel of Conches, the wife of a Norman baron of about the year 1100, was described by a contemporary writer as generous, daring, and high-spirited: "In war she rode among the knights, dressed as a knight herself."

Isabel was a newsworthy exception to the male domination in warfare, but women could be influential in other ways as well. For if the aristocracy was a warrior class, it was also a class of hereditary landholders, and women could play a key role in the inheritance of land. In the absence of sons, a daughter might become a wealthy and coveted heiress; even if she had brothers, a well-born daughter might bring a large estate to her husband as a dowry. And a widow normally received a third of her late husband's lands (their eldest son received the rest). Thus, heiresses, widows, and well-dowered daughters were extremely desirable commodities on the marriage market. A strong king might compel a wealthy maiden or widow to marry some royal favorite, who would usually be expected to pay the king for the privilege. In the financial accounts of King Henry I of England (1100–1135) one finds such items as these: "Robert de Venuiz renders account to the king for sixteen shillings eighteenpence for the daughter of Herbert the Chamberlain with her dowry"; "The sheriff of Hampshire renders account to the king for a thousand silver marks for the office, lands, and daughter of the late Robert Mauduit." And one great English heiress, the thrice-widowed Lucy countess of Chester, was charged a handsome sum for the privilege of not having to remarry for five years.

Favorable marriages could bring wealth and greatness to a family. Many a family fortune was built on strategic marriages of heirs to heiresses. In a landed society such as medieval Europe's, marriages were crucial to a family's well-being, and marriages for love alone were luxuries that no noble family could afford. Hence the tendency toward extramarital love affairs in the troubadour songs—and sometimes in the real world as well.

In feudal law, wives were very much under their husbands' control. A wife could not plead in court without her husband or make a will without his consent. He had complete authority over her property; only when she reached widowhood did she acquire any degree of legal independence, and even then (as we have seen with Lucy) she might find herself under pressure to remarry. Legally, the husband was boss, but in the actual day-by-day functioning of family life, the wife might exercise a great deal of power. She usually ran the castle and the barony when her husband was absent (as husbands often were—on wars or Crusades). If the castle was attacked while the lord was away, his wife frequently commanded its defense.

Even when the lord was home, the wife might enjoy considerable authority. In medieval marriages as in modern ones, husband and wife might relate in a wide variety of ways. Some husbands were cruel and domineering. Others were ineffectual cupcakes, in which case—despite social and legal conventions—the wife ruled the castle. One such person was Avicia countess of Évreux:

❝ The count of Évreux's intellect was by nature somewhat feeble as well as being blunted with age. And putting perhaps undue trust in his wife's ability, he left the government of his county entirely in her hands. The countess was distinguished for her wit and beauty. She was one of the tallest women in all Évreux, and of very high birth . . . . Disregarding the counsels of her husband's barons, she chose instead to follow her own opinion and ambition. Often inspiring bold measures in political affairs, she readily engaged in rash enterprises. **❞**

The Norman monk who wrote these words clearly disapproved, but his description of the Countess Avicia brings us much closer to reality than do the arid accounts of legal custom and the romances of the troubadours.

The Evolution of Agrarian Life

The new social and economic conditions of the late eleventh and twelfth centuries gave rise to an immense expansion of arable land, which transformed the north-European countryside. The vast primeval forest that once had blanketed northern Europe was reduced to patches. Swamps and marshes were drained, and in the Low Countries dikes were built to reclaim land from the sea. These prodigious clearing and draining operations were stimulated by the growing population and the rising money economy. Agricultural surpluses could now be sold to townspeople and thereby converted into cash. Consequently, the peasant was motivated to produce as far in excess of the consumption level as he possibly could. Every new field was likely to bring a profit.

The initial result was to increase peasants' income and elevate their legal status. Slavery, common in Carolingian times, was diminishing by the eleventh century and virtually disappeared in the course of the twelfth. The tillers of the land were now chiefly freemen and serfs. Often the freeman owned his own small farm, but the serf was generally to be found on a manor. Normally, it will be remembered, the manor included the peasants' fields intermixed with the lord's fields (demesne), the produce of which went directly to the lord. Among the obligations that the serf usually owed his lord was labor service for a stipulated number of days per week on the lord's demesne. In Carolingian times, manorial lords had augmented the part-time serf labor by using slaves. But in the twelfth century, with slavery dying out, the lord was faced with a labor shortage on his demesne.

As a result of this problem, and in keeping with the trend toward transforming service obligations into money payments, some lords abandoned demesne farming altogether. They leased out their demesne fields to peasants and, in return for a fixed-money payment, released their serfs from the traditional obligation to work part-time on the demesne. At about the same time, many lords were translating the serf's rent-in-kind from his own fields into a money rent. By freeing the serf of his labor obligation they transformed him, in effect, into a tenant farmer, thereby improving his legal status immensely. The obligations of the peasant, like those of the feudal vassal, were gradually being placed on a fiscal basis.

Throughout much of the eleventh and twelfth century, lords were under some pressure to improve the condition of their peasants in order to keep them from fleeing to the towns or to newly cleared lands. The peasant was in demand, and enterprising land developers who were turning woods and marshes into fields competed for his services. As a consequence, the twelfth century witnessed the elevation of innumerable peasants from servile status to freedom. One of the clearest expressions of this trend was the emergence of rural communes—communities of peasants whose lord had granted a charter freeing them from servile obligations and permitting them to pay their dues collectively, on the pattern of the chartered town.

But even in the booming twelfth century, the reduction of demesne farming and the freeing of serfs occurred slowly and unevenly. And by the thirteenth, these trends were beginning to reverse. For population growth was gradually outstripping the increase in arable lands, creating a rise in land values and a surplus of peasant labor. As land became more valuable than laborers, lords throughout much of northern Europe began farming their demesnes more intensively than before, often employing landless peasants at low wages or strictly enforcing the labor services of their remaining serfs.

Moreover, the thirteenth century witnessed a growth of legal consciousness and a hardening of custom that gave rise to stricter class divisions and made it much more difficult for serfs to gain their freedom. On the other hand, a freeman might all too easily sink back into serfdom. It was the custom of some districts, for example, that a free peasant forfeited his freedom by marrying a servile woman, and a free woman suffered the same descent if she married a serf. In thirteenth-century England there are even instances of landless free peasants submitting to serfdom in return for a plot of land. And quite apart from the matter of legal status, peasants of the thirteenth century, lacking the leverage they had enjoyed in the earlier generations of land clearance and labor shortage, were subjected to heavy economic exploitation by their lords. They were burdened with higher rents and taxes, higher fines at the lord's court, higher charges for the use of his mill, winepress, and ovens. If a peasant refused to pay he could be replaced by someone else from among the growing body of landless laborers that the high-medieval population explosion produced.

Again, these processes varied a great deal from place to place and from region to region. But generally speaking, the combined effects of population growth and land clearance profited lords and peasants alike throughout the later eleventh century and much of the twelfth, but worked to the peasants' disadvantage during the thirteenth, when land clearance and advances in farming techniques failed to keep pace with a continually rising population. Western Europe remained prosperous throughout most of the thirteenth century, but the easy years of limitless land were passing, and there was trouble ahead.

Life in a North-European Peasant Village

By today's standards, the life of a high-medieval peasant is almost beyond our imagining. Village life was tied to the cycle of the seasons and vulnerable to the whims of nature—drought, flooding, epidemics among humans and animals, crop diseases, the summer's heat and the winter's chill. Today we are insulated from nature by a screen of modern technological wonders: central heating, air conditioning, a secure food supply, plumbing, deodorants, modern medicine, and much more. We enjoy the protection of police and fire departments; we defy distance and terrain with our freeways and jets. All these things and others we take for granted, but they are all products of the recent past. They were undreamed of in the eleventh century and remained unknown for centuries thereafter.

From the viewpoint of modern suburban America, the medieval peasantry lived in unspeakable poverty and filth. A typical peasant's house was built largely of mud with a thatched roof. Often it consisted of a single room, bare of furniture. The straw on which the family slept was apt to be crawling with vermin. The smells of sweat and manure were always present, and therefore largely unnoticed. Flies buzzed everywhere. The single room might shelter not only a large family but its domestic livestock as well: chickens, dogs, geese, and sometimes even cattle. Windows, if any, were small and few (and, of course, had no glass). The floor was usually of earth; it froze in the wintertime and turned damp and oozy with the coming of a thaw. Arthritis and rheumatism must have been common, along with countless other diseases whose cure lay far in the future. A simple fire served for cooking and heating, but in the absence of chimneys the smoke filled the room before escaping through holes or cracks in the ceiling. Candles were luxury items, and peasants had to make do with smoky, evil-smelling torches made of rushes soaked in fat. And there was always the danger that a stray spark might set the thatched roof afire.

The daily routine of a family of village-dwelling serfs might run more or less as follows: there would be a pre-dawn breakfast—perhaps of coarse black bread (don't try it!) and diluted ale—after which the father would head out with his elder sons into the fields encircling the village to work from daybreak to nightfall—plowing, sowing, weeding, or harvesting, depending on the season. Or in winter, when the fields were often frozen, the men of the family might stay indoors constructing or repairing their tools. All the year round the women cared for the children and domestic animals, made the family's clothes, and did the milking, cheese-making, and cooking. The evening meal might consist of a pot of meatless soup and more coarse black bread (and possibly even an egg). Then it was early to bed, to rest for the toils of the following day.

Even this somber picture is a bit idealized. Often one or more members of the peasant family would be immobilized by illness (for which there were no available doctors and no effective medicines) or tormented by injuries, wounds, aches, and pains (no aspirin). Wives had to endure one pregnancy after another; childbirth was hazardous to mother and baby alike, and infant mortality was very high. Indeed, women of all classes in medieval lay society were tied down for long periods of their lives by the bearing and nursing of children, many of whom never reached adulthood.

Occasionally famine would strike a large region, as in 1125 when a great August flood inundated numerous villages of eastern England: "Many people drowned and bridges collapsed and grain and meadows were utterly ruined, and famine and disease afflicted people and cattle." Worse still, the frequency of feudal warfare meant that a peasant village might be pillaged or burned by its lord's enemy, or might even become a battleground. From a twelfth-century French poem comes this chilling tale:

“ They start to march. The scouts and the incendiaries lead. After them come the foragers who are to gather the spoils and load them into the great baggage train. The tumult begins. The peasants, having just come out to the fields, turn back uttering loud cries. The shepherds gather their flocks and drive them toward the neighboring woods in the hope of saving them. The incendiaries set the villages afire and the foragers visit and plunder them. The distracted inhabitants are burned to death or led away with tied hands to be held for ransom. Everywhere alarm bells ring. Fear spreads from one side to another and becomes general. Everywhere one sees helmets shining, pennons floating, and horsemen covering the plain. Here money is seized; there cattle, donkeys, and flocks are taken. The smoke spreads; the flames rise; the terrified peasants and shepherds flee in all directions. **”**

Such disasters were rare in the life of a single village, but when they occurred the helpless inhabitants had no choice but to rebuild, replant, and pray for survival through a cold, hungry winter.

In a typical peasant village the most substantial buildings were apt to be the lord's or bailiff's residence (sometimes a castle) and the parish church. To the manor house the peasants would bring portions of their crops, which they owed as customary dues. Here, too, they would bring their disputes to be settled in their lord's court. The parish church, often standing at the center of the village, was in the charge of a priest who was himself of peasant birth. The village priest was seldom well-educated, though he might have learned the rudiments of reading and writing. He played a central role in the villagers' lives—baptizing infants, presiding at marriages and burials, and regularly celebrating the Mass. The church was likely to be painted inside with scenes from the Bible or the life of the local patron saint; such paintings provided an elementary form of religious instruction to a totally illiterate congregation.

The church usually doubled as a village meeting hall, and on festival days it was used for dancing, drinking, and revelry. The feast days of the Christian calendar—Christmas, Easter, and many lesser holy days (holidays)—must have provided joyous relief from an otherwise grinding routine. In some districts the feast of Candlemas (February 2) was celebrated by a candlelight procession followed by a pancake dinner. On the eve of May Day the young men of some villages would cut branches in the forest and lay them at the doors of houses inhabited by attractive young women. St. John's Day (midsummer) brought bonfires and dancing. And throughout the year, time could be found for informal sports—wrestling, archery, rooster fights, drinking contests, and a rough, primitive form of soccer.

But for most of their days the medieval peasants labored to raise the food on which their families and communities depended for survival. An English writer of the late tenth century attributes these words to an imaginary serf of his times:

❦ I work hard. I go out at daybreak, driving the oxen to the field, and then I yoke them to the plow. Be the winter ever so stark, I dare not linger at home for awe of my lord; but having yoked my oxen, and fastened plowshare and coulter, every day I must plow a full acre or more . . . . I have a boy, driving the oxen with an iron goad, who is hoarse with cold and shouting. Mighty hard work it is, for I am not free. **❞**

The New Frontiers

European frontiers were open and expanding in the High Middle Ages. The clearing of forests and the draining of swamps represents the conquest of a great internal frontier. It is paralleled by external expansion all along the periphery of Western Christendom that brought areas of the Arab, Byzantine, and Slavic worlds within the ballooning boundaries of European civilization and added wealth to the flourishing economy.

Western Europe had been expanding ever since Charles Martel repelled the Arabs in 732. Charlemagne had introduced Frankish government and Christianity into much of Germany and had established a Spanish bridgehead around Barcelona. The stabilization and conversion of Hungary, Scandinavia, Bohemia, and Poland around the turn of the millennium pushed the limits of Western Civilization far northward and eastward from the original Carolingian core. Now, in the eleventh, twelfth, and thirteenth centuries, the population boom produced multitudes of landless aristocratic younger sons who sought land and military glory on Christendom's frontiers. And the ever-proliferating European peasantry provided a potential labor force for the newly conquered lands. While the warrior of the frontier was carving out new estates for himself, he was also storing up treasures in heaven by pushing Western Christianity into Muslim Spain, Sicily, Syria, and great tracts of Slavic Eastern Europe. Land, gold, and eternal salvation—these were the alluring rewards of the medieval frontier.

Spain

So it was that knightly adventurers from all over Christendom—and particularly from feudal France—flocked southwestward into Spain during the eleventh century to aid in the reconquest of the Iberian Peninsula from Islam. The powerful Moorish Caliphate of Cordova had broken up after 1002 into

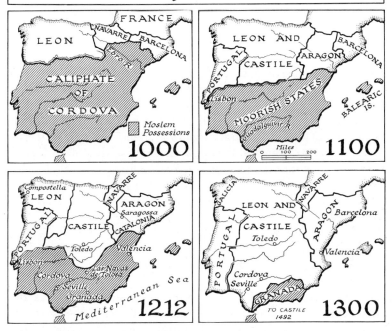

THE RECONQUEST OF SPAIN

1000 — LEON, NAVARRE, BARCELONA, CALIPHATE OF CORDOVA, Moslem Possessions

1100 — LEON AND CASTILE, ARAGON, BARCELONA, PORTUGAL, Lisbon, MOORISH STATES, Guadalquivir, BALEARIC IS., Miles 0 100 200

1212 — Compostella, LEON, NAVARRE, ARAGON, Saragossa, CASTILE, CATALONIA, PORTUGAL, Lisbon, Toledo, Valencia, Cordova, Las Navas de Tolosa, Seville, Granada, Mediterranean Sea

1300 — GALICIA, LEON AND CASTILE, NAVARRE, Barcelona, ARAGON, PORTUGAL, Toledo, Valencia, Cordova, Seville, GRANADA TO CASTILE 1492

small, warring fragments, thereby providing the Christians a superb opportunity. The Christians, however, were themselves divided into several
kingdoms and seldom capable of united action. Taking the lead in the reconquest, the Christian kingdom of Castile captured the great Muslim city of
Toledo in 1085. In later years Toledo became a crucial contact point between
Islamic and Christian culture. Here Arab scientific and philosophical works
were translated into Latin and then disseminated throughout Europe to
challenge and invigorate the mind of the West.

Early in the twelfth century the Spanish Christian kingdom of Aragon
contested the supremacy of Castile and undertook an offensive of its own
against the Moors. In 1140 Aragon was strengthened by its unification with
the county of Barcelona—the Spanish March of Charlemagne's time. And
meanwhile still another Christian state, Portugal, was establishing itself as an
independent kingdom in the far west, facing the Atlantic. Yet for more than a
century following Toledo's fall in 1085, the reconquest made little progress.
Muslim resistance stiffened, while the Christian kingdoms exhausted
themselves fighting one another or intervening in the affairs of southern
France. It was not uncommon for a Christian state to ally with Muslims
against another Christian state.

Finally, in 1212, Pope Innocent III proclaimed a crusade against the
Spanish Muslims. The king of Castile advanced from Toledo with a pan-

Iberian army and won a decisive victory over the Moors at the battle of Las Navas de Tolosa. Thereafter, Moorish power was permanently crippled. Cordova itself fell to Castile in 1236, and by the later thirteenth century the Moors were confined to the small southern kingdom of Granada where they remained in power until 1492. Castile now dominated central Spain, and the work of re-Christianization proceeded apace as Christian peasants were imported *en masse* into the newly conquered lands. Aragon, in the meantime, was overrunning the Muslim islands of the western Mediterranean and establishing a powerful maritime empire.

The High Middle Ages thus witnessed the reconquest and Christianization of nearly all the Iberian Peninsula and its organization into three major Christian kingdoms: Castile, Aragon, and Portugal. Generations thereafter, Castile and Aragon would unite into the kingdom of Spain. And Spain, along with Portugal, would one day lead Europe's expansion into America, Africa, and the Far East. The high-medieval reconquest was an essential precondition for these Atlantic ventures.

Southern Italy and Sicily

The most militant force in Europe's eleventh-century awakening was the warrior-aristocracy of Normandy. Largely Viking in ancestry, the Normans were by now thoroughly adapted to French culture. French in tongue, Christian in faith, feudal in social organization, they plied their arms across the length and breadth of Europe: in the reconquest of Spain, on the Crusades to the Holy Land, on the battlefields of England and France, and in southern Italy and Sicily.

Normandy itself was growing in prosperity and political centralization, and the pressure of an ever-increasing population drove the greedy and adventurous Norman warriors far and wide on distant enterprises. The impression that they made on contemporaries is suggested by a passage from an Italian chronicler:

❝ The Normans are a cunning and revengeful people; eloquence and deceit seem to be their hereditary qualities. They can stoop to flatter, but unless curbed by the restraint of law they indulge in the licentiousness of nature and passion and, in their eager search for wealth and power, despise whatever they possess and seek whatever they desire. They delight in arms and horses, the luxury of dress, and the exercise of hawking and hunting, but on pressing occasions they can endure with incredible patience the inclemency of every climate and the toil and privation of a military life. ❞

The key figures in the Norman conquest of southern Italy were sons of a minor baron of northwest Normandy named Tancred de Hauteville. Tancred had twelve sons, and eight of them headed off to Italy in the 1030s and 1040s, poor in goods but rich in ambition. Even before the first of them arrived, other Norman adventurers had already been drifting south to serve as hired soldiers for the Byzantine coastal cities, Lombard principalities and seaport republics that were struggling for power in the military-political snake pit of eleventh-century southern Italy. In the words of a contemporary observer, these Norman newcomers moved about the south Italian countryside "hoping to find someone willing to employ them; for they were sturdy men and well-built, and also most skilled in the use of arms." They made their presence felt, and before long were building principalities of their own.

In 1047 there arrived the most formidable of Tancred de Hauteville's sons, Robert Guiscard ("the cunning"). A contemporary Byzantine princess describes him as a man

❝ of tyrannical temper, cunning in mind, brave in action, tall and well-proportioned. His complexion was ruddy, his hair blond, his shoulders broad, and his eyes all but emitted sparks of fire. His shout was loud enough to terrify armies . . . . and he was ready to submit to nobody in all the world. **❞**

Finding no one to employ him Robert Guiscard went into business for himself—as a bandit leader. Swooping down from his hideaway in the barren mountains of southern Italy, he plundered villagers and travelers and terrorized the countryside. Successful at this, he expanded his activities to conquest. And demonstrating his warlike prowess with victories over his neighbors, he gradually rose to become the leader of the south-Italian Normans. In 1059 his authority over southern Italy was recognized formally by the pope himself in the Treaty of Melfi: Guiscard agreed to become a papal vassal and received in return the title of duke.

From the Treaty of Melfi onward, the conquests of the southern Normans were "holy wars," and the papacy—which was becoming increasingly hostile toward the Holy Roman Empire to its north—came more and more to depend on the military support of Duke Robert Guiscard. In 1060, with papal blessing, Guiscard invaded the populous Muslim island of Sicily—driven less by Christian zeal than by Norman greed. The island was prosperous and well-defended, and its conquest consumed over thirty years. Once the invasion was well underway, Guiscard turned the campaign over to a younger brother named Roger and launched an attack against the Byzantine holdings in southern Italy. In 1071 he captured Bari, Byzantium's chief Italian seaport. Then, returning to Sicily, he combined forces with his brother Roger to seize the great Muslim metropolis of Palermo in 1072. Palermo had been one of the leading urban centers of the Islamic world. It was larger and richer than any other city in Western Christendom, and its bustling harbor was the key to the central Mediterranean. With Palermo, Bari, and all of southern Italy under his control, Guiscard was now in a position to dominate Mediterranean commerce.

His ambitions were limitless. In 1080, again with papal backing, he launched a "crusade" against the Byzantine Empire, lusting for Constantinople itself. But in 1084, in the midst of his Byzantine campaign, he was summoned back to Italy by Pope Gregory VII, whose conflicts with the Holy Roman Empire had brought the emperor and his army to Rome. With Pope Gregory besieged in a fortress within his own city, Robert Guiscard returned to rescue him, and the news of his coming was enough to send the Holy Roman emperor fleeing northward.

Guiscard entered Rome in triumph. But shortly afterwards a dispute between some boisterous Norman knights and a group of Roman townsmen exploded into violence. Enraged, the Normans proceeded to plunder and destroy the city of Rome, causing greater devastation than the fifth-century Visigoths. Afterwards Guiscard's followers sold many of Rome's leading citizens into Muslim slavery.

In 1085 Guiscard died at Salerno amidst plans for still another campaign. His rags-to-riches career displays in full measure the limitless opportunities and ruthlessness of his age. His epitaph is brief but memorable:

**   Here lies Guiscard, the terror of the world,**
   Who out of Rome the Roman emperor hurled. **"**

The Norman Kingdom of Sicily

In the generations following Robert Guiscard's death, his Italian-Sicilian dominions became one of the wealthiest and best-governed states in medieval Europe. The lord-vassal structure of Norman feudalism was blended with the sophisticated administrative techniques of the Italian Byzantines and Sicilian Muslims. The mixing of cultures is vividly apparent in the Capella Palatina (Palace Chapel), built by Norman rulers of the twelfth century in their palace at Palermo. The structural design of high nave and lower side aisles probably derives from other churches of Western Christendom; the interior glitters with mosaics in the Byzantine style; and the decor of the vaulted ceiling suggests a Muslim paradise, inhabited by djinns instead of Christian angels. The overall effect of the church, despite its diverse cultural ingredients, is one of unity— echoing the achievement of the southern Norman state in unifying peoples of many tongues and many pasts into a single, cohesive realm.

This achievement was given formal recognition in 1130 when a pope sanctioned the coronation of Guiscard's nephew, Roger the Great (d. 1154), as king of Sicily and southern Italy. The new Norman state came to be known officially as the "kingdom of Sicily," and its capital was the Sicilian metropolis of Palermo. But the kingdom, despite its name, included southern Italy as well. Roger the Great ruled strongly but tolerantly over the assorted peoples of his realm—Normans, Byzantines, Muslims, Jews, Italians, and Lombards—with their variety of faiths, customs, and languages. Palermo, with its superb harbor and magnificent palace, its impressive public buildings and luxurious villas, was at once a great commercial center and a crucial point of cultural exchange. Known as the city of the threefold tongue, Palermo drew its administrators and scholars from the Latin, Byzantine, and Arabic traditions.

The legal structure of the kingdom included elements from Justinian's *Corpus Juris* and subsequent Byzantine law, from Lombard law, and from Norman feudalism. The royal court was the hub of an efficient, centralized bureaucracy with special departments of justice and finance. The administration profited from the inclusion of an important non-noble professional class,

The Capella Palatina in Palermo (1132-1140); note the mosaics on the inside of the arches and on the floor.

Mosaic of Christ from the Cathedral in Monreale, Sicily: twelfth century.

devoted to the king and to the efficient execution of its duties. Drawing on the long experience of Byzantium and Islam, Roger's government was far in advance of most other states in Latin Christendom.

Under Roger and his successors the kingdom enjoyed a vital and diverse intellectual life. Its history was well chronicled by talented historians; the Muslim scholar Idrisi, the greatest geographer of his age, contributed a comprehensive geographical work that drew from classical and Islamic sources. Idrisi dedicated his masterpiece to Roger the Great, and the work bears the title, "The Book of Roger." Sicily, like Spain, became a significant source of translations from Arabic and Greek into Latin. The Sicilian translators provided Western European scholars with a steady stream of texts drawn from both classical-Greek and Islamic sources, and these texts, together with others passing into Europe from Spain, served as the essential foundations for the intellectual achievements of thirteenth-century Christendom.

In many ways Norman Sicily was Western Europe's most interesting and fruitful frontier state. Having been carved out partially at Byzantine and Muslim expense, it was representative of twelfth-century Europe's advancing territorial frontier, and as a vibrant center of cultural interplay, it demonstrated that the frontier was not only advancing but also open. Europe besieged had given way to a new, expanding Europe, exposed to the invigorating influences of surrounding civilizations. And nowhere was this cultural contact more intense than in Norman Sicily. East and West met in Roger the Great's glittering, sundrenched realm, and worked creatively side by side to make his kingdom the most sophisticated European state of its day.

The Crusades

The crusading movement, which proved so costly to Europe's Jews, was the most famous and self-conscious episode of Western Christian expansion in the High Middle Ages, though not the most lasting. The Crusades came in response to a major political crisis in the Near East. During the eleventh century a new warlike tribe from Central Asia, the Seljuk Turks, had swept into Persia, taken up the Islamic faith, and turned the Abbasid caliphs of Baghdad into their pawns. In 1071 the Seljuk Turks inflicted a nearly fatal wound on the Byzantine Empire by smashing a Byzantine army at the battle of Manzikert.* Their victory at Manzikert gave the Turks Asia Minor, which had been for centuries a vital reservoir of Byzantine manpower. Stories began filtering into the West of Turkish atrocities against Christian pilgrims to Jerusalem, and when the desperate Byzantine emperor, Alexius Comnenus, swallowed his pride and appealed to the West for help, Europe, under the leadership of a reinvigorated papacy, was glad to respond.

The Crusades represented a fusion of three characteristic medieval impulses: piety, pugnacity, and greed. All three were essential. Without Christian idealism the Crusades would be inconceivable, yet the dream of liberating Jerusalem and the Holy Land from the infidel and reopening them to Christian pilgrims was reinforced mightily by the lure of new lands and unimaginable wealth. The Crusaders were provided a superb opportunity to employ their knightly skills in God's service—and to make their fortunes in the bargain.

It was to Pope Urban II that Emperor Alexius Comnenus sent his envoys asking for military aid against the Turks, and Urban II, a masterful reform pope, was quick to grasp the opportunity. The Crusade presented many advantages to the Church. It enabled the papacy to put itself at the forefront of an immense popular movement and grasp the moral leadership of Europe. Moreover, the pope saw in the Crusade a partial solution to the problem of endemic private warfare in Europe. The Church had long been trying to pacify the warrior nobility; through such principles as the "Truce of God," it had sought to outlaw warfare on holy days and during holy seasons. The Crusade promised to be a more effective means of domestic pacification, drawing off warlike and restive members of the European nobility and turning their ferocity outward against the Muslims. When Urban proclaimed the Crusade, he also proclaimed a peace throughout Latin Christendom. Then, too, as a rescue mission to Byzantium, the Crusade opened the possibility of reuniting the Eastern and Western Churches that had been in schism for more than a generation. Finally, Urban shared with many other Europeans of his day the beguiling dream of winning the holy city of Jerusalem for Christendom.

Accordingly in 1095 Pope Urban summoned the European nobility to take up the Cross and reconquer the Holy Land. He delivered a spellbinding ad-

---

*For a discussion of the Seljuk Turks and the battle of Manzikert see p. 37. The fall of Bari to Robert Guiscard in the same year was an added blow to Byzantium, though a less crippling one.

dress to the Frankish aristocracy at Clermont-Ferrand, calling upon them to emulate the brave deeds of their ancestors, to avenge the Turkish atrocities (which he described in gory detail), to win the Biblical "land of milk and honey" for Christendom and drive the infidel from Jerusalem. Finally, he promised those who undertook the enterprise the highest of spiritual rewards: "Undertake this journey for the remission of your sins, with the assurance of the imperishable glory of the kingdom of Heaven."

The response was overwhelming. With shouts of "God wills it!" Frankish warriors poured into the crusading army. By 1096 the First Crusade was under way. A great international military force—with a large nucleus of knights from central and southern France, Normandy, and Norman Sicily—made its way across the Balkans and assembled at Constantinople. Altogether the warriors of the First Crusade numbered around twenty-five or thirty thousand, a relatively modest figure by modern standards but immense in the eyes of contemporaries. Emperor Alexius was gravely disturbed by the magnitude of the western European response. Having asked for some military support, he had, as he put it, a new barbarian invasion on his hands. Cautious and apprehensive, he demanded and obtained from the Crusaders a promise of homage for all the lands they might conquer.

From the beginning there was friction between the Crusaders and the Byzantines, for they differed both in temperament and in aim. The Byzantines wished only to recapture the lost provinces of Asia Minor, whereas the Crusaders were determined on nothing less than the conquest of the Holy Land. Alexius promised military aid, but it was never forthcoming, and not long after the Crusaders left Constantinople, they broke with the Byzantines altogether. Hurling themselves southeastward across Asia Minor into Syria, they encountered and defeated Muslim forces, captured ancient Antioch after a long and complex siege, and in the summer of 1099 took Jerusalem itself.

The Crusaders celebrated their capture of Jerusalem by plundering the city and pitilessly slaughtering its Muslim inhabitants (as they had slaughtered Jews on their journey eastward). A Christian eyewitness describes the sack of Jerusalem in these words:

❝ If you had been there you would have seen our feet colored to our ankles with the blood of the slain. But what more shall I relate? None of them were left alive; neither women nor children were spared . . . . Afterward, all, clergy and laymen, went to the Sepulcher of the Lord and his glorious temple, singing the ninth chant. With fitting humility they repeated prayers and made their offering at the holy places that they had long desired to visit. **❞**

With the capture of Jerusalem after only three years of vigorous campaigning, the goal of the First Crusade had been achieved. No future crusade was to enjoy such success as the first, and during the two centuries that followed, the original conquests were gradually lost. For the moment, however, Europe rejoiced at the triumph of its Crusaders. Some of them returned to their homes and received heroes' welcomes. Others remained in Latin Syria to enjoy the fruits of their conquests. A long strip of territory along the eastern Mediterranean shore had been wrested from Islam and was now divided, according to feudal principles, among the Crusader knights. These warriors consolidated their conquests by erecting elaborate castles, whose ruins attract tourists to this day.

The conquered lands were organized into four Crusader States: the county of Edessa, the principality of Antioch (ruled by a son of Robert Guiscard), the county of Tripolis, and the kingdom of Jerusalem. This last was the most important of the four states, and the king of Jerusalem was theoretically the feudal overlord of all the crusader territories. In fact, however, he had difficulty enforcing his authority outside his own kingdom, and sometimes even within it. Indeed, the feudal knights who settled in the Holy Land were far too proud and warlike for their own good, and the Crusader States were tormented from the beginning by rivalries and dissensions.

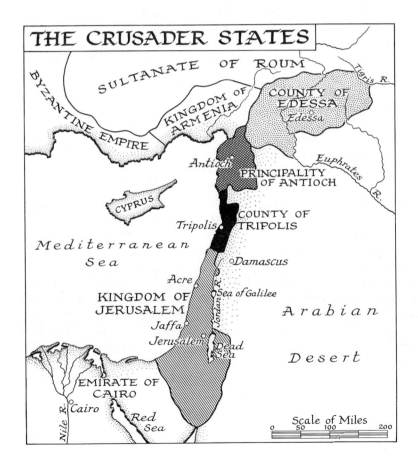

THE CRUSADER STATES

Gradually over the years, the Muslims began to recover their lost lands. In 1144 the county of Edessa fell before Islamic pressure, and the disaster gave rise to a renewal of crusading fervor in Europe. But the Second Crusade (1147–48), although preached by the renowned abbot, St. Bernard, and led by the kings of France and Germany, was a total disaster. The Crusaders returned home shamefaced and emptyhanded, prompting St. Bernard to describe the campaign as "an abyss so deep that I must call him blessed who is not scandalized thereby."

The 1170s and 1180s witnessed the rise of a new, unified Islamic state centered in Egypt and galvanized by the skilled leadership of a warrior-prince named Saladin. Chivalrous as well as able, Saladin at first engaged in a truce with the Crusader States, but the rise of his new principality was nevertheless an ominous threat to Latin Syria. The truce was broken by a Christian robber baron, a characteristic product of grassroots feudal enterprise, who persisted in attacking Muslim caravans. Saladin responded by moving against Jerusalem, and in 1187 he captured it. Jerusalem was not to be retaken by a Christian army for the remainder of the Middle Ages.

This new catastrophe resulted in still another major crusading effort. The Third Crusade (1189–93) was led by three of medieval Europe's most illustrious monarchs: Emperor Frederick Barbarossa of Germany, King Philip Augustus of France, and King Richard the Lion-Hearted of England.* But Frederick Barbarossa drowned on the way and most of his army trudged back to Germany; Philip Augustus quarreled with King Richard and went home; and Richard failed to take Jerusalem. Worse yet, Richard fell into hostile hands on his return journey and became the prisoner of Frederick Barbarossa's son, Emperor Henry VI, who released his royal captive only after England had paid the staggering sum of 100,000 pounds—quite literally, a king's ransom.

Within a decade Europe was ready for still another attempt on Jerusalem. Although lacking the distinguished royal leaders of the previous campaign, the Fourth Crusade (1201–4) had as its instigator the most powerful of the medieval popes: Innocent III. Like the First Crusade, it was led not by kings but by great feudal lords such as Baldwin IX, count of Flanders. It was, withal, the oddest of the Crusades. It never reached the Holy Land at all, yet in its own way it was spectacularly successful.

The Crusaders resolved to avoid the perils of overland travel by crossing to the Holy Land in Venetian ships. The doge of Venice was both a Christian and a man of business. He demanded as payment for the service of his ships a sum of money greater than the Crusaders could afford. He agreed, however, to take what money the Crusaders had and to transport them to the Holy Land if in return they would do him an errand on the way. They were to capture for Venice the port of Zara which had recently come into the hands of the king of Hungary. Pope Innocent III was infuriated by this bargain that diverted the crusading army against a king who was not only a Catholic, but a papal vassal

---

*All three will be encountered in subsequent chapters.

as well. The Crusaders were excommunicated when they attacked Zara, and Innocent washed his hands of the whole enterprise.

Nevertheless, the warriors went doggedly on. Capturing Zara in 1202, they were then diverted still again, this time by a political dispute in Constantinople involving the succession to the Byzantine throne. One of the two claimants, having recently fled to the West, contacted the Crusaders and begged their support, promising them immense wealth, aid against the Muslims, and reunion of the Eastern and Western Churches under Rome. Rising to the challenge, the crusading army moved on Constantinople. The emperor-in-residence panicked and fled the city, and a delegation of citizens, realizing that further resistance was useless, opened Constantinople's gates to the Crusaders. Their imperial claimant was installed in power but was murdered shortly afterwards by one of his anti-Latin countrymen. Meanwhile, the Crusaders had withdrawn from the city as a result of growing hostility and violence between Greeks and Latins. But now, having expended considerable effort in what was apparently a fruitless cause, they resolved to take the city for themselves. Their plan was to elect a new Byzantine emperor from their own ranks and to divide the Eastern Empire among them.

Accordingly, the Crusaders besieged Constantinople and took it by storm in 1204. The impregnable Byzantine capital had fallen at last to enemy conquerors; the Crusaders had succeeded where hordes of Muslims, Persians, Avars, and Germanic tribesmen had failed. Count Baldwin IX of Flanders became emperor, and he and his successors ruled in Constantinople for over half a century. A nucleus of the old Byzantine state held out in Asia Minor, gathering its strength, until in 1261 the Latin Empire was overthrown and Greek emperors reigned once again in Constantinople. But the Fourth Crusade had delivered a blow from which Byzantium never entirely recovered.

The wealth of Constantinople permanently diverted the warriors of the Fourth Crusade from the Holy Land. The Eastern and Western Churches were temporarily reunited, however. A Latin patriarch now sat in Constantinople, and a Latin hierarchy presided over a captive Greek Church. Innocent III, who had absolved the Crusaders from excommunication after the fall of Zara and had excommunicated them anew for attacking Constantinople, readmitted them once again to communion when he realized the "great blessings" that had befallen Christendom by the capture of the schismatic city.

The Crusaders, for their part, returned to Europe with immense booty from the Byzantine metropolis: precious gems, money, and gold such as few of them had imagined. But the greatest prize of all was the immense store of relics that the westerners liberated from the Byzantine capital and brought home. Bones, heads, and arms of saints, Jesus' crown of thorns, St. Thomas the Apostle's doubting finger, and many similar treasures passed into Western Europe at this time. Perhaps more important, the West was given additional access to the intellectual legacy of Greek and Byzantine Civilization. But the old hostility between Greeks and Latins was aggravated by the events of the Fourth Crusade into a virtually insurmountable wall of hatred.

During the thirteenth century, crusading fervor gradually waned. The papacy cheapened the crusading ideal by calling for repeated crusades not only against Muslims in the Holy Land and Spain, but also against Albigensian heretics in southern France and even the Holy Roman emperor. In 1212 a visionary, ill-organized enterprise known as the "Children's Crusade" ended in tragedy. Thousands of boys and girls flocked into the ports of southern Europe, gripped by religious fervor and convinced that the Mediterranean would dry up before them to provide them a miraculous pathway into the Holy Land. Many of them returned home sadder but wiser, and the rest were sold into Muslim slavery.

The next major crusading effort, the Fifth Crusade (1217–1221), was directed not at the Holy Land but at Egypt—the real center of Muslim power in the Near East. The Crusaders captured the key Egyptian port of Damietta in 1219 and refused a Muslim offer to trade Jerusalem for it. But dissension tore the crusader ranks, and when they moved against Cairo they were caught between a Muslim army and the flooding Nile. The results were military disaster, the abandonment of Damietta, and another joyless homecoming.

Three additional crusades of importance were undertaken in the thirteenth century. The first, led by the brilliant emperor Frederick II, was at once the most fruitful and least violent of the three. Frederick negotiated with the sultan of Egypt rather than fighting him, and in 1229 obtained possession of Jerusalem by treaty. The triumph was ephemeral, however, for Jerusalem fell into Muslim hands once again in 1244. And because of the absence of bloodshed, Frederick II's crusade was never dignified by being given a number.

The Sixth and Seventh Crusades were led by the saint-king of France, Louis IX. One was undertaken against Egypt in 1248, the other against Tunisia in 1270. Both failed, and the second cost St. Louis his life. Crusades continued to be organized and mounted in subsequent generations, but as the thirteenth century closed, crusading enthusiasm was dying out. In 1291, the fall of Acre—the last Christian bridgehead on the Syrian coast—brought an end to the Crusader States in the Holy Land.

One scholar has called the Crusades "medieval Europe's Lost Weekend." But they were more than simply a romantic and bloody fiasco. During the greater part of the High Middle Ages Christian lords ruled portions of the Holy Land. Their activities caught the imagination of Europe and held it for two centuries, uniting Western Christendom in a single vast effort. At the same time European merchants established permanent bases in Syria and enormously enlarged their role in international commerce. When the Crusaders departed the merchants remained. Knights and barons who participated in the Crusades broadened their perspective through contacts with other civilizations. The effect of such contacts in dissolving the provincial narrow-mindedness of the European nobility is incalculable.

The Crusades gave rise to several religious orders of Christian warriors, bound by monastic rules and dedicated to fighting the Muslims and advancing the crusading cause in every possible way. One such order was the Knights

Hospitalers, which drew chiefly on the French for its membership. Another was the Knights Templars, an international brotherhood that acquired great wealth through pious gifts and intelligent estate management, and gradually became involved in far-flung banking activities. A third order, the Teutonic Knights, was composed chiefly of Germans. In the thirteenth century the Teutonic Knights transferred their activities from the Holy Land to northern Germany where they devoted themselves to the eastward thrust of German-Christian civilization against the Slavs. Orders of a similar sort arose on other frontiers of Western Christendom. The Knights of Santiago de Compostella, for example, were dedicated to fighting the Muslims in Spain and furthering the Christian reconquest of the Iberian peninsula. These crusading orders, bridging as they did the two great medieval institutions of monasticism and knighthood, represent the ultimate synthesis of the military and the Christian life.

The German Eastward Expansion

Eastern Germany was still another of medieval Europe's expanding frontiers. The German eastward drive was not a product of active royal policy but rather a movement led by enterprising local aristocrats, in particular, the dukes of Saxony. It was a gradual advance with a great deal of momentum behind it. Over a drawn-out period between 1125 and 1350, it succeeded in pushing the eastern boundary of German settlement far to the north and east at Slavic expense (see the map). German military gains were consolidated by the building of innumerable agrarian villages and by a massive eastward migration of German peasants. Consequently, the new areas were not only conquered; they were in large part Christianized and permanently Germanized.

The later phases of the German push were spearheaded by the Teutonic Knights who penetrated temporarily far northward into Lithuania, Latvia, and Estonia, and even made an unsuccessful bid to conquer Russia. During the fourteenth and fifteenth centuries the Teutonic Knights lost some of their conquests, but much of the German expansion proved to be permanent. The epoch between 1125 and 1350 witnessed the conquest and Germanization of large portions of modern East Germany and western Poland.

In the later thirteenth and early fourteenth centuries European expansion was coming to an end. The internal frontiers of forest and swamp had by then been won. The best farmlands had been reclaimed. And Europe's external frontiers were everywhere hardening, sometimes even receding, as in the Holy Land. The closing of the frontiers was accompanied by cultural change and diminishing prosperity. For the culture of the High Middle Ages was the product of a buoyant, expanding, frontier society, fired by religious confidence, driven by immense ambitions, and captivated by a world in which, so it seemed, anything was possible.

THE GERMAN EASTWARD PENETRATION

Legend:
- German before 800
- 800–1400
- Large minorities 1400
- Small minorities 1400

FINNS

SWEDES

DANES

Baltic Sea

ESTONIANS

LETTS

Dvina R.

RUSSIANS

Königsberg

Lübeck

Niemen R.

Elbe R.

Berlin

Vistula R.

GERMANS

Magdeburg

Leipzig

Oder

POLES

Weser R.

Dresden

Breslau

Rhine R.

Prague

BOHEMIANS

Cracow

Dniester

MORAVIANS

Danube R.

Vienna

Theiss R.

Buda

HUNGARIANS

ITALIANS

Drave R.

Venice

CROATS

Po R.

Adriatic Sea

Danube R.

Scale of Miles
0   100   200   300   400

Spain	Sicily	Holy Land
1002: Breakup of Caliphate of Cordova	c. 1016: Norman infiltration begins	
	1060–91: Sicily conquered	
1085: Capture of Toledo	1085: Death of Robert Guiscard	1095: Calling of First Crusade
1140: Aragon unites with Catalonia	1130: Coronation of Roger the Great	1099: Crusaders take Jerusalem
	1154: Death of Roger the Great	
		1187: Crusaders lose Jerusalem
1212: Christian victory at Las Navas de Tolosa		1204: Crusaders take Constantinople
1236: Castile takes Cordova		1291: Crusaders driven from Holy Land

Chapter 10

New Dimensions in Medieval Christianity

The Church in the High Middle Ages

⁋ The expansion of civilization during the High Middle Ages has been viewed thus far as a series of advancing economic and territorial frontiers. In a
broader sense, however, frontiers of all sorts were being explored and extended. Scholars were pioneering in new intellectual frontiers; artists and
writers were adding ever-new dimensions to Western culture. Administrators
were pushing forward the art of government. And underlying all these phenomena—which will be explored in the next chapters—was a deepening of the
religious impulse that manifested itself in many different ways: in the rise of a
vigorous papacy dedicated to reform and the creation of a Christian world
order,* in the development of new forms of monasticism, in the rapid expansion of ecclesiastical administration and Church activities, in the intensification of lay piety, and in the growth of heresy.

Medieval religion followed many different paths. It could be devoutly orthodox, it could be anticlerical, and it could be openly heretical. Yet its basic
institutional expression was the Catholic Church, and the most obvious

*See Chapter 11.

characteristic that the vast majority of Western Christians had in common was their Catholicism. Nationalism was scarcely yet alive, and the allegiance of Europeans tended to be at once local and international. In the twelfth and thirteenth centuries the majority of Europeans were still intensely parochial in their outlook, only vaguely aware of what was going on beyond their immediate surroundings. But alongside their localism was an element of cosmopolitanism—a consciousness of belonging to the international commonwealth of Western Christendom, fragmented politically, but united culturally and spiritually by the Church.

The Church in the High Middle Ages was a powerful unifying influence. It had made notable progress since the half-heathen pre-Carolingian era. A flourishing parish system was by now spreading across the European countryside to bring the sacraments and a modicum of Christian instruction to the peasantry. New bishoprics and archbishoprics were formed, and old ones were becoming steadily more active. The papacy never completely succeeded in breaking the control of kings and secular lords over their local bishops, but by the twelfth century it was coming to exercise a very real authority over European bishops. And the growing efficiency of the papal bureaucracy evoked the envy and imitation of the rising royal governments.

The Sacraments

The buoyancy of high medieval Europe is nowhere more evident than in the accelerating impact of Christian piety on European society. The sacraments of the Church introduced a significant religious dimension into the life of ordinary Europeans: their births were sanctified by the sacrament of *baptism*, in which they were cleansed of the taint of original sin and initiated into the Christian fellowship. At puberty they received the sacrament of *confirmation*, which reaffirmed their membership in the Church and gave them the additional grace to cope with the problems of adulthood. Christian couples were united in the sacrament of *matrimony*. And if a man chose the calling of the Christian ministry, he was spiritually transformed into a priest and "married" to the Church by the sacrament of *holy orders*. As death approached, the sacrament of *extreme unction* prepared the soul for its journey into the next world. And throughout their lives, Christians could receive forgiveness from the damning consequences of mortal sin by repenting their past transgressions and humbly receiving the comforting sacrament of *penance*. Finally they might partake regularly of the central sacrament of the Church—the *eucharist*—receiving the body of Christ into their own bodies by consuming the eucharistic bread. Thus, the Church, through its seven sacraments, brought God's grace to all its members, great and humble, at every critical juncture of their lives. The sacramental system, which only assumed final form in the High Middle Ages, was a source of comfort and reassurance: it made communion with God not merely the elusive goal of a few mystics but the periodic experience of all believers. And, of course, it established the Church as the essential intermediary between God and humanity.

The Evolution of Piety

The ever-increasing scope of the Church, together with the rising self-awareness of the new age, resulted in a deepening of popular piety throughout Western Europe. The High Middle Ages witnessed a profound shift in religious attitude, from the awe and mystery characteristic of earlier Christianity to a new emotionalism and dynamism. This shift is evident in ecclesiastical architecture, as the earthbound Romanesque style gave way in the later twelfth century to the tense, upward-reaching Gothic.* A parallel change is evident in devotional practice, as the divine Christ sitting in judgment gave way to the tragic figure of the human Christ suffering on the Cross for the sins of humanity. And it was in the High Middle Ages that the Virgin Mary came into her own as the compassionate intercessor for hopelessly lost souls. A legend of the age told of the devil complaining to God that the tender-hearted Queen of Heaven was cheating Hell of its most promising candidates. Christianity became, as never before, a doctrine of love, hope, and compassion. The God of Justice became the merciful, suffering God of Love.

Like other human institutions, the medieval Church fell short of its ideals. Corrupt churchmen were in evidence throughout the age, and certain historians have delighted in cataloguing instances of larcenous bishops, gluttonous priests, and licentious nuns. But cases such as these were clearly exceptional. The great shortcoming of the high-medieval Church was not gross corruption but rather a creeping complacency that resulted sometimes in a shallow, even mechanical attitude toward the Christian religious life and an obsession with ecclesiastical property. The medieval Church had more than its share of saints, but among much of the clergy the profundity of the Faith was often lost in the day-to-day affairs of the pastoral office, the management of far-flung estates, disputes over land and privileges, and ecclesiastical status seeking. These flaws reflect less on the medieval Church than on humanity's enduring capacity to compromise ideals in the pursuit of power, money, and prestige.

The Crisis in Benedictinism

The drift toward complacency has been a recurring problem in Christian monasticism. Again and again, the lofty idealism of a monastic reform movement has been eroded and transformed by time and success until, at length, new reform movements arose in protest against the growing worldliness of old

*See pp. 240 ff.

ones. This cycle has been repeated countless times. Indeed, the sixth-century Benedictine movement was itself a protest against the excesses and inadequacies of earlier monasticism. St. Benedict had regarded his new order as a means of withdrawing from the world and devoting full time to communion with God. But Benedictinism, despite Benedict's ideal, quickly became involved in teaching, evangelism, and ecclesiastical reform, and by the tenth and eleventh centuries the whole Benedictine movement had become deeply immersed in worldly affairs. Benedictine monasteries controlled vast estates, supplied significant contingents of knights to feudal armies, and worked closely with secular princes in affairs of state. Early in the tenth century the Cluniac movement, which was itself Benedictine in spirit and rule, arose as a protest against the worldliness and complacency of contemporary Benedictine monasticism.* But by the early twelfth century the Congregation of Cluny had come to terms with the secular establishment and was beginning to display traces of the very complacency against which it had originally rebelled. Prosperous, respected, and secure, Cluny was too content with its majestic abbeys and priories, its elaborate liturgical program, and its bounteous fields to give its wholehearted support to the radical transformation of Christian society for which many Christian reformers were now struggling.

St. Benedict had sought to create monastic sanctuaries in which Christians might retire from the evils and temptations of society, but the High Middle Ages witnessed an endeavor to sanctify society itself. The new goal, pioneered by the reform papacy of the eleventh century, was not *withdrawal* but *conversion*. Instead of retiring from the world, the reformers sought to transform the social order into something more in tune with their Christian ideals. During the eleventh and twelfth centuries, these two contrary tendencies—withdrawal and conversion—both had a profound impact upon monastic reform.

In the early generations of the High Middle Ages the Benedictine movement was showing signs of exhaustion. During the long, troubled centuries of the early Middle Ages, Benedictine teachers and missionaries, scribes and political advisers, had provided indispensable services to society. Benedictine monasteries had served as the spiritual and cultural foci of Christendom. But in the twelfth century the Benedictines saw their educational monopoly broken by the rising cathedral schools and universities of the new towns. These urban schools produced increasing numbers of well-trained scholars who gradually superseded the Benedictine monks as scribes and advisers to princes. In other words, the urbanizing impulse of the High Middle Ages drastically diminished the traditional Benedictine contribution to society.

Still, the Benedictines retained their great landed wealth. The Benedictine monastery was scarcely the sanctuary from worldy concerns that St. Benedict had planned. Nor was it any longer the vital force it once had been in Christianizing the world. Twelfth-century Benedictines followed neither the path of withdrawal nor the path of conversion, and even in the arena of secular affairs

*See pp. 117-118.

they were losing their grip. The Benedictine life was beginning to appear tarnished and unappealing to sensitive religious spirits caught up in the piety of the new age.

Carthusians and Cistercians

The monastic revolt against Benedictinism followed the two divergent roads of uncompromising withdrawal from society and ardent participation in the Christianization of society. The impulse toward withdrawal pervaded the Carthusian order that arose in eastern France in the later eleventh century and spread across Christendom in the twelfth. Isolated from the outside world, the Carthusians lived in small groups, worshiping together in communal chapels but otherwise living as hermits in individual cells. This austere order has survived to the present day and, unlike most monastic movements, its severe spirituality has seldom waned. Yet even in the spiritually-charged atmosphere of the twelfth century it was a small movement, offering a way of life for only an heroically holy minority. Too ascetic for the average Christian, the Carthusian order was much admired but seldom joined.

The greatest monastic force of the twelfth century, the Cistercian order, managed for a time to be both austere and popular. The mother house of the order, Cîteaux, was established by a little group of Benedictine dissidents in 1098 on a wild, remote site in eastern France. The Cistercian order grew slowly at first, then gradually acquired momentum. In 1115 it had four daughter houses; by the end of the century it had five hundred.

The success of the Cistercians demonstrates the immense appeal of withdrawal to the Christians of the twelfth century. Like Cîteaux, the daughter houses were deliberately built in remote wilderness areas. The abbeys themselves were stark and primitive in contrast to the elaborate Cluniac architecture. Cistercian life was stark and primitive, too—less severe than that of the Carthusians but far more so than that of the Cluniacs. Refusing to accept gifts of manors or serfs, the Cistercians sought to resurrect the strict, simple life of primitive Benedictinism. Their houses were unheated, even in the bitter north-European winters; their diet was limited to black bread, water, and a few stewed vegetables; they were forbidden to speak, except when it was absolutely essential. The numerous Cistercian houses were bound together not by the authority of a central abbot, as at Cluny, but by an annual council of all Cistercian abbots meeting at Cîteaux. Without such centralized control it is unlikely that the individual houses could have clung for long to the harsh, ascetic ideals on which the order was founded.

The key figure in twelfth-century Cistercianism was St. Bernard, whom we have already encountered preaching the Second Crusade. As a young man, Bernard joined the community of Cîteaux in 1112 and three years later became the founder and abbot of Clairvaux, one of Cîteaux's earliest daughter houses. St. Bernard of Clairvaux was the foremost Christian of his age—a mystic, an eloquent religious orator, and a crucial figure in the meteoric rise of the Cistercian order. His moral influence was so immense that he became Europe's leading arbiter of political and ecclesiastical disputes. Besides inducing the king of France and the Holy Roman emperor to participate in the Second Crusade, he persuaded Christendom to accept his candidate in the years following a hotly disputed papal election in 1130. On one occasion he even succeeded in reconciling the two great warring families of Germany, the Welfs and Hohenstaufens. He rebuked the pope himself: "Remember, first of all, that the Holy Roman Church, over which you hold sway, is the mother of churches, not their sovereign mistress—that you yourself are not the lord of bishops, but one among them." And he took an uncompromising stand against one of the rising movements of his day: the attempt to reconcile the Catholic faith with human reason, led by the brilliant philosopher, Peter Abelard. In the long run Bernard failed to halt the growth of Christian rationalism, but he succeeded in making life miserable for Abelard and in securing the official condemnation of certain of Abelard's teachings.*

Above and beyond his obvious talents for diplomacy and persuasion, St. Bernard won the devotion of twelfth-century Europe through his reputation for sanctity. He was widely regarded as a saint in his own lifetime, and stories of his miracles circulated far and wide. Pilgrims flocked to Clairvaux to be healed by his touch. This aspect of Bernard's reputation made his skillful preaching and diplomacy even more effective than it would otherwise have been. For here was a holy man, a miracle worker, who engaged in severe fasts, overworked himself to an extraordinary degree, wore coarse clothing, and devoted himself singlemindedly to the service of God.

On one occasion St. Bernard commanded Duke William of Aquitaine to reinstate certain bishops whom the duke had driven from their sees. When, after much persuasion, the duke remained obstinate, St. Bernard celebrated a High Mass for him. Holding the consecrated host in his hands, Bernard advanced from the altar toward the duke and said,

❝ We have besought you, and you have spurned us. The united multitude of the servants of God, meeting you elsewhere, have entreated you and you have scorned them. Behold! Here comes to you the Virgin's Son, the Head and Lord of the Church which you persecute! Your Judge is here, at whose name every knee shall bow . . . Your Judge is here, into whose hands your soul is to pass! Will you spurn him also? Will you scorn him as you have scorned his servants? **❞**

The duke threw himself on the ground and submitted to Bernard's demands.

Bernard's career demonstrates the essential paradox of Cistercianism. For although the Cistercians strove to dissociate themselves from the world, Bernard was drawn into the vortex of secular affairs. Indeed, as the twelfth cen-

*See pp. 265-266.

tury progressed, the entire Cistercian movement became increasingly involved in the world outside. And like the later Puritans, the Cistercians discovered that their twin virtues of austere living and hard work resulted in an embarrassing accumulation of wealth and a corrosion of their spiritual simplicity. Their efforts to clear fields around their remote abbeys placed them in the vanguard of the internal frontier movement. They became pioneers in scientific farming and introduced notable improvements in the breeding of horses, cattle, and sheep. The English Cistercians became the great wool producers of the realm. Altogether the Cistercians exerted a powerful, progressive influence on European husbandry and came to play a prominent role in the agrarian economy. Economic success brought ever-increasing wealth to the order. Cistercian abbey churches became more elaborate, and the austerity of Cistercian life was progressively relaxed. In later years there emerged new offshoots, such as the Trappists, which returned to the strict observance of original Cistercianism.

Monasticism in the World

The Cistercians had endeavored to withdraw from the world, yet became a powerful force in twelfth-century Europe. At roughly the same time, other orders were being established with the deliberate aim of participating actively in society and working toward its regeneration. The Augustinian Canons, for example, submitted to the rigor of a rule, yet carried on normal ecclesiastical duties in the world, serving in parish churches and cathedrals. The fusion of monastic discipline and worldly activity culminated in the twelfth-century Crusading orders—the Knights Templars, Knights Hospitalers, Teutonic Knights, and similar groups—whose ideal was a synthesis of the monastic and the military life for the purpose of expanding the political frontiers of Western Christendom. These and other efforts to direct the spiritual vigor of monastic life toward the Christianization of society typify the visions and hopes of the new, emotionally-charged religiosity that animated twelfth-century Europe.

Heresies and the Inquisition

The surge of popular piety also resulted in a flood of criticism against the Church itself. It was not that churchmen had grown worse, but rather that the laity had begun to judge them by more rigorous standards. Popular dissatisfaction toward the workaday Church spurred the rush toward the austere twelfth-century monastic orders. Yet the majority of Christians could not become monks, and for them, certain new heretical doctrines began to exert a powerful appeal.

The heresies of the High Middle Ages flourished particularly in the rising towns of southern Europe. The eleventh-century urban revolution had caught the Church unprepared. The new towns were becoming centers of a burgeoning lay piety, yet the Church, with its roots in the older agrarian order, seemed unable to minister effectively to the vigorous and widely literate new burgher class. Too often the urban bishops appeared as political oppressors and enemies of burghal independence rather than spiritual directors. Too often the Church failed to understand the town dwellers' problems and aspirations or to anticipate their growing suspicion of ecclesiastical wealth and power. Although most townspeople remained loyal to the Church, a minority, particularly in the south, turned to new, anticlerical sects. In their denunciation of ecclesiastical wealth, these sects were doing nothing more than St. Bernard and the Cistercians had done. But many of the anticlerical sects crossed the narrow line between orthodox reformism and heresy by preaching without episcopal or papal approval. Far more important, they denied the exclusive right of the priesthood to perform sacraments.

One such sect, the Waldensians, was founded by a merchant of Lyons named Peter Waldo who, around 1173, gave all his possessions to the poor and took up a life of apostolic poverty. He and his followers worked at first within the bounds of orthodoxy, but gradually their criticism of priestly wealth and their denial of special priestly powers earned them the condemnation of the Church. Similar groups, some orthodox, some heretical, arose in the communes of Lombardy and were known as the *Humiliati*. These groups proved troublesome to the local ecclesiastical hierarchies, but generally they escaped downright condemnation, unless they themselves took the step of denying the authority of the Church. Many of them did take that step, however, and by the opening of the thirteenth century heretical, anticlerical sects were spreading across northern Italy and southern France, and even into Spain and Germany.

The most popular heresy in southern France was associated with a group known as the *Cathari* (the pure) or the Albigensians—after the town of Albi where they were particularly strong. The Albigensians represented a fusion of two traditions: (1) the anticlerical protest against ecclesiastical wealth and power, and (2) an exotic theology derived originally from Persia. The Albigensians recognized two gods: the god of good who reigned over the universe of the spirit, and the god of evil who ruled the world of matter. The Old Testament God, creator of the material universe, was their god of evil; Christ, whom they regarded as a purely spiritual being with a phantom body, was the god of good. The Albigensians believed in reincarnation, and their goal was to break free of the endless cycles of physical rebirth. Their morality stressed a rigorous rejection of all material things—of physical appetites, wealth, worldly vanities, and sexual intercourse—in the hope of one day escaping from the prison of the body and ascending to the realm of pure spirit. In reality this severe ethic was practiced only by a small elite known as the *perfecti;* the rank and file normally ate well, made love, and participated only vicariously in the rejection of the material world—by criticizing the affluence of the Church. Indeed,their opponents accused them of gross licentiousness. And although such accusations were grotesquely exaggerated, it does seem likely that certain Provençal nobles were attracted to the new teaching by the opportunity of appropriating Church property in good conscience.

As the thirteenth century dawned, Albigensianism was spreading so swiftly that it posed a dangerous threat to the unity of Christendom and the authority of the Church. Pope Innocent III, recognizing the gravity of the situation, tried with every means in his power to eradicate the heresy. At length, in 1208, he responded to the murder of a papal legate in southern France by summoning a crusade against the Albigensians. The Albigensian Crusade was a ruthless, savage affair that succeeded in its purpose only after many years of bloodshed and at the cost of ravaging the vibrant civilization of southern France.* The French monarchy intervened in the Crusade's final stages and brought it to an end at last in 1229. The Crusade succeeded in reversing the drift toward heresy in southern France, and in the process it disclosed the brutality of which the Church was capable when sufficiently threatened.

In the years immediately following the Albigensian Crusade, there emerged an institution that will always stand as a grim symbol of the medieval Church at its worst: the Inquisition. Christian persecution of heretics dates from the later fourth century, but it was not until the High Middle Ages that heterodox views presented a serious problem to European society. Traditionally, the problem of converting or punishing heretics was handled at the local level, but in 1233 the papacy established a central tribunal for the purpose of standardizing procedures and increasing efficiency in the suppression of heresies. The methods of the Inquisition included the use of torture, secret testimony, conviction on the testimony of only two witnesses, the denial of legal counsel to the accused, and other procedures offensive to the Anglo-American legal tradition but not especially remarkable by standards of the times. Indeed, many of these procedures—including torture—were drawn from the customs of Roman law.

Some historians have adduced further arguments in an attempt to defend an indefensible institution. Let us say here merely that the Christian faith was far more important to the people of medieval Europe than national allegiance. The medieval Church, with its elaborate charitable activities, its hospitals and universities, and its other social services, performed many of the functions of the modern state, and medieval heresy was therefore akin to modern treason. To the medieval Catholic, heresy was a hateful thing, an insult to Christ, and a source of contamination to others. An Albigensian preaching in the streets of thirteenth-century Paris would have been approximately as popular as a Ku Klux Klansman preaching white supremacy on a modern campus. Today, when political and economic doctrines are more important to most people than religious creeds, the closest parallels to medieval Waldensianism or Albigensianism are to be found in the Nazi party in modern America, Zionism in Saudi Arabia, and Soviet Marxism in Peking. In examining opposition to

*See pp. 233-236.

movements such as these, we can gain an inkling of the state of mind that produced the medieval Inquisition.

Mendicantism

The thirteenth-century Church found an answer to the heretical drift that was far more compassionate and effective than the Inquisition. In the opening decades of the century two new religious orders emerged—the Dominican and Franciscan—which were devoted to a life of poverty, preaching, and charitable deeds. Rejecting the life of the cloister, they dedicated themselves to religious work in the world—particularly in the towns. Benedictines had traditionally taken vows of personal poverty, but their monasteries could and did acquire great corporate wealth. The Dominicans and Franciscans, on the contrary, were pledged to both personal and corporate poverty and were therefore known as mendicants (beggars). Capturing the imagination of thirteenth-century Christendom, they drained urban heterodoxy of much of its former support by demonstrating to the townspeople of Europe that Christian orthodoxy could be both relevant and compelling.

The Dominicans

St. Dominic (1170–1221), a well-educated Spaniard, spent his early manhood in Castile serving as an Augustinian canon. In his mid-thirties he traveled to Rome, met Pope Innocent III, and followed the pope's bidding to preach in southern France against the Albigensians. For the next decade, between 1205 and 1215, he worked among the heretics, leading an austere, humble life. His eloquence and simplicity won him considerable renown, but few converts.

The Dominican order evolved out of a small group of volunteers who joined Dominic in his work among the Albigensians. Gradually Dominic came to see the possibility of a far larger mission: to preach and win converts to the faith throughout the world. In 1215 Dominic's friend the bishop of Toulouse gave the group a church and a house in the city, and shortly thereafter, the papacy recognized the Dominicans as a separate religious order and approved the Dominican rule.

The congregation founded by Dominic was to be known as the Order of Friars Preachers. It assumed its permanent shape during the years between its formal establishment in 1216 and Dominic's death in 1221, by which time it had grown to include some five hundred friars and sixty priories organized into eight provinces embracing the whole of Western Europe. The Dominicans stood in the vanguard of thirteenth-century piety. Their order attracted people of imagination and unusual religious dedication, who could not be satisfied with the enclosed and tradition-bound life of earlier monasticism but were challenged by the austerity of the Dominican rule, the disciplined vitality of the order, and the goal of working toward the moral regeneration of society.

The Dominican rule drew freely from the earlier rule of the Augustinian Canons that Dominic had known in his youth, but added new elements and provided a novel direction for the religious life. The order was to be headed by a minister-general, elected for life, and a legislative body that met annually. The friars themselves belonged not to a particular house, but to the order at large. Their place of residence and sphere of activity were determined by the minister-general. Their life, strictly regulated and austere, included rigors such as midnight services, total abstinence from meat, frequent fasts, and prolonged periods of mandatory silence. And the entire order was strictly bound by the rule of poverty which Dominic had learned from his contemporary, St. Francis. Not only should poverty be the condition of individual Dominicans as it was of individual Benedictines; it was to be the condition of the order itself. The Dominican order was to have no possessions, except churches and priories. It was to have no fixed incomes, no manors, but was to subsist through charitable gifts. It was, in short, a mendicant order.

The Dominican order expanded at a phenomenal rate during the course of the thirteenth century. Dominican friars carried their evangelical activities across Europe and beyond, into the Holy Land, Central Asia, Tartary, Tibet, and China. Joining the faculties of the rising universities, they became the leading proponents of Aristotelian philosophy and included in their numbers such notable scholars as St. Albertus Magnus and St. Thomas Aquinas. Dominic himself had insisted that his followers acquire broad educations before undertaking their mission of preaching and that each Dominican priory maintain a school of theology. Within a few decades after his death his order included some of the foremost intellects of the age.

The Dominicans were, above all, preachers, and their particular mission was to preach among heretics and non-Christians. Their contact with heretics brought them into close involvements with the Inquisition, and in later years their reputation was darkened by the fact that they themselves became the leading inquisitors. The grand inquisitor of Spain, for example, was customarily a Dominican. They took pride in their nickname *"Domini canes"*—hounds of God—which suggested their role as watchdogs of the Catholic Faith. To religious rebels, the nickname bore an ominous connotation.

The Dominican order still flourishes. The rule of corporate poverty was softened increasingly; finally, in the fifteenth century, it was dropped altogether in deference to the great truth that scholar-teachers cannot be expected to beg or do odd jobs. But long after their original mendicant ideals were modified, the Dominicans remained committed to their central mission of championing Catholic orthodoxy by word and pen.

Saint Francis

Dominic's remarkable achievements were overshadowed by those of his contemporary, St. Francis (c.1182–1226)—a warm, appealing man who is widely regarded as Christianity's ideal saint. Francis was a product of the medieval urban revolution. He was the son of a wealthy cloth merchant of Assisi, a town in central Italy with an influential Albigensian minority. As a youth he was generous, high-spirited, and popular, and in time he became the leader of a boisterous but harmless teenage gang. He was by no means dissolute but rather, as one writer has aptly expressed it, he "seems altogether to have been rather a festive figure."

In his early twenties St. Francis underwent a profound religious conversion that occurred in several steps. It began on the occasion of a banquet that he was giving for some of his friends. After the banquet Francis and his companions went into the town with torches, singing in the streets. Francis was crowned with garlands as king of the revelers, but after a time he disappeared and was found in a religious trance. Thereafter, he devoted himself to solitude, prayer, and service to the poor. He went as a pilgrim to Rome where he is reported to have exchanged clothes with a beggar and spent the day begging with other beggars. Returning to Assisi, he encountered an impoverished leper and, notwithstanding his fear of leprosy, he gave the poor man all the money he was carrying and kissed his hand. Thenceforth he devoted himself to the service of lepers and hospitals.

To the confusion and consternation of his bourgeois father, Francis now went about Assisi dressed in rags, giving to the poor. His former companions pelted him with mud, and his father, fearing that Francis's almsgiving would consume the family fortune, disinherited him. Francis left the family house singing a French song and spent the next three years of his life in the environs of Assisi, living in abject poverty. He ministered to lepers and social outcasts and continued to embarrass his family by his unconventional behavior. It was at this time that he began to frequent a crumbling little chapel known as the Portiuncula. One day in the year 1209, while attending Mass there, he was struck by the words of the Gospel that the priest was reading:

❝ Everywhere on your road preach and say, 'The kingdom of God is at hand.' Cure the sick, raise the dead, cleanse the lepers, drive out devils. Freely have you received; freely give. Carry neither gold nor silver nor money in your belts, nor bag, nor two coats, nor sandals, nor staff, for the workman is worthy of his hire.* **❞**

Francis at once accepted this injunction as the basis of his vocation and immediately thereafter—even though a layman—began to preach to the poor.

Disciples now joined him, and when he had about a dozen followers he is

*Matthew, 10:7–10.

This much restored painting of St. Francis, ascribed to the half-legendary thirteenth-century Italian painter Cimabue (*c.* 1240-1302), is taken from a series of frescoes in the Upper Church of St. Francis in Assisi.

said to have remarked, "Let us go to our Mother, the Holy Roman Church, and tell the pope what the Lord has begun to do through us and carry it out with papal approval." This may seem a naive approach to the masterful, aristocratic Pope Innocent III, yet when Francis came to Rome in 1210, Innocent sanctioned his work. Doubtless the pope saw in the Franciscan mission a potential orthodox counterpoise to the Waldensians, Albigensians, and other heretical groups who had been winning masses of converts from the Church by the example of their poverty and simplicity. For here was a man whose loyalty to Catholicism was beyond question and whose own artless simplicity might bring erring souls back into the Church. Already Innocent III had given his blessing to movements similar to that of Francis. An orthodox group of Humiliati had received his sanction in 1201, and in 1208 he permitted a converted Waldensian to found an order known as the "Poor Catholics," which was dedicated to lay preaching. In Francis's movement the pope must have seen still another opportunity to encourage a much-needed wave of reform within the orthodox framework. And it may well be that Francis's glowing spirituality appealed to the sanctity of Innocent himself, for the pope, even though a great man of affairs, was genuinely pious. However this may be, thirteenth-century Europe deserves some credit for embracing a movement that in many other ages would have been persecuted or ridiculed. Rome crucified Christ, whereas the medieval West took Francis to its heart and made him a saint. But the hard edges of Franciscan religious austerity were blunted in the process.

Immediately after the papal interview Francis and his followers returned to the neighborhood of Assisi. They were given the Portiuncula as their own chapel, and over the years it continued to serve as the headquarters of the Franciscan movement. Around it the friars built huts of branches and twigs. The Portiuncula was a headquarters but not a home, for the friars were always on the move, wandering in pairs over the country, dressed in peasants' clothing, preaching, serving, and living in conscious imitation of Christ.

During the next decade the order expanded at a spectacular rate. Franciscans were soon to be found throughout northern Italy; by Francis's death, in 1226, Franciscan missions were active in France, Germany, England, Hungary, Spain, Morocco, Turkey, and the Holy Land, and the friars numbered in the thousands. The captivating personality of Francis himself was doubtless a crucial factor in his order's popularity, but it also owed much to the fact that its ideals harmonized with the highest religious aspirations of the age. Urban heresy lost some of its allure as the cheerful, devoted Franciscans began to pour into Europe's cities, preaching in the crowded streets and setting a living example of Christian sanctity.

The Franciscan ideal was based above all on the imitation of Christ. Fundamental to this ideal was the notion of poverty, both individual and corporate. The Franciscans subsisted by working and serving in return for their sustenance. Humility also was a part of the ideal; Francis named his followers the Friars Minor (little brothers). Preaching was an important part of their mission, and it answered an urgent need in the cities where the Church had hitherto responded inadequately to the growing religious hunger of the townspeople. Perhaps most attractive of all was the quality of joyousness, akin to the joyousness that Francis had shown prior to his conversion, but directed now toward spiritual ends. Contemporaries referred to Francis affectionately as "God's own troubadour."

Pious people of other times have fled the world; the Albigensians renounced it as the epitome of evil. But Francis embraced it joyfully as the handiwork of God. In his "Song of Brother Sun" he expressed poetically his holy commitment to the physical universe:

Praise be to you, my Lord, for all your creatures,
Above all Brother Sun
Who brings us the day, and lends us his light;
Beautiful is he, radiant with great splendor,
And speaks to us of you, O most high.
Praise to you, my Lord, for Sister Moon and for the stars;
In heaven you have set them, clear and precious and fair.
Praise to you, my Lord, for Brother Wind,
For air and clouds, for calm and all weather
By which you support life in all your creatures.
Praise to you, my Lord, for Sister Water
Which is so helpful and humble, precious and pure.
Praise to you, my Lord, for Brother Fire,
By whom you light up the night.
And fair is he, and joyous, and mighty, and strong.
Praise to you, my Lord, for our sister, Mother Earth,
Who sustains and directs us,
And brings forth varied fruits, and plants,
and flowers bright.
Praise and bless my Lord, and give him thanks,
And serve him with great humility.

Early Franciscanism was too good to last. The order was becoming too large to retain its original disorganized simplicity. Francis was no administrator, and well before his death the movement was passing beyond his control. In 1219–20 he traveled to Egypt in an effort to convert its Muslim inhabitants—a hopeless task, but Francis was never dismayed by the impossible—and while he was away it became apparent that his order required a more coherent organization than he had seen fit to provide it. Many perplexing questions now arose: With thousands of friars invading the begging market, what would become of the common tramp? Would Europe's generosity be overstrained? Above all, how could these crowds of friars be expected to cleave to the ideal without an explicit rule and without Francis's personal presence to inspire and guide them? In short, could the Franciscan ideal be practical on a large scale? For the movement was proliferating at a remarkable rate. Besides the Friars Minor themselves, a Second Order was established—a female order directed by Francis's friend, St. Clare—known as the Poor Clares. And a third group, consisting of part-time Franciscans known as Tertiaries, dedicated themselves to the Franciscan way while continuing their former careers in the world. The little band of Franciscan brothers had evolved into a multitude.

On his return from the Near East, Francis prevailed on a powerful friend, Cardinal Hugolino—later Pope Gregory IX—to become the order's protector. On Hugolino's initiative a formal rule was drawn up in 1220 that provided a certain degree of administrative structure to the order. A probationary period was established for initiates who, after completing it, were required to take lifetime vows. And the rule of absolute poverty was softened. In 1223 a shorter, somewhat laxer rule was instituted, and over the years and decades that followed, the movement continued to evolve from the ideal to the practical.

St. Francis himself withdrew more and more from involvement in the order's administration. At the meeting of the general chapter in 1220, he resigned his formal leadership of the movement with the words, "Lord, I give you back this family that you entrusted to me. You know, most sweet Jesus, that I no longer have the power and qualities to continue to take care of it." In 1224, St. Francis underwent a mystical experience atop Mt. Alverno in the Apennines, and legend has it that he received the *stigmata** on that occasion. It is not entirely clear how St. Francis reacted to the evolution of his order, but in his closing years his mysticism deepened, his health declined, and he kept much to himself. At his death in 1226 he was universally mourned, and the order that he had founded remained the most powerful and attractive religious movement of its age.

As Franciscanism became increasingly modified by the demands of practicality, it also became increasingly rent with dissension. Some friars, wishing to draw on Francis's prestige without being burdened with his spiritual dedication, advocated an exceedingly lax interpretation of the Franciscan way. Others insisted on the strict imitation of Francis's life and struggled against its modification. These last, known in later years as "Spiritual Franciscans," sought to preserve the apostolic poverty and artless idealism of Francis himself. By the fourteenth century they had become vigorously antipapal and anticlerical.

The majority of Franciscans, however, were willing to meet reality halfway. Although Francis had disparaged formal learning as irrelevant to salvation, Franciscan friars began devoting themselves to scholarship and took their places alongside the Dominicans in the thirteenth- and fourteenth-century universities. Indeed, Franciscan scholars, such as Roger Bacon in thirteenth-century England, played a vital role in the revival of scientific investigation, and the minister-general of the Franciscan order in the later thirteenth century, St. Bonaventure, was one of the most illustrious theologians of the age.

*The stigmata, which have been attributed to several saints, consist of wounds or scars, supposedly of supernatural origin, that correspond to those sustained by Christ in his crucifixion.

The very weight and complexity of the Franciscan organization forced it to compromise its original ideal of corporate poverty. Although it neither acquired nor sought the immense landed wealth of the Benedictines or Cistercians, it soon possessed sufficient means to sustain its members. It is interesting to see how the minister-general Bonaventure, a holy man and a brilliant philosopher, instituted and justified some of the changes that the order underwent in the thirteenth century. Although an intense admirer of St. Francis, Bonaventure was not himself a beggar by nature, nor a wandering minstrel, nor a day laborer, but a scholar-administrator burdened with the task of adapting a way of life designed for a dozen friars living in huts of twigs to an international order of many thousands. Contrary to Francis, Bonaventure encouraged scholarship as an aid to preaching and evangelism. St. Francis had told his followers that "manual labor should be done with faith and devotion." Bonaventure, after demonstrating the superiority of contemplation to manual labor, concluded that Franciscans were under no compulsion to engage in physical work, although if any wished to do so they should by all means do it "with faith and devotion."

Necessary though they were, these compromises robbed the Franciscan movement of a good measure of the radical idealism that Francis had instilled in it. In the progress from huts of twigs to halls of ivy, something precious was left behind. The Franciscans continued to serve society, but by the end of the thirteenth century they had ceased to inspire it.

The Passing of the High Middle Ages

The pattern of religious reform in the High Middle Ages is one of rhythmic ebb and flow. A reform movement is launched with high enthusiasm and lofty purpose, it galvanizes society for a time, then succumbs gradually to complacency and gives way to a new and different wave of reform. But with the passing of the High Middle Ages, one can detect a gradual waning of spiritual vigor in orthodox Catholicism. The frontiers were closing as the fourteenth century dawned. Western political power was at an end in Constantinople and the Holy Land, and the Spanish reconquest had ceased. The economic boom was giving way to an epoch of depression, declining population, peasants' rebellions, and debilitating wars. And until the time of the Protestant Reformation, no new religious order was to attain the immense social impact of the thirteenth-century Franciscans and Dominicans. Popular piety remained strong, particularly in northern Europe where succeeding centuries witnessed a surge of mysticism. But in the south a more secular attitude was beginning to emerge. Young men and women no longer flocked into monastic orders; soldiers no longer rushed to crusades; papal excommunications no longer wrought their former terror. The electrifying appeal of a St. Bernard, a St. Dominic, and a St. Francis was a phenomenon peculiar to their age. By the fourteenth century their age was passing.

910:	Founding of Cluny
1084:	Establishment of Carthusian Order
1098:	Establishment of Cîteaux
1112–53:	Career of St. Bernard of Clairvaux as a Cistercian
1128:	Original rule of the Knights Templars
c.1173:	Beginning of the Waldensian movement
1208:	Innocent III calls the Albigensian Crusade
1210:	Innocent III authorizes the Francisan order
1216:	Dominican Rule sanctioned by the papacy
1226:	Death of St. Francis
1233:	Inquisition established

Chapter 11

✺

Empire
and
Papacy

Papacy and Church in the Mid-Eleventh Century

The role of the popes in the changing religious patterns of the High Middle Ages was scarcely touched upon in the previous chapter. For although the papacy contributed much to the spiritual development of the period, it was also closely associated with the politics of empire and kingdom, which is the central topic of this chapter. So we must return now to the mid-eleventh century, the age when Cluny still stood in the vanguard of European monasticism, when Cîteaux was yet an untouched wilderness and the mendicant movement lay in the distant future.

With the dawning of the High Middle Ages there emerged a newly invigorated papacy, dedicated to ecclesiastical reform and the spiritual regeneration of Christian society. Almost at once the reform papacy became involved in a struggle with the Holy Roman Empire—a tragic conflict that dominated European politics for more than two centuries. On the eve of the conflict, Germany was the mightiest monarchy in Western Christendom and the German king, or "Roman Emperor," dominated the papacy. By 1300 Germany was fragmented, and the papacy, after 250 years of political prominence, was on the brink of a long downward slide.

✺

Prior to the beginnings of papal reform in the mid-eleventh century, a chasm had existed between the papal theory of Christian society and the realities of the contemporary Church. The papal theory, with a venerable tradition running back to the fifth-century pope, Leo the Great, envisaged a sanctified Christian commonwealth in which lords and kings accepted the spiritual direction of priests and bishops who, in turn, submitted to the leadership of the papacy. The popes claimed to be the successors and representatives of St. Peter, who was thought to have been the first bishop of Rome—the first pope. Just as St. Peter was the chief of Christ's apostles, they argued, the pope was the monarch of the apostolic Church. And as eternal salvation was more important than earthly prosperity—as the soul was more important than the body—so the priestly power overshadowed the power of secular lords, kings, and emperors. The properly ordered society, the truly Christian society, was one dominated by the Church which, in turn, was dominated by the pope. In the intellectual climate of the High Middle Ages this view had great pertinence and caught the imagination of many thoughtful people. It provided a persuasive justification for the idea of papal monarchy.

The reality of mid-eleventh-century society was far different. Almost everywhere the Church was under the control of aristocratic lay proprietors. Manorial lords appointed their priests; dukes and kings selected their bishops and abbots. As we have seen, the Holy Roman emperors used churchmen extensively in the administration of Germany. In France, the Church provided warriors from its estates for feudal armies, advisers for kings and magnates, and clerks for their administrations. The Church played a vital role in the operation of tenth- and early-eleventh-century society, but it was usually subordinate to the lay ruling class. Its spiritual and sacramental role was compromised by its secular, administrative responsibilities. As was bound to happen under such conditions, the Church tended to neglect its sacred mission. From the lay standpoint it was an effective administrative tool, but from the spiritual standpoint it was inadequate and sometimes corrupt. Monasteries all too frequently ignored the strict Benedictine rule. Some priests had concubines, and many had wives, despite the canonical requirement of priestly celibacy. Lay lords often sold important ecclesiastical offices to the highest bidder, and the new prelate customarily recouped the purchase price by exploiting his tenants and subordinates. This commerce in ecclesiastical appointments was known as *simony*. It was regarded by some contemporary reformers as the arch-sin of the age.

Ecclesiastical corruption was nowhere more evident than in Rome itself. The papacy of the earlier eleventh century had fallen into the soiled hands of the Roman nobility and had become a prize disputed among the several leading aristocratic families of the city. In 1032 the prize fell to a young aristocratic libertine who took the name of Benedict IX. His pontificate was scandalous even by contemporary Roman standards. Benedict sold the papacy, then changed his mind and reclaimed it. By 1046 his right to the papal throne was challenged by two other claimants; the papacy had fallen into a three-way schism.

Ecclesiastical Reform

Such were the conditions of the European Church as the mid-eleventh century approached. A Church dominated by lay proprietors had long existed in Europe and had long been accepted. But with the upsurge of lay piety that accompanied the opening of the High Middle Ages, the comfortable church-state relationship of the previous epoch seemed monstrously wrong to many sensitive spirits. This was the epoch in which Christians were beginning to join hermit groups such as the Carthusians; they would soon be flocking into the austere Cistercian order. Such people as these were responding to the spiritual awakening of their age by following the path of withdrawal from worldly society. Others chose the more novel and adventurous approach of reforming the Church and the world. The dream of sanctifying society, which was later to find such vivid expression in the career of St. Francis, was shared by many Christians of the High Middle Ages. During the second half of the eleventh century it manifested itself in a powerful movement of ecclesiastical reform that was beginning to make itself felt across Western Christendom. At the heart of this movement was the reform papacy.

In general, the reformers fell into two groups. One consisted of moderate reformers who sought to eliminate simony, enforce clerical celibacy, and improve the moral caliber of churchmen, but without challenging the Church's traditional subordination to the lay nobility—a subordination that had been sweetened by countless gifts of lands and privileges to submissive prelates. The second group was much more radical. Its goal was to demolish the tradition of lay control and to rebuild society on the pattern of the papal monarchy theory. The radical reformers struggled to establish an ideal Christian commonwealth in which laymen no longer appointed churchmen—in which kings deferred to bishops and a reformed papacy ruled the Church. The moderate reformers endeavored to heal society; the radicals were determined to transform it.

The Congregation of Cluny, firm in its spiritual rectitude yet at peace with the existing social order, leaned toward moderate reform. Its ideals were shared by several princes of the age, among them Emperor Henry III of Germany. Shocked by the antics of Pope Benedict IX and the three-way tug-of-war for the papal throne, Henry III intervened in Italy in 1046, arranged the deposition of Benedict and his two rivals, and drastically improved the quality of the papal leadership by appointing the first of a series of reform popes. The ablest of these imperial appointees, Pope Leo IX (1049–54), carried on a vigorous campaign against simony and clerical marriage, holding yearly synods at Rome, sending legates far and wide to enforce reform, and traveling constantly himself to preside over local councils and depose guilty churchmen. Leo's reform pontificate opened dramatically when, at the Roman Synod of 1049, the bishop of Sutri was condemned for simony and promptly fell dead in the presence of the whole assembly.

Leo IX labored mightily for reform, and his pontificate constitutes the opening phase in the evolution of the high-medieval papacy. His vigorous assertion of papal authority aggravated the long and deepening hostility between the churches of Rome and Constantinople, and in 1054 two of his legates placed a papal bull on the high altar of Sancta Sophia excommunicating the eastern patriarch. More than anything else, Leo struggled to enforce canon law and to purge the Church of simony and clerical marriage. In most of his enterprises, he could count on the support of Emperor Henry III. In these early years empire and papacy worked hand in glove to raise the moral level of the European Church.

But whatever the success of Leo's reforms, there were those who felt that he was not going far enough. The real evil, in the view of the radical reformers, was lay supremacy over the Church. To them Henry III's domination of papal appointments, however well-intentioned, was the supreme example of a profound social sin. A number of ardent reformers were to be found among the cardinals whom Pope Leo appointed and gathered around him. These newcomers, who dominated the reform papacy for the next several decades, came for the most part from monastic backgrounds. Many of them were influenced by the piety surging through the towns of eleventh-century northern Italy, a piety that was stimulating the widespread revival of hermit monasticism.

One such reformer was St. Peter Damiani, a leader of the northern-Italian hermit movement before he was brought to Rome by Leo IX and made a cardinal. Zealous and saintly, Damiani was deeply respected by his contemporaries. He was a mystic and, like St. Bernard after him, a vigorous opponent of the growing tendency among Christian intellectuals to elucidate the faith by reason and logic. Damiani served the reform papacy tirelessly, traveling far and wide to enforce the prohibitions against simony and clerical marriage and to reform the clergy. Yet he drew back from what seemed to him the irresponsible efforts of his more radical associates to challenge and destroy the social order. Spurred by the new piety and dedicated to the papacy, Damiani was nevertheless one of the less extreme of Leo IX's new cardinals.

The real leaders of the radical group were Humbert and Hildebrand. Both were cardinals under Leo; both had, like Damiani, left monastic lives to join the Roman curia. Humbert was a German from Lorraine, probably of aristocratic background, who used his subtle, well-trained intellect to support papal reform in its most radical aspect. He was one of Pope Leo's legates to Constantinople during the dispute with the Eastern Church, where his uncompromising attitudes on papal supremacy clashed with the equally intransigent views of the eastern patriarch. Indeed, it was Humbert himself who precipitated the schism of 1054 by laying a bull excommunicating the patriarch on the high altar of Sancta Sophia. A few years later Humbert produced a bitter, closely reasoned attack against the lay-dominated social order in the West, *Three Books Against the Simoniacs,* in which he extended the meaning of simony to include not merely the buying or selling of ecclesiastical offices but any instance of lay interference in clerical appointments. In Humbert's view the Church ought to be utterly free of lay control and supreme in European society.

Hildebrand, an Italian, lacked the originality and intellectual depth of Humbert but had a remarkable ability to draw ideas from the minds of others and formulate them into a clearly articulated program. Intellectually, Hildebrand was a disciple of Humbert, but as a spellbinding leader and mover of events, he was second to none. Contemporaries described Hildebrand as a small, ugly, pot-bellied man, but they also recognized that a fire burned inside him—a holy or unholy fire depending on one's point of view. For Hildebrand was the most controversial figure of his age. Consumed by the ideal of a Christian society dominated by the Church and a Church dominated by the papacy, Hildebrand served with prodigious vigor and determination under Pope Leo IX and his successors. At length he became pope himself, taking the name Gregory VII (1073–85).His pontificate was to be one of the most violent and tragic of the Middle Ages.

So long as Henry III lived, radicals such as Humbert and Hildebrand remained in the background. But in 1056 the emperor died in the prime of life, leaving behind him a six-year-old heir, Henry IV, and a weak regency government. Henry III's death was a catastrophe for the empire and a godsend to the radicals who longed to wrest the papacy from imperial control. At the death of Henry III's last papal appointee in 1057, the reform cardinals began electing popes on their own. In 1059, under the influence of Humbert and Hildebrand, they issued a daring declaration of independence known as the *Papal Election Decree,*which stated that thenceforth the pope would be chosen by cardinals. The emperor and the Roman laity would merely give formal approval to the candidate whom the cardinals elected. In the years that followed, this revolutionary proclamation was challenged by both the empire and the Roman aristocracy, but in the end the cardinals won out. The papacy had broken free of lay control and was in the hands of the reformers. For now the cardinals elected the pope and the pope appointed the cardinals. The Decree of 1059 created at the apex of the ecclesiastical hierarchy a reform oligarchy of the most exclusive sort.*

---

*Strictly speaking, the Decree of 1059 provided that the pope should be elected not by all cardinals but by the cardinal bishops alone. The other cardinals—cardinal priests and cardinal deacons— were empowered to participate in papal elections by a decree of the twelfth century.

The Investiture Controversy

The next step in the program of the radical reformers was infinitely more difficult. It involved nothing less than the annihilation of lay control over the Church. At a time when the Church possessed perhaps a third of the land in Europe, the total realization of such a goal would cripple secular power and revolutionize European society. Yet only by its realization, so the radical reformers believed, could a justly-ordered Christian commonwealth be achieved.

One of the first arenas of conflict was the city of Milan, with its proud archbishopric renowned since St. Ambrose's time. Milan was in the grip of the new commercial revival and, like many other Lombard towns of the eleventh century, was seething with activity. Most Lombard cities of this era were, as we have seen, dominated by their bishops who were inclined to cooperate with the Holy Roman Empire and were supported by an elite group of landholding nobles. As a group, the Lombard bishops tended to ignore the new wave of reform, and some were themselves guilty of simony. Throughout Lombardy, and in Milan in particular, their rule was being challenged by the growing class of merchants and artisans, backed by day workers and peasants. In Milan and elsewhere, these dissidents were referred to by their enemies as *patarenes* (ragpickers). Hostile to the domination of the traditional ruling group and fired by the new piety, the patarenes made common cause with the reform papacy against their unreformed and oppressive bishops. The reformers in Rome had no sympathy for the Lombard bishops and were especially antagonistic toward the archbishop of Milan who was, in effect, an imperial agent and who, by condoning simony and marriage among his clergy, symbolized the old proprietary Church at its worst.

In 1059 Cardinal Peter Damiani journeyed to Milan to enforce reform. Backed by the patarenes and the authority of Rome, he humbled the archbishop and the higher clergy, made them confess their sins publicly, and wrung promises of amendment from them. Thus, the Milanese church, despite its traditional cooperation with the Empire and independence of Roman authority, was made to submit to the power of the papacy. Over the next fifteen years, the struggle continued between the patarenes and the noble-ecclesiastical ruling group, and the city was torn by murder and mob violence. When, in 1072, the young Emperor Henry IV ordered the consecration of an anti-reformer as archbishop of Milan, he was at once faced with the combined wrath of the papacy and patarenes. The patarenes rioted and the pope excommunicated Henry's counselors. The most significant aspect of this entire affair is the way in which it typifies the close alliance between radical urban piety and papal reform. During the second half of the eleventh century, the papacy placed itself at the forefront of the new piety and drew upon the energy of the revolutionary social-spiritual movement that was sweeping Europe. At odds with much of the traditional ecclesiastical establishment, the radical reformers in Rome were in tune with the most vigorous forces of the age.

The struggle over lay control of ecclesiastical appointments broke out in earnest in 1075 when Hildebrand, now Pope Gregory VII, issued a proclamation banning lay investiture. Traditionally, a newly chosen bishop or abbot was invested by a lay lord with a ring and a pastoral staff, symbolic of his marriage to the Church and his duty to be a good shepherd to his Christian flock. Gregory attacked this custom of lay investiture as the crucial symbol of lay authority over churchmen. Its prohibition was a challenge to the established social order. It threatened to compromise the authority of every ruler in Christendom, and none more than the Holy Roman emperor himself. For the imperial system of administration was particularly dependent on the German and Lombard Churches.

By Gregory VII's time, Henry IV had grown to vigorous manhood and was showing promise of becoming as strong a ruler as his father. When Gregory VII suspended a group of uncooperative, imperially-appointed German bishops, Henry IV responded with a vehement letter of defiance. He asserted his authority as a divinely appointed sovereign to lead the German Church without papal interference and challenged Gregory's very right to the papal throne. The letter was addressed to Gregory under his previous name, "Hildebrand, not pope but false monk." It concluded with the dramatic words, "I, Henry, king by grace of God, with all my bishops, say to you: 'Come down, come down, and be damned throughout the ages.'"

Henry's letter was in effect a defense of the traditional social order of divinely ordained priest-kings ruling over a docile Church. Gregory's view of society was vastly different: he denied the priestly qualities of kings and emperors, suggested that most of them were gangsters destined for hell, and repudiated their right to question his status or his decrees. Emperors had no power to appoint churchmen, much less depose popes. But the pope, as the ultimate authority in Christendom, had the power to depose kings and emperors. Accordingly, Gregory responded to Henry's letter with a startling exercise of his spiritual authority that was, nevertheless, perfectly in accord with his conception of Christian society: he excommunicated and deposed Henry. It was for the pope to judge whether or not the king was fit to rule, and Gregory had judged. His action was nothing less than revolutionary, for in banning lay investiture and deposing the king of Germany he was putting into practice the papal theory in its most radical form and striking at the bedrock of the traditional order.

Radical though it was, the deposition was effective. Under the relatively calm surface of monarchical authority in Germany, a powerful aristocratic opposition had long been gathering force. Subdued during the reign of Henry III, local and regional particularism asserted itself during the long regency following his death, and Henry IV, on reaching maturity, had much ground to recover. In 1075 he succeeded in stifling a long, bitter rebellion in Saxony and seemed to be on his way toward reasserting his father's power when the controversy with Rome exploded. Gregory VII's excommunication and deposition—awesome spiritual sanctions to the minds of eleventh-century

Christians—unleashed in Germany all the latent hostility that the centralizing policies of the Salian dynasty had evoked. Many Germans, churchmen and aristocrats alike, refused to serve an excommunicated sovereign. The German nobles took the revolutionary step of threatening to elect a new king in Henry's place, thereby challenging the ingrained German tradition of hereditary kingship with the counterdoctrine of elective monarchy. The elective principle, which crippled the later-medieval and early-modern German monarchy, had its real inception at this moment.

Desperate to keep his throne, Henry crossed the Alps into Italy to seek the pope's forgiveness. In January 1077, at the castle of Canossa in Tuscany, the two men met in what was perhaps medieval history's most dramatic encounter—Henry IV humble and barefoot in the snow, clothed in rough, penitential garments; Gregory VII torn between his conviction that Henry's change of heart was a mere political subterfuge and his priestly duty to forgive a repentant sinner. Finally, Gregory lifted Henry's excommunication and the monarch, promising to amend his ways, returned to Germany to rebuild his authority.

Through the centuries Canossa has symbolized the ultimate royal degradation before the power of the Church. Perhaps it was—but in the immediate political context it was a victory, and a badly needed one, for Henry IV. It did not prevent a group of German nobles from electing a rival king, nor did it restore the powerful centralized monarchy of Henry III; but it did save Henry IV's throne. Restored to communion, he was able to rally support, to check for a time the forces of princely particularism, and to defeat the rival king.

As his power waxed, Henry ignored his promises at Canossa. In 1080 Gregory excommunicated and deposed him a second time, only to find that Henry had consolidated his political position to such a degree that he could now withstand these papal weapons. In the early 1080s Henry returned to Italy, this time with an army. Gregory summoned his vassal and ally, the Norman Robert Guiscard, to rescue him from his situation; but Robert's boisterous Normans, although they frightened Henry away, became involved in a destructive riot against the Roman townspeople. The commoners of Rome had always supported Gregory, but now they turned furiously against him and he was obliged, for his own protection, to accompany the Normans when they withdrew to the south. In 1085 Gregory died at Salerno, consumed by bitterness and a conviction of failure. His last words were these: "I have loved justice and hated iniquity; therefore I die in exile."*

Although Gregory VII failed to transform Europe into what he conceived to be a proper Christian society, his theory of papal monarchy retained its potency. The reform papacy soon fell into the expert hands of Urban II (1088–99), a former prior of Cluny, who seized the moral leadership of Europe

*An ironic twist to Psalm 45, verse 7: "You have loved justice and hated iniquity; therefore God, your God, has anointed you with the oil of gladness, above all your rivals."

by calling the First Crusade. Urban steered a more moderate course than Gregory had done, yet he and his successors continued to harass the unlucky Henry IV, stirring up rebellions in Germany and eroding the power of the imperial government. In 1106 Henry died as unhappily as Gregory had. In the end Henry's own son and heir, Henry V, led an army of hostile nobles against his father. As Henry IV died, his empire seemed to be collapsing around him.

Henry V (1106–25) enjoyed a happier reign than his father's, but only because he foresook his father's struggle to recover the fullness of imperial power as it had existed in the mid-eleventh century. The independence-minded aristocracy consolidated the gains it had made during the preceding era of chaos, and Henry V could do little about it.

Toward the end of his reign, Henry V worked out a compromise settlement with the Church that brought the Investiture Contest to an end at last. Already the controversy had been settled by compromise in England and France, where the church-state struggle had been considerably less bitter than in Germany. As time progressed both papacy and empire tended to draw back from the extreme positions they had taken during Gregory VII's pontificate, and in 1122 they reconciled their differences in the Concordat of Worms. Henry agreed to give up lay investiture, while the pope conceded to the emperor the important privilege of bestowing on the new prelate the symbols of his *territorial* and *administrative* jurisdiction. Bishops and abbots were thenceforth to be elected according to the principles of canon law, by the monks of a monastery or the canons of a cathedral, but the emperor had the right to be present at such elections and to make the final decision in the event of a dispute. These reservations enabled the emperor to retain a considerable degree of de facto control over the appointment of important German churchmen. The exercise of royal control over a "canonical election" is illustrated in the later twelfth century by a command of King Henry II of England to the monks at Winchester: "I order you to hold a free election, but nevertheless I forbid you to elect anyone except Richard, my clerk, the archdeacon of Poitiers."

There was no real victor in the Investiture Controversy. The Church had won its point—lay investiture was banned—but monarchs still exercised considerable control over their churches. The theory of papal monarchy over a reconstituted Christian society remained unrealized, and the old tradition of peaceful cooperation between kings and prelates was shaken. The papacy, however noble its intentions, had become politicized as never before. And by asserting its authority across Europe, it evoked hostile royalist propaganda and growing anticlericalism.

Still, the papal-imperial balance of power had changed radically since the mid-eleventh century. The papacy was now a mighty force in Europe, and the power of the emperor had declined. During the chaotic half-century between the onset of the controversy in 1075 and Henry V's death in 1125, feudalism came to Germany. In these decades of civil strife a powerful new aristocracy emerged. Ambitious landowners rose to great power, built castles, extended their estates, and usurped royal rights. They forced minor neighboring noblemen to become their vassals and, in some instances, forced free peasants to become their serfs. The monarchy was helpless to curb this ominous process of fragmentation.

The Investiture Controversy resulted in the crippling of imperial authority in northern Italy. The fierce patarene struggle in Milan was repeated throughout Lombardy, and in the anarchy wrought by the papal-imperial conflict, the pro-imperial Lombard bishops lost the wide jurisdictional powers they had formerly exercised over their cities. Lombard burghers, under the banner of papal reform, rebelled against the control of nobles, bishops, and emperor alike, and established quasi-independent city states. By 1125, Milan and her sister cities were free urban communes, and imperial authority in Lombardy had become nominal.

In Germany and Italy alike, imperial power was receding before the whirlwind of local particularism, invigorated by the Investiture Controversy and the soaring popular piety of the age. Well before the Concordat of Worms, the decline of the medieval empire had begun.

The Age of Frederick Barbarossa

The Salian dynasty died out with the passing of Henry V in 1125. During the next quarter century, Germany reaped the harvest of princely particularism. Disregarding the principle of direct hereditary succession, the nobles reverted to the elective principle that they had asserted at the time of Canossa. Their choice always fell to a man of royal blood but never to the most direct heir. In the decades between 1125 and 1152 a rivalry developed between two great families that had risen to power in the anarchic era of the Investiture Controversy: the Welfs of Saxony and the Hohenstaufens of Swabia. In 1152 the princes elected as king a talented Hohenstaufen, Frederick I, "Barbarossa" (the Red-Bearded), duke of Swabia, who took as his mission the revival and reconstruction of the German monarchy.

Emperor Frederick Barbarossa recognized that the mighty imperial structure of Henry III was beyond recovery. His goal was to harness the new feudal forces of his age to the royal advantage. He deliberately encouraged the great princes of the realm to expand their power and privileges at the expense of the lesser lords, but at the same time he forced them to recognize his own feudal authority over all the kingdom. In other words, he succeeded in establishing an effective lordship over the leading feudal magnates, making them his obedient vassals—his tenants-in-chief. He was the supreme overlord at the apex of the feudal pyramid.

But as the sorry state of the early French monarchy well illustrates, feudal overlordship was an ephemeral thing if the royal overlord lacked the power and resources to support his position. Therefore, Frederick Barbarossa set about to increase his revenues and extend the territories under his direct authority. A strong feudal monarchy required a substantial territorial core under exclusive royal control—an extensive royal demesne—to act as a counterweight to the great fiefs of the chief vassals of the realm. Frederick enlarged his demesne territories, most of which were concentrated in Swabia, by bringing many of the new monasteries and rising towns under imperial jurisdiction. The crux of his imaginative policy was the reassertion of imperial authority over the wealthy Lombard cities. With Lombardy under his control and its revenues pouring into the imperial treasury, no German lord could challenge him.

Barbarossa's Lombard policy earned him the hostility of the papacy, which had always feared the consolidation of imperial power in Italy, and of the intensely independent Lombard cities, which were determined to give up as little of their wealth and autonomy as they possibly could. And should he become too deeply involved in Italy, Barbarossa exposed himself to rebellion on the part of the German aristocrats and high nobility—in particular, the Welf family, which was vigorously represented at the time by Duke Henry the Lion of Saxony.

The papacy of the mid-twelfth century was having problems of its own. Pope Hadrian IV (1154–59), who was to become one of Frederick Barbarossa's most bitter foes, was faced at the beginning of his pontificate with the problem of maintaining the papacy's hold on Rome itself. A gifted man of humble origins, Hadrian IV was the one Englishman ever to occupy the papal throne. Rome was turbulent during his years, for the patarene movement had reached the Holy City and had turned violently antipapal. The revolutionary social forces that had earlier allied with the papacy in breaking the power of an archbishop in Milan were now challenging the pope's authority over Rome. In the 1140s the city was torn by a rebellion whose leaders struggled to drive out the pope and dreamed of reestablishing the ancient Roman Republic. Very quickly this antipapal communal movement spread to other cities in the Papal States, and for a time the pope himself was forced into exile.

Before long, the Roman rebellion fell under the leadership of Arnold of Brescia, a gifted scholar and spiritual revolutionary, whose goal it was to strip the Church of its wealth and secular authority. Suppressed by the Norman troops of Roger the Great in the 1140s, Arnold's revolution reasserted itself under Hadrian, and the pope was driven to the desperate expedient of placing Rome itself under interdict, ordering the suspension of church services throughout the city. The interdict proved an effective weapon. Among other things it afflicted Rome's economy by discouraging pilgrimages. The revolution collapsed and Arnold of Brescia was driven from the city. Hadrian and Barbarossa joined forces to hunt him down, and once he fell into their hands he was hanged, burned, and thrown into the Tiber (1155). Thus, Arnold was emphatically eliminated and his relics were put out of the reach of any future admirers. But his movement persisted as an anticlerical heresy—an early example of the opposition to ecclesiastical wealth and power that was soon to find expression among the the Waldensians and Albigensians and, by implication, among the Franciscans.

The growing split between the papacy and the Roman townspeople was an ominous indication that papal leadership over urban reform movements was at an end. The papacy was no longer able to make common cause with the explosive forces of popular piety, as it had under Gregory VII, but was now beginning to suppress them. Pope Hadrian actually had little choice but to defend himself in whatever way possible against Arnold of Brescia, yet in laying Rome under interdict he was following a path that would lead within a century to the Albigensian Crusade and the Inquisition. This split between papal leadership and popular piety was a factor of decisive importance in the ultimate decline of the papacy in the late Middle Ages.

Hadrian IV and Frederick Barbarossa first met on the occasion of the imperial coronation in Rome in 1155. The two men had collaborated against Arnold of Brescia, but thereafter they became enemies. At their initial encounter, Hadrian insisted that Frederick follow ancient tradition and lead the papal mule.* At first Frederick refused to humble himself in such a manner, but when it appeared that there would be no coronation at all, he grudgingly submitted. This small conflict was symbolic of far greater ones, for Hadrian and his successors proved to be implacable opponents of Frederick's drive to win control of the Lombard cities.

The Lombard struggle reached its height in the pontificate of Alexander III (1159–81), Hadrian's successor. Shrewd and learned, Alexander was the greatest pope of the twelfth century and Frederick Barbarossa's most formidable opponent. Whereas most of the early reform popes had been monks, Alexander and many of his successors were canon lawyers. Hildebrand himself had urged the study of canon law and the formulation of canonical collections in order to provide intellectual ammunition to support papal claims. During the later eleventh and twelfth centuries the study of canon law was pursued vigorously in north Italian schools, particularly the great law school at Bologna, and a good number of twelfth and thirteenth century popes were products of these schools. Alexander III was one of the ablest of them.

Determined to prevent Frederick Barbarossa from establishing himself strongly in northern Italy, Alexander rallied the Lombard towns that had long been engaged in intercity warfare but now combined forces against the empire. They formed an association called the Lombard League and organized a powerful interurban army. Frederick had meanwhile thrown his support behind a rival claimant to the papal throne, and Alexander responded by excommunicating the emperor. There followed a prolonged struggle involving Alexander, Barbarossa, and the Lombard League, ending in the total victory of the Lombard army at the battle of Legnano in 1176.

---

*The tradition of ceremonial mule-leading seems to have originated in the eighth-century forgery, the "Donation of Constantine."

THE HOLY ROMAN EMPIRE IN 1190

Barbarossa submitted with as much good cheer as he could manage. He granted *de facto* independence to the Lombard cities in return for their admission of a vague imperial overlordship. Pope and emperor tearfully embraced. Barbarossa led Alexander's mule and promised to be a dutiful son of the Roman See.

But Barbarossa did not abandon his designs on Italy; he merely shifted his theater of operations. Leaving Lombardy severely alone, he redirected his efforts southward and succeeded in gaining control of Tuscany, the rich province just to the north of the Papal States. At about the same time he arranged a marriage between his son and the future heiress of the Norman kingdom of southern Italy and Sicily—a marriage that ultimately brought that opulent realm into the imperial fold. Outmaneuvered and outwitted, the papacy faced the chilling prospect of imperial encirclement. In 1180 Barbarossa tightened his hold on Germany by crushing the most formidable of his vassals, Henry the Lion, the Welf duke of Saxony. After Alexander III's death in 1181, the papacy ceased for a time to be a serious threat, and the far-sighted emperor was at the height of his power in 1190 when he died while leading his army toward the Holy Land on the Third Crusade.

Henry VI: 1190–97

Barbarossa had taken pains to circumvent the princely policy of elective monarchy by forcing the princes, prior to his death, to elect his eldest son, Henry VI. In 1190 Henry succeeded to the German throne without difficulty, and in 1194 he made good his claim to the Kingdom of Sicily. The Papal States were now an island completely surrounded by Holy Roman Empire, and the papacy was powerless to alter the situation. The bounteous revenues of southern Italy and Sicily fattened the imperial.purse. The territories under imperial rule had never been so extensive.

But for an age in which the emperor had to remain always on the watch for regional rebellion, particularly among his great vassals in Germany, the imperial frontiers had become dangerously overextended. It remained uncertain whether a single monarch could rule Italy and Germany concurrently. Whether Henry VI might have accomplished this task we cannot tell, for he died prematurely in 1197 leaving as his heir his infant son, Frederick II. The problems the empire faced in 1197 would have taxed the ablest of leaders, yet at this moment imperial leadership failed. The papacy had its opportunity.

The High Noon of the Medieval Papacy: Innocent III

During the twelfth century, the papacy lost much of its former zealous reform spirit as it evolved into a huge, complex administrative institution. Revenues flowed into its treasury from all the states of Western Christendom; bishops traveled vast distances to make their spiritual submission to the Roman pontiff; the papal curia served as a court of last appeal for an immense network of ecclesiastical courts across Christendom. Papal authority over the European Church had increased immeasurably since the mid-eleventh century. And as the dream of papal monarchy came nearer realization, the traditional theory of papal supremacy over Christian society was increasingly magnified and elaborated by the canon lawyers. These subtle ecclesiastical scholars were beginning to dominate the papal curia and, like Alexander III, to occupy the papal throne itself.

Innocent III (1198–1216), the greatest of all the lawyer popes, came to power in the year following Emperor Henry VI's death. It was he who seized the opportunity offered by the succession of an infant to the throne of the overextended empire. Innocent was history's most powerful pope—an astute diplomat, an imperious, self-confident aristocrat who, while genuinely pious, was aloof from the surging religious emotionalism of the humbler Christians of his age. He had the wisdom and sensitivity to support the Franciscans, and the ruthlessness to mount the Albigensian Crusade.*

Animated by the theory of papal monarchy in its most uncompromising form, Innocent forced his will on the leading monarchs of Europe, playing off one ruler against another with consummate skill. In the course of a long struggle with King John of England over the appointment of an archbishop of Canterbury, Innocent laid John's kingdom under interdict, threatened to depose John himself, and urged King Philip Augustus of France to send an army against him. The struggle ended with John's complete submission. Innocent's man was installed as archbishop of Canterbury, and John consented to papal lordship over England.

Innocent had earlier clashed with Philip Augustus over the king's refusal to repudiate an uncanonical second marriage and return to his first wife. After laying France under interdict and excommunicating Philip, Innocent obtained his submission.† It has already been shown how Innocent instigated the Fourth Crusade, which was aimed at Jerusalem but ended in Constantinople, and how he mounted crusades against the Albigensians and the Spanish Moors. These diverse activities illustrate the unprecedented political and moral sway that Innocent exercised over Christendom.

A mighty force in the secular politics of his age, Innocent also dominated the Church more completely than any of his predecessors had done. In 1215 he summoned a general Church council in Rome—the Fourth Lateran Council—which produced a remarkable quantity of significant ecclesiastical legislation: clerical dress was strictly regulated, a moratorium was declared on new religious orders, Jews were required to wear special badges, clerics were forbidden to participate in the ancient Germanic legal procedure of the ordeal,‡ fees for the administration of sacraments were forbidden, cathedral churches were ordered to maintain schools and to provide sermons at their services, and all Catholics were bound to receive the sacraments of penance and the

---

*See pp. 167-168.

†Philip Augustus's submission was less complete, however, than might have been wished. His controversial second wife had died—conveniently but naturally—and his reconciliation with his first wife was a mere formality.

‡See pp. 17-18.

eucharist at least once a year. The efficient organization of the Fourth Lateran Council, and the degree to which Pope Innocent dominated and directed it, are illustrated by the fact that the churchmen in attendance—more than twelve hundred bishops, abbots, and priests—produced their important new legislation in meetings that lasted a total of only three weeks. By contrast, the fifteenth-century Council of Basel met off and on for eighteen years and the Council of Trent for nineteen.

The range of Innocent III's activities was seemingly boundless. But throughout his pontificate one political issue took precedence over all others: the problem of the German imperial succession. It was a marvelously complex problem that taxed even Pope Innocent's diplomatic skill. Involved were the questions of whether or not the Kingdom of Sicily would remain in imperial hands, whether the imperial throne would pass to the Welfs or the Hohenstaufens, and whether an accommodation could be achieved between the traditionally hostile forces of papacy and empire. The German succession problem also touched the interests of the French and English monarchies: the Welf claimant, Otto of Brunswick, was a nephew and favorite of King John of England and could usually count on his support, whereas the Hohenstaufens enjoyed the friendship of the French king, Philip Augustus.

The direct Hohenstaufen heir was the infant Frederick, son of the late Henry VI. But since a child could hardly be expected to wage a successful fight for the throne in these anxious years, the Hohenstaufen claim was taken up by Frederick's uncle, Philip of Swabia, younger brother of the former emperor. The young Frederick remained in Sicily while Philip of Swabia and the Welf, Otto of Brunswick, battled for the imperial throne. Innocent recognized the German princes' right to elect their own monarch but, as it happened, Philip and Otto had both been elected, each by a different group of nobles. In the case of a disputed election such as this, Innocent claimed the right to intervene by virtue of the traditional papal privilege of crowning the emperor. He delayed his decision considerably, and in the meantime civil war raged in Germany. At length he settled on Otto of Brunswick. Otto had promised to support the papal interests in Germany and to abandon almost entirely the policy of imperial control of the German church. Further, a Welf emperor would have no claim on the Hohenstaufen kingdom of Sicily, and Otto's coronation would therefore realize the papal goal of separating the two realms.

Despite Innocent's decision, the civil war continued in Germany until Philip of Swabia's death in 1208. Otto was crowned emperor in 1209, but now, having no rival to oppose him, he repudiated his promises to Innocent, asserted his mastery over the German church, and even launched an invasion of southern Italy. Innocent responded to this breach of faith by deposing and anathematizing Otto and throwing his support behind the young Frederick of Hohenstaufen. From its inception the Kingdom of Sicily had been, at least nominally, a papal vassal state, and Innocent claimed the overlord's privilege of being guardian of its underage king. But before undertaking to back Frederick, Innocent wrung promises from him: to abdicate as king of Sicily and sever the Sicilian kingdom from the empire, to lead a crusade, to follow the spiritual direction of the papacy, and in general to confirm the pledges that Otto of Brunswick had made and then broken.

Innocent's decision in favor of Frederick revived the Hohenstaufen cause in Germany and renewed the civil war. Innocent employed all his diplomatic skill and leverage to win over German nobles to Frederick's cause. He was supported in these maneuverings by King Philip Augustus of France, now on friendly terms with the papacy, traditionally sympathetic to the Hohenstaufens, and hostile to the English and their Welf allies.

The complex currents of international politics in Innocent's pontificate reached their climax and their resolution in 1214. King John invaded France from the west while Otto of Brunswick led a powerful army against Philip Augustus from the east—an army heavily subsidized by England and consisting of the combined forces of pro-Welf princes from Germany and the Low Countries. John's invasion bogged down and accomplished nothing; Otto's army met the forces of Philip Augustus in pitched battle at Bouvines and was decisively defeated.

The battle of Bouvines of 1214 was an epoch-making engagement. Philip Augustus emerged as Europe's mightiest monarch, Otto's imperial dreams were dashed, and Frederick became emperor in fact as well as in theory. Bouvines was a triumph not only for Philip Augustus and Frederick but also for Innocent III. His ward was now emperor-elect and was pledged to sever the kingdom of Sicily from Germany and free the German Church of imperial control.

Germany itself was in a state of chaos. The solid achievements of Frederick Barbarossa, which might have served as the foundation for a revival of imperial power, were compromised by the subsequent imperial involvement in the affairs of the Sicilian kingdom and were demolished by long years of dynastic strife, during which the German princes usurped royal privileges and royal lands on a vast scale. By the time of Innocent's death the imperial authority that Barbarossa had achieved was almost beyond recovery.

The policies of Innocent III were everywhere triumphant. Yet Innocent, by the very range of his political activites, had involved the papacy in secular affairs to such a degree that its spiritual authority was becoming tarnished. Innocent had won his battles, but he had chosen a dangerous battleground. His successors, lacking his skill and his luck, could do little to arrest the gradual ebbing of papal political authority during the middle and later decades of the thirteenth century and across the centuries that followed. For papal power was based ultimately on spiritual prestige, and the thirteenth-century popes, despite their piety, despite their continuing concern for ecclesiastical reform, were lawyers, administrators, and diplomats rather than charismatic spiritual leaders. The papacy was a mighty force in the world of the thirteenth century, but it was failing more and more to satisfy the spiritual hunger of devoted Christians. Piety remained strong, but many of the pious were coming to doubt that the papal government, with its vast wealth and bureaucratic efficiency, was indeed the true spiritual center of the apostolic Church and the citadel of Christ's kingdom on earth. The popes were doing what they had to do, and in playing the game of international politics they continued to dream of a regenerated Christian society led and inspired by the Church. But as time went on they dreamed less and plotted more, permitting their political means to overshadow their spiritual ends.

The impressive diplomatic success of Innocent III's pontificate ended abruptly with his death in 1216. Once Innocent was gone, his former ward, Frederick II, now a grown man, made it clear that he would ignore his promises as completely as Otto of Brunswick had earlier done. Frederick ruled exactly as he pleased, and in the course of his long reign he became the medieval papacy's most ferocious adversary.

Frederick II (1211-1250)

Frederick II, whose Sicilian childhood had exposed him to several faiths, grew up to be a brilliant, anticlerical skeptic, more concerned with his harem and his exotic menagerie than with his soul. He dazzled his contemporaries and earned the name *Stupor Mundi*, the "Wonder of the World." His vision of unifying all Italy and making it the nucleus of his empire earned him the hatred of the papacy. Some churchmen regarded Frederick quite literally as the incarnate antichrist.

Frederick II was a talented, many-sided man—perhaps the most flamboyant product of an intensely creative age. He was a writer of considerable skill and an amateur scientist, curious about the world around him, but in some matters deeply superstitious. After much delay he kept his promise to lead a crusade (1228), but instead of fighting the Muslims he negotiated with them and did so with such success that Jerusalem itself came into his hands for a time. The amicable spirit of Frederick's crusade against the infidel struck many churchmen as unholy, and its success infuriated them.

Frederick II ruled his kingdom of Sicily in the autocratic and enlightened manner of a Renaissance despot. He established a uniform legal code, tightened and broadened the centralized administrative system of his Norman-Sicilian predecessors, encouraged agriculture, industry, and commerce, abolished interior tariffs and tolls, and founded a great university in Naples. Although he had promised Innocent III that he would sever Sicily from his empire, he made no effort to keep his word. He had always preferred his urbane, sunny Sicilian homeland to the dark forests and gloomy castles of Germany. Like Frederick Barbarossa, he tried to expand the royal demesne in Germany and to enforce the feudal obligations of his great German vassals. But he did so half-heartedly. For to Frederick II, Germany was important chiefly as a source of money and military strength with which to carry out his policy of bringing all Italy under his rule.

As it happened, this policy proved disastrous to the Holy Roman Empire.

Frederick's aggressions in Italy evoked the opposition of a revived Lombard League and the implacable hostility of the papacy. He gave up lands and royal rights in Germany with an almost careless abandon in order to keep the peace with the German princes and win their support for his persistent but inconclusive Italian campaigns. In the end, he was even obliged to tax his beloved Sicily to the point of impoverishment in order to support his endless wars. Astute lawyer-popes such as Gregory IX and Innocent IV devoted all their diplomatic talents and spiritual sanctions to blocking Frederick's enterprises, building alliances to oppose him, and hurling anathemas against him. In 1245 Innocent IV presided over a universal council of the Church, at Lyons, which condemned and excommunicated the emperor. Frederick was deposed, a rival emperor was elected in his place, and a crusade was called to rid the empire of its ungodly tyrant. Revolts now broke out against Frederick throughout his empire. The royal estates in Germany slipped more and more from his grasp, and his Italian holdings were riddled with rebellion. Against this unhappy background Frederick II died in 1250.

The Decline of the Medieval Empire

In a very real sense, the hopes of the medieval empire died with him. His son succeeded him in Germany but died in 1254 after a brief and unsuccessful reign. For the next nineteen years, Germany suffered a crippling interregnum (1254–73) during which no recognized emperor held the throne. In 1273 a vastly weakened Holy Roman Empire reemerged with papal blessing under Rudolph of Hapsburg, the first emperor of a family that was destined to play a crucial role in modern European history. Rudolph attempted to rebuild the shattered royal demesne and shore up the foundations of imperial rule, but it was much too late. The monarchy's one hope had been to strengthen and extend the crown lands to the point where they provided resources overwhelmingly superior to those of any magnate. This was the policy on which the medieval French monarchy had risen to a position of dominance in France; it was the policy that Frederick Barbarossa had pursued so promisingly in Germany. But it aroused the unremitting opposition of the German princes, who had no desire to see their own rights and territories eaten away by royal expansion and would much prefer to extend their own principalities at the expense of the crown.

The civil strife during Innocent's pontificate, the Italian involvements of Frederick II, and the Interregnum of 1254–73 gave the princes their opportunity, and by 1273 the crown lands were hopelessly shrunken and disorganized. Germany was now drifting irreversibly toward the loose confederation of principalities and the anemic elective monarchy that characterized its constitutional structure from the fourteenth to the later-nineteenth century. The tragic failure of the medieval empire doomed Germany to six hundred years of disunity—a heritage which may well have contributed to her catastrophic career in the first half of the present century.

Italy, too, emerged from the struggles of the High Middle Ages hopelessly fragmented. The Papal States, straddling the peninsula, were torn with unrest and disaffection, and the papacy had trouble maintaining its authority over the inhabitants of Rome itself. North of the Papal States, Tuscany and Lombardy had become a chaos of totally independent warring city-states—Florence, Siena, Venice, Milan, and many others—whose rivalries would form the political backdrop of the Italian Renaissance.

Southern Italy and Sicily

The Kingdom of Sicily, established by the Normans and cherished by the Hohenstaufens, passed shortly after Frederick II's death to his illegitimate son, Manfred. The papacy, determined to rid Italy of Hohenstaufen rule, bent all its energies toward securing Manfred's downfall. At length it offered the Sicilian crown to Charles of Anjou, a younger brother of King Louis IX of France (St. Louis). The pope's intention was that the power of France be used to drive Manfred out of the Sicilian kingdom. Charles of Anjou—dour, cruel, and ambitious—defeated and killed Manfred in 1266 and established a new, French dynasty on the throne of the kingdom.

The inhabitants of the realm, particularly those on the island of Sicily, had become accustomed to Hohenstaufen rule and resented Charles of Anjou. They looked on his French soldiers as an army of occupation. When, on Easter Monday 1282, a French soldier mishandled a young married woman on her way to evening vesper services in Palermo, he was struck down, and on all sides was raised the cry, "Death to the French!" The incident resulted in a spontaneous uprising and a general massacre of Frenchmen, which spread swiftly throughout the island. When the French retaliated, the Sicilians offered the crown to Peter III of Aragon, Manfred's son-in-law, who claimed the Hohenstaufen inheritance and led an army to Sicily.

There ensued a long, bloody, indecisive struggle known by the romantic name, "the War of the Sicilian Vespers." For twenty years Charles of Anjou and his successors, backed by the French monarchy and the papacy, fought against the Sicilians and Aragonese. In the end, southern Italy remained under Charles of Anjou's heirs, who ruled it from Naples, while Sicily passed under the control of the kings of Aragon. The dispute between France and Aragon over southern Italy and Sicily persisted for generations and was an important factor in the politics of early modern Europe.

The chaotic strife of the thirteenth century destroyed Sicilian prosperity. Once the wealthiest and most enlightened state in Italy, the Kingdom of Sicily became pauperized and divided—a victim of international politics and of the ruthless struggle between Church and state.

The Papacy After Innocent III

To judge by the disintegration of the Holy Roman Empire in the thirteenth century, one might conclude that the papacy had won an overwhelming victory. But the triumph was an empty one. As popes like Innocent III, Gregory IX, and Innocent IV became increasingly involved in power politics, their spiritual role was more and more obscured. In the thirteenth century the papacy's international religious mission was being steadily subordinated to its local political interests. Slowly, almost imperceptibly, it was losing its hold on the hearts of European Christians. Papal excommunication, after several centuries of overuse—often for political purposes—was no longer the terrifying weapon it once had been. To call a crusade against Frederick II was doubtless an effective means of harassment, but the crusading ideal was debased in the process.

As the papacy became a great political power and a big business, it found itself in need of ever-increasing revenues. By the end of the thirteenth century the papal tax system was admirably efficient, with the result that the papacy acquired an unsavory reputation for greed. As one contemporary observer complained, the supreme pastor of Christendom was supposed to lead Christ's flock but not to fleece it. Ironically, the fiscal and political cast of the later medieval papacy came as a direct consequence of its earlier dream of becoming the spiritual dynamo of a reformed Christendom. Rising to prominence in the eleventh century upon the floodtide of the new popular piety, the papacy became in the twelfth and thirteenth centuries increasingly insensitive to the deeper spiritual aspirations of Christians, as it became more and more absorbed in the problems of politics.

The papacy humbled the empire only to be humbled itself by the rising power of the new centralized monarchies of northern Europe. By the end of the thirteenth century a new concept of royal sovereignty was in the air. The kings of England and France were becoming less and less willing to tolerate the existence of a semi-independent, highly privileged, internationally controlled Church within their realms. By endeavoring to bring these ecclesiastical "states within states" under royal control, the two monarchies encountered vigorous papal opposition. The issue of papal versus royal control of the Church was an old one, but the ancient controversy now took a new form. The growing monarchies of the late thirteenth century found themselves increasingly in need of money. This was particularly true after 1294 when England and France became locked in a series of costly wars. Both monarchies adopted the novel policy of systematically taxing the clergy of their realms, and Pope Boniface VIII (1294–1303) retaliated in 1296 with the papal bull *Clericis Laicos* that expressly forbade this practice. Once again, Church and state were at an impasse.

Boniface VIII was another lawyer-pope—proud, aged, and inflexible—whose visions of papal power transcended even Innocent III's. He made it known that the pope is the "emperor sent from heaven" and "can do whatever God can do." But Boniface failed to grasp the momentous implications of the new centralized monarchies of late thirteenth-century Europe. His great weakness was his inability to bend his stupendous concepts of papal authority to the realities of contemporary European politics.

In King Philip the Fair* of France (1285–1314) Boniface had a ruthless antagonist. Philip ignored the papal bull prohibiting clerical taxation; he set his agents to work spreading scandalous rumors about the pope's morals and exerted financial pressure on Rome by cutting off all papal taxes from his French realm. Boniface was obliged to submit for the moment, and Philip taxed his clergy unopposed. But a vast influx of pilgrims into Rome in the Jubilee year of 1300 restored the pope's confidence. He withdrew his concession to Philip the Fair on clerical taxation and in 1302 issued the famous bull *Unam Sanctam,* which asserted the doctrine of papal monarchy in uncompromising terms: ". . . We declare, announce, affirm and define that, for every human creature, to be subject to the Roman pontiff is absolutely necessary for salvation."

Philip the Fair now summoned a kingdom-wide assembly, and before it he accused Boniface of every imaginable crime from murder to black magic to keeping a demon as a pet. A small French military force crossed into Italy in 1303 and took Boniface prisoner at his palace at Anagni with the intention of bringing him to France for trial. Anagni, the antithesis of Canossa, symbolized the humiliation of the medieval papacy. The French plan failed—Boniface was freed by local townspeople a couple of days later—but the proud old pope died shortly thereafter, outraged and chagrined that armed Frenchmen had dared to lay hands on his person.

The great age of the medieval papacy was now at an end. In 1305 the cardinals elected the Frenchman Clement V (1305–14), who pursued a policy of cautious subservience to the French throne. Clement submitted on the question of clerical taxation and repudiated *Unam Sanctam.* He even conceded that Philip the Fair, in accusing Pope Boniface, had shown "praiseworthy zeal." A few years after his election, Clement abandoned faction-ridden Rome for a new papal capital at Avignon on the Rhône river, where the papacy remained for the next several generations. At Avignon the papal administration continued to grow, and papal spiritual prestige continued to diminish. The town of Avignon belonged to the papacy, not to the French crown, yet France's enemies could never be confident of the Avignon papacy's political objectivity. The French kings were strong, and they were nearby.

It is easy to criticize the inflexibility of a Boniface VIII or the limpness of a Clement V, but the waning of papal authority in the later Middle Ages did not result primarily from personal shortcomings. Instead, it stemmed from an ever-widening gulf between papal government and the spiritual thirst of ordinary Christians, combined with the hostility to Catholic internationalism on the part of increasingly powerful centralized states such as England and France. It would be grossly unfair to describe the high medieval papacy as "corrupt." Between 1050 and 1300 men of good intentions and high purposes

*That is, the handsome; see pp. 226-228.

sat on the papal throne. Not satisfied merely to chide the society of their day by innocuous moralizing from the sidelines, they plunged into the world and struggled to sanctify it. Tragically, perhaps inevitably, they soiled their hands.

CHRONOLOGY OF THE PAPAL-IMPERIAL CONFLICT

1039-1056: Reign of Henry III
    1046: Henry III deposes three rival popes,
        inaugurates papal reform movement
1049-1054: Pontificate of Leo IX
1056-1106: Reign of Henry IV
    1059: Papal Election Decree
1073-1085: Pontificate of Gregory VII
    1075: Gregory VII bans lay investiture
    1076: Gregory VII excommunicates and deposes Henry IV
    1077: Henry IV humbles himself at Canossa
    1080: Second excommunication and deposition of Henry IV
1088-1099: Pontificate of Urban II
1106-1125: Reign of Henry V
    1122: Concordat of Worms
1152-1190: Reign of Frederick I, "Barbarossa"
1154-1159: Pontificate of Hadrian IV
    1155: Execution of Arnold of Brescia
1159-1181: Pontificate of Alexander III
    1176: Lombards defeat Barbarossa at Legnano
    1180: Barbarossa defeats Duke Henry the Lion of Saxony
1190-1197: Reign of Henry VI
    1194: Henry VI becomes king of Sicily.
1198-1216: Pontificate of Innocent III
1211-1250: Reign of Frederick II
    1214: Philip Augustus defeats Otto of Brunswick at Bouvines
    1215: Fourth Lateran Council
1227-1241: Pontificate of Gregory IX
1243-1254: Pontificate of Innocent IV
    1245: Council of Lyons
1254-1273: Interregnum in Germany
1273-1291: Reign of Rudolph of Hapsburg
1282-1302: War of the Sicilian Vespers
1294-1303: Pontificate of Boniface VIII
    1302: Boniface VIII issues *Unam Sanctam*
    1303: Boniface VIII humiliated at Anagni
1305-1314: Pontificate of Clement V. Papacy moves to Avignon

Chapter 12

ॐ

England
and
France

The Anglo-Norman Monarchy

While empire and papacy were engaged in their drawn-out struggle, England and France were evolving into centralized states. Strong monarchy came to England sooner than to France, yet in the long run it was the English who were the more successful in limiting royal power. French royal absolutism and English parliamentary monarchy are both rooted in the High Middle Ages.

More than that, the rise of effective royal law and administration was an early, crucial step in the evolution of the political environment that surrounds us today. The secret of writing entertaining administrative history has yet to be discovered, but the tedious details of medieval governance in England and France mark the genesis of the modern state and all that it implies. These details can be overlooked only at the peril of missing one of the most fundamental medieval contributions to modern civilization.

The Anglo-Saxon period of English history came to an end when Duke William of Normandy won the English crown with his victory at Hastings in 1066. In the generations that followed, England was tied to the continent, for her kings ruled wide dominions on both sides of the English Channel. As kings

ॐ

of England they were masterless, but the French monarchy claimed the overlordship of their possessions in France. England's continental involvement continued, with various ups and downs, from 1066 until the mid-sixteenth century. It led to generations of hostility between the two monarchies, but it was also a source of power and wealth to the kings of England. Throughout much of the period between 1066 and 1204, England was merely one important component of a great trans-channel realm that played a dominant part in twelfth-century politics. When the English monarchy lost the bulk of its French dominions in 1204 its power declined sharply, while the kings of France became the foremost monarchs of thirteenth-century Christendom.

The English kingdom that William the Conqueror won in 1066 was already centralized and well-governed by the standards of mid-eleventh-century Europe. Its kings had enjoyed the direct allegiance of all their subjects. Its army was subject only to the commands of the king or his representatives; private armies and private war were largely unknown. An informal royal council of nobles and household officials known as the *witenagemot* advised the king on important matters and approved the succession of new kings. The chief officers in the royal household were gradually coming to assume important administrative responsibilities: issuing writs that carried royal decisions and commands to local officials in the countryside, administering the royal finances, and performing other governmental functions. Although the pre-Conquest royal household was constantly on the move, traveling around England from one royal estate to another, the treasury had become fixed permanently at Winchester in Wessex.

England in 1066 had long been divided into regional units known as shires (or counties), each with its own shire court and administered by a royal officer called a "shire reeve," or sheriff. The sheriff presided over the shire court, the membership of which was drawn from important men of the district. The customs and procedures of the shire courts were rooted in the traditions of the locality rather than in royal mandates. In operation as in membership, the shire courts were local phenomena and are often described as folk courts. The sheriff, too, was usually a local figure whose sympathies were apt to be divided between his native shire and the king. The subtle interplay between local initiative and royal authority—a significant characteristic of Anglo-Saxon government—persisted over the post-conquest centuries to give medieval England a political balance lacking in many contemporary states.

The English shires were subdivided into smaller administrative units known as hundreds. Each hundred had its own court which handled less important cases than those brought to the shire courts. Like the shire courts, the hundred courts were local in membership and legal custom yet were presided over by royal officials. By 1066 a number of hundreds had passed into the hands of private lords—lay or ecclesiastical—in which case the royal official was replaced by an official of the lord.

The sheriff was responsible for administering the unique Anglo-Saxon land tax, the danegeld, which varied somewhat in amount but in most instances provided the crown with about ten pounds from each hundred. It was also the sheriff's task to assemble the shire's military contingent when the king summoned the army—the *fyrd,* as it was then called. Our evidence suggests that by 1066 it had become customary for each hundred to provide about twenty armed men for the fyrd and to supply their sustenance during their period of duty.

Such were some of the more important institutions which William the Conqueror inherited when he won the English crown. He came to England not as an open aggressor but as a legitimate claimant to the throne, related (distantly) to the Anglo-Saxon royal family and designated—so he claimed—by King Edward the Confessor who died childless early in 1066. On the Confessor's death, the witenagemot had chosen his brother-in-law, Harold earl of Wessex, to succeed him. But William regarded Harold as a usurper, and when Harold was killed at Hastings and his army put to flight, William took the position that he was passing into his rightful inheritance. Although another five years were required to put down the last vestiges of English resistance, William was crowned king of England in London on Christmas Day, 1066, and turned at once to the problem of governing his new realm.

Taking up his role as Edward the Confessor's proper successor, William promised to preserve the laws and customs of Edward's day. Indeed, it was to his advantage to do so, since many of these customs were exceedingly beneficial to the monarchy. He maintained the danegeld, as well he might; he continued to summon the fyrd whenever he needed it; he perpetuated the folk courts of shire and hundred; and he drew needed strength from the Anglo-Saxon custom of general allegiance to the crown.

The Conqueror preserved much, but he also built energetically on the system that he inherited. The changes and additions that he introduced were derived in part from customs that he had known in Normandy, in part from his own creative imagination, and in part from his unique position as unquestioned master of a conquered land. If the government of Anglo-Saxon England was remarkably strong, the government of Norman England was far stronger, and its strength was in some measure a consequence of William the Conqueror's practical intelligence.

In the years immediately following the conquest, William divided much of England among the leading warriors of his victorious army, thereby introducing into the kingdom a new, knightly, French-speaking aristocracy. He established a feudal regime in England more-or-less on the Norman pattern but more systematically organized and more directly subordinate to the royal will. Most English estates, both lay and ecclesiastical, were transformed into fiefs, held by crown vassals in return for a specified number of mounted knights and certain other feudal obligations. The greatest of the new magnates tended to acquire their lands piecemeal as the kingdom passed progressively under William's control, with the result that their estates were scattered across various shires rather than coalescing into territorial blocs. This dispersion of great fiefs shaped England's political future, giving the baronage a kingdom-wide perspective at a time when France and Germany—segmented into regional princedoms—remained politically provincial. And William was careful to reserve for his own royal demesne about a sixth of the lands of England (similarly scattered), so that he and his successors would not be mere nominal overlords like the early Capetian kings of France and the later Hohenstaufen emperors in Germany and Italy.

The English crown vassals, or tenants-in-chief, in order to raise the numerous knights required by the monarchy, subdivided portions of their fiefs into smaller fiefs and granted them to knightly subvassals. In other words, the process of subinfeudation proceeded rather in the way that it had centuries earlier on the continent, but much more swiftly and systematically. As a byproduct of the establishment of feudalism in England, scores of castles were quickly erected across the land by the king and his barons. Most of these early castles were simply square wooden towers built on earthen mounds and encircled by wooden palisades. Only later did they become elaborate works of stone.

Feudalism in England was by no means accompanied by political disintegration as it had been in Carolingian Frankland. With the resources of their vast royal domain on which to draw, the Norman kings of England were firmly established at the apex of the feudal pyramid and were generally successful in keeping their vassals under tight rein. Their authoritative position in the Anglo-Norman feudal structure owed much to the centralizing traditions of the Anglo-Saxon monarchy. The new barons established feudal courts, as had been their custom in Normandy, but alongside these baronial courts there persisted the older courts of shire and hundred. The new feudal army could be an effective force, but when it proved inadequate or unreliable, the monarchy would summon the Old English fyrd or use the royal revenues to hire mercenary troops.

Feudal particularism was diminished by the Anglo-Saxon custom of general allegiance to the crown, which enabled the Norman kings to claim the direct and primary loyalty of every vassal and subvassal in the English feudal hierarchy. A knight's allegiance to his lord was now secondary to his allegiance to the crown. Private war between vassals was prohibited, and private castles could be built only by royal license. In brief, the new institution of feudalism was molded by the powerful Anglo-Saxon tradition of royal supremacy, and by William the Conqueror's authority, into something far more centralized than the feudalism of the continent.

On the Conqueror's death, his kingdom passed in turn to his two sons, William II (1087–1100) and Henry I (1100-35). Both were strong leaders, but Henry I was the abler of the two. A skillful diplomat and administrative innovator, Henry I rid England of rebellion and exploited the growing prosperity of his day through heavy taxes. He was not a kindly man, but his was an age in which firmness and military strength were the chief requisites to successful rule and excessive geniality was bad politics. His great service to his English and Norman subjects was his severe enforcement of the peace.

The reigns of William the Conqueror and his sons witnessed a significant growth in royal administrative institutions. The unique survey of land holdings known as *Domesday Book*—the product of a comprehensive census of the realm undertaken by royal order in 1086—testifies to the administrative vigor of William the Conqueror's regime. Between 1066 and 1135 the royal administration became steadily more elaborate and efficient. By the close of Henry I's reign royal justices were traveling about England hearing cases in the shire courts, extending the king's jurisdiction far and wide across the land. The baronial courts and ecclesiastical courts continued to function, as did the ancient folk courts of shire and hundred (under tightening royal control). But royal justice was on the march, and Henry I's innovations mark the initial step in a long, significant process whereby folk and private courts were gradually overshadowed by the king's courts.

Administrative efficiency and royal centralization were the keynotes of Henry I's reign. Royal dues were collected systematically by the king's sheriffs, who delivered their revenues to a remarkable new central auditing board known as the *exchequer*. A powerful royal bureaucracy was gradually coming into being. The growing efficiency of the exchequer and the expansion of royal justice were both motivated in part by the king's desire for larger revenues. For the more cases the royal justices handled, the more fines went into the royal coffers; the more closely the sheriffs were supervised, the less likely it was that royal taxes would stick to their fingers. The Norman kings discovered that strong government was good business.

The Anglo-Norman church was ornamented by two exceptionally able archbishops of Canterbury: Lanfranc (d. 1089) and St. Anselm (d. 1109). Both were theologians; both, in different ways, were deeply involved in the politics of their day; and both were Italians who had migrated to the Benedictine monastery of Bec in Normandy.

William the Conqueror drew Lanfranc from Normandy in 1070 to become archbishop of Canterbury and primate of the English Church. William and Lanfranc were contemporaries of Hildebrand and could not help but become involved in the raging controversy over ecclesiastical reform. The king and archbishop were both sympathetic to reform, but neither was receptive to the Gregorian notion of an independent Church under tight papal control. William was more than willing to work toward moderate church reform, and Lanfranc supported him vigorously. But when Gregory insisted on becoming William's overlord, the Conqueror flatly refused: "I have not consented to pay fealty nor will I now, because I never promised it, nor do I find that my predecessors ever paid it to your predecessors."

Gregory VII, preoccupied with his struggle against the Holy Roman emperor, could not afford to alienate William, who was, after all, friendly toward reform. Accordingly, the specific issue of lay investiture did not emerge in England until after Gregory's death. It was raised by St. Anselm, who had followed Lanfranc to Bec and was chosen in 1093 to succeed him as archbishop of Canterbury. Lanfranc and William the Conqueror had worked in close cooperation with one another, but St. Anselm's relations with the Norman monarchy were turbulent. Already advanced in years when he assumed the archbishopric, Anselm was the greatest theologian of his age and perhaps the most profound philosopher that Western Christendom had produced since St. Augustine's time. He was also devoted to the Gregorian notion of ecclesiastical independence.

This notion no Norman king could accept, and Anselm came into bitter conflict with both William II and Henry I. He spent much of his tenure as archbishop in exile, and it was not until 1107 that a compromise on the investiture issue was ratified between Henry, the papacy, and himself. As in the later Concordat of Worms, the agreement of 1107 prohibited lay investiture as such, but permitted the king to retain a certain control over important ecclesiastical appointments. Ecclesiastical tenants-in-chief were to continue their traditional practice of rendering homage to the king. More important than the settlement itself is the fact that Anselm died two years thereafter, and Henry, rid at last of his troublesome saint, dominated the English church through pressure and patronage. Anselm had won his point, but the Church remained generally subservient to the Norman monarchy.

Henry I's death in 1135 was followed by a period of unrest brought on by a disputed royal succession. Henry was survived by a daughter, Matilda, who was wed to Geoffrey Plantagenet, count of Anjou. Henry had arranged the marriage with the hope of healing the long rivalry between the two great powers of northern France: Normandy and Anjou. In the years just prior to Henry's death Matilda bore him two grandsons, the eldest of whom, Henry Plantagenet, would ultimately rule a vast territory including Anjou, Aquitaine, Normandy, and England. But when the old king died, Henry Plantagenet was only two years old, and the crown was seized by Henry I's nephew, Stephen of Blois (1135-1154). For nineteen troubled years Stephen struggled with Matilda, Geoffrey, and their growing son for control of the Anglo-Norman realm, while the barons, some supporting one side and some the other, built unlicensed castles and usurped royal rights. Tormented by warfare, people of all classes looked back longingly toward the peaceful days of Henry I.

Henry II (1154–1189)

Toward the end of Stephen's embattled reign, Henry Plantagenet had grown to vigorous manhood, and his prospects were brightening year by year. He became duke of Normandy in 1150 and inherited Anjou on the death of his father Geoffrey in 1151. His territories were extended still further by his marriage in 1152 to Eleanor, heiress of the large southern French duchy of Aquitaine. In 1153 King Stephen was forced by his declining military fortunes to name Henry as his heir, and when Stephen died the following year, Henry peacefully assumed the throne as King Henry II of England (1154–89). He now held sway over an immense constellation of territories north and south of the English Channel, which historians have termed the "Angevin Empire"—Angevin because Henry II and his heirs descended in the male line from counts of Anjou. On the map, these Angevin dominions dwarf the modest territory controlled by the king of France. But Henry II, and his sons who succeeded him, had difficulty in keeping order throughout these vast, diverse territories. They were a source of wealth, power, and prestige to their rulers, but a burden as well.

Henry was an energetic, brilliant, exuberant man—short, burly, and red-headed. Named after his grandfather, he was far more flamboyant than Henry I yet ruled in his imperious tradition and consciously imitated him. In many respects he was a creature of his age—a product of the intellectual and cultural outburst of twelfth-century Europe. He was a literate monarch who consorted with scholars, encouraged the growth of towns, and presided over an age of economic boom. A chaos of feverish activity pervaded his court, which was constantly on the move and, in the opinion of one court scholar, was "a perfect portrait of hell."

Henry pursued the interdependent goals of preserving the Angevin dominions, strengthening royal authority, and increasing his revenues. He began his reign by ordering the destruction of unlicensed castles that English barons had thrown up during the previous anarchic period and was cautious thereafter in permitting new private castles to be built. At once he began to recover the royal privileges that had been eroding during Stephen's reign and, in some cases, to expand them considerably. During the thirty-five years of his rule in England, the royal administration grew in complexity and effectiveness. The maturity of Henry's exchequer is illustrated not only by a series of annual financial accounts—known as *Pipe Rolls*—but also by a comprehensive, detailed treatise on the exchequer's organization and methods—the *Dialogue of the Exchequer*—written by one of the king's financial officers. The royal secretarial office—the chancery—was similarly increasing in efficiency and scope. Indeed, the entire royal administration was growing more specialized, more professional, and more self-conscious. Separate administrative departments were evolving, and public records became fuller and more extensive. Many were delighted at the return of peace and order; others were uneasy over the steady rise of "Big Government."

Throughout the twelfth century, commerce was becoming ever more vigorous and the circulation of money was rapidly increasing. Under the pressure of royal ambition and the growing money economy, the older feudal relationship of service in return for land was giving way to wage service. By the time of Henry II it had become commonplace for feudal tenants-in-chief to pay scutage to the crown in lieu of their military-service obligation. Dues from the royal demesne estates were being collected in coin rather than in kind, and royal troops, servants, and administrators customarily served for wages. These trends can be traced back to the reign of Henry I and beyond, but under Henry II they were accelerating. The baronage remained powerful, but feudal

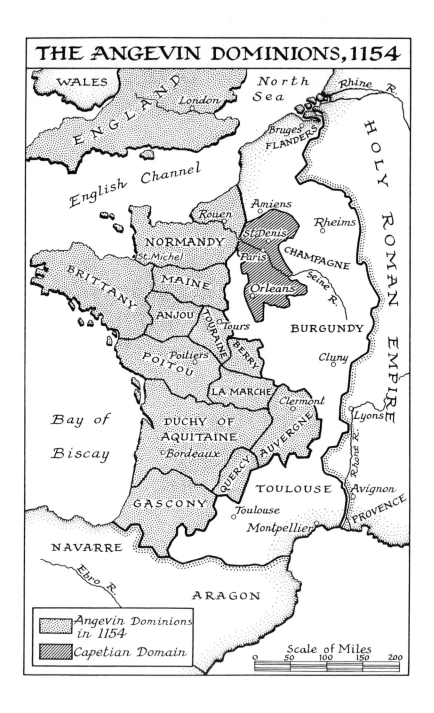

THE ANGEVIN DOMINIONS, 1154

WALES

ENGLAND

London

North
Sea

Rhine R.

English Channel

Bruges
FLANDERS

HOLY ROMAN EMPIRE

Amiens

Rouen

Rheims

St Denis

NORMANDY

Paris

CHAMPAGNE

St Michel

BRITTANY

MAINE

Seine R.

ANJOU

TOURAINE

Orleans

Tours

BURGUNDY

BERRY

Poitiers

POITOU

Cluny

LA MARCHE

Clermont

Bay of

Biscay

DUCHY OF
AQUITAINE

Lyons

AUVERGNE

Bordeaux

QUERCY

Rhone R.

TOULOUSE

Avignon

GASCONY

Toulouse

PROVENCE

Montpellier

NAVARRE

Ebro R.

ARAGON

Angevin Dominions
in 1154

Capetian Domain

Scale of Miles
0   50   100   150   200

obligations were being translated into fiscal terms. Both the economy and the administration were steadily increasing in complexity and sophistication.

Of necessity, the authority of the king and the efficiency of his central administrative system depended upon an effective local government and the maintenance of strong bonds between court and countryside. The two were linked under Henry II, as under Henry I, by the activites of sheriffs and itinerant royal justices. Henry II broadened the scope of these itinerant justices, thereby making royal justice more accessible than ever before. Itinerant royal justices now made periodic circuits of the countryside, bringing the king's law to considerable numbers who had previously been untouched by it.

The sheriffs were responsible for enforcing the king's orders, which continued to issue from the chancery in the form of writs. It also remained the sheriff's duty to collect royal dues and fines and to render a periodic accounting of them at the exchequer. In these respects and others, the sheriffs had long been subject to the king's central administration. Yet they also had interests of their own to pursue, not always parallel to the royal interests. Most were wealthy landholders in their localities, who used their official status to become wealthier still—sometimes at their neighbors' expense and sometimes at the king's. In 1170 Henry II ordered a searching investigation of his sheriffs' behavior—the Inquest of Sheriffs—and subsequently replaced most of them with new and more tractable men.

Henry II has been called the father of the English common law. Like his predecessors he favored the extension of royal jurisdiction, partly for its financial rewards to the crown, and in his quest for ever-greater judicial revenues he was able to advance the powers of the royal courts well beyond their former limits. His *Assize of Clarendon* of 1166 widened the scope of royal justice to include the indictment and prosecution of local criminals. It provided that regional inquest juries should meet periodically under royal auspices to identify and denounce notorious neighborhood criminals, whose guilt or innocence was then to be determined by the ordeal of cold water.* The inquest jury was more akin to the modern grand jury than to the modern trial jury, for its duty was to investigate and indict rather than to judge guilt. Inquest juries had been used before: they were assembled under William the Conqueror to provide information for the Domesday survey; there is a reference to one such jury in the records of late Anglo-Saxon times; and bodies of a similar nature were employed in the administration of Carolingian Frankland. Never before, however, had they been used in such a systematic fashion.

Henry also extended royal jurisdiction over the tangled jungle of land disputes. Here again local juries were employed to determine the rightful possessors or heirs of disputed estates. The most important of Henry's "possessory assizes," the *Assize of Novel Disseisin*, was designed to protect property rights by providing a legal action for anyone who was wrongfully

*See pp. 17-18.

dispossessed of an estate. Regardless of whether the plaintiff had a just claim to the estate in question, if he had been dispossessed without legal judgment he was entitled to purchase a royal writ commanding the sheriff to assemble a jury to determine the facts of the case. If the jury concluded that the plaintiff had indeed been wrongfully dispossessed, the sheriff, acting with full royal authority, would see that the estate was restored. Another of the new legal actions provided by Henry II—the *Grand Assize*—used a similar procedure of purchased writ and jury to determine not whether the plaintiff had been improperly dispossessed, but whether he had, in fact, the best title to the land in question.

These and similar assizes carried the king's justice into an area that had once been dominated by the feudal courts, which usually settled questions of land possession by the crude procedure of trial by combat. Previous kings had intervened in quarrels over property, but only on an *ad hoc* basis, never in such a consistent, systematic way. Now, English landholders turned *en masse* to Henry II's courts for quick, rational justice. The baronial courts, with their archaic and time-consuming procedures, lost out in the competition. Gradually the patchwork of local laws and customs which had so long divided England was giving way to a uniform royal law—a *common law* by which all free subjects were ruled. The *political* unification of the tenth-century kings of Wessex was consummated by a process of *legal* unification that advanced significantly under the Angevin kings.

Predictably, Henry II also sought to expand royal justice at the expense of the ecclesiastical courts. A separate system of ecclesiastical jurisdiction had long been in effect, distinct from the various secular courts—local, feudal, and royal. The ecclesiastical court system can be regarded as one manifestation of the complex government of the international Church, which—as it grew steadily more elaborate—came increasingly into conflict with the proliferating governmental structures of England and other secular states. The two governments, royal and ecclesiastical, were both expanding in the twelfth century, and conflicts between them were bound to occur. The first great conflict centered on Anselm, the second on Becket.

In 1162 Henry sought to bring the English church under strict royal control by appointing to the archbishopric of Canterbury his chancellor and good friend, Thomas Becket. But in raising Becket to the primacy, Henry had misjudged his man. As chancellor Becket had been a devoted royal servant, but as archbishop of Canterbury he became a fervent defender of ecclesiastical independence and an implacable enemy of the king. Henry and Becket became locked in a furious quarrel over the issue of royal control of the English Church. In 1164 Henry issued a list of pro-royal provisions relating to church-state relations known as the *Constitutions of Clarendon*, which, among other things, prohibited appeals to Rome without royal license and established a degree of royal control over the Church courts. Henry maintained that the Constitutions of Clarendon represented ancient custom; Becket regarded them as unacceptable infringements on the freedom of the Church.

At the heart of the quarrel was the issue of whether churchmen accused of crimes should be subject to royal jurisdiction after being found guilty and punished by Church courts. The king complained that "criminous clerks" were often given absurdly light sentences by the ecclesiastical tribunals. A murderer, for example, might simply be defrocked and released, whereas in the royal courts the penalty was execution or mutilation. The Constitutions of Clarendon provided that once a cleric was tried, convicted and defrocked by an ecclesiastical court, the Church should no longer prevent his being brought to a royal court for further punishment. Becket replied that nobody ought to be put in double jeopardy. In essence, Henry was challenging the competence of an agency of the international Church, whereas Becket, as primate of England, felt bound to defend the ecclesiastical system of justice and the privileges of churchmen. Two worlds were in collision.

Henry turned on his archbishop, accusing him of various crimes against the kingdom, and Becket, denying the king's right to try an archbishop, fled England to seek papal support. Pope Alexander III, who was in the midst of his struggle with Frederick Barbarossa, could not afford to alienate Henry; yet neither could he turn against such an ardent ecclesiastical champion as Becket. The great lawyer-pope was forced to equivocate—to encourage Becket without breaking with Henry—and Becket remained in exile for the next six years. At length, in 1170, the king and his archbishop agreed to a truce. Most of the outstanding issues between them remained unsettled, but Becket was permitted to return peacefully to England and resume the archbishopric. At once, however, the two antagonists had another falling out. Becket excommunicated a number of Henry's supporters; the king flew into a rage, and four overenthusiastic knights of the royal household went to Canterbury cathedral and murdered Becket at the high altar.

This dramatic crime made a deep impact on the age. Becket was regarded as a martyr; miracles were alleged to have occurred at his tomb, and he was quickly canonized. For the remainder of the Middle Ages, Canterbury was a major pilgrimage center and the cult of St. Thomas enjoyed immense popularity. Henry, who had not ordered the killing but whose anger had prompted it, suffered acute embarrassment. He was obliged to do penance by walking barefoot through the streets of Canterbury and submitting to a flogging by the Canterbury monks. But his campaign against the ecclesiastical courts was delayed only momentarily. Although forced to give in on specific matters such as royal jurisdiction over criminous clerks and unlicensed appeals to Rome, he obtained through indirection and maneuvering what he had failed to win through open conflict. He succeeded generally in arranging the appointment to high ecclesiastical offices of men friendly to the crown, and by the end of his reign royal justice had made significant inroads on the authority of the Church courts. The monarchy had succeeded in bringing the English Church under tight rein. Here, as elsewhere, Henry was remarkably successful in steering England toward administrative and legal centralization.

Throughout his reign Henry divided his time between England and the other territories of his "Angevin Empire." Strictly speaking, these trans-channel dominions did not constitute an empire in any real sense, nor were they called an empire at the time. They were, instead, a multiplicity of individual political units, each with its own customs and administrative structure, bound together by their allegiance to Henry Plantagenet. The French monarchy did what it could to break up this threatening configuration, encouraging rebellions on the part of Henry's dutiless sons and his estranged wife, Eleanor of Aquitaine. Henry put down the rebellions one by one, relegated Eleanor to comfortable imprisonment in a royal castle, and sought to placate his sons. It did little good. The rebellions persisted, and as Henry neared death in 1189 his two surviving sons, Richard and John, were both in arms against him. In the end the aged monarch was outmaneuvered and defeated by his offspring and their French allies; he died with the statement, "Shame, shame on a conquered king."

Richard and John

Although Henry's final days were saddened by defeat, the Angevin dominions remained intact, passing into the hands of his eldest surviving son, Richard I, "the Lion-Hearted" (1189–99). This warrior-king devoted himself chiefly to two projects: defending his possessions in France against the French crown and crusading against the Muslims. He was a skillful general who not only won renown on the Third Crusade but also foiled every attempt of the French monarchy to reduce his continental territories. He was far less impressive as an administrator and, indeed, spent less than six months of his ten-year reign in England. During his protracted absences, the administrative system of Henry II proved its worth. It governed England more or less satisfactorily for ten kingless years and even produced the huge ransom demanded by Emperor Henry VI, who had imprisoned Richard on his homeward journey from the Holy Land.

The fortunes of the Angevin dominions veered sharply with the accession of King John (1199–1216), Richard the Lion-Hearted's younger brother. John is an enigmatic figure—brilliant in certain respects, a master of administrative detail, but suspicious, unscrupulous, and mistrusted. His crisis-prone career was sabotaged repeatedly by the half-heartedness with which his vassals supported him—and the energy with which some of them opposed him.

In Philip Augustus of France (1180–1223) John had a shrewd, unremitting antagonist. Philip took full advantage of his position as overlord of John's continental possessions. In 1202 John was summoned to the French royal court to answer charges brought against him by one of his own Aquitainian vassals. When John refused to come, Philip Augustus declared his French lands forfeited and proceeded to invade Normandy. The duchy quickly fell into Philip's hands (1203–4). John's demoralized Norman vassals began to defect, one after another, and John himself fled to England—leaving his remaining loyalists twisting in the wind. In the chaos that followed, Philip Augustus was able to wrest Anjou and other French dominions from John's control. Only portions of distant Aquitaine retained their connection with the English monarchy. King John had sustained a monstrous political and military disaster.

For the next ten years John wove a dextrous web of alliances against King Philip in hopes of regaining his lost possessions. His careful plans were shattered by Philip's decisive victory over John's Flemish and German allies at the battle of Bouvines in 1214.* With Bouvines went John's last hope of recovering Normandy and Anjou.

In the decade between the loss of Normandy and the catastrophe at Bouvines, John engaged in a bitter quarrel with Pope Innocent III. At stake was royal control over the appointment of an archbishop of Canterbury. According to canon law and established custom, a bishop or archbishop was to be elected by the canons of the cathedral chapter. The Investiture Controversy notwithstanding, such elections were commonly controlled by the king, who would overawe the canons into electing the candidate of his choice. Canterbury differed from most European cathedrals in that a body of monks performed the functions that were ordinarily the responsibility of cathedral canons; it was the monks who customarily elected the archbishop, but they, no less than canons, were usually susceptible to royal control. In 1205, however, the monks of Canterbury, declining to wait for royal instructions, elected one of their own number as archbishop and sent a delegation to Rome to obtain Pope Innocent's confirmation. Going personally to Canterbury, John forced the monks to hold another election and to select his own nominee. In the course of events several delegations went from England to Rome, and Innocent, keenly interested in the enforcement of proper canonical procedures, quashed both elections. He ordered those Canterbury monks who were then in Rome—quite a number by this time—to hold still another election, and under papal influence they elected Stephen Langton, a learned Englishman who had spent some years as a scholar in Paris.

Furious that his own candidate should have been passed over, John refused to confirm Langton's appointment or admit him into England. For the next six years, 1207–13, John held to his position, while Innocent used every weapon at his disposal to make the king submit. England was laid under interdict; John retaliated by confiscating all ecclesiastical revenues. John was excommunicated, and Innocent even threatened to depose him. This threat, together with the danger of a projected French invasion of England with full papal backing, forced John to submit at last. In 1213 he accepted Stephen Langton as archbishop of Canterbury. Going still further, John conceded to Innocent the overlordship of England that Gregory VII had fruitlessly demanded of William the Conqueror long before. John agreed to hold his kingdom thenceforth as a papal fief and render a substantial annual tribute to Rome.

*See p. 194.

Having lost the struggle over the archbishopric, John was anxious to transform his papal antagonist into a devoted friend, and his concession of the overlordship had precisely that effect.

John had won the papal friendship, but many of his own barons were regarding him with increasing hostility. The Bouvines disaster of 1214, coming at the end of a long series of expensive and humiliating diplomatic failures, diminished John's prestige still further. It paved the way for the English baronial uprising that culminated on the field of Runnymede in 1215 with the signing of *Magna Carta*.

John's baronial enemies had reason to oppose him. He had pushed the centralizing tendencies of his Norman and Angevin predecessors to new limits and was taxing his subjects with grim efficiency. The baronial reaction of 1215 was both a protest against John himself and an effort to reverse the long trend toward royal authoritarianism.

Magna Carta has been interpreted in contradictory ways: as the fountainhead of England's later constitutional monarchy, and as a reactionary, backward-looking document designed to favor the particularistic feudal aristocracy at the expense of the enlightened Angevin regime. But in historical perspective, Magna Carta was both feudal and constitutional, both backward-looking and forward-looking. Still more to the point, its authors were looking neither forward nor backward but were contending with problems of the moment. Magna Carta's more important clauses were designed to keep the king within the bounds of popular and feudal custom. Royal taxes not sanctioned by custom, for example, were to be levied only by the common counsel of the kingdom. But implicit in the traditional doctrine that the lord had to respect the rights of his vassals and rule according to good customs was the constitutional principle of government under the law. In striving to make King John a good feudal lord, the barons in 1215 were moving uncertainly and unconsciously toward constitutional monarchy. Thus, one finds in Magna Carta the notion that the king is bound by traditional legal limitations in his relations with all classes of free Englishmen. It would be misleading to lay too much stress on the underlying principles of this intensely practical document, which was concerned primarily with correcting specific royal abuses of feudal custom. But it would be equally misleading to ignore the implication in Magna Carta, derived from the feudal ideology, of an overarching body of law which limited and circumscribed royal authority.

The chief constitutional problem in the years following Magna Carta was the question of how an unwilling king might be forced to stay within the bounds of law. A series of royal promises was obviously insufficient to control an ambitious monarch who held all the machinery of the central government in his grasp. Magna Carta itself relied on a committee of twenty-five barons who were empowered, should the king violate the charter, to call upon the English people "to distrain and distress him in every possible way." Thus, the monarch was to be held in check by the threat of baronial and popular rebellion—a desperate and unwieldy weapon against an unscrupulous king.

John himself seems to have had no intention of carrying out his promises. He repudiated Magna Carta at the first opportunity, with the full backing of his papal overlord. The result was a full-scale revolt that ended only with John's death in 1216.

The crown now passed, without objection, to John's nine-year-old son, Henry III (1216–72) who was supervised during his minority by a baronial council. In the decades that followed, Magna Carta was reissued many times, but the great task of the new age was to create political institutions capable of uniting king, bureaucracy, and baronage in the governance of England. The ultimate solution to this problem was found in Parliament.

Henry III

Henry III was a petulant, erratic monarch: pious without being holy, bookish without being wise. Surrounding himself with foreign favorites and intoxicated by grandiose, impractical foreign projects, he ignored the advice of his barons and gradually lost their confidence.

Ever since its beginning, the English monarchy had customarily arrived at important decisions of policy with the advice of a royal council of nobles, prelates, and officials. In Anglo-Saxon times, this council was called the witenagemot; after 1066 it was known as the *curia regis*. Its composition had always been vague, and it had never possessed anything resembling a veto power over royal decisions. But many of the king's subjects, particularly among the upper classes, valued the tradition of royal policy being framed in consultation with the lay and ecclesiastical lords.

Traditionally, English royal councils were of two types. Ordinary royal business was conducted in a small council that perambulated with the king, consisting of household officials along with royal favorites and others who happened to be at court at the time. But on great ceremonial occasions such as Christmas and Easter, or at other times when some important decision was pending, the kings supplemented their normal coterie of advisers by assembling around them all the important noblemen and churchmen of the realm. It was these great councils that eventually evolved into Parliament.

Accompanying the evolution from great council to Parliament was a gradual trend, beginning in the thirteenth century, toward including representatives of the country gentry and the burghers alongside the great barons, prelates, and royal officials. This development resulted from the royal policy, particularly common after Magna Carta, of summoning great councils for the purpose of winning approval of some uncustomary tax. As royal justice and royal taxation gradually expanded to include all free persons of the realm, the magnates lost the power and confidence to commit the wealth of their tenants and social inferiors. Accordingly, the king found it expedient on occasion to obtain the consent of these lesser orders to new royal taxes by summoning their representatives to great councils.

The baronial opposition to Henry III arose primarily from his habit of summoning great councils not for the purpose of consulting his magnates but chiefly to seek their consent to new taxes. For advice he depended heavily on his wife's relatives from southern France. His barons resented being asked to finance hair-brained foreign schemes on which they had not been consulted and of which they heartily disapproved. They refused Henry's fiscal demands from the first, and by 1258 the monarch's diplomatic initiatives, military blunders, and soaring debts had brought on a financial crisis of major proportions. To obtain desperately needed monetary support, Henry submitted to a set of baronial limitations on royal power known as the *Provisions of Oxford*.

These Provisions of 1258 went far beyond Magna Carta in creating machinery to force the king to govern in accordance with good custom and in consultation with his magnates. Great councils, now called parliaments, were to be assembled three times a year. They were to include, along with their usual membership, twelve men "elected" by the "community"—in other words, chosen by the barons. These twelve were empowered to speak for all the magnates, so that even if heavily outnumbered in a parliament, their authority would be great. The Provisions of Oxford also established a *Council of Fifteen*, chiefly barons, which shared with the king control over the royal administration. Specifically, this council was given authority over the exchequer and the power to appoint the chancellor and other high officers of state.

The Provisions of Oxford proved premature, and the governmental system they established turned out to be unworkable because of baronial factionalism. But they do cast precious light on the attitude of many mid-thirteenth-century barons toward the royal administration. These magnates had no thought of abolishing the administrative and legal advances of the past two centuries or of weakening the central government. Their interests were national rather than provincial; they sought to exert a degree of control over the royal administration rather than dismantle it. They were motivated not by constitutional abstractions but by the need, as they saw it, to curb an incompetent, arbitrary, spendthrift king.

With the failure of the Provisions of Oxford, Henry III resumed exclusive control of his administration and returned to the arbitrary and inept governance that his barons found so distasteful. At length, discontent exploded into open rebellion. A group of dissidents led by Simon de Montfort, earl of Leicester, defeated the royal army at Lewes in 1264 and captured King Henry himself.

For the next fifteen months Simon de Montfort ruled England in the king's name. He shared his authority with two baronial colleagues and a committee of magnates, augmented periodically by parliaments. Simon's government was a product of the same impulse toward baronial participation that had evoked the Provisions of Oxford. But Simon was supported by only a portion of the baronage, along with townspeople and lesser landholders. Many barons remained royalists, as was usually the case in such crises. And with their backing the monarchy rallied under the leadership of the Lord Edward, Henry III's talented son. Edward defeated Simon's army at Evesham in 1265 and the rebellion dissolved.

The Evolution of Parliament

Earlier in 1265 Simon de Montfort had summoned a parliament that included, for the first time, all the classes that were to characterize the parliaments of the late Middle Ages. It included, in addition to great lords and royal officials, two knights from every shire and two burghers from every town. Shire knights and burghers had been called to earlier great councils, but only rarely and for some specific purpose—and never jointly. Simon's chief motive for summoning them was probably to broaden the base of his rebellion, but they continued to be included, from time to time, in the parliaments of subsequent years.

The barons, burghers and shire knights all brought with them a wealth of local political experience. The burghers in parliament were usually veterans of town government. The shire knights had long been involved in the administration of the counties and county courts. Intermediate between the barons and the peasantry, these men represented a separate, emerging class of country gentry, rooted to their shires and their ancestral estates, experienced in local government. But for several generations, burghers and shire knights were summoned only on occasion. Through the thirteenth century and beyond, parliaments consisted primarily of great lords, royal judges and administrators, and, of course, the king himself.

In 1272 Henry III was succeeded by his son, Edward I, a strong-willed monarch who had the sagacity to take the barons into his confidence. Edward summoned parliaments often and experimented endlessly in their composition. Like Simon de Montfort, he sometimes included shire knights and townsmen, particularly in the later years of his reign. But it was not until well into the fourteenth century that the knights and burghers began meeting separately from the barons, giving birth to the great parliamentary division into Lords and Commons.

As the thirteenth century closed, the powers of parliaments remained vague and their composition was still fluid. Barons might bargain discreetly with the king in parliament for concessions in return for the granting of a special tax. But parliaments remained primarily instruments to serve the king's purposes and to assist him in the governance of the realm. They did so in many ways: by sitting as a high court of law, by settling thorny issues of law and administration, by hearing petitions of complaint from subjects seeking the redress of grievances (particularly those arising from the misconduct of royal officials), by giving counsel on important matters of state, and by declaring their support in moments of crisis.

Edward I, backed by his officials and usually by a sympathetic baronial majority, was the controlling figure in all his parliaments. There was nothing remotely democratic about them. Edward regarded these assemblies as tools of royal policy and used them to aid and strengthen the monarchy rather than limit it. He would have been appalled to learn that his royal descendants would one day be figurehead monarchs and that Parliament was destined to rule England. Only then would it become evident that Parliament was the crucial institutional bridge spanning the chasm between medieval feudalism and modern democracy.

Edward I (1272–1307)

The reign of Edward I witnessed the culmination of many trends in English law and administration that had been developing throughout the High Middle Ages. Edward was a great systematizer, and in his hands the royal administrative structure and the common law acquired the shape and coherence that they were to retain through future centuries.

The four chief agencies of royal government under Edward I were the chancery, the exchequer, the council, and the household. Chancery and exchequer were by now both permanently established at Westminster. The chancery remained the royal secretarial office, and its chief officer, the chancellor, was the custodian of the great seal by which royal documents were authenticated. A staff of professional chancery clerks prepared the numerous letters and charters by which the king made his will known and preserved copies of them for future reference. The exchequer, headed by a royal official known as the treasurer, continued to serve, as it long had, as the king's accounting agency. By now it supervised the accounts not only of sheriffs but of many other local officials who were charged with collecting royal revenues.

Unlike the chancery and exchequer, the council and household accompanied the king on his endless travels. Since meetings of the great council were coming more and more to be referred to as "parliaments," the "council" in Edward's government is to be identified with the earlier "small council." It was a permanent royal entourage of varied and changing membership, consisting of judges, administrators, magnates, and prelates, who advised the king on routine matters. In the Provisions of Oxford the barons had tried to wrest control of the council from the king, but in Edward's reign it was firmly under royal control. The household was a royal government in miniature, with its own writing clerks, supervised by the keeper of the privy seal, and its own financial office known as the "wardrobe." By means of his household administration the king could govern on the move, without the necessity of routing all his business through Westminster.

Royal government in the countryside continued to depend on sheriffs and itinerant justices, whose duties and responsibilities were defined and regularized as never before. But now other royal servants were working alongside them: coroners, who were charged with investigating felonies; keepers of the peace, whose duty it was to apprehend criminals; assessors, tax collectors, customs officials, and others—local men, for the most part, who were responsible for serving the king in their native districts.

The royal legal system was also taking permanent form. Cases of singular importance were brought before the king himself, sitting in Parliament or surrounded by his council. Less important cases were handled by the king's itinerant justices or by one of the three royal courts sitting at Westminster. These three were the courts of the *king's bench*, which heard cases of particular royal concern; *exchequer* which, besides its fiscal responsibilities, heard cases touching on the royal revenues; and *common pleas*, which had jurisdiction over most remaining types of cases. These courts were all staffed with highly trained professionals—lawyers or, in the case of the exchequer, experienced accountants. By Edward I's day the royal judicial system had come of age.

Like his predecessors, Edward worked toward the expansion of royal justice over private justice. From the beginning of his reign he issued numerous writs of *quo warranto* (by what warrant?), which obliged lords who claimed the right of private legal jurisdiction to prove their claim by producing a royal charter to that effect. In 1290 Edward issued the statute of *Quo Warranto,* which quashed all private jurisdictions unsupported by royal charter or ancient custom. By means of these policies, Edward eliminated a good number of private jurisdictional franchises and asserted his right to exercise some supervision over those that remained. If a lord seriously abused his jurisdictional authority, Edward was prepared to seize his lands. The ultimate supremacy of the king's jurisdiction was thus established beyond question.

Edward's reign was marked by the appearance of a great many royal statutes—issued by the king in Parliament—which elaborated and systematized royal administrative and legal procedures in many different ways. Law had formerly been regarded as a matter of custom; the king might interpret or clarify it, but he seldom made a new law. As ancient Germanic tradition had it, the king was bound by the customs of his people. It is not always possible to distinguish between the act of clarifying or elaborating old law and making new law, and many of Edward's predecessors had been lawmakers in fact, if not in theory. But in the later thirteenth century the English government began to legislate on a larger scale than before. Even in Edward's day, original legislation was such a solemn affair that the king issued his statutes only with the approval of the "community of the realm" as expressed in his parliaments. Edward dominated his parliaments, and his statutes were unquestionably products of the royal initiative, but it is nevertheless significant that the role of parliaments in the making of law was clearly conceded. In the course of the fourteenth century, Parliament employed its power of approving royal taxes to win control of the legislative process itself.

Thus, Edward I completed the work of his predecessors in creating an effective and complex royal administrative system, bringing feudal justice under royal control, and building a comprehensive body of common law. More than that, he solidified the concept of original legislation and nurtured the developing institution of Parliament, setting into motion forces that would have an immense impact on England's future.

Edward was also a skillful and ambitious warrior. He brought to a decisive end the centuries-long military struggle along the Welsh frontier by conquering Wales altogether in a whirlwind campaign during 1282 and 1283. He granted his eldest son the title "Prince of Wales," which male heirs-apparent to the English throne have held ever since. By a ruthless exploitation of the traditional English overlordship over the Scottish realm he came very near to conquering Scotland and was foiled only by the dogged determination of the Scottish hero-king, Robert Bruce. His war with Philip IV of France was expensive and inconclusive, but it did succeed in preserving English lordship over Gascony which had been seriously threatened.* These wars gradually exhausted the royal treasury, and during the latter portion of his reign, Edward was faced with growing baronial and popular opposition to his expensive policies. But the king was able to ride out this opposition by making timely concessions—reissuing Magna Carta and recognizing Parliament's right to approve all extraordinary taxation.

At his death in 1307, Edward left behind him a realm exhausted by his prodigious foreign and domestic activities but firmly under his control. Edward's England was still, in spirit, a feudal kingdom rather than a modern nation, but feudalism was waning and the initial steps toward nationhood had been taken.

The Early Capetians

When William of Normandy conquered England in 1066, the king of France exerted unsteady control over a modest territory around Paris and Orléans known as the Île de France and was virtually powerless in the lands beyond.† To be sure, the French monarchy claimed the overlordship of great princes such as the dukes of Normandy and Aquitaine and the counts of Anjou, Flanders, and Champagne, but only gradually did it acquire the power and respect to make good this claim. In theory the anointed king of the French was a mighty figure—with his priestly charisma, with the sovereign power traditionally associated with royalty, and with the supreme feudal overlordship. But in grim reality he was impotent to control the feudal princes and unable to keep order in the Île de France itself. All France was tormented by incessant warfare, and the king could do nothing to curb it.

Since 987 the French crown had been held by the Capetian dynasty. The achievement of the Capetians in the first century or so of their rule was modest

---

*Gascony was a portion of Aquitaine that the kings of England continued to control after losing the remainder of their French possessions under John.
†See map, p. 225.

enough. Their one success was in keeping the crown within their own family. The Capetians had gained the throne originally by virtue of being elected by the magnates of the realm, but from the first they sought to purge the monarchy of its elective character and make it hereditary. This they accomplished by managing to produce male heirs at the right moment and by arranging for the new heir to be crowned before the old king died. They may have been aided by the fact that the crown was not a sufficiently alluring prize to attract powerful usurpers.

In the early twelfth century the Capetians remained no stronger than several of their own vassals. While feudal principalities like Normandy and Anjou were becoming increasingly centralized, the Capetian Île de France was still ridden with fiercely insubordinate barons. If the Capetians were to realize the potential of their royal title they had three great tasks before them: (1) to master and pacify the Île de France; (2) to expand their political and economic base by bringing additional territories under direct royal authority; and (3) to make their lordship over the great feudal principalities real rather than merely theoretical.

During the twelfth and thirteenth centuries a series of able Capetian kings pursued and achieved these goals. Their success was so complete that by the opening of the fourteenth century the Capetians controlled all France, either directly or indirectly, and had developed an efficient, sophisticated royal bureaucracy. They followed no hard and fast formula. Their success depended instead on a combination of luck and ingenuity—on their clever exploitation of the powers which, potentially, they had always possessed as kings and overlords. They were successful in avoiding the family squabbles that had at times paralyzed Germany and the Anglo-Norman dominions. Unlike the German monarchs, they maintained comparatively good relations with the papacy. They had the enormous good fortune of an unbroken sequence of direct male heirs from 987 to 1328. Above all, they seldom overreached themselves: they avoided grandiose schemes and spectacular strokes of policy, preferring instead to pursue modest, realistic goals. They extended their power gradually and cautiously by favorable marriages, by confiscating the fiefs of vassals who died without heirs, and by dispossessing vassals who violated their feudal obligation toward the monarchy. Yet the majority of the Capetians had no desire to absorb the territories of all their vassals; rather they sought to build a kingdom with a substantial core of royal domain lands surrounded by the fiefs of loyal, obedient magnates.

Philip I, Louis VI, and Louis VII

The first Capetian to work seriously toward the consolidation of royal control in the Île de France was King Philip I (1060–1108), a bloated, repugnant man who grasped the essential fact that the Capetian monarchy had to make its home base secure before turning to loftier goals. Philip's realistic policy was pursued far more vigorously by his son, Louis VI, "the Fat" (1108–1137)—gluttonous and mediocre, but blessed with an intelligent wife, Adelaide of Murienne. Encouraged by Queen Adelaide, Louis the Fat battled dissident barons of the Île de France year after year, until he could no longer find a horse with the strength to carry him. Besieging baronial castles one by one, he at last reduced the Île de France to obedience. At his death in 1137 it was relatively orderly and prosperous, and the French monarchy was stronger than it had been since Carolingian times.

Louis the Fat received invaluable assistance in the later part of his reign from Abbot Suger of the great royal monastery of Saint-Denis. This talented statesman served as chief royal adviser from 1130 to 1151 and labored hard and effectively to extend the king's sway, to systematize the royal administration, and, incidentally, to augment the wealth and prestige of Saint-Denis.

Suger provided an invaluable element of continuity between the reigns of Louis the Fat and his son, Louis VII (1137–80). Pious and gentle, Louis VII was, in the words of one contemporary observer, "a very Christian king, if somewhat simple-minded." When Abbot Suger died in 1151, Louis was left to face unaided a new and formidable threat to the French monarchy. The Angevin dominions were just then in the process of formation, and in 1154 the ominous configuration was completed when Henry Plantagenet, count of Anjou and duke of Normandy and Aquitaine, acceded to the English throne as King Henry II. Louis VII sought to embarrass his mighty vassal by encouraging Henry's sons to rebel, but his efforts were too halfhearted to be successful.

Still, Louis' reign witnessed a significant extension of royal power. Indeed, as one historian has aptly said, it was under Louis VII that "the prestige of the French monarchy was decisively established." * The great vassals of the crown, fearful of their powerful Angevin colleague and respectful of Louis' piety and impartiality, began for the first time to bring cases to the court of their royal overlord and submit their disputes to his judgment. Churchmen and townspeople alike sought his support in struggles with the nobility. These developments resulted not so much from royal initiative as from the fundamental trends of the age toward peace, order, and growing commercial activity. Frenchmen in increasing numbers were turning to their genial, unassuming monarch for succor and justice. Little by little, Louis began to assume his place as feudal suzerain and supreme sovereign of the realm.

Philip Augustus: 1180-1223

The French monarchy came of age under Louis VII's talented son, Philip II "Augustus." By remorseless insistence on his rights as overlord, and by a policy of dextrous opportunism, Philip Augustus enlarged the royal territories enormously and, beyond the districts of direct royal jurisdiction, transformed

*Robert Fawtier, *The Capetian Kings of France* (London: Macmillan & Co., 1960), p. 23.

the chaotic anarchy of the vassal states into a more ordered hierarchy subordinate to the king.

Philip Augustus's great achievement was the destruction of the Angevin territorial configuration and the establishment of royal jurisdiction over Normandy, Anjou, and their dependencies. For two decades he plotted with dissatisfied members of the Angevin family against King Henry II and King Richard the Lion-Hearted, but it was not until the reign of King John (1199–1216) that his efforts bore fruit. Against John's notorious faithlessness and greed, Philip was able to play the role of the just lord rightfully punishing a disobedient vassal. And when Philip Augustus moved against Normany in 1203–4, John's unpopularity played into his hands. The prize that Philip had sought so long was now won with surprising ease. And once Normandy was conquered, John's remaining fiefs in northern France fell quickly. Ten years later, in 1214, Philip extinguished John's last hope of recovering the lost territories by winning his decisive victory over John's German allies at Bouvines.* Settling for good the question of Normandy and Anjou, Bouvines was also a turning point in the power balance between France and Germany in the High Middle Ages. Thereafter the Capetian monarchy overshadowed the faltering kingdom of Germany and the much reduced territories of the kings of England. France became the great power in thirteenth-century Christendom.

Under Philip Augustus and his predecessors significant developments were occurring in the royal administrative system. The curia regis had assumed its place as the high feudal court of France and was proving an effective instrument for the assertion of royal rights over the dukes and counts. Hereditary noblemen who had traditionally served as local administrators in the royal territories were gradually replaced by salaried officials known as *baillis*. These new officials, whose functions were at once financial, judicial, military, and administrative, owed their positions to royal favor and were fervently devoted to the interests of the crown. Throughout the thirteenth century the baillis worked tirelessly and often unscrupulously to erode the privileges of the feudal aristocracy and extend the royal sway. This intensely loyal and highly mobile bureaucracy, without local roots and without respect for feudal or local traditions, became in time a powerful instrument of royal absolutism. The baillis stood in sharp contrast to the local officials in England—the sheriffs and shire knights—who were customarily drawn from the local gentry and whose loyalties were divided between the monarch whom they served and the region and class from which they sprang.

Louis VIII: 1223–1226

The closing years of Philip Augustus's reign were concurrent with the Albigensian Crusade, called by Innocent III against the dualist heretics of southern

*See pp. 194, 213.

France.* Philip Augustus declined to participate personally in the crusade, but his son, Prince Louis, took an active part in it. And when the prince succeeded to his father's throne in 1223 as Louis VIII (1223–26), he threw all the resources of the monarchy behind the southern campaign. The crusade succeeded in eliminating the Albigensian heresy, but only by devastating large portions of Languedoc and exterminating the brilliant culture that had previously flourished there.† Thenceforth southern France tended to be dominated by northern France, and the authority of the French monarchy was extended to the Mediterranean.

It may perhaps be surprising to discover that Louis VIII, who inherited from his father a vastly expanded royal jurisdiction and extended it still further himself, gave out about a third of the hard-won royal territories as fiefs to junior members of the Capetian family. These family fiefs, carved out of the royal domain, are known as *apanages.* Their creation should serve as a warning that the growth of the Capetian monarchy cannot be understood simply as a linear process of expanding the royal territories. The Capetians had no objection to vassals so long as they were obedient and subject to royal control. Indeed, given the limited transportation and communication facilities of twelfth and thirteenth-century France, the kingdom was far too large to be controlled directly by the monarchy. The new vassals, bound to the crown by strong family ties, played an essential role in the governance of the realm. For the time being, at least, they strengthened rather than weakened the effectiveness of Capetian rule.

St. Louis: 1226–1270

Louis VIII died prematurely in 1226, leaving the land in the skillful hands of his pious Spanish widow, Blanche of Castile, who acted as regent for the boy‑king Louis IX (1226–70), later St. Louis. Even after St. Louis came of age in 1234 he remained devoted to his mother, and Queen Blanche continued for years to play a dominant and highly capable role in the royal government.

St. Louis possessed both his mother's sanctity and his mother's firmness. He was a strong monarch, determined to rule justly and to promote moral rectitude throughout the kingdom of France. His sanctity, although thoroughly genuine, was too conventional; he took it as his duty to punish heretics and crusade against the Muslims. But in other respects he pursued his religious goals with a measure of compassion and good sense. He hated Judaism and undertook a major effort to persuade Jewish children to become Christians; yet he protected his Jewish subjects from grassroots violence much more effectively than, for example, King Henry III was protecting the Jews in England.

*See pp. 167-168.
†See pp. 233-236.

He made war against the Muslims but worked toward peace in Christendom, arranging treaties with Henry III and with the king of Aragon that settled all outstanding disputes. He played the role of peacemaker among Christian princes and was even called upon to arbitrate between Henry III and his barons (who were outraged when he decided solidly in favor of the royal authority).

St. Louis was content, in general, to maintain the royal rights established by his predecessors. His baillis and other officials were actually far more aggressive than he in extending the royal power. As one modern historian puts it, "in this reign monarchical progress was the complex result of the sanctity of a

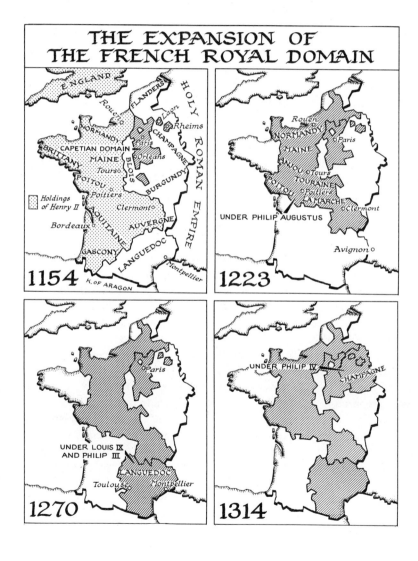

THE EXPANSION OF THE FRENCH ROYAL DOMAIN

revered ruler, and the patient and obstinately aggressive policy of the king's servants." Indeed, St. Louis went to the length of establishing a system of itinerant royal inspectors—*enquêteurs*—who reported local grievances and helped keep the ambitious local officals in check.

In France under Louis IX, medieval culture reached its climax. Town life flourished under St. Louis's rule, and in the towns magnificent Gothic cathedrals were rising. This was the great age of the medieval universities, and at the most distinguished university of the age, the University of Paris, some of the keenest intellects of medieval Europe—St. Bonaventure, St. Albertus Magnus, St. Thomas Aquinas—were assembled concurrently. Besides philosophers and theologians, the universities produced subtle, ambitious lawyers—men of a more secular cast who devoted their talents to the king and swelled the ranks of the royal bureaucracy. The Capetian government became steadily more complex, more efficient and, from the standpoint of the feudal nobility, more oppressive.

Philip the Fair: 1285–1314

St. Louis died in the midst of his last crusade. Under his successors the bureaucracy pursued its centralizing policies without restraint. The saint-king was succeeded by his inept son, Philip III (1270–85), and his icy, enigmatic grandson, Philip IV, "the Fair" (1285–1314). Philip IV was a strange, silent figure, conventionally pious, but with a flair for choosing thoroughly unprincipled ministers—chiefly middle-class lawyers from southern France—who devoted themselves singlemindedly to the exaltation of the French monarchy.

The reign of Philip the Fair was an age of unceasing royal aggression against the territories of neighboring states, against the papacy, and against the traditional privileges of the French nobility. Philip waged an indecisive war against King Edward I of England over Edward's remaining fiefs in southern France. He made a serious effort to absorb Flanders, imprisoning the Flemish count and ruling the district directly through a royal agent, but he was foiled by a bloody uprising of Flemish nobles and burghers who routed his army at the battle of Courtrai in 1302. More successful was his drawn-out policy of nibbling aggression to the east against the faltering Holy Roman Empire.

Like Edward I, Philip IV was constantly in need of money for his wars. And he was prepared to raise it by any means, no matter how tyrannical. In 1306 he arrested all the Jews in his domain, and after seizing their property and their claims as creditors he had them expelled from France. Edward I had treated English Jews in the same cruel fashion in 1290, and for similar reasons. Equally unscrupulous was Philip's attack on the rich crusading order of Knights Templars, from which he had been borrowing heavily. He ruined their reputation by a campaign of vituperative propaganda, confiscated their wealth, and had fifty of them burned as heretics. We have already seen him launching a similar propagandistic campaign against Pope Boniface VIII in the conflict over royal taxation of the French clergy, and sending his agents to arrest the proud old pope at Anagni.*

Against his nobles, Philip pursued a rigorously anti-feudal policy. Short-circuiting the feudal hierarchy, he demanded direct allegiance and obedience from all the French. These activities were manifestations of the prevailing political philosophy of his reign: that the French king was by rights the secular and spiritual master of France and the dominating figure in Western Europe. We encounter a similar philosophy in ambitious French statesmen of succeeding centuries: in Cardinal Richelieu; in Louis XIV; and, stripped of its monarchical trappings, in Napoleon and De Gaulle.

Throughout the thirteenth century the French royal bureaucracy had been developing steadily. The royal revenues came to be handled by a special accounting bureau, roughly parallel to the English exchequer, called the *chambre des comptes*. The King's judicial business became the responsibility of a high court known as the *Parlement of Paris*, which was to play a significant political role in later centuries. Under Philip the Fair the bureaucracy became a refined and supple tool of the royal interest; its middle-class background and tenacious royalism gave the king a degree of independence from the nobility that was quite unknown in contemporary England.

Still, the king could not rule without a certain amount of support from his subjects. Philip's victory over the papacy on the issue of royal taxation of the clergy and his rape of the Jews and Knights Templars brought additional money into his treasury. But the soaring expenses of government and warfare forced him to seek ever-new sources of revenue and, as in England, to secure his subjects' approval of extraordinary taxation. Instead of summoning a great assembly—a parliament—for this purpose, he usually negotiated individually with various taxpaying groups.

Nevertheless it was under Philip the Fair that France's first kingdom-wide representative assemblies were summoned. Beginning in 1302, the *Estates General* was assembled from time to time, primarily for the purpose of giving formal support to the monarchy in moments of crisis—during the struggle with Pope Boniface VIII, for example, or in the midst of the Knights Templars controversy. The assembly included members of the three great social classes or "estates": the clergy, the nobility, and the townspeople. It continued to meet occasionally over the succeeding centuries, but it never became a real organ of government as did Parliament in England. Its failure resulted in part from a premature and unsuccessful bid for power during the fourteenth century in the midst of the Hundred Years' War. But even under Philip the Fair, the Estates General lacked the potential of the contemporary parliaments of England. It had no real voice in royal taxation and was therefore not in a position to bargain with the king through increasing control of the purse strings. It was not, as in England, an evolutionary outgrowth of the royal council, but rather an entirely separate, exotic body. There was no real opportunity for the

*See p. 199.

townsmen and the gentry to join ranks as in the English House of Commons; lacking the important responsibilities in local government which fell on English shire knights, the knights of France remained an inarticulate and subordinate part of the aristocratic class. Above all, the French nobility and bourgeoisie lagged far behind the English in developing a national consciousness. Late-thirteenth-century France was too large, too segmented into cohesive principalites, and too recently brought under royal authority for its inhabitants to have acquired a strong sense of identification as a people. Their outlook remained provincial.

Yet despite the significant differences between the English Parliament and the French Estates General, the two institutions had much in common. Both were products of Europe's evolution out of feudal monarchy, expressions of the vague but pervading medieval notion of government under the law or government by the consent of the realm. Similar representative institutions were emerging concurrently all over Western Christendom: in the Christian kingdoms of Spain, in Italy under Frederick II, in the principalities of Germany, and in innumerable counties, duchies, and communes across Europe. Of these many experiments only the English Parliament survives today. But Parliament was not merely the outgrowth of an isolated English experience; it was one particular expression of a broad and fundamental trend in medieval civilization.

CHRONOLOGY OF THE ENGLISH AND FRENCH
MONARCHIES IN THE HIGH MIDDLE AGES

England	France
1066: Norman Conquest of England	987–1328: Rule of the Capetian Dynasty
1066–1087: Reign of William the Conqueror	1060–1108: Reign of Philip I
1087–1100: Reign of William II	
1100–1135: Reign of Henry I	1108–1137: Reign of Louis VI, "the Fat"
1135–1154: Disputed succession; King Stephen	
1154–1189: Reign of Henry II	1137–1180: Reign of Louis VII
1189–1199: Reign of Richard I, "the Lion-Hearted"	1180–1223: Reign of Philip II, "Augustus"
1199–1216: Reign of John	
1203–1204: Loss of Normandy	1214: Battle of Bouvines
1215: Magna Carta	1223–1226: Reign of Louis VIII
1216–1272: Reign of Henry III	1226–1270: Reign of St. Louis IX
1264–1265: Simon de Montfort's rebellion	1270–1285: Reign of Philip III
	1285–1314: Reign of Philip IV, "the Fair"
1272–1307: Reign of Edward I	

Chapter 13

❦

Literature
and
Art

The Dynamics of High Medieval Culture

Thirteenth-century Paris has been described as the Athens of medieval Europe. And despite all the obvious and fundamental differences that separate the golden age of Pericles from the golden age of St. Louis, these two epochs did have something in common. Both developed within the framework of traditional beliefs and customs that had long existed but were being challenged and transformed by powerful new forces—a new rationalism, a new art, a burgeoning commerce, an expansion of frontiers, and an influx of ideas from other cultures. The socio-religious world of the early Middle Ages, like the socio-religious world of the early Greek polis, was parochial and tradition bound. As the two cultures passed into their golden ages, the values of the past were assailed by new intellectual currents, and the old economic patterns were expanded and transformed. Yet for a time, these dynamic new forces resulted in a heightened cultural expression of the old values. The Parthenon, dedicated to the venerable civic goddess Athena, and the Gothic cathedrals of Notre Dame (Our Lady) that were rising at Paris, Chartres, Reims, Amiens, and elsewhere, were all products of a new creativity harnessed to the service of an older ideology. In the long run, the new creative impulses would subvert

❦

the old ideologies, but for a time, both ancient Greece and medieval Europe achieved an elusive equilibrium between old and new. The results, in both cases, were spectacular.

Twelfth- and thirteenth-century Europe succeeded, by and large, in keeping its vibrant culture within the bounds of traditional Catholic Christianity. And the Christian world view gave form and orientation to the new creativity. Despite the intense dynamism of the period, it can still be called, with some semblance of accuracy, an Age of Faith.

Europe in the High Middle Ages underwent an artistic and intellectual awakening that affected every imaginable form of expression. Significant creative work was done in literature, architecture, sculpture, law, philosophy, political theory, even science. By the close of the period, the foundations of the Western cultural tradition were firmly established. The pages that follow will provide only a glimpse at these achievements.

Latin Literature

The literature of the High Middle Ages was abundant and richly varied. Poetry was written both in the traditional Latin—the universal scholarly language of medieval Europe—and in the vernacular languages of ordinary speech that had long been evolving in the various districts of Christendom. Traditional Christian piety found expression in a series of somber and majestic Latin hymns, whose mood is illustrated—through the clouded glass of translation—by these excerpts from "Jerusalem the Golden" (twelfth century):

The world is very evil, the times are waxing late,
Be sober and keep vigil; the judge is at the gate.
   . . .
Brief life is here our portion; brief sorrow, short-lived care.
The life that knows no ending, the tearless life, is there.
   . . .
Jerusalem the Golden, with milk and honey blessed,
Beneath thy contemplation sink heart and voice oppressed.
I know not, O I know not, what social joys are there,
What radiancy of glory, what light beyond compare.

At the opposite end of the medieval Latin spectrum one encounters poetry of quite a different sort, composed by young, wandering scholars and older non-students. The deliberate sensuality and blasphemy of their poems is an expression of student rebelliousness against traditional ideals:

For on this my heart is set, when the hour is nigh me,
Let me in the tavern die, with a tankard by me,
While the angels, looking down, joyously sing o'er me . . .

One of these wandering-scholar poems is an elaborate and impudent parody of the Apostles' Creed. The phrase from the Creed, "I believe in the Holy Ghost, the Holy [Catholic] Church . . ." is embroidered as follows:

I believe in wine that's fair to see,
And in the tavern of my host
More than in the Holy Ghost
The tavern will my sweetheart be,
And the Holy Church is not for me.

These sentiments do not betoken a sweeping trend toward agnosticism. Instead, they are distinctively medieval expressions of the perennial student irreverence toward established institutions. A student activist of the late 1960s shouting obscenities in a faculty meeting would have created much the same effect, though less cleverly.

Vernacular Literature: the Epic

For all its originality, the Latin poetry of the High Middle Ages was outstripped both in quantity and in variety of expression by vernacular poetry. The drift toward emotionalism, which we have already noted in medieval piety, was closely paralleled by the evolution of vernacular literature from the martial epics of the eleventh century to the delicate and sensitive romances of the thirteenth. Influenced by the sophisticated romanticism of the southern troubadour tradition, the bellicose spirit of northern France gradually softened.

In the eleventh and early twelfth centuries, heroic epics known as *chansons de geste* (songs of great deeds) were enormously popular among the northern French aristocracy. These chansons arose out of the earlier heroic tradition of the Teutonic north that had produced moody and violent masterpieces such as *Beowulf*. The hero Beowulf is a lonely figure who fights monsters, slays dragons, and pits his strength and courage against a wild, windswept wilderness. The chansons de geste reflect the somewhat more civilized and Christianized age of feudalism. Still warlike and heroic in mood, they often consisted of exaggerated accounts of events in the reign of Charlemagne. The most famous of all the chansons de geste, the *Song of Roland*, tells of a heroic, bloody battle between a horde of Muslims and the detached rearguard of Charlemagne's army as it was withdrawing from Spain. Like old-fashioned Westerns, the chansons de geste were packed with action, and their heroes tended to steer clear of sentimental entanglements with women. Warlike prowess, courage, and loyalty to one's lord and fellows-in-arms were the virtues stressed in these heroic epics. The battle descriptions, often characterized by gory realism, tell of Christian knights fighting with almost superhuman strength against fantastic odds. The heroes of the chansons are not only proud, loyal, and skilled at arms, but also capable of experiencing deep emotions—weeping at the death of their comrades and appealing to God to receive the souls of the fallen. In short, the chansons de geste mirror the bellicose spirit and sense of military brotherhood that characterized the feudal knighthood of eleventh-century Europe:

Turpin of Reims, his horse beneath him slain,
And with four lance wounds he himself in pain,
Hastens to rise, brave lord, and stand erect.
He looks on Roland, runs to him, and says
Only one thing: "I am not beaten yet!
True man fails not, while life in him is left."
He draws Almace, his keen-edged steel-bright sword,
And strikes a thousand strokes amid the press.
. . . . .
Count Roland never loved a recreant,
Nor a false heart, nor yet a braggart jack,
Nor knight that was not faithful to his lord.
He cried to Turpin—churchman militant—
"Sir, you're on foot, I'm on my horse's back.
For love of you, here will I make my stand,
And side by side we'll take both good and bad.
I'll not leave you for any mortal man."
. . . .
Now Roland feels that he is nearing death;
Out of his ears the brain is running forth.
So for his peers he prays God call them all,
And for himself St. Gabriel's aid implores.

Roland and his rearguard are slain to a man, but the Lord Charlemagne returns to avenge them, and a furious battle ensues:

Both French and Moors are fighting with a will.
How many spears are shattered! lances split!
Whoever saw those shields smashed all to bits,
Heard the bright hauberks grind, the mail rings rip,
Heard the harsh spear upon the helmet ring,
Seen countless knights out of the saddle spilled,
And all the earth with death and deathcries filled,
Would long recall the face of suffering!

The French are victorious. Charlemagne himself defeats the Moorish emir in single combat, and Roland is avenged:

The Muslims fly, God will not have them stay.
All's done, all's won, the French have gained the day.

It should not be supposed that any such battle actually occurred. By and large, Charlemagne's Spanish campaign was a fiasco, and it was left to the *Song of Roland* to supply the happy ending.

The Lyric

During the middle and later twelfth century the martial spirit of northern French literature was gradually transformed by the influx of the romantic troubadour tradition of southern France. In Provence, Toulouse, and Aquitaine a rich, colorful culture had been developing in the eleventh and twelfth centuries, and out of it came a lyric poetry of remarkable sensitivity and enduring value. The lyric poets of the south were known as *troubadours*. Many of them were court minstrels, but some, including Duke William IX of Aquitaine, were members of the upper nobility. Their poems were far more intimate and personal than the chansons de geste, and placed much greater emphasis upon romantic love. The wit, delicacy, and romanticism of the troubadour lyrics disclose a more genteel and sophisticated nobility than that of the feudal north—a nobility that preferred songs of love to songs of war. Indeed, medieval southern France, under the influence of Islamic courtly poetry and ideas, was the source of the romantic-love tradition of Western Civilization. It was from southern France that Europe derived such concepts as the idealization of women, the importance of male gallantry and courtesy, and the impulse to embroider relations between man and woman with potent emotional overtones of eternal oneness, undying devotion, agony, and ecstasy. One of the favorite themes of the lyric poets was the hopeless love—the unrequited love from afar:

I die of wounds from blissful blows,
And love's cruel stings dry out my flesh,
My health is lost, my vigor goes,
And nothing can my soul refresh.
I never knew so sad a plight,
It should not be, it is not right.
. . . .
I'll never hold her near to me,
My ardent joy she'll ever spurn,
In her good grace I cannot be,
Nor even hope, but only yearn.
She tells me nothing, false or true,
And neither will she ever do.

The author of these lines, Jaufré Rudel (fl. 1148), unhappily and hopelessly in love, finds consolation in his talents as a poet, of which he has an exceedingly high opinion. The poem concludes on a much more optimistic note:

*M*ake no mistake, my song is fair,
With fitting words and apt design.
My messenger would never dare
To cut it short or change a line.
. . . .
My song is fair, my song is good,
'Twill bring delight, as well it should.

Many such poems were written in twelfth-century southern France. Their recurring theme is the poet's passionate love for a woman. Occasionally, however, the pattern is reversed, as in this lyric poem by the poetess Beatritz de Dia (fl. 1160):

I live in grave anxiety
For one fair knight who loved me so.
It would have made him glad to know
I loved him too—but silently.
I was mistaken, now I'm sure,
When I withheld myself from him.
My grief is deep, my days are dim,
And life itself has no allure.

I wish my knight might sleep with me
And hold me naked to his breast,
And on my body take his rest,
And grieve no more, but joyous be.
My love for him surpasses all
The loves that famous lovers knew.
My soul is his, my body, too,
My heart, my life, are at his call.

My most beloved, dearest friend,
When will you fall into my power?
That I might lie with you an hour,
And love you 'til my life should end.
My heart is filled with passion's fire.
My well-loved knight, I grant thee grace
To hold me in my husband's place,
And do the things I so desire.

Not all the lyric poems of southern France took love or life quite so seriously. In some, one encounters a refreshing lightness and wit. The following verses, by Duke William IX of Aquitaine (1071–1127), typify the vivacious spirit of the South. They parody both the romantic seriousness of the love lyric and the heroic mood of the chansons de geste:

Minstrels playing the harp, the flute, and the pipe and tabor.

I'll make some verses just for fun,
Not of myself or anyone,
Nor of great deeds that knights have done
Nor lovers true.
I made them riding in the sun,
My horse helped, too.

When I was born, I'm not aware.
I'm neither glad nor in despair,
Nor stiff, nor loose, nor do I care,
Nor wonder why.
Since meeting an enchantress fair,
Bewitched am I.

Living for dreaming I mistake,
I must be told when I'm awake,
My mood is sad, my heart may break,
Such grief I bear!
But never mind, for heaven's sake,
I just don't care.

I'm sick to death, or so I fear,
I cannot see, but only hear..
I hope that there's a doctor near,
No matter who.
If he can heal me, I'll pay dear,
If not, he's through.

My lady fair is far away,
Just who, or where, I cannot say,
She tells me neither yea nor nay,
Yet I'm not blue,
So long as all those Normans stay
Far from Poitou.

My distant love I so adore,
Though me she has no longing for,
We've never met, and furthermore—
To my disgrace—
I've other loves, some three or four,
To fill her place.

This verse is done, as you can see,
And by your leave, dispatched 'twill be
To one who'll read it carefully
In far Anjou.
Its meaning he'd explain to me
If he but knew.

These verses, only a brief sampling of the fascinating lyrics of southern France—and distorted by translation—may provide some feeling for the rich civilization that flourished there in the twelfth century and disintegrated with the savage horrors of the Albigensian Crusade.

The Romance

Midway through the twelfth century, the southern troubadour tradition began to filter into northern France, England, and Germany. As its influence grew, the northern knights discovered that more was expected of them than loyalty to their lords and a life of carefree slaughter. They were now expected to be gentlemen as well—to be courtly in manner and urbane in speech, to exhibit delicate, refined behavior in feminine company, and to idolize some noble woman. Such, briefly, were the ideals of what has been called "courtly love." Their impact on the actual behavior of knights was limited, but their effect on the literature of northern Europe was revolutionary. Out of the convergence of vernacular epic and vernacular lyric there emerged a new poetic form known as the romance.

Like the chanson de geste, the romance was a long narrative, but like the southern lyric, it was sentimental and concerned with love. It was commonly based on some theme from the remote past: the Trojan War, Alexander the Great, and above all, King Arthur—the half-legendary sixth-century British king. Arthur was transformed into an idealized twelfth-century monarch surrounded by charming ladies and chivalrous knights. His court at Camelot, as described by the late-twelfth-century French poet, Chrétien de Troyes, was a center of romantic love and refined religious sensibilities where knights worshipped their ladies and went on daring quests in a world of magic and fantasy.

In the chanson de geste the great moral imperative was loyalty to one's lord; in the romance it was love for one's lady. Several romances portray the old and new values in conflict. An important theme in both the Arthurian romances and the twelfth-century romance of *Tristan and Iseult* is a love affair between a vassal and his lord's wife. Love and feudal loyalty stand face to face, and love wins out. Tristan loves Iseult, the wife of his lord, King Mark of Cornwall. King Arthur's beloved knight Lancelot loves Arthur's wife, Guinevere. In both stories the lovers are ruined by their love, yet love they must—they have no choice—and although the conduct of Tristan and Lancelot would have been regarded by earlier standards as nothing less than treasonable, both men are presented sympathetically in the romances. Love destroys the lovers in the end, yet their destruction is romantic—even glorious. Tristan and Iseult die together, and in their very death their love achieves its deepest consummation.

Alongside the theme of love in the medieval romances, and standing in sharp contrast to it, is the theme of Christian purity and dedication. The rough-hewn knight of old, having been instructed to be courteous and loving, was now instructed to be holy. Lancelot was trapped in the meshes of a lawless love, but his son, Galahad, became the prototype of the Christian knight—worshipful and chaste. And Perceval, another knight of the Arthurian circle, quested not for a lost loved one but for the Holy Grail of the Last Supper.

The romance flourished in twelfth- and thirteenth-century France and among the French-speaking nobility of England. It spread also into Italy and Spain and became a crucial factor in the evolution of vernacular literature in Germany. The German poets, known as Minnesingers, were influenced by the French lyric and romance but developed these literary forms along highly original lines. The Minnesingers produced their own deeply sensitive and mystical versions of the Arthurian stories that, in their exalted symbolism and deep emotion, surpass even the works of Chrétien de Troyes and his French contemporaries.

Aucassin et Nicolette; the Romance of the Rose

As the thirteenth century drew toward its close, the romance was becoming conventionalized and drained of inspiration. The love story of *Aucassin et Nicolette*, which achieved a degree of popularity, was actually a satirical romance in which the hero is much less heroic than heroes usually are, and a battle is depicted in which the opponents cast pieces of cheese at each other. Based on earlier Byzantine material, *Aucassin et Nicolette* makes mortal love take priority over salvation itself. Indeed, Aucassin is scornful of Heaven:

" For into Paradise go only such people as these: There go those aged priests and elderly cripples and maimed ones who day and night stoop before altars and in the crypts beneath the churches; those who go around in worn-out cloaks and shabby old habits; who are naked and shoeless and full of sores; who are dying of hunger and thirst, of cold and misery. Such folks as these enter Paradise, and I will have nothing to do with them. I will go to hell. For to hell go the fair clerics and comely knights who are killed in tournaments and great wars, and the sturdy archer and the loyal vassal. I will go with them. There also go the fair and courteous ladies who have loving friends, two or three, together with their wedded lords. And there go the gold and silver, the ermine and all rich furs, the harpers and the minstrels, and the happy folk of the world. I will go with these, so long as I have Nicolette, my very sweet friend, at my side. **"**

Another important product of thirteenth-century vernacular literature, the *Romance of the Rose*, was in fact not a romance in the ordinary sense but an allegory of the whole courtly love tradition in which the thoughts and emotions of the lover and his lady are personified in actual characters such as Love, Reason, Jealousy, and Fair-Welcome. Begun by William of Lorris as an idealization of courtly love, the *Romance of the Rose* was completed after William's death by Jean de Meun, a man of limited talent and bourgeois origin. Jean's contribution was long-winded and encyclopedic, and the poem as a whole lacks high literary distinction; yet it appealed to contemporaries and enjoyed a great vogue.

Fabliaux and Fables

Neither epic, lyric, nor romance had much appeal below the level of the landed aristocracy. The inhabitants of the rising towns had a vernacular literature all their own. From the bourgeoisie came the high medieval *fabliaux*, short satirical poems filled with vigor and crude humor, which devoted themselves chiefly to ridiculing conventional morality. Priests and monks were portrayed as lechers, merchants' wives were easily and frequently seduced, and clever young men perpetually made fools of sober and stuffy merchants.

Medieval urban culture also produced the fable, or animal story, an allegory in the tradition of Aesop in which various stock characters in medieval society were presented as animals—thinly disguised. Most of the more popular fables dealt with Renard the Fox and were known collectively as the *Romance of Renard*. These tales constituted a ruthless parody of chivalric ideals in which the clever, unscrupulous Renard persistently outwitted King Lion and his loyal but stupid vassals. Thus, paradoxically, the medieval town, which produced such powerful waves of piety, was responsible for literary forms characterized chiefly by secularism, lasciviousness, and the ridiculing of customs and conventions. To balance the impression conveyed by the fabliaux and fables one must consider the great Romanesque and Gothic cathedrals, the *Song of Brother Sun* composed by that illustrious son of a medieval merchant, St. Francis of Assisi, and the deeply religious poetry of the Florentine, Dante.

Dante

Vernacular poetry matured late in Italy, but in the works of Dante (1265–1321) it achieved its loftiest expression. Dante wrote on a wide variety of subjects, sometimes in Latin, more often in the Tuscan vernacular. He composed a series of lyric poems celebrating his love for the lady Beatrice, which are assembled, with prose commentaries, in his *Vita Nuova* ("the New Life"). Dante's lyrics reflect a more mystical and idealized love than that of the troubadours:

A shining love comes from my lady's eyes,
All that she looks on is made lovelier,
And as she walks, men turn to gaze at her,
Whoever meets her feels his heart arise.

. . .

Humility, and hope that hopeth well,
Come to the mind of one who hears her voice,
And blessed is he who looks on her awhile.
Her beauty, when she gives her slightest smile,
One cannot paint in words, yet must rejoice
In such a new and gracious miracle.

Firmly convinced of the literary potential of the Tuscan vernacular, Dante urged its use in his *De Vulgari Eloquentia*, which he wrote in Latin so as to appeal to scholars and writers who scorned the vulgar tongue. And he filled his own vernacular works with such grace and beauty as to convince by example those whom he could not persuade by argument. In his hands the Tuscan vernacular became the literary language of Italy.

Dante was immersed in the politics of his age. His experience brought him to the opinion that Italy's hope for peace lay in imperial domination and in divorcing the papacy from politics. Although futile and anachronistic in view of the empire's impotence in Dante's time, these views were expressed forcefully in his great political essay, *On Monarchy*.

Dante's masterpiece was the *Divine Comedy*, written in the Tuscan vernacular. Abounding in allegory and symbolism, it encompasses in one majestic vision the entire medieval universe. Dante tells of his own journey through hell, purgatory, and paradise to the very presence of God. This device permitted the poet to make devastating comments on past and contemporary history by placing all those of whom he disapproved—from local politicians to popes—in various levels of hell. Virgil, the archetype of ancient rationalism, is Dante's guide through hell and purgatory; the lady Beatrice, a symbol of purified love, guides him through the celestial spheres of paradise; and St. Bernard, the epitome of medieval sanctity, leads him to the threshold of God. The poem closes with Dante alone in the divine presence:

Eternal Light, thou in thyself alone
Abidest, and alone thine essence knows,
And loves, and smiles, self-knowing and self-known . . . .
. . .
Here power gave way to high sublimity,
But my desire and will were turned—as one—
And as a wheel that turneth evenly,
By Holy Love, that moves the stars and sun.

The Romanesque Style

The High Middle Ages is one of the great epochs in the history of western architecture. Stone churches, large and small, were built in prodigious numbers: in France alone, more stone was quarried during the High Middle Ages than by the pyramid and temple builders of ancient Egypt throughout its 3000-year history. But the real achievement of the medieval architects lay not in the immense scope of their activities but in the splendid originality of their aesthetic vision. Two great architectural styles dominated the age: the Romanesque style flourished in the eleventh century and early twelfth, and during the middle decades of the twelfth century it gave way gradually to the Gothic style. From about 1150 to the early 1300s the most famous of the medieval Gothic cathedrals were built. Thereafter the Gothic builders, having exhausted the

Romanesque exterior: Sainte-Foy in Conques (*c.* 1050–*c.* 1120).

structural possibilities of their style, turned from basic innovation to decorative elaboration. But during the High Middle Ages Gothic architecture constituted one of humanity's most audacious and successful architectural experiments.

The evolution of high-medieval church architecture was shaped by two

Romanesque interior: Saint-Etienne in Nevers (*c.* 1083–1097).

fundamental trends in medieval civilization. First, the great cathedrals were products of the urban revolution—of rising wealth, civic pride, and intense urban piety. Second, the change from Romanesque to Gothic mirrors the shift in literature, piety, and aristocratic life style toward emotional sensitivity and romanticism. Romanesque architecture, though characterized by an exceeding diversity of expression, tended toward the solemnity of earlier Christian piety and the rough-hewn power of the chansons de geste. The Gothic style, on the other hand, is dramatic, upward-reaching, aspiring. It embodies the heightened sensitivity that one finds in the romance.

The development from Romanesque to Gothic can be understood, too, as an evolution in the principles of structural engineering. The key architectural ingredient in the Romanesque churches was the round arch, which appears in their portals, their windows, their arcades, and the massive stone vaulting of their roofs. Romanesque roof design was based on various elaborations of the round arch, such as the barrel vault and the cross vault (see illustration). The immense downward and outward thrusts of these heavy stone roofs required massive pillars and thick supporting walls.

 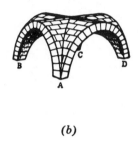

(a)   (b)

(a) Barrel Vault. (b) Cross Vault.

Romanesque tympanum: Sainte-Foy in Conques (c. 1130).

"Adoration of the Magi," Cloister capital, Moissac (c. 1100).

The great engineering achievement of the Romanesque architects was to replace flat wooden ceilings with stone vaulting, thereby creating buildings less susceptible to fire and more unified. In achieving this goal, the Romanesque builders constructed stone vaults far larger than ever before. The glittering mosaics and wooden roofs, which characterized the churches of late-

Roman, Byzantine, and Carolingian times, gave way to the domination of stone as the key material in both Romanesque architecture and Romanesque sculpture. Indeed, the inventive religious sculpture of the age—ornamenting the capitals of Romanesque columns and the semicircular area between the

Detail of right portal, Vézelay (begun 1120).

Cloister capital, Moissac (1100).

lintel and round arch of the portal (the *tympanum*)—were totally architectonic—completely fused into the structure of the church itself.

By the standards of the later Gothic style, the Romanesque interior is dark—characterized by heavy masses and relatively small windows. Graceful and richly decorated in southern Europe, the style tends to become increasingly severe as one moves northward. A church in the fully developed Romanesque style conveys a feeling of artistic unity and solidity. Its sturdy arches, vaults, and walls, and its somber, shadowy interior give the illusion of mystery and otherworldliness, yet suggest at the same time the steadfast might of the universal Church.

The Gothic Style

During the first half of the twelfth century, new structural elements began to be employed in the building of Romanesque churches: first, ribs of stone that crisscrossed the vaulting, carrying its weight down to the supporting columns and thus relieving the strain on the walls; next, pointed arches that permitted greater height in the vaults and arcades. By the middle of the century these novel features— vault rib and pointed arch—were providing the basis for an entirely new style of architecture, no longer Romanesque but Gothic. They were employed with such effect by Abbot Suger in his new abbey church of Saint-Denis near Paris around 1140 that Saint-Denis is regarded as the first true Gothic church.

French Gothic churches of the late twelfth century such as Notre Dame of Paris disclose the development of vault rib and pointed arch into a powerful, coherent style. During these exciting years, every decade brought new experiments and opened new possibilities in church building; yet Notre Dame of Paris and the churches of its period and region retain some of the heaviness and solidity of the earlier Romanesque. Not until the 1190s were the full potentialities of Gothic architecture realized. The use of the vault rib and pointed arch, and of a third Gothic structural element—the flying buttress—made it possible to support weights and stresses in a new way. The traditional building, of roof supported by walls, was transformed into a radically new kind of building—a skeleton—in which the stone vault rested not on walls but on slender columns and graceful exterior supports. The walls became mere screens—structurally unnecessary. With the passage of time, they were replaced increasingly by huge windows of stained glass which flooded the church interior with light and color. For concurrent with the Gothic architectural revolution was the development, in twelfth-century Europe, of the new art of stained-glass making. The glowing windows created in the twelfth and thirteenth centuries, with episodes from the Bible and religious legend depicted in shimmering blues and reds, have never been equalled.

The Gothic innovations of vault rib, pointed arch, and flying buttress

Nave looking east (showing vault ribs), Notre Dame in Paris (begun 1163).

created the breathtaking illusion of stone vaulting resting on walls of glass. The new churches rose upward in seeming defiance of gravity, losing their earthbound quality and reaching toward the heavens. By about the mid-thirteenth century all the structural possibilities of the Gothic skeleton design were fully realized, and in the towns of central and northern France there now rose churches of delicate, soaring stone with walls of lustrous glass. Never before in history had windows been so immense or buildings so lofty; and seldom since has European architecture been at once so daring and so assured.

Gothic sculpture, like Romanesque, was intimately related to architec-

High Gothic facade: Amiens Cathedral (showing the three west portals decorated with sculpture: thirteenth century).

ture, yet the two styles differed markedly. Romanesque fantasy, exuberance, and distortion gave way to a serene, self-confident naturalism. Human figures were no longer crowded together on the capitals of pillars; often they stood as statues—great rows of them—in niches on the cathedral exteriors: saints, prophets, kings, and angels, Christ and the Virgin Mary, depicted as tall, slender figures, calm yet warmly human, often young and sometimes smiling. The greatest Gothic churches of thirteenth-century France—Bourges, Chartres, Amiens, Reims, Sainte-Chapelle—are among the most impressive

High Gothic exterior: Reims Cathedral (showing the great clerestory windows around the rounded east end, and the decorated flying buttresses: thirteenth century).

buildings on earth. They bring together many separate arts: architecture, sculpture, stained glass, liturgical music—all directed to the single end of providing a majestic background for the central act of Christian worship, the reenactment of Christ's Last Supper and sacrificial death, the Mass itself.

Cathedral Life in the Middle Ages

Stepping inside a medieval cathedral today, one finds an atmosphere of awesome quiet that contrasts sharply with the bustle of the surrounding city. But in the Middle Ages, cathedrals were centers of urban life rather than refuges from it. The cathedral bells announced the hours of the business day, called university students to their studies, and proclaimed great public events—a victory in battle, the death of a famous person, the birth of a prince or princess. Townspeople flocked to their cathedral not for the Mass alone, but for marriages, baptisms, funerals, civic and religious festivals, excommunications, and victory celebrations. Famous traveling preachers addressed huge crowds from cathedral pulpits and sometimes stirred them into frenzied enthusiasm. Often a cathedral was the site of a great assembly of nobles and princes or of a public meeting of the town council. On major feast days— Easter, Christmas, Pentecost, and others—the cathedral would be ablaze with candles. Colorful processions would march noisily along its aisles and then out through its portals into the narrow streets of the city.

Every cathedral prided itself in possessing the relics of saints, and these

High Gothic interior: Amiens Cathedral looking east toward the rounded
apse (thirteenth century).

relics might attract pilgrims from far and wide—many of them crippled or ill,
desperate for a miraculous cure. At night, pilgrims might be found sleeping on
the cathedral's straw-covered floor in company with local beggars and drunks.
On great feast days, the church would be swarming with pilgrims and local
worshipers. Abbot Suger, describing a boisterous multitude that pressed into
his abbey church of St. Denis, complained of "howling men" and of women
who screamed "as though they were giving birth." The crowd of visitors,
shoving and struggling to see the relics of St. Denis, forced the abbey's monks
"to flee through the windows, carrying the relics with them."

Even larger crowds were drawn to Canterbury Cathedral to visit the
wonder-working tomb of St. Thomas Becket. If we could travel backwards in
time to witness the scene, we would be appalled at the sight of cripples
writhing on the floor near the tomb, the ear-shattering cries of the mentally
deranged, the suffocating odor of poverty and disease. We would hear people
shouting out their prayers in the half-darkness, or see them offering their pen-
nies and homemade candles in desperate appeal for the saint's help. Someone

High Gothic sculpture: Apostle's head, from Sens Cathedral (central France, c. 1190-1200).

is loudly explaining his miraculous cure to a monk; someone else is vomiting in a corner. Well-dressed nobles are there, too, along with some high officials of the Church; they ignore the crowds of poor and diseased as they await their opportunity to present offerings of silver or gems.*

Canterbury Cathedral was a singularly popular pilgrimage center. Few holy relics were as famed for miraculous cures as those of St. Thomas Becket. But all across medieval Europe the cathedrals teemed with women and men from all social levels. One would encounter there the commotion and stench, the hopes and griefs, of a turbulent cross section of humanity.

* R.C. Finucane, "The Use and Abuse of Medieval Miracles," *History*, 60 (1975), 1.

Head of the Virgin Mary, from the west facade of Reims Cathedral; first half of the thirteenth century.

Chapter 14

❦

The
World of
Intellect

The Rise of Universities

Like the Gothic cathedral, the university was a product of the medieval town. The urban revolution of the eleventh and twelfth centuries brought about the decline of the old monastic schools which had done so much to preserve culture over the previous centuries. They were superseded north of the Alps by cathedral schools and in Italy by semi-secular municipal schools. Both the cathedral schools and the municipal schools had long existed, but it was only in the eleventh century that they rose to prominence. Many of these schools now became centers of higher learning of a sort that Europe had not known for centuries. Their enrollments increased and their faculties grew until, in the twelfth century, some of them evolved into universities.

In the Middle Ages, *university* was a vague term. A university was simply a group of persons associated for any purpose. The word was commonly applied to the merchant guilds and craft guilds of the rising towns. A guild or "university" of students and scholars engaged in the pursuit of higher learning was given the more specific name, *studium generale*. When we speak of the medieval university, therefore, we are referring to an institution that would have been called a *studium generale* by a person of the thirteenth century. It

❦

differed from lesser schools in three significant respects: (1) the *studium generale* was open to students from many lands, not simply those from the surrounding districts; (2) the *studium generale* was a large school with a number of specialist teachers rather than merely one versatile master; (3) the *studium generale* offered both elementary and advanced curricula. It offered a basic program of instruction in the traditional "seven liberal arts": astronomy, geometry, arithmetic, music, grammar, rhetoric, and logic; and also instruction in one or more of the "higher" disciplines: theology, law, and medicine. Upon the successful completion of his liberal arts curriculum, the student could apply for a license to teach, but he might also wish to continue his studies by specializing in medicine, theology, or civil or canon law.

Fundamentally, then, the medieval university was neither a campus nor a complex of buildings, but a guild—a privileged corporation of teachers, or sometimes of students. With its classes normally held in rented rooms, it was a highly mobile institution, and on more than one occasion, when a university was dissatisfied with local conditions it won important concessions from the townspeople simply by threatening to move elsewhere.

In the thirteenth century, universities flourished at Paris, Bologna, Naples, Montpellier, Oxford, Cambridge, and elsewhere. Paris, Oxford, and a number of others were dominated by guilds of instructors in the liberal arts. Bologna, whose pattern was followed by other universities of southern Europe, was governed by a guild of students. The Bologna student guild managed to reduce the exorbitant local prices of food and lodgings by threatening to move collectively to another town and established strict rules of conduct for the instructors. Professors, for example, were placed under the outrageous obligation to begin and end their classes on time and to cover the prescribed curriculum. Since Bologna specialized in legal studies, its pupils were older professional students for the most part—students who had completed their liberal arts curriculum and were determined to secure sufficient training for successful careers in law.

Notwithstanding the enormous differences between medieval and modern university life, the modern university is a direct outgrowth of its high-medieval predecessor. We owe to the medieval university such customs as the formal teaching license, the practice—unknown to antiquity—of group instruction, the awarding of academic degrees, the notion of a liberal arts curriculum, and the tradition of honoring commencement day by dressing in clerical garb (caps and gowns).

Student Life at the University of Paris

Thirteenth-century student life can best be described by looking at a particular university at a particular time. Let us imagine ourselves at the University of Paris in the days of St. Louis and St. Thomas Aquinas. Here the intellectual environment was alive with philosophical disputes and passionate intellectual rivalries. And besides these battles of words, there were frequent tavern brawls, sometimes exploding into full-scale battles between students and townspeople, or among rival student gangs. New students were hazed unmercifully and imaginatively, while unpopular professors were hissed, shouted down, or, as a last resort, pelted with stones.

Students came to the University of Paris from all over Western Christendom. Most of them were from the middle social stratum of town dwellers and lesser landholders. Poor boys occasionally made it, but the sons of the high aristocracy did not flock in until a later era; university educations did not become fashionable in high society until after 1500. And there were no women students at all. (Until recent years women were excluded from most Oxford and Cambridge colleges and denied admission to some of America's foremost private universities.)

The letters of medieval students to their parents or guardians have a curiously modern ring:

❝ The city is expensive and makes many demands: I have to rent lodgings, buy necessities, and provide for many other things that I cannot specify. Therefore I beg your paternity that by the prompting of divine pity you may assist me, so that I may be able to complete what I have so well begun. **❞**

A father replies to his son:

❝ I have recently learned that you live dissolutely, preferring play to work, and strumming your guitar while others are at their studies. **❞**

In the course of the thirteenth century, wealthy benefactors founded residential colleges at Paris where poor students could receive room and board. Some students were monks or friars and lived in houses built and supported by their orders. But most students found whatever rented rooms they could afford, and more than one student riot was inspired by the high prices charged by burghers for food and housing.

Students in thirteenth-century Paris began their day at five or six in the morning, when the great bells of Notre Dame Cathedral summoned them to work. They would flock out of their rooms and boarding houses into the narrow, noisy streets and on to the lecture halls, which were scattered about the university quarter of the city. These halls were bare and bitterly cold in the winter. Some of them had rough benches; in others the students had to sit on a straw-covered floor, using their knees to support the wax tablets on which they took their lecture notes. The teacher mounted a platform at one end of the room and sat down to deliver a lecture that might run on all morning, unenlivened by audio-visual aids.

In the afternoon, students would congregate in the meadows outside the city walls to join in various sports: races, long-jump contests, lawn bowling, swimming, ball games of different sorts, and free-for-all fights pitting students from one region of Europe against those from another. In the evenings, serious students retired to their rooms for study, while the funlovers gathered in Paris's numerous taverns.

To many students, a university education opened the way to a successful career in medicine, law, or teaching, or to a desirable administrative post in the Church or royal government. Some students were devoted scholars, fascinated by their subjects. Others were ambitious climbers, eager to raise themselves above the status of their parents. Still others were devotees of wine, women, and song. And many were a bit of each.

Medicine

The chief medical school of medieval Europe was the University of Salerno in southern Italy. Here, in a land of vigorous cultural intermingling, scholars were able to draw from the medical heritage of Islam and Byzantium. In general, medieval medical scholarship was a bizarre medley of cautious observation, common sense, and gross superstition. In one instance we encounter the good advice that a person should eat and drink in moderation. But we are also instructed that onions will cure baldness, that the urine of a dog is an admirable cure for warts, and that all one must do to prevent a woman from conceiving is to bind her head with a red ribbon. Yet in the midst of all this, important progress was being made in medical science. The comprehensive medical writings of the second-century scientist Galen were studied and digested, along with the important works of Arab medical scholars. And to this invaluable body of knowledge Europeans were now making their own original contributions on such subjects as the curative properties of plants and the anatomy of the human body. It is probable that both animal and human dissections were performed by the scholars of twelfth-century Salerno. These doctors, crude and primitive though their methods were, laid the foundations on which Western European medical science was to rise.

Civil and Canon Law

Medieval legal scholarship addressed itself to two distinct bodies of material: civil law and canon law. The legal structure of early medieval society was largely Germanic in inspiration and custom-based, particularly in northern Europe where Roman law had virtually disappeared. Customary law remained strong throughout the High Middle Ages: it governed the relationships among the feudal aristocracy and determined the obligations of the medieval peasantry. It limited the prerogatives of kings, and underlay Magna Carta. But from the late eleventh century on, Roman law was studied in Bologna and other European universities. Christendom was now exposed to a distinctly different legal tradition—coherent and logical—that began to compete with Germanic law, to rationalize it, and in some instances to replace it.

The foundation of medieval Roman law was the *Corpus Juris Civilis* of Justinian, which was all but unknown in the West throughout most of the early Middle Ages but reappeared at Bologna in the last quarter of the eleventh century. Italy remained the center of Roman legal studies throughout the High Middle Ages. The traditions of Roman law had never entirely disappeared there, and the Italian peninsula therefore provided the most fertile soil for their revival. From Italy the study of Roman law spread northward. A great school of law emerged at Montpellier in southern France, and others flourished at Orléans, Paris, and Oxford. But Bologna remained the foremost center of Roman legal studies. There, scholars known as "glossators " wrote analytical commentaries on the *Corpus Juris,* elucidating difficult points and reconciling apparent contradictions. Later on they began to produce textbooks and important original treatises on the *Corpus* and to reorganize it into a coherent sequence of topics. Eventually such an extensive body of supplementary material existed that the glossators turned to the task of glossing the glosses— elucidating the elucidations. Around the mid-thirteenth century the work of the earlier glossators was brought to culmination with a comprehensive work by the Bolognese scholar Accursius—the *Glossa Ordinaria*—which was a composite synthesis of all previous commentaries on the *Corpus Juris.* Thereafter the *Glossa Ordinaria* became the authoritative supplement to the *Corpus Juris* in courts of Roman law.

The impact of the glossators was particularly strong in Italy and southern France where elements of Roman law had survived as local custom. By the thirteenth century Roman law was beginning to make a significant impact in the north as well, for by then civil lawyers trained in the Roman tradition were achieving an increasingly dominant role in the courts of France, Germany, and Spain. These men devoted themselves wholeheartedly to the royal service and used their legal training to exalt their monarchs. Although the Roman legal tradition had originally contained a strong element of constitutionalism, it inherited from Justinian's age an autocratic cast that the court lawyers of the rising monarchies put to effective use. Thus as Roman law gained an increasingly firm hold in the states of continental Europe it tended to make their governments at once more systematic and more autocratic. In France, for example, civil lawyers played an important part in the gradual transformation of the Capetian feudal monarchy into the royal absolutism of early modern times. And the development and durability of the parliamentary regime in England owed much to the fact that a strong monarchy, founded on the principles of Germanic law with its custom-based limitations on royal authority, was already well established before northern Europe felt the full impact of the Roman law revival.

Canon law developed alongside Roman law and derived a great deal from it. Methods of scholarship were similar in the two fields—commentaries and glosses were common to both—and the ecclesiastical courts borrowed much from the principles and procedures of Roman law. But whereas Roman law was based on the single authority of Justinian's *Corpus Juris,* canon law drew from many sources: the Bible, the writings of the ancient Church fathers, the canons of Church councils, and the decretals of popes. The *Corpus Juris,* although susceptible to endless commentary, was fundamentally complete in itself; popes and councils, on the other hand, continued to issue decrees, and canon law was therefore capable of unlimited development.

Canon law, like civil law, first became a serious scholarly discipline in eleventh-century Bologna and later spread to other major centers of learning. The study of canon law was strongly stimulated by the Investiture Controversy and subsequent church-state struggles, for the papacy looked to canon lawyers to support its claims with cogent, documented arguments and apt precedents. But the medieval scholars of canon law were far more than mere papal propagandists. They were grappling with the formidable problem of systematizing their sources, explaining what was unclear, reconciling what seemed contradictory—in other words, imposing order on the immense variety of dicta, opinions, and precedents upon which their discipline was based.

The essential goal of the canon lawyers was to assemble their diverse sources—their canons—into a single coherent work. It was up to them, in short, to accomplish the task that Justinian had performed for Roman law back in the sixth century. The civil lawyers had their *Corpus Juris Civilis;* it was up to the canon lawyers to create their own "Corpus Juris Canonici." The first attempts to produce comprehensive canonical collections date from the early Middle Ages, but it was not until the eleventh-century revival at Bologna that serious scholarly standards were applied to the task. The definitive collection was completed around 1140 by the great Bolognese canon lawyer Gratian. Originally entitled *The Concordance of Discordant Canons,* Gratian's work is known to posterity as the *Decretum.*

Gratian not only brought together an immense body of canons from a bewildering variety of sources; he also framed them in a logical, topically-organized scheme. Using methods that were just beginning to be employed by scholastic philosophers, he raised questions in logical sequence, quoted the relevant canons, and endeavored to reconcile contradictions. The result was an ordered body of general legal principles validated by passages from the Bible, the fathers, and papal and conciliar decrees. The *Decretum* became the authoritative text in ecclesiastical tribunals and the basis of all future study in canon law.

As time passed, and new decrees were issued, it became necessary to supplement Gratian's *Decretum* by collecting the canons issued after 1140. One such collection was made in 1234 under the direction of the lawyer-pope Gregory IX, another in the pontificate of Boniface VIII, and still others in later generations. Together, the *Decretum* and the supplementary collections were given the title, *Corpus Juris Canonici,* and became the ecclesiastical equivalent of Justinian's *Corpus.* These two great compilations, ecclesiastical and civil, reflect the parallel growth of Medieval Europe's two supreme sources of administrative and jurisdictional authority: church and monarchy.

The Background of High Medieval Philosophy

It is only to be expected that an age which witnessed such sweeping economic and political changes and such vigorous creativity in religious and artistic expression would also achieve notable success in the realms of abstract thought. Medieval philosophy is marked by avid curiosity and heated controversy. Although every important philosopher in the High Middle Ages was a churchman of one sort or another, ecclesiastical authority did not stifle speculation. Catholic orthodoxy, which hardened noticeably at the time of the Protestant Reformation, was still flexible in the twelfth and thirteenth centuries, and the philosophers of the age were far from being timid apologists for official dogmas. If some of them were impelled by conviction to provide the Catholic faith with a logical substructure, others asserted vigorously that reason does not lead to the truth of Christian revelation. And among those who sought to harmonize faith and reason there was sharp disagreement as to what form the logical substructure should take. All were believers—all were Catholics—but their doctrinal unanimity did not limit their diversity or curb their spirit of adventure.

The high medieval philosophers drew nourishment from five earlier sources: (1) From the Greeks they inherited the great philosophical systems of Plato and Aristotle. At first these two Greek masters were known in the West only through a handful of translations and commentaries dating from late Roman times. By the thirteenth century, however, new and far more complete translations were coming into Christendom from Spain and Sicily, and Aristotelian philosophy became a matter of intense interest and controversy in Europe's universities. (2) From the Islamic world came a flood of Greek scientific and philosophical works that had long before been translated into Arabic and were now retranslated from Arabic into Latin. These works came into Europe accompanied by extensive commentaries and original writings of Arab philosophers and scientists, for the Arabs had come to grips with Greek learning long before the advent of the High Middle Ages. Islamic thought made a particularly vital contribution to European science. In philosophy it was enriched by the work of Jewish scholars such as Moses Maimonides (1135–1204), whose *Guide for the Perplexed*—a penetrating reconciliation of Aristotle and Scripture—influenced the work of thirteenth-century Christian philosophers and theologians. (3) The early Church fathers, particularly Ambrose, Jerome, and Augustine, had been a dominant intellectual force throughout the early Middle Ages and their authority remained strong in the twelfth and thirteenth centuries. St. Augustine retained his singular significance and was, indeed, the chief vessel of Platonic and Neoplatonic thought in the medieval universities. No philosopher of the High Middle Ages could ignore him, and some of the most distinguished of them were conscious and devoted Augustinians. (4) The early medieval scholars themselves contributed significantly to the high medieval intellectual revival. Gregory the Great, Isidore of Seville, Bede, Alcuin, Raban Maur, John the Scot, and Gerbert of Aurillac were all studied in the new universities. The original intellectual contributions of these men were less important, however, than the fact that they and their contemporaries had kept learning alive, fostering and perpetuating the classical tradition in Europe, and thus creating the intellectual climate that made possible the reawakening of philosophical speculation in the eleventh century. (5) The high-medieval philosophers looked back beyond the scholars of the early Middle Ages, beyond the fathers of the early Church, to the Hebrew and primitive Christian religious traditions as recorded in Scripture. Among medieval theologians the Bible, the chief written source of divine revelation, was the fundamental text and the ultimate authority.

Such were the chief elements—Greek, Islamic-Jewish, Patristic, early medieval, and scriptural—that underlay the thought of the scholastic philosophers. Strictly defined, scholasticism is simply the philosophical movement associated with the high medieval schools—the cathedral and monastic schools and later the universities. More basically it was a movement concerned above all with exploring the relationship between rationalism and theism—reason and revelation. All medieval scholastics were theists; all were committed, to some degree, to the life of reason. Many of them were immensely enthusiastic over the intellectual possibilities inherent in the careful application of Aristotelian logic to basic human and religious problems. Some believed that the syllogism was the master key to a thousand doors and that with sufficient methodological rigor, with sufficient exactness in the use of words, the potentialities of human reason were all but limitless.

The scholastics applied their logical method to a multitude of problems. They were concerned chiefly, however, with matters of basic significance to human existence: the nature of human beings, the purpose of human life, the existence and attributes of God, the fundamentals of human morality, the ethical imperatives of social and political life, the relationship between God and humanity. It would be hard to deny that these are the most profound sorts of questions that one can ask, although many philosophers of our own day are inclined to reject them as unanswerable. Perhaps they are. But the scholastics, standing near the beginning of Europe's long intellectual journey, and lacking the modern sense of disillusionment, were determined to make the attempt.

The Relationship of Faith and Reason

Among the diverse investigations and conflicting opinions of the medieval philosophers, three central issues deserve particular attention: the degree of interrelationship between faith and reason; the relative merits of the Platonic-

Augustinian and the Aristotelian intellectual traditions; and the reality of the Platonic archetypes, or, as they were called in the Middle Ages, "universals."

The issue of faith *vs.* reason was perhaps the most far-reaching of the three. Ever since Tertullian in the third century, there had been Christian writers who insisted that God so transcended reason that any attempt to approach him intellectually was useless and, indeed, blasphemous. It was the mystic who knew God, not the theologian. Tertullian had posed the rhetorical questions,

❝ What has Athens to do with Jerusalem? What concord is there between the Academy and the Church? . . . Let us have done with all attempts to produce a bastard Christianity of Stoic, Platonic, and dialectic composition! We desire no curious disputation after possessing Christ Jesus, no logical analyses after enjoying the Gospel! ❞

Tertullian had many followers in the Middle Ages. St. Peter Damiani, standing at the source of the new medieval piety, rejected the intellectual road to God in favor of the mystical. Damiani had insisted that God, whose power is limitless, cannot be bound or even approached by logic. He was followed in this view by such later mystics as St. Bernard, who denounced his brilliant rationalist contemporary Peter Abelard, and St. Francis, who regarded intellectual speculation as irrelevant and perhaps even dangerous to salvation. A later spiritual Franciscan, Jacopone da Todi, expressed the anti-intellectual position in verse:

*P*lato and Socrates may oft contend,
And all the breath within their bodies spend,
Engaged in disputations without end.
What's that to me?
For only with a pure and simple mind
Can one the narrow path to heaven find,
And greet the King; while lingers far behind,
Philosophy.

The contrary view was just as old. Third-century theologians such as Clement and Origen in the school of Alexandria had labored to provide Christianity with a sturdy philosophical foundation and did not hesitate to elucidate the faith by means of Greek—and particularly Platonic—thought. The fourth-century Latin Doctors, Ambrose, Jerome, and Augustine, had wrestled with the problem of whether a Christian might properly use elements from the pagan classical tradition in the service of the faith, and all three ended with affirmative answers. As Augustine expressed it,

❝ If those who are called philosophers, and especially the Platonists, have said anything that is true and in harmony with our faith, we must not only not shrink from it, but claim it for our own use from those who have unlawful possession of it. **"**

Such is the viewpoint that underlies most of high medieval philosophy—that reason has a valuable role to play as a servant of revelation. St. Anselm, following Augustine, declared, "I believe so that I may know." Faith comes first, reason second; faith rules reason, but reason can perform the useful service of illuminating faith. Indeed, faith and reason are separate avenues to a single body of truth. By their very nature they cannot lead to contradictory conclusions, for truth is one. Should their conclusions ever *appear* to be contradictory, the philosopher can be assured that some flaw exists in his logic. Reason cannot err, but our use of it can, and revelation must therefore be the criterion against which reason is measured.

This, in general, became the common position of later scholastic philosophers. The intellectual system of St. Thomas Aquinas was built on the conviction that reason and faith were harmonious. Even the arch-rationalist of the twelfth century, Peter Abelard, wrote: "I do not wish to be Aristotle if it must separate me from Christ." Abelard believed that he could at once be a philosopher and a Christian, but his faith took first priority.

Among some medieval philosophers the priorities were reversed. Averroës, a profound Aristotelian Muslim of twelfth-century Spain, boldly asserted the superiority of reason over faith. He affirmed the truth of several propositions that were logical byproducts of Aristotle's philosophy but were directly contrary to Islamic and Christian doctrine. Averroës taught, following Aristotle, that the world had always existed and was therefore uncreated—that all human actions were determined—that there was no personal salvation but only the return of human raindrops to the divine ocean. In the thirteenth century a Christian philosophical school known as Latin Averroism became active at the University of Paris and elsewhere. Latin Averroists such as Siger of Brabant took the position that reason and revelation led to radically contrary conclusions. As Christians they accepted the teachings of the Church as ultimate truth, but as scholars they insisted that the conclusions of Aristotle and Averroës, being logically airtight, were "philosophically necessary." This position came to be called the doctrine of the "twofold truth."

The Latin Averroists shared with anti-intellectuals such as Damiani the belief that reason did not lead to the truth of revelation; they shared with Anselm and Aquinas the conviction that ultimate truth was revealed truth. Yet unlike most scholastics they abandoned altogether the effort to harmonize reason and revelation, and unlike the anti-intellectuals they did not reject philosophy but made it their profession. As believers they conceded the supremacy of dogma; as philosophers they insisted on the supremacy of reason. And although Siger of Brabant and most of his contemporaries appear to have held this awkward position in full sincerity, some of their successors became outright religious skeptics and only paid the necessary lip service to Christian doctrine. The fourteenth-century Latin Averroist John of Jandun, for example, never lost an opportunity to poke subtle fun at any Christian dogma that seemed to him contrary to reason. On the subject of the Creation, John points out that according to reason the world has always existed. He concludes—with tongue in cheek—that as Christians we must nevertheless believe that God created the world; "Let it be added that creation very seldom happens; there has been only one, and that was a very long time ago."

Platonism-Augustinianism versus Aristotelianism

Thus, medieval thought produced a diversity of views on the proper relationship of reason and revelation. The same is true of the other two issues that we are to consider: the rivalry between Platonism and Aristotelianism, and the controversy over universals. The conflict between the intellectual systems of Plato-Augustine and Aristotle did not emerge clearly until the thirteenth century when the full body of Aristotle's writings came into the West in Latin translations from Greek and Arabic. Until then, most efforts at applying reason to faith were based on the Platonic tradition transmuted and transmitted by Augustine to medieval Europe. St. Anselm, for example, was a dedicated Augustinian, as were many of his twelfth-century successors. The tradition was carried on brilliantly and sensitively in the thirteenth century by the Franciscan, St. Bonaventure. Many thoughtful Christians of the thirteenth century were deeply suspicious of the newly recovered Aristotelian writings, and the rise of Latin Averroism served to deepen their apprehensions. They regarded Aristotle as pagan in viewpoint and dangerous to the faith. Other thirteenth-century intellectuals, such as St. Thomas Aquinas, were much too devoted to the goal of reconciling faith and reason to reject the works of a man whom they regarded as antiquity's greatest philosopher. St. Thomas sought to Christianize Aristotle much as Augustine had Christianized Plato and the Neoplatonists. In the middle decades of the thirteenth century, as high medieval philosophy was reaching its crescendo, the Platonic and Aristotelian traditions flourished side by side, and in the works of certain English scientific thinkers of the age they achieved a singularly fruitful synthesis.

The Conflict over Universals

The contest between Platonism and Aristotelianism carried with it the seeds of yet another controversy: the argument over archetypes or universals. Plato had taught that terms such as "dog" or "cat" not only describe particular creatures but also are language-symbols for things that have reality in themselves—that individual cats are imperfect reflections of a model cat, an archetypal or universal cat. Similarly, there are many examples of circles, squares, or triangles. Were we to measure these individual figures with sufficiently refined instruments we would discover that they were imperfect in one respect or another. No circle in this world is absolutely round. No square or triangle has perfectly straight sides. They are merely crude approximations of a perfect "idea." In "heaven," Plato would say, the perfect triangle exists. It is the source of the concept of triangularity that lurks in our minds and of all the imperfect triangles that we see in the physical world. The heavenly triangle is not only perfect but *real.* The earthly triangles are less real, less significant, and less worthy of our attention. Or, to take still another example, we call certain acts "good" because they partake, imperfectly, of a universal good that exists in heaven. In short, these universals—cat, dog, circle, triangle, beauty, goodness, etc.—exist apart from the multitude of individual dogs, cats, circles, triangles, and beautiful and good things in this world. And the person who seeks knowledge ought to meditate on these universals rather than study the world of phenomena in which they are only imperfectly reflected.

St. Augustine accepted Plato's theory of universals but not without amendment. Augustine taught that the archetypes existed in the mind of God rather than in Plato's abstract "heaven." And whereas Plato had ascribed our knowledge of the universals to dim memories from a prenatal existence, Augustine maintained that God puts a knowledge of universals directly into our minds by a process of "divine illumination." Plato and Augustine agreed, however, that the universal existed apart from the particular and, indeed, was *more real* than the particular. In the High Middle Ages, those who followed the Platonic-Augustinian approach to universals were known as *realists*—they believed that universals were real.

The Aristotelian tradition brought with it another viewpoint on universals: they existed, to be sure, but only in the particular. Only by studying particular things in the world of phenomena could one gain a knowledge of universals. The human mind drew its knowledge of the universal from its observation of the particular by a process of abstraction. The universals were real, but in a sense less real—or at least less independently real—than Plato and Augustine believed. Accordingly, philosophers who inclined toward the Aristotelian position have been called *moderate realists.*

Medieval philosophers were by no means confined to a choice between these two points of view. Several of them worked out subtle solutions of their own. As early as the eleventh century the philosopher Roscellinus declared that universals were not real at all. "Dog," "cat," and "triangle" are mere words—names that we have concocted for bunches of individual things that we have lumped into arbitrary categories. These categories, or "universals," have no objective existence whatever. Reality is not to be found in them, but rather in the multiplicity and variety of individual objects which we can see, touch, and smell in the world around us. Those who followed Roscellinus in this view were known as *nominalists:* for them, the universals had no reality apart from their *nomina*— "names." Nominalism remained in the intellectual background during the twelfth and thirteenth centuries but was revived in the fourteenth. Many churchmen regarded it as a dangerous doctrine, since its emphasis on the particular over the universal seemed to suggest that the Church was not, as Catholics believed, a single universal body but rather a vast accumulation of individual Christians.

St. Anselm

Having examined three central issues of high medieval philosophy—the relationship of reason to revelation, the relative validity of the Platonic-Augustinian and Aristotelian systems of thought, and the problem of universals—we shall now see how they developed in the minds of individual philosophers between the eleventh and fourteenth centuries.

The scholastic philosophers first made their appearance in the later eleventh century as an aspect of the general reawakening that Europe was just then beginning to experience. The earliest important figure in scholasticism was St. Anselm (ca. 1033–1109), the Italian philosopher who became abbot of Bec in Normandy and later, as archbishop of Canterbury, brought the Investiture Controversy into England. During his eventful career he found time to write profoundly on a variety of philosophical and theological subjects.

As an Augustinian, Anselm took the realist position on the problem of universals. It was from Augustine, too, that he derived his attitude on the relationship of faith and reason. He taught that faith must precede reason, but that reason could serve to illuminate faith. His conviction that reason and faith were compatible made him a singularly important pioneer in the development of high medieval rationalism. He worked out several proofs of God, and in his important theological treatise, *Cur Deus Homo* (Why God became Man), he subjected the doctrines of the incarnation and atonement to rigorous logical analysis.

Anselm's emphasis on reason, employed within the framework of a firm Christian conviction, set the stage for the significant philosophical developments of the following generations. With Anselm, Western Christendom regained at last the intellectual level of the fourth-century Latin Doctors.

Abelard

The twelfth-century philosophers, intoxicated by the seemingly limitless possibilities of reason and logic, advanced across new intellectual frontiers at the very time that their contemporaries were pushing forward the territorial frontiers of Europe. The most audacious of these twelfth-century Christian rationalists was Peter Abelard (1079–1142), a celebrated teacher whose dazzling career ended in tragedy and defeat.

Abelard is perhaps best known for his love affair with the young Heloise, a relationship that ended with Abelard's castration at the hands of thugs hired by Heloise's enraged uncle. The lovers separated permanently, both taking

.nonastic vows, and in later years Abelard wrote regretfully of the affair in his autobiographical *History of My Calamities.* There followed a touching correspondence between the two lovers in which Heloise, now an abbess, confessed her enduring love, and Abelard, writing almost as a father confessor, offered her spiritual consolation but nothing more. Abelard's autobiography and the correspondence with Heloise survive to this day, providing modern students with a tender, intimate picture of romance and pathos in a society far removed from our own.*

Abelard was the supreme logician of the twelfth century. Writing several decades before the great influx of Aristotelian thought in Latin translation, he anticipated Aristotle's position on the question of universals by advocating a theory rather similar to Aristotle's moderate realism. Universals, Abelard believed, have no separate existence; our knowledge of them is derived from particular things by a process of abstraction. In a famous work entitled *Sic et Non* ("Yes and No"), Abelard collected opinions from the Bible, the Latin fathers, the councils of the Church, and the decrees of the papacy on a great variety of theological issues, demonstrating that these authorities often disagreed on important religious matters. Others before him had collected authoritative opinions on various theological and legal issues, but never so thoroughly or systematically. Abelard, in his *Sic et Non,* employed a method of inquiry that was developed and perfected by canon lawyers and philosophers over the next several generations. We have already seen how the canonist Gratian, in his *Decretum,* used the device of lining up conflicting authorities and reconciling them. Similarly, Abelard's successors in theology sought to reconcile contradictions and arrive at conclusions, whereas Abelard had earned the enmity of his conservative contemporaries by leaving the issues unresolved. Abelard was a devoted Christian, if something of an intellectual show-off, but many regarded him as a budding skeptic. Thus he left himself open to attacks by St. Bernard, who was deeply hostile to the Christian rationalist movement and called Abelard's theology a "fool-ology." The brilliant teacher was driven from one place to another until at length his opinions were condemned by an ecclesiastical council in 1141. Retiring to Cluny, he died in 1142. The abbot of Cluny wrote Heloise a touching letter (definitely authentic) praising Abelard's late-blooming humility and assuring her that on the day of the Lord's coming "His grace will restore him to you."

Peter Lombard and Hugh of Saint-Victor

Twelfth-century rationalism was far more than a one-man affair, and the attacks on Abelard failed to halt its growth. His student Peter Lombard (c. 1100–60) produced an important theological text, the *Book of Sentences,*

---

*It has recently been argued that the autobiography and correspondence are forgeries. Is nothing sacred?

which set off conflicting opinions on the pattern of the *Sic et Non*, but which, like Gratian's *Decretum*, took the further step of reconciling the contradictory authorities. Lombard's *Book of Sentences* remained for centuries a fundamental text in schools of theology.

The Augustinian tradition was best represented in Abelard's time at the school of Saint-Victor in Paris, and in particular by the distinguished scholar, Hugh of Saint-Victor (d. 1141). Hugh was a Christian rationalist, but he believed that reason was only the first step in one's approach to God. Beyond reason lay mysticism, and God could not be circumscribed by logic alone. Hugh and his school emphasized the subordination of the material to the spiritual, and—drawing on the ancient tradition of Biblical allegory—interpreted the entire natural world as a multitude of symbols pointing to spiritual truths.

John of Salisbury

The intellectual mood of the twelfth century was one of immense excitement at the possibilities of logic or dialectic. In this atmosphere, the remaining liberal arts—and especially the study of humanistic disciplines such as Latin literature—began to lose out in the competition. Cathedral schools of northern France such as Chartres, Paris, and Laon were important centers of literary studies in the eleventh century and remained so throughout much of the twelfth. But as the century progressed, as more and more Aristotelian texts became available, and as the vision of rational solutions to the great questions became ever more captivating, the interest of students and scholars shifted increasingly from literature to logic. The accomplished twelfth-century English scholar, John of Salisbury (c. 1115–80), was a pupil of Abelard's, a student of Greek, and a well-trained logician, but he was above all a humanist—a devotee of classical literature. He approved of dialectic but regretted that it was growing at the expense of other studies; he complained that the schools were tending to produce narrow logicians rather than broadly educated scholars.

In his *Policraticus* (1159), John of Salisbury made a major contribution to medieval political philosophy. Drawing on the thought of Classical Antiquity and the early Middle Ages, he stressed the divine nature of kingship but emphasized equally its responsibilities and limitations. The king drew his authority from God but was commissioned to rule for the good of his subjects rather than himself. He was bound to give his subjects peace and justice and to protect the Church. If he abused his commission and neglected his responsibilities he lost his divine authority, ceased to be a king, and became a tyrant. As such he forfeited his subjects' allegiance and was no longer their lawful ruler. Under extreme circumstances, and if all else failed, John of Salisbury recommended tyrannicide. A good Christian subject, although obliged to obey his king, might kill a tyrant. Apart from the highly original doctrine of tyrannicide, the views expressed in the *Policraticus* mirror the general political attitudes of the twelfth century—responsible limited monarchy and government in behalf of the governed. These theories, in turn, were idealized reflections of the actual feudal monarchies of the day that were deterred from autocracy by the power of the nobility, the authority of the Church, and ancient custom.

Translation and System-Building

In the later twelfth and early thirteenth centuries the movement of Christian rationalism was powerfully reinforced by the arrival of vast quantities of Greek and Arabic writings in Latin translation. For the first time, significant portions of the philosophical and scientific legacy of ancient Greece became available to European scholars. Above all, the full Aristotelian corpus now came into the West through the labors of translators in Spain, Sicily, and the Latin Empire of Constantinople.

These translations came in answer to a deep hunger on the part of Western thinkers for a fuller knowledge of the classical heritage in philosophy and science. The introduction of certain new Aristotelian works provoked a crisis in Western Christendom, for they contained implications that seemed hostile to the faith. And with them, as we have seen, came the skeptical and intellectually impressive works of the Islamic Spaniard Averroës, which gave rise to the doctrine of the "twofold truth." For a time it seemed as though reason and revelation were sundered, and the Church reacted in panic by condemning certain of Aristotle's writings. It was one of the major goals of thirteenth-century thought to refute the Latin Averroists—to rescue Aristotle and, indeed, reason itself for Western Christianity.

The thirteenth century differed sharply in spirit from the twelfth. The philosophers of the twelfth century were daring pioneers embarking on a great adventure. The thirteenth century, although by no means lacking in originality, was preeminently an age of consolidation and synthesis. Its scholars digested the insights and conclusions of the past and cast them into comprehensive systems of thought. Vincent of Beauvais (d. 1264) attempted in his *Speculum Majus* to bring together all knowledge of all imaginable subjects into one immense compendium. At a much higher level, theologians such as Alexander of Hales (d. 1245), Albertus Magnus (1193–1280), and Thomas Aquinas (1225–74) produced great systematic treatises on theology, known as summas, which provided structure and unity to the theological speculations of theirs and past ages.

St. Bonaventure

The thought of Aristotle loomed large in the thirteenth-century schools, but the Platonic-Augustinian tradition was well represented, too. There was a tendency for the Dominican scholars to espouse Aristotle, and the Franciscans to follow Plato and Augustine. Thus, the outstanding thirteenth-century exponent of Platonism-Augustinianism was the Franciscan St. Bonaventure (1221–74), an Italian of humble origin who rose to become a cardinal of the Church and minister-general of the Franciscan order.

Bonaventure was at once a philosopher and a mystic. Following in the Augustinian tradition, he was a realist on the matter of universals and a rationalist who stressed the subordination of reason to faith. He accepted the nature symbolism of Hugh of Saint-Victor, and visualized the whole physical universe as a multitude of symbols pointing to God and glorifying Him. For example, he regarded everything in the natural world that could possibly be divided into three parts as a reflection of the Holy Trinity. Bonaventure's universe was eternally reaching upward toward the Divine Presence.

Bonaventure believed that, as mortals, we stand at the fulcrum of creation. Our bodies make us the kin of beasts; our souls give us kinship with the angels. We perceive the physical universe through our senses, but we know the spiritual world—the world of universals—through the grace of divine illumination. The road to God and to truth, therefore, lies in introspection, meditation, and worship, not in observation and experiment.

Bonaventure's philosophy is not coldly intellectual but warm and deeply spiritual. His discussion of God's attributes becomes a litany—an act of worship. His emphasis is less on knowledge than on love, and his entire system of thought is a kind of prayer in praise of God.

The New Aristotelianism; St. Albertus Magnus

While Bonaventure was bringing new dimensions to traditional Platonism-Augustinianism, several of his contemporaries were coming to grips with the great Aristotelian-Averroistic challenge to orthodox Christian rationalism. The conflicting intellectual currents of the age were brilliantly represented by philosophers and theologians on the faculty of the mid-century University of Paris—the Augustinian Bonaventure, the Latin Averroist Siger of Brabant, and the orthodox Aristotelians Albertus Magnus and Thomas Aquinas.

Albertus and his student, Thomas Aquinas, were both Dominicans, and both devoted themselves wholeheartedly to the reconciliation of reason and faith through the fusion of Aristotelianism and Christianity. They sought to confound the Latin Averroists by demonstrating that reason and revelation pointed to one truth, not two. A native of Germany, Albertus Magnus was a scholar of widely ranging interests who made important contributions to natural science—especially biology—as well as to philosophy and theology. He was a master of Aristotelian thought and a summa writer, whose goal was to purge Aristotle of the heretical taint of Averroism and transform his philosophy into the intellectual foundation of Christian orthodoxy. Albertus

Magnus came near to realizing this goal, but its full achievement was left to his gifted student, Thomas Aquinas.

St. Thomas Aquinas

St. Thomas was born of a Norman-Italian noble family in 1225. His parents intended him to become a Benedictine monk and to rise in due course to a lucrative abbacy. But in 1244 he shocked them by joining the radical new Dominican Order. He went to the University of Paris shortly thereafter and spent his ensuing years traveling, teaching, and writing. Unlike Augustine he had no youthful follies to regret. Unlike Anselm and Bernard, he played no great role in the political affairs of his day. He persevered in his academic tasks until, late in life, he suddenly declared that all his books were worthless and devoted his remaining days to mysticism. At his death, the priest who heard his final confession described it as being as innocent as that of a five-year-old.

From the standpoint of intellectual history St. Thomas is a figure of singular interest and significance. In his copious writings—particularly his great comprehensive work, the *Summa Theologica*—he explored all the great questions of philosophy and theology, political theory and morality. He used Aristotle's logical method and Aristotle's categories of thought but arrived at conclusions that were in complete harmony with the Christian faith. Like Abelard, St. Thomas assembled every possible argument, pro and con, on every subject that he discussed, but unlike Abelard he drew conclusions and defended them with cogent arguments. Few philosophers before or since have been so generous in presenting and exploring opinions contrary to their own, and none has been so systematic and exhaustive.

St. Thomas created a vast, unified intellectual system, ranging from God to the natural world, logically supported at every step. His theological writings have none of the fiery passion of St. Augustine, none of the literary elegance of Plato; rather, they have an *intellectual* elegance, an elegance of system and organization akin to that of Euclid's geometry. His *Summa Theologica* is organized into an immense series of separate sections, each section dealing with a particular philosophical question. In Part I of the *Summa*, for example, Question 2 takes up the problem of God's existence. The *Question* is subdivided into three *Articles:* (1) "Whether God's existence is self-evident" (St. Thomas concludes that it is not); (2) "Whether it can be demonstrated that God exists" (St. Thomas concludes that it can be demonstrated); and (3) "Whether God exists" (here St. Thomas propounds five separate proofs of God's existence).

In each *Article,* St. Thomas takes up a specific problem and subjects it to rigorous formal analysis. First, he presents a series of *Objections (Objection 1, Objection 2,* etc.) in which he sets forth as effectively as he possibly can all the arguments *contrary* to his final conclusion. For example, *Question 2, Article 3,*

"Whether God exists," begins with two *Objections* purporting to demonstrate that God does not exist. One of them runs as follows:

** *Objection 1.*** It seems that God does not exist, because if one of two contraries can be infinite, the other would be altogether destroyed. But the name "God" means that He is infinite goodness. Therefore, if God existed there would be no evil discoverable; but there is evil in the world. Therefore God does not exist. ** **

After presenting the *Objections,* St. Thomas then turns to the second step in his analysis, the appeal to authority. This appeal is always introduced by the phrase, *On the contrary,* followed by a quotation from Scripture or from some authoritative patristic source that supports St. Thomas's own opinion on the subject. In the *Article* on God's existence the *Objections* are followed by the statement, "On the contrary, it is said in the person of God: 'I am Who I am' (Exodus, 3:14)." Having cited his authority, St. Thomas next appeals to reason and subjects the problem to his own logical scrutiny, beginning always with the formula, I *answer that . . . ,* for example, "I answer that, The existence of God can be proved in five ways" (followed by a presentation of five proofs of the existence of God). Here is one:

** ** The fifth way is taken from the governance of the world. We see that things which lack knowledge, such as natural bodies, act for an end, and this is evident from their acting always or nearly always in the same way, so as to obtain the best result. Hence it is clear that they achieve their end not only by chance but by design. Now whatever lacks knowledge cannot move toward an end unless it be directed by some being endowed with knowledge and intelligence, as the arrow is directed by the archer. Therefore some intelligent being exists by whom all natural things are directed to their end; and this being we call God. ** **

The analysis concludes with refutations of the earlier *Objections:*

** *Reply to Objection 1.*** As Augustine says, 'Since God is the highest good, He would not allow any evil to exist in His works unless His omnipotence and goodness were such as to bring good even out of evil.' This is part of the infinite goodness of God, that He should allow evil to exist, and out of it to produce good. ** **

Having completed his analysis, St. Thomas then turns to the next *Article* or the next *Question* and subjects it to precisely the same process of inquiry: *Objections; On the Contrary; I answer that;* and *Reply to Objections.* As in Euclidian geometry so in Thomistic theology, once a problem is settled the conclusion can be used in solving subsequent problems. Thus the system grows, problem by problem, step by step, as St. Thomas's wide-ranging mind takes up such matters as the nature of God, the attributes of God, the nature and destiny of man, human morality, law, and political theory. The result is an imposing, comprehensive edifice of thought, embracing all major theological issues.

As the Gothic cathedral was the artistic embodiment of the high medieval world, so the philosophy of Aquinas was its supreme intellectual expression. Both were based on clear and obvious principles of structure. St. Thomas shared with the cathedral builders the impulse to display rather than disguise the structural framework of his edifice. Like the boldly executed Gothic flying buttress, the Thomistic *Questions, Articles,* and *Objections* allowed no doubt as to what the builder was doing, where he was going, or how he was acheiving his effects.

As a Christian and Aristotelian, Aquinas contended against both the Augustinians, who would reject Aristotle altogether, and the Latin Averroists, who would make a heretic of him. St. Thomas distinguished carefully between revelation and reason but endeavored to prove that they could never contradict one another. Since human reason was a valid avenue to truth, since Christian revelation was authoritative, and since truth was one, then philosophy and Christian doctrine had to be compatible and complementary. "For faith rests upon infallible truth, and therefore its contrary cannot be demonstrated." This was the essence of St. Thomas's philosophical position.

As against the Augustinianism of St. Anselm, Hugh of Saint-Victor, and St. Bonaventure, Aquinas emphasized the reality of the physical world as a world of things rather than symbols. Embracing the moderate realism of Aristotle, he declared that universals were to be found in the world of phenomena and nowhere else—that knowledge came from observation and analysis, not from divine illumination. He shared with St. Francis and others the notion that the physical world was deeply significant in itself, that matter mattered.

Similarly the state, which previous Christian thinkers had commonly regarded as a necessary evil—an unfortunate but indispensable consequence of the Fall of Adam—was accepted by Aquinas as a good and natural outgrowth of humanity's social impulse. He echoed Aristotle's dictum that "Man is a political creature" and regarded the justly governed state as a fitting part of the divine order. Like John of Salisbury, St. Thomas insisted that kings must govern in their subjects' behalf and that a willful, unrestrained ruler who ignored God's moral imperatives was no king but a tyrant. Just as the human body could be corrupted by sin, the body politic could be corrupted by tyranny. But although the Christian must reject both sin and tyranny, he should nevertheless revere the body, the state, and indeed all physical creation as worthy products of God's will, inseparable from the world of spirit, and essential ingredients in the unity of existence.

Aquinas sought to encompass the totality of being in a vast existential unity. At the center was God, the author of physical and spiritual creation, the maker of heaven and earth, who himself had assumed human form and redeemed mankind on the cross, who discloses portions of the truth to man through revelation, permits him to discover other portions through the operation of his intellect, and will lead him into all truth through salvation. Ultimately, God *is* truth, and it is our destiny, upon reaching heaven, to stand unshielded in the divine presence—to love and to know. Thus the roads of St. Thomas, St. Bonaventure, St. Bernard, and Dante, although passing over very different terrain, arrive finally at the same destination. It is not so surprising, after all, that in the end St. Thomas rejected the way of the philosopher for the way of the mystic.

Critics of St. Thomas

To this day there are people of keen intelligence who accept the philosophy of St. Thomas. On the other hand, many of his own thirteenth-century contemporaries rejected it in whole or in part, and it remained a source of intense controversy in the centuries that followed. Franciscans such as Bonaventure were particularly suspicious of the intellectual *tour de force* of this gifted Dominican. Bonaventure was a rationalist, but a cautious one, and his Franciscan successors came increasingly to the opinion that reason was of little or no use in probing metaphysical problems. The Scottish Franciscan Duns Scotus (d. 1308) undertook a subtle critique of St. Thomas's theory of knowledge. And in the philosophy of the astute English Franciscan, William of Ockham (c. 1300–1349), reason and revelation were divorced altogether.* Christian doctrine, Ockham said, could not be approached by reason at all but had to be accepted on faith. The Thomist synthesis was a mirage. Reason's province was the natural world and that alone.

Science

The Ockhamist position, with its duality of mysticism and empiricism, blazed two paths into the future: pietism uninhibited by reason and science uninhibited by revelation. In Ockham's time Western science was already well evolved. As far back as the later decades of the tenth century, Gerbert of Aurillac had visited Moorish Spain, familiarized himself with Islamic thought, and made his own modest contributions to scientific knowledge.† Gerbert built a simple "planetarium" of balls, rods, and bands to illustrate the rotation of the stellar sphere and the motions of the planets. He introduced the abacus and Arabic numerals into the West and, following the Greeks and Arabs, he taught that the earth was round.

*See below, pp. 309-310.
†See p. 109.

Islamic science continued thereafter to inspire western scholars, particularly in the late-eleventh and twelfth centuries. Men such as Adelard of Bath (d. 1150) retraced Gerbert's pilgrimage into Islamic lands and returned with a new respect for scientific inquiry—as well as an abundance of astrological texts. Among the works that Adelard translated from Arabic into Latin were Euclid's *Elements* and an important Muslim work on arithmetic that used Arabic numerals. Through the labors of the twelfth-century translators, the great scientific works of Greece and Islam were made known in the West—Aristotle's *Physics*, Ptolemy's *Almagest*, Arabic books on algebra, astrology, and medicine, and many others. And now Western scholars began to write scientific books of their own, such as Adelard of Bath's *Natural Questions*. Such works, however, were mere summaries of Greek and Arabic knowledge. The purely assimilative phase of western science continued until the thirteenth century when, particularly among the Franciscans, the first serious original work began.

Thirteenth-century Franciscans, anticipating the later duality of Ockham, were inclined toward both pietism and the investigation of nature. The mysticism of St. Bonaventure represents one pole of Franciscan thought; at the other stand a group of scientific thinkers, who, inspired perhaps by St. Francis's love of nature, applied their logical tools to the task of investigating the physical world. Thirteenth-century Oxford became Europe's chief scientific center; it was there that Western science began to be creative.

The key figure in the development of medieval science was the English scholar, Robert Grosseteste (1168–1253), who, although not a Franciscan himself, was chief lecturer to the Franciscans at Oxford. Grosseteste was on intimate terms with Platonic and Neoplatonic philosophy, Aristotelian physics, and the scientific legacy of Islam. At bottom, he was a Platonist and an Augustinian, but he wrote important commentaries on the scientific works of Aristotle and was able to draw on both traditions. From Plato Grosseteste derived the notion that mathematics is a basic key to understanding the physical universe; the fundamental importance of numbers is very much in keeping with the Platonic realist interpretation of universals, and Plato himself had once asserted that "God is a mathematician." From Aristotle Grosseteste learned the importance of abstracting knowledge from the world of phenomena by means of observation and experiment. Thus, bridging the two traditions, Grosseteste brought together the mathematical and experimental components that together underlie the rise of modern science. More than that, drawing on the suggestive work of his Islamic predecessors he worked out a far more rigorous experimental procedure than is to be found in the pages of Aristotle. A pioneer in the development of scientific method, he outlined a system of observation, hypothesis, and experimental verification that was elaborated by his successors into the methodology that modern physical scientists still employ.

Like other pioneers, Grosseteste followed many false paths. He was better at formulating a scientific methodology than in applying it to specific problems, and his explanations of such phenomena as heat, light, color, comets, and rainbows were rejected in later centuries. But the experimental method that he formulated was to become in time a powerful intellectual tool. The problem of the rainbow, for example, was largely solved by the fourteenth-century scientist Theodoric of Freiburg, who employed a refined version of Grosseteste's experimental methodology. The great triumphs of European science lay far in the future, but with the work of Robert Grosseteste the basic instrument had been forged.

Grosseteste's work was carried further by his disciple, the Oxford Franciscan Roger Bacon (c. 1214–94). The author of a fascinating body of scientific sense and nonsense, Roger Bacon dabbled in the mysteries of alchemy, and his curiosity carried him along strange roads. He was critical of the deductive logic and metaphysical speculations that so fascinated his scholastic contemporaries: "Reasoning," he wrote, "does not illuminate these matters; experiments are required, conducted on a large scale, performed with instruments and by various necessary means."

At his best, Roger Bacon was almost prophetic:

❝ Experimental science controls the conclusions of all other sciences. It reveals truths which reasoning from general principles would never have discovered. Finally, it starts us on the way to marvelous inventions which will change the face of the world. **❞**

Conclusion

The world of the High Middle Ages is described in some outworn books as stagnant, gloomy, and monolithic. At the other extreme, it has been portrayed as an ideally constituted society, free of modern fears and tensions, where people of all classes could live happily and creatively, finding fulfillment in their service to the common good. In reality, the medieval era was neither of these things. It was an age of striking contrasts, of dark fears and high hopes, poverty and commercial vitality, crudeness yet growing sophistication in many areas of human life and expression. Above all, it was an age in which Europeans awoke to the rich variety of possibilities that lay before them. A thirteenth-century poet, in his celebration of springtime, captured the spirit of this awakening:

*T*he earth's ablaze again with lustrous flowers.
The fields are green again, the shadows, deep.
Woods are in leaf again, and all the world
Is filled with joy again; this long-dead land
Now flames with life again: the passions surge,
Love is reborn, and beauty wakes from sleep.

SUGGESTED READINGS

The asterisk indicates a paperback edition.

GENERAL WORKS

The High Middle Ages are covered splendidly in two sequential textbooks, both in paperback: CHRISTOPHER BROOKE, *Europe in the Central Middle Ages, 962–1154* (1963); and JOHN H. MUNDY, *Europe in the High Middle Ages, 1150–1309* (1973).

*JOHN W. BALDWIN, *The Scholastic Culture of the Middle Ages: 1000–1300* (1971). Universities, thought, and Gothic architecture are placed in their urban setting.

*CHRISTOPHER BROOKE, *The Structure of Medieval Society* (1971). Perceptive essays on medieval people and their ideas and customs, using Francis's meeting with Innocent III as the point of departure.

*CAROLLY ERICKSON, *The Medieval Vision* (1976). A sensitively written account of how medieval people perceived their "enchanted" world.

*R.W.SOUTHERN, *The Making of the Middle Ages* (1953). A brilliant, sympathetic interpretation of the eleventh and twelfth centuries.

TOWN, COUNTRYSIDE, AND FRONTIER

*ISRAEL ABRAHAMS, *Jewish Life in the Middle Ages* (1969). Recreates the Jewish urban communities.

*ROBERT-HENRI BAUTIER, *The Economic Development of Medieval Europe* (1971). A valuable work, superbly illustrated.

*DAVID DOUGLAS, *The Norman Achievement* (1969), and *The Norman Fate* (1976). Expert, readable studies of Norman activities in Normandy, Syria, Italy-Sicily, and England, 1050–1154.

GEORGES DUBY, *Rural Economy and Country Life in the Medieval West* (1968). A seminal, highly innovative work, translated from the French.

*J.K. HYDE, *Society and Politics in Medieval Italy, 1000–1350* (1973). A study of socio-economic and cultural changes among the urban governing classes.

N.J.G. POUNDS, *An Economic History of Medieval Europe* (1974). A good, analytical survey, written for students.

*ROBERT S. LOPEZ, *The Commercial Revolution of the Middle Ages, 950–1350* (1971). Advances the thesis that the medieval commercial revolution was unique in world history and an essential precondition to later industrialization.

*STEVEN RUNCIMAN, *A History of the Crusades* (3 vols., 1964–1967). Comprehensive and authoritative.

CHRISTIANITY

RUSSELL'S *History of Medieval Christianity* (above, p. 119) remains useful throughout the medieval period.

EDWARD A. ARMSTRONG, *St. Francis: Nature Mystic* (1973). A graceful, sophisticated study of Francis's perceptions of God's creation.

CHRISTOPHER BROOKE, *Medieval Church and Society* (1971). Perceptive essays on Gregory VII, medieval forgery, Becket, heresy, Francis and Dominic, and other topics.

DOM DAVID KNOWLES, *From Pachomius to Ignatius* (1966). A brief, authoritative account of the organization of religious orders, emphasizing the period from the rise of Cluny through the death of Dominic. For a comprehensive treatment of the Benedictines and later religious orders in England, see, by the same author, *The Monastic Order in England* (2nd ed., 1963), and *The Religious Orders in England* (3 vols., 1948–1959).

*JEAN LECLERQ, *The Love of Learning and the Desire for God* (1961). The best short study of monasticism in English.

PAUL SABATIER, *St. Francis of Assisi* (1894). A warm and deeply sympathetic older work.

*R.W. SOUTHERN, *Western Society and the Church in the Middle Ages* (1970). A masterful survey and interpretation showing the interactions between the Church and the secular world.

EMPIRE AND PAPACY

*GEOFFREY BARRACLOUGH, *The Medieval Papacy* (1968). A thoughtful, interpretive survey, beautifully illustrated.

FRIEDRICH HEER, *The Holy Roman Empire* (1968). A lively defense of the empire as a viable "federal" system.

MARCEL PACAUT, *Frederick Barbarossa* (1970). An "unashamed work of popularization" by an able scholar who argues that Barbarossa, "better than anyone else, expressed the imperial ideal."

GERD TELLENBACH, *Church, State and Christian Society at the Time of the Investiture Contest* (1940). This remains the best analysis of the Investiture Controversy in English.

WALTER ULLMANN, *The Growth of Papal Government in the Middle Ages* (2nd ed., 1962). An intellectual history of the medieval papal ideology.

ENGLAND AND FRANCE

Two general treatments, in paperback, are CHRISTOPHER BROOKE, *From Alfred to Henry III* (1966); and C.W. HOLLISTER, *The Making of England* (3rd ed., 1976).

*R. ALLEN BROWN, *the Normans and the Norman Conquest* (1969). A well-written, pro-Norman account of the Conquest and its background and aftermath.

*DAVID DOUGLAS, *William the Conqueror* (1964). The best account of the Conqueror's career. Due attention is given to William's background and achievements in Normandy.

*ROBERT FAWTIER, *The Capetian Kings of France* (1960). A short, masterful treatment.

*C.W. HOLLISTER, ed., *The Impact of the Norman Conquest* (1969). A collection of modern opinions and original sources.

*JAMES C. HOLT, ed., *Magna Carta and the Idea of Liberty* (1972). An exploration of original sources and modern scholarly writings relating to Magna Carta and its influence over subsequent centuries, with an illuminating section on similar charters of liberties issued elsewhere in medieval Europe.

*AMY KELLY, *Eleanor of Aquitaine and the Four Kings* (1950). Entertaining and thorough.

DOM DAVID KNOWLES, *Thomas Becket* (1970). A short, well-balanced biography.

*JOHN LE PATOUREL, *the Norman Empire* (1976). Stresses the unity of Norman politics in England and northern France to 1154.

*G.O. SAYLES, *The King's Parliament of England* (1974). A brief but important interpretation of medieval parliament as a response to the problems of contemporaries.

THOUGHT, LETTERS, AND THE ARTS

*CHRISTOPHER BROOKE, *The Twelfth-Century Renaissance* (1969). A well-illustrated, sensitively-written essay on cultural figures of twelfth-century Europe.

*EDWARD GRANT, *Physical Science in the Middle Ages* (1971). Stresses the impact of Aristotelian physical science on the medieval mind after c. 1200.

*C.H. HASKINS, *The Renaissance of the Twelfth Century* (1927). A pioneering book, particularly strong on Latin literature.

*C.H. HASKINS, *The Rise of the Universities* (1923). Brief, informative, and a delight to read.

*GEORGE HENDERSON, *Gothic* (1967). A well-illustrated study of the Gothic style in its historical and cultural context.

*DAVID KNOWLES, *The Evolution of Medieval Thought* (1964). A short, lucid survey.

*JOHN C. MOORE, *Love in Twelfth-Century France* (1972). Short, learned, and graceful.

*R.W. SOUTHERN, *Medieval Humanism and Other Studies* (1970). Important related essays on medieval thought and life, containing a reinterpretation of medieval humanism.

WHITNEY STODDARD, *Monastery and Cathedral in France* (1966). A superbly illustrated account of French Romanesque and Gothic art.

*WALTER ULLMANN, *A History of Political Thought: The Middle Ages* (1965). A short synthetic work that points to the medieval background of modern political thought.

SOURCES

*DANTE ALIGHIERI, *The Divine Comedy.* Many translations.

ANGEL FLORES, *An Anthology of Medieval Lyrics.* English translations of medieval lyric poems from France, Italy, Germany, and Spain.

The Correspondence of Pope Gregory VII, ed. and tr. EPHRAIM EMERTON.

*GUIBERT OF NOGENT, *Self and Society in Medieval France,* tr. JOHN F. BENTON. The revealing autobiography of a twelfth-century abbot and scholar, to which Benton gives a Freudian twist in his provocative introduction.

*BENNETT D. HILL, *Church and State in the Middle Ages.* Sources and modern interpretive essays.

*OTTO OF FREISING, *The Deeds of Frederick Barbarossa,* tr. C. C. MIEROW and RICHARD EMERY.

ANTON C. PEGIS, ed. *Introduction to St. Thomas Aquinas.* Intelligently chosen selections with a stimulating introduction.

The Song of Roland, tr. D. L. SAYERS.

*VILLEHARDOUIN and DE JOINVILLE, *Memoirs of the Crusades,* tr. SIR FRANK MARZIALS.

Part III

The Late Middle Ages

The ordeal
of transition

Chapter 15

ℭ

Church and State in the 14th and 15th Centuries

Changing Culture and Changing Values

¶ Like most eras of transition, the fourteenth and fifteenth centuries were violent and unsettled. They were marked by a gradual ebbing of confidence in the values on which high-medieval civilization had rested. Prosperity gave way to sporadic depression, optimism to disillusionment, and the thirteenth-century dream of fusing the worlds of matter and spirit faded. Social behavior ran to extremes—to rebellion, sensualism, flagellation, cynicism, and witchcraft. Powerful creative forces were at work in these centuries, but they were less evident to many observers than the forces of disintegration and decay. The shrinking of Europe's economy, population, and territorial frontiers was accompanied by a mood of pessimism and claustrophobia, exploding periodically into frenzied enthusiasm or blind rage. The literature and art of the period were often preoccupied with fantasy, eccentricity, and death. England and France were torn by war, and both were ruled for a time by madmen. The Black Death struck in the mid-fourteenth century and returned periodically, carrying off millions of victims and darkening the spirits of those who survived.

These varied symptoms of social and psychological disorder were

ℭ

associated with a gradual shift in Western Europe's political orientation—from a Christian commonwealth to a constellation of territorial states. The Roman Catholic Church fared badly during the late Middle Ages. The Western kingdoms were racked by civil and external war and, at times, by a near-breakdown of royal government. Yet during the final half-century of the period (c. 1450–1500) strong monarchies emerged in England, France, and Spain. These three states were destined to dominate Western European politics far into the future. By 1500 the monarchies were replacing the Church as the object of their inhabitants' highest allegiance. The pope had become mired in local Italian politics, and medieval Christian internationalism was breaking up into sovereign fragments.

The Church in the Late Middle Ages

The late-medieval evolution from Christendom toward nationhood was not so much a transformation as a shift in balance. Even during the High Middle Ages the ideal of a Christian commonwealth, guided by pope and clergy, had never been fulfilled. At best, popes could win momentary political victories over kings and could achieve an uneasy equilibrium between royal and clerical authority. By the later thirteenth century the balance was already tipping in favor of monarchs such as Edward I of England and Philip the Fair of France. The trend accelerated during the late Middle Ages until, by 1500, the papacy had become far weaker as an international force and the monarchies stronger. "Nationhood," by any strict definition, had not yet come, but papal authority over the churches of the various kingdoms was becoming tenuous. The prince-ly electors of Germany had long before denied the papacy any role in imperial elections or coronations, and papal influence in the appointment of French, English, and Spanish prelates had ebbed. More important still, the late Middle Ages witnessed a collapse of papal spiritual prestige and a widening chasm be-tween Christian piety and the organized Church.

Mystics and Reformers

Christianity did not decline noticeably during this period; it merely became less ecclesiastical. The powerful movement of lay piety, which had been drift-ing away from papal leadership all through the High Middle Ages, now became increasingly hostile to ecclesiastical wealth and privilege, increasingly individualistic, and increasingly mystical. The wave of mysticism that swept across late-medieval Europe was not, for the most part, openly heretical. But by stressing the spiritual relationship between the individual and God, the mystics tended to de-emphasize the role of the ordained clergy and the sacraments as channels of divine grace. Although they believed in the efficacy of the Holy Eucharist, mystics devoted themselves chiefly to the direct apprehension of God, for which no clerical hierarchy, no popes, and no sacraments were needed.

Mysticism had always been an element in Christian devotional life, and it was well known to the High Middle Ages. But with the growth of complacency and corruption within the Church, mysticism became, for the first time, a large-scale movement among the laity. Early in the fourteenth century, the great Dominican mystic, Meister Eckhart (d. 1327), taught that humanity's true goal is utter separation from the world of the senses and absorption into the Divine Unknown. Eckhart had many followers, and as the century progressed, several large mystical communities were formed. Loosely-organized associations of pious laywomen known as Beguines flourished in the Low Countries and spread into Germany, and they were paralleled by mystical brotherhoods and sisterhoods of a similar sort.

Around 1375 the highly influential Brethren of the Common Life was founded by the Flemish lay preacher Gerard Groot, a student of one of Eckhart's disciples. The Brethren of the Common Life devoted themselves to simple lives of preaching, teaching, and charitable works. Their popularity in fifteenth-century northern Europe approached that of the Franciscans two centuries before, but the Brethren, unlike the Franciscans, took no lifetime vows. Their schools were among Europe's finest and produced some of the leading mystics, humanists, and reformers of the fifteenth and sixteenth centuries. Erasmus and Luther were both products of the Brethren's schools, as was Thomas à Kempis (d. 1471), whose *Imitation of Christ* stands as the supreme literary expression of late-medieval mysticism.* The *Imitation of Christ* typifies the mystical outlook in its emphasis on adoration over speculation, inner spiritual purity over external "good works," and direct experience of God over the sacramental avenues to divine grace. The *Imitation* remained well within the bounds of Catholic orthodoxy, yet it contained ideas that had great appeal to the sixteenth-century Protestant reformers. The emphasis on individual piety, common to all the mystics, tended to erode the medieval idea of a Christian commonwealth by viewing the Catholic Church as a multitude of individual souls, each groping toward salvation alone.

This element of Christian individualism was carried at times to the point of heresy. John Wycliffe (d. 1384), a professor at Oxford, anticipated the later Protestants by placing the authority of Scriptures over the pronouncements of popes and councils. Extending the implications of contemporary mysticism to their limit, Wycliffe stressed the individual's inner spiritual journey toward God, questioned the real presence of Christ in the Holy Eucharist, de-emphasized the entire sacramental system, and spoke out strongly against ecclesiastical wealth. This last protest had been implicit in the thirteenth-century Franciscan movement, although St. Francis had shown his devotion to apostolic poverty by living it rather than forcing it on others. The com-

---

*Although most scholars attribute *The Imitation of Christ* to Thomas à Kempis, the attribution is not certain.

promises of later Franciscanism on the matter of property had given rise to a zealous splinter group—the "Spiritual Franciscans"—whose insistence on universal ecclesiastical poverty had made them anticlerical and antipapal. John XXII (1316–1334), the shrewd Avignonese "financier-pope," had seen fit in 1323 to denounce their doctrine of apostolic poverty as heretical. And Wycliffe, more than a half century later, was stripped of his professorship and convicted of heresy. Owing to his powerful friends at court, and to the unpopularity of the papacy in fourteenth-century England, he was permitted to die peacefully, but his followers, the Lollards, were less fortunate. Their fate is suggested by the title of a parliamentary act of 1401: "The Statute on the Burning of Heretics." There were to be no Lollards in England to celebrate King Henry VIII's break with Rome in the 1530s.

English Lollardy represented an extreme expression of a growing discontent with the official Church. Wycliffe's doctrines spread to faraway Bohemia where they were taken up by the reformer John Hus. The Hussites used Wycliffe's anticlericalism as a weapon in the struggle for Czech independence from German political and cultural influence. John Hus was burned at the stake at the Council of Constance in 1415, but his followers survived into the Reformation era as a dissident national group. Both Wycliffe and Hus represented, in their oppositon to the organized international Church, a reconciliation of personal religious faith with the idea of national sovereignty. If Christianity was to be an individual affair, then the political claims of popes and prelates were meritless, and secular rulers might govern without ecclesiastical interference. Thus the radical thrust of late medieval Christianity, by its very anticlericalism, tended to support the growing concept of secular sovereignty. Ardent religious spirits such as John Hus—and Joan of Arc, burned as a heretic in 1431—could fuse Christian mysticism with the beginnings of patriotism.

Popes and Councils

The mystics and reformers, implicitly or explicitly, rejected the pope as the chief link connecting God and the Christian community. And the late-medieval papacy was vulnerable to their attacks. Early in the fourteenth century, as we have seen, the papacy had moved to Avignon on the Rhône River, just outside the domain of the French monarchy. There a series of able French popes ruled from 1309 to 1376. The Avignon popes were subservient to the French crown only on occasion; for the most part they were capable of strong, independent action. But their very location suggested to France's enemies that they were no longer an impartial international force. Attempts were made to return the papacy to Rome, but they were foiled by the violent factionalism of the Holy City. Meanwhile the Avignon popes carried the thirteenth-century trend toward administrative and fiscal efficiency to its ultimate degree. The large, well-tuned bureaucracy of papal Avignon provided revenues and personnel sufficient to make the papacy an even stronger international power than before. But the administrative machinery failed to inspire mystics and reformers, and France's neighbors resented the taxation and interference of what they mistakenly regarded as a tool of the French crown. Thus, while the papacy was growing wealthier and more efficient, its spiritual capital was diminishing.

At length, in 1376, Pope Gregory XI moved the Holy See back to Rome. Chagrined by the turbulent conditions he encountered there, Gregory made plans to return to France but died in 1378 before he could carry them out. Urged on by a Roman mob, the cardinals—most of them homesick Frenchmen—grudgingly elected an Italian to the papal throne. The new pope, Urban VI, had previously been a colorless functionary in the ecclesiastical establishment. Now, to everyone's surprise, he became a zealous reformer and began taking steps to reduce the cardinals' revenues and influence. The French cardinals fled Rome, canceled their previous election on the grounds of mob intimidation, and elected a French pope who returned with them to Avignon. Back in Rome, Urban VI appointed new cardinals, and for the next thirty-seven years the Universal Church was torn by schism. When the rival popes died, their cardinals elected rival successors. Excommunications were hurled to-and-fro between Rome and Avignon, and the states of Europe chose their sides according to their interests. France and its allies supported Avignon, England and the Holy Roman Empire backed Rome, and the Italian states shifted from one side to the other as it suited their purposes. Papal prestige was falling in ruin, yet in the face of age-long papal claims to absolute spiritual authority, there seemed no power on earth that could purport to arbitrate between two rival popes. The Church was at an impasse.

As the schism dragged on, increasing numbers of Christians became convinced that the only solution was the convening of a general church council. Both popes argued that councils were inferior to them and could not judge them, and Christians were perplexed as to who, if not the popes, had the authority to summon a council. At length some of the cardinals themselves, in both camps, called a council to meet in Pisa. There, in 1409, a group of 500 prelates deposed both popes and elected a new one. Since neither pope recognized the conciliar depositions, the effect of the Council of Pisa was to transform a two-way schism into a three-way schism. The situation was not only scandalous but ludicrous. Finally the Holy Roman emperor arranged for the summoning of great churchmen from all across Europe to the Council of Constance (1415–1418). Here at last the schism was ended. Two popes were deposed, the third resigned, and the Church was reunited by the election of a conciliar pope, Martin V (1417–1431).

To many thoughtful Christians the healing of the schism was not enough. The papacy stood discredited, and it was argued that future popes should be guided by general councils meeting regularly and automatically. The role of councils and assemblies was familiar enough to contemporary secular governments. Why shouldn't the Church, too, be governed "constitutionally"? Such views were being urged by political philosophers such as Marsilius of Padua in the fourteenth century and Nicholas of Cusa in the fifteenth, and they were widely accepted among the prelates at Constance. That these delegates were essentially conservative is suggested by their decision to burn John Hus, who came to Constance with an imperial promise of safe conduct. Yet the Council of Constance made a genuine effort to reform the constitution of the Church along conciliar lines. The delegates affirmed, against papal objection, the ultimate authority of councils in matters of doctrine and reform, and they decreed that thenceforth general councils would convene at regular intervals.

These broad principles, together with a number of specific reforms voted by the Council of Constance, met with firm opposition from Pope Martin V and his successors, who insisted on absolute papal supremacy. The popes reluctantly summoned a council in 1423 and another in 1431, but worked to make them ineffective. The last of the important medieval councils, the Council of Basel (1431–1449), drifted gradually into open schism with the recalcitrant papacy and petered out ingloriously. By then Europe's enthusiasm for conciliarism was waning; the conciliar movement died, and a single pope ruled unopposed once more in Rome.

The men who sat on the papal throne between the dissolution of Basel (1449) and the beginning of the Protestant Reformation (1517) were radically different from their high-medieval predecessors. Abandoning much of their former jurisdiction over the international Church, they devoted themselves to the beguiling culture and bitter local politics of Renaissance Italy. By now the popes were mostly Italian, and so they would remain on into the future. Struggling to strengthen their hold on the Papal States, maneuvering through the shifting sands of Italian diplomacy, they conceded to northern monarchs an extensive degree of control over Church and clergy in return for a formal recognition of papal authority and an agreed division of Church revenues between pope and king.

The fifteenth century ended with the pontificate of the Borgia pope, Alexander VI (1492–1503), whose scandalous behavior and bastard offspring were sufficient even to raise eyebrows in high-Renaissance Italy. Alexander's pontificate is a caricature of all that ailed the papacy at the end of the Middle Ages. Devoting himself to the advancement of his own family, he gave full support to the unprincipled military and diplomatic activities of his son, Caesar, who used assassination, treachery, and force to carve out a great Borgia state in central Italy.

As the Borgia pontificate vividly illustrates, the papacy by 1500, had ceased to be an international spiritual power. Fourteen years after Alexander VI's death, the Protestant Reformation exploded, and the tremendous popular response to Luther's rebellion bespeaks the failure of the late-medieval popes. Europeans were by no means prepared to abandon Christianity, but they were willing, in large numbers, to desert tarnished Rome.

1309–1376:	Avignon papacy prior to the Great Schism
1327:	Meister Eckhart dies
c.1375:	Gerard Groot founds the Brethren of the Common Life
1378–1415:	Great Schism: Rome *versus* Avignon
1384:	John Wycliffe dies
1409:	Council of Pisa: three-way schism
1415–1418:	Council of Constance: schism healed; beginning of conciliarism
1415:	John Hus burned at the stake
1417–1431:	Pontificate of Martin V
1431–1449:	Council of Basel: waning of conciliarism
1492–1503:	Pontificate of Alexander VI, the Borgia pope
1517:	Outbreak of Lutheran Reformation

The Western Monarchies

The late-medieval trend from international Catholicism toward secular sovereignty found forceful expression in Marsilius of Padua's important treatise, the *Defensor Pacis* (1324). Here the dilemma of conflicting sovereign jurisdictions, secular and ecclesiastical, was resolved uncompromisingly in favor of the state. The Church, Marsilius argued, should be stripped of political authority, and the state should wield sovereign power over all its subjects, lay and clerical alike. Thus the Church, united in faith, would be divided politically into dozens of state churches obedient to their secular rulers and not to the pope. In its glorification of the sovereign state, the *Defensor Pacis* foreshadowed the evolution of late-medieval and early-modern politics.

It was only after 1450, however, that the western monarchies were able to assert their authority with any consistency over the nobility. During the period from the early-fourteenth to the mid-fifteenth century, the high-medieval trend toward royal centralization seemed to have reversed itself. The major Iberian powers—Aragon, Castile, and Portugal—were tormented by sporadic internal upheavals and made no progress toward reducing Granada, the remaining Islamic enclave in the peninsula. For most of the period, England and France were involved in the Hundred Years' War (1337–1453), which drove England to the brink of bankruptcy and ravaged the French countryside and population.

England

Nevertheless, the unwritten English constitution developed significantly during these years. In the course of the fourteenth century, Parliament changed from a body that met occasionally to a permanent institution and split into Lords and Commons. The House of Commons, consisting of representative townsmen and shire knights, bargained with a monarchy hard pressed by the expenses of the Hundred Years' War. Commons traded its fiscal support for important political concessions, and by the century's end it had gained the privilege of approving or disapproving all taxation not sanctioned by custom. With control of the royal purse strings, Commons exerted increasing influence on legislation. Adopting the motto, "redress before supply," it refused to pass financial grants until the king had approved its petitions, and, in the end, the king almost always acquiesced.

Yet the late-medieval House of Commons was by no means the independent voice of a rising middle class. By and large, it was controlled by the force or manipulation of powerful aristocrats. Elections could be rigged; representatives could be bribed or overawed. And although Parliament deposed two English kings in the fourteenth century—Edward II in 1327 and Richard II in 1399—in both instances it was simply ratifying the results of aristocratic power struggles. It is significant that such parliamentary ratification should seem necessary, but one must not conclude that Parliament had yet become a free agent. Symbolically, it represented the will of the English community; actually, it remained sensitive to royal and aristocratic force and tended to affirm decisions already made in castles or on battlefields.

The Hundred Years' War, which proved such a stimulus to the growth of parliamentary privileges, also constituted a serious drain on English wealth and lives. Beginning in 1337, the war dragged on fitfully for 116 years with periods of savage warfare alternating with prolonged periods of truce. Broadly speaking, the conflict was a continuation of the Anglo-French rivalry that dated from the Norman Conquest. Since 1066 England and France had battled on numerous occasions. In 1204 the Capetian crown had won the extensive northern French territories of the Angevin Empire, but the English kings retained a tenuous lordship over Gascony in the southwest. The English Gascon claim, cemented by a brisk commerce in Bordeaux wine and English cloth, gave rise to an expensive but inconclusive war (1294–1303) between Philip the Fair of France and Edward I of England. Competing English and French claims to jurisdiction in Gascony constituted one of several causes for the resumption of hostilities in 1337.

Another cause of the Hundred Years' War was the Anglo-French diplomatic struggle for control of Flanders, which France needed to round out its territories and which England needed to secure its profitable wool trade. Tension mounted when in 1328 the last Capetian king of France died without sons, throwing the royal succession into dispute. The French crown was claimed by King Edward III of England (1327–77), whose mother was a daughter of King Philip the Fair. But Edward's claim was contested by Philip of Valois, son of Philip the Fair's younger brother. The French nobility, arguing unhistorically that the right to inherit cannot pass through a woman, raised Philip of Valois to the throne. As King Philip VI (1328–1350), he became the first of a long line of Valois kings who ruled France until 1589. Edward III accepted the decision initially, but in 1337, when other reasons prompted him to take up arms, he revived his claim and titled himself king of France and England.

None of these causes can be considered decisive, and war might yet have been avoided. But Edward III and Philip VI were both chivalrous, high-spirited romantics who delighted in heroic clashes of arms. And the nobles of both sides were infected by similar attitudes. The French lost most of their ardor when English longbowmen won smashing victories at Crécy (1346) and Poitiers (1356). The English revered Edward III so long as English arms were victorious, but they deposed his successor, Richard II (1377–1399), who preferred reducing the power of his nobles to fighting Frenchmen. Henry V (1413–1422) revived hostilities and gained the adulation of his English subjects by winning a momentous victory over the French at Agincourt in 1415. But Henry V's early death, and the subsequent career of Joan of Arc,* turned the tide of war against the English. By 1453, when the long struggle ended at last, England had lost all of France except the port of Calais. The centuries-long process of Anglo-French disentanglement was completed, and Joan of Arc's vision was realized: the Valois Charles VII ruled France unopposed.

The Hundred Years' War had been over for scarcely two years when England entered an era of civil strife between the rival houses of York and Lancaster. The Wars of the Roses, which raged off and on between 1455 and 1485, were the medieval English nobility's last hurrah. Nobles and commoners alike grew tired of endless bloodshed and longed for firm royal governance. They achieved it, to a degree, in the reign of the Yorkist Edward IV (1461–1483). And after a final burst of warfare, strong monarchy came permanently to England with the accession of the first Tudor king, Henry VII (1485–1509). Both Edward IV and Henry VII sought peace, a full treasury, and effective government, and by the late fifteenth century these goals were coming within

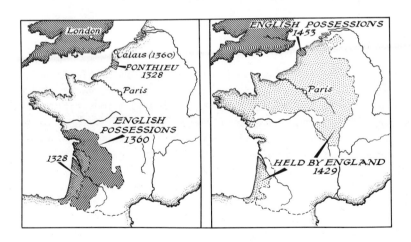

*See p. 293.

reach. The economy was reviving, many of the more troublesome nobles had perished in the Wars of the Roses, and the English were more than willing to exchange anarchy for obedience and peace. All that was needed now was strong royal leadership, and that was supplied in full measure by the willful, determined Tudors.

France

The Hundred Years' War was a far greater trial to France than to England. All the fighting took place on French soil, and mercenary companies continually pillaged the French countryside, even when they were not engaged in actual warfare. King John the Good (1350–1364)—a very bad king indeed—was powerless to cope with the English or bring order to a demoralized, plague-ridden land. In 1356, a decade after the French military debacle at Crécy and eight years after the onset of the Black Death, France was stunned by a crushing defeat at Poitiers. French nobles fell in great numbers, and King John himself was taken prisoner by the English.

The Estates General, meeting in Paris under the leadership of a Parisian cloth merchant named Etienne Marcel, momentarily assumed the reins of government. In 1357 they forced King John's son, the young Dauphin* Charles, to issue a radical constitutional statute known as the "Great Ordinance." This statute embodied the demands of the bourgeois-dominated Estates General to join with the monarchy in the governance of France. The Estates General were thenceforth to meet on regular occasions and to supervise the royal finances, courts, and administration through a small standing committee. The Dauphin Charles, deeply hostile to this infringement of royal authority, submitted for a time, then fled Paris to gather royalist support in the countryside.

By 1358 the horrors of plague, depression, and mercenary marauders had goaded the French peasantry into open revolt. The Jacquerie—as the rebellious peasants were called—lacked coherent goals and effective leaders, but they managed for two memorable weeks to terrorize portions of the northern French countryside. On one occasion they are reported to have forced an aristocratic wife to eat her roasted husband, after which they raped and murdered her. But the aristocracy and urban elites quickly crushed the uprising with a savagery worthy of the rebels themselves. The Jacquerie rebellion of 1358 evoked a longing for law and order and a return to the ways of old. This conservative backlash resulted in a surge of royalism that doomed Etienne Marcel's constitutional movement in Paris. Marcel himself was murdered in midsummer, 1358, and the Dauphin Charles returned to the city in triumph.

The Great Ordinance of 1357 became a dead letter after Marcel's fall, and in later centuries the Estates General met less and less frequently. The Dauphin

*Crown prince.

Charles, who became the able King Charles V (1364–1380), instituted new tax measures that largely freed the monarchy from its financial dependence on assemblies and made it potentially the richest in Europe. The Estates General, unlike the English Parliament, failed to become an integral part of the government, and French kings reverted more and more to their high-medieval practice of dealing with their subjects through local assemblies. There were "Parlements" in France—outgrowths of the central and regional courts—but their functions remained judicial; they did not deliberate on the granting of taxes, and they did not legislate. French national cohesion continued to lag behind that of England, because France was much larger, more populous, and more culturally diverse. During the late Middle Ages its great dukes still ruled whole provinces with little interference from Paris. In the absence of an articulate national parliament, the only voice that could claim to speak for all the French people was the voice of their king.

Charles V succeeded in turning the tide of war by avoiding pitched battles. His armies harassed the English unceasingly and forced them, little by little, to draw back. By Charles's death the French monarchy was recovering. The English, reduced to small outposts around Bordeaux and Calais, virtually abandoned the war for a generation.

But Charles V was succeeded by the incompetent Charles VI (1380–1422)—"Charles the Mad"—who grew from a weak child into an unstable adult, periodically insane. His reign was marked by a bloody rivalry between the houses of Burgundy and Orléans. The duke of Orléans was Charles the Mad's brother, the duke of Burgundy his uncle. In Capetian times, such powerful fief-holding members of the royal family had usually cooperated with the king, but now, with a madman on the throne, Burgundy and Orléans struggled for control of the kingdom. In the course of the fifteenth century, the Orléanist faction became identified with the cause of the Valois monarchy, and Burgundy evolved into a powerful independent state between France and Germany. But at the time of Charles the Mad, all was uncertain.

With France ravaged once again by murder and civil strife, King Henry V of England resumed the Hundred Years' War and, in 1415, won his overwhelming victory at Agincourt. At this the Burgundians joined forces with the English, and Charles the Mad was forced to make Henry V his heir. But both kings died in 1422, and while Charles the Mad's son, Charles VII (1422–1461), carried on a half-hearted resistance, the Burgundians and English divided northern France between them and prepared to crush the remaining power of the Valois monarchy.

At the nadir of his fortunes, Charles VII, as yet uncrowned, accepted in desperation the military services of the peasant visionary Joan of Arc. Joan's victory at Orléans, her insistence on Charles's coronation in Reims, and her capture and death at the stake in 1431 have become legendary. The spirit that she kindled raised French hopes, and in the two decades following her death Charles VII's armies went from victory to victory. The conquest of France had always been beyond English resources, and English successes in the Hundred

Years' War had been largely a product of wretched French leadership and paralyzing internal division. Now, as the war drew at last to a close, Charles VII could devote himself to the rebuilding of the royal government. He was supported in his task by secure tax revenues, a standing army, and the steady development of effective administrative institutions.

Centralization was carried still further by Louis XI (1461–83), known as the "Spider King"—a name befitting both his appearance and his politics. Son and heir of Charles VII (whom he despised), Louis XI wove webs about his various rivals, removing them by murder, beheadings, and treachery. The Burgundian threat dissolved in 1477 when the last duke of Burgundy died fighting Louis' Swiss allies, and the Spider King swiftly confiscated the entire duchy. Plotting his way through a labyrinth of shifting alliances and loyalties, he advanced significantly toward the goals of French unification and Valois absolutism.

By 1500 the French monarchy was ruling through a central administration of middle-class professional bureaucrats. The nobility was highly favored and apparently tamed, the towns were flourishing, and new royal armies were carrying the dynastic claims of the Valois kings into foreign lands.

CHRONOLOGY OF LATE-MEDIEVAL ENGLAND AND FRANCE

England	France
1307-1327 : Reign of Edward II	1328–1589: Valois Dynasty
1327–1377: Reign of Edward III	1328–1350: Reign of Philip VI
1337–1453: Hundred Years' War	1337–1453: Hundred Years' War
1346: Battle of Crécy	1346: Battle of Crécy
1348–1349: Black Death	1348–1349: Black Death
	1350–1364: Reign of John "the Good"
1356: Battle of Poitiers	1356: Battle of Poitiers
	1357: The Great Ordinance
	1358: Jacquerie Rebellion
1377–1399: Reign of Richard II	1364–1380: Reign of Charles V
1381: Peasants' Revolt	1380–1422: Reign of Charles VI, "The Mad"
1413–1422: Reign of Henry V	
1415: Battle of Agincourt	1415: Battle of Agincourt
1455–1485: Wars of the Roses	1422–1461: Reign of Charles VII
1461–1483: Reign of Edward IV	1429–1431: Career of Joan of Arc
1485–1509: Reign of Henry VII; beginning of Tudor Dynasty	1461–1483: Reign of Louis XI

Spain

The course of Spanish history in the late Middle Ages runs parallel to that of England and France, with generations of internal turmoil giving way in the later fifteenth century to political coherence and royal consolidation. As the high-medieval *Reconquista* rolled to a stop around 1270, the Iberian Peninsula contained three strong Christian kingdoms—Castile, Aragon, and Portugal— and Muslim Granada in the extreme south. Of the major kingdoms, Castile was the largest and Aragon the most urbanized and imperialistic. During the thirteenth and fourteenth centuries Aragonese kings conquered the Mediterranean islands of Majorca, Minorca, Sardinia, and Sicily, and Aragonese merchants began moving into international commerce.

Aragon and Castile were both plagued by civil turbulence during the late Middle Ages. The Aragonese monarchy strove with only limited success to placate the nobility and townspeople by granting significant concessions to the Cortes, the regional representative assemblies. A prolonged revolt by the mercantile class in the Aragonese province of Catalonia was put down in 1472 only with the greatest difficulty. Castile, in the meantime, was torn by constant aristocratic uprisings and disputed royal successions. Peace and strong government came within reach at last when Ferdinand of Aragon married Isabella of Castile in 1469. Isabella inherited her throne in 1474; Ferdinand inherited his in 1479. And thereafter, despite the continuation of regional Cortes, tribunals, and customs, an efficient central administration governed the two realms and eventually transformed them into the Kingdom of Spain.

In 1492 the new kingdom completed the *Reconquista* by conquering Muslim Granada. Working tirelessly to enforce obedience, unity, and orthodoxy, the Spanish monarchy presented its Muslim and Jewish subjects with the choice of conversion or banishment, and the consequent Jewish exodus drained the kingdom of valuable mercantile and intellectual talent. The Catholic Inquisition became a tool of the state and, as an instrument of both political and doctrinal conformity, it brought the crown not only religious unity but lucrative revenues as well. The nobility was persuaded that its best interests lay in supporting the monarchy rather than opposing it, and regional separatism was curbed. With unity established and with the immense wealth of the New World soon to be pouring in, Spain in 1500 was entering a period of rich cultural expression and international power.

The wealth of Spain and Portugal in the sixteenth century resulted from their strategic location at the extreme west of Europe, facing the Atlantic. Important advances in shipbuilding and navigation opened the way for long ocean voyages, and by 1500 European captains had traversed the Atlantic and Indian Oceans. The conquest of these seas brought Spain a New World empire and the wealth of the Incas and Aztecs. It brought Portugal a direct sea route to India and a vast commercial empire in the Far East. The first Atlantic explorations, however, were pioneered by Italian seamen who could draw on their experience in Mediterranean commerce. In the early fourteenth century,

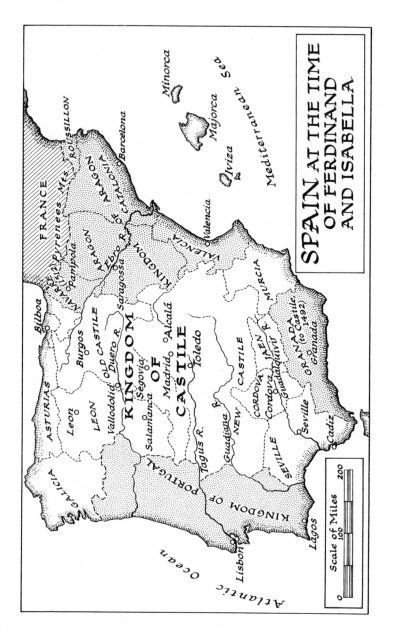

SPAIN AT THE TIME OF FERDINAND AND ISABELLA

Venetian galley fleets were making yearly expeditions through the Straits of Gibraltar to England and Flanders, and Genoese merchants were trading with the Canary Islands. By the mid-fifteenth century the Canaries, Madeiras, Azores, and Cape Verde Islands had all passed into Spanish or Portuguese hands, but the ships of the Iberian monarchies continued to depend often on the skill of Italian captains and crews. It was the Genoese captain, Columbus, who brought the Spanish monarchy its claim to the New World.

Missionary zeal, curiosity, and greed were the mixed motives of these explorations. In the long run, greed was the primary consideration of both the sponsoring monarchies and the captains and private merchants who stood to make their fortunes from successful voyages. But the great patron of Portuguese West-African exploration, Prince Henry the Navigator (1394–1460), seems to have been driven in large measure by the hope of Christian evangelism and the longing to discover unknown lands. From his court at Sagres, ships were sent westward to the Atlantic islands and southward down the African coast. And at Sagres itself Prince Henry collected an invaluable store of geographical and navigational data for the instruction of his captains. The Portuguese West-African voyages continued intermittently after Prince Henry's death and reached their climax in 1497–1499 when Vasco da Gama rounded the Cape of Good Hope and reached India. The six-thousand percent profit realized by da Gama's voyage demonstrated emphatically the commercial potentialities of this new, direct route to the Orient. The old trade routes were short-circuited, and the Ottoman Empire and Renaissance Italy both underwent a gradual commercial decline. The future lay with the rising Atlantic monarchies.

Germany and Italy

Late medieval Germany and Italy suffered from much the same sort of regional particularism that afflicted England, France, and the Iberian Peninsula, but the late fifteenth century brought no corresponding trend toward centralization. Both lands passed into the modern era divided internally and incapable of competing with the Western monarchies. The weak, elective Holy Roman Empire that emerged in Germany from the papal-imperial struggles of the High Middle Ages was given formal sanction in the Golden Bull of 1356. The Bull made no mention of any papal role in the imperial appointment or coronation, but left the choice of succession to the majority vote of seven great German princes. These "electors" were the archbishops of Mainz, Trier, and Cologne, the count palatine of the Rhine, the duke of Saxony, the margrave of Brandenburg, and the king of Bohemia. The electoral states themselves remained relatively stable, as did other large German principalities such as the Hapsburg duchy of Austria, but the empire itself became powerless. Germany in 1500 was a Chinese puzzle of more than a hundred principalities—fiefs, ecclesiastical city-states, free cities, counties, and duchies—their boundaries shifting periodically through war, marriage, and inheritance. Imperial authority in Italian politics was as dead as papal authority in imperial elections. Germany and Italy were disengaged at last, but both continued to suffer the prolonged consequences of their former entanglement.

Through the domination of small states by larger ones, the political crazy-quilt of late-medieval Italy had evolved by the fifteenth century into a delicate power balance between five strong political units: the Kingdom of Naples, the

Papal States, and the three northern city-states of Florence, Milan, and Venice. Naples was ruled first by a French dynasty, and later by Aragon. Central Italy remained subject to a tenuous papal control, compromised by the particularism of local aristocrats and the political turbulence of Rome itself. Milan, and later Florence, ceased to be republics and fell under the rule of self-

made despots. Throughout this period, Venice remained a republic dominated by a narrow commercial oligarchy.

The despots, ruling without the sanction of royal anointment or legitimate succession, governed by their wits and by the realities of power, uninhibited by traditions or customs. They have often been regarded as symbols of the "new Renaissance man," but in fact their opportunism was a quality well known to the northern monarchs, and their ruthlessness would have surprised neither William the Conqueror nor Philip the Fair. Yet the very insecurity of their positions and the fragile equilibrium of the five major Italian powers gave rise to a considerable refinement of traditional diplomatic practices. Ambassadors, skilled at compliments and espionage, were exchanged on a regular basis, and emerging from the tendency of two or three weaker states to combine against a stronger one came the shifting alliances known as the "balance of power" principle.

The Italian power balance was upset in 1494 when a powerful French army invaded the peninsula. For generations thereafter Italy was a battleground for French-Spanish rivalries, and the techniques and concepts of Italian Renaissance diplomacy passed across the Alps to affect the relations of the northern kingdoms. The modern tendency to ignore moral limitations and ecclesiastical mediation—to base diplomacy on a calculated balance of force—was growing throughout late-medieval Europe. But it reached fruition first in Renaissance Italy.

Eastern Europe

Eastern Europe was, in general, no more successful than Germany and Italy in achieving political cohesion. Poland, Lithuania, and Hungary (as well as the Scandinavian states to the north) were all afflicted by aristocratic turbulence and dynastic quarrels. The Teutonic Knights were humbled by Slavic armies and internal rebellions, and most of the Balkan peninsula was overwhelmed by the Ottoman Turks. Only the Russians and Ottomans were able to build strong states, and both, by 1500, were uncompromisingly autocratic.

Poland had become a Catholic-Christian kingdom around A.D. 1000, but throughout the High Middle Ages it had been paralyzed by aristocratic factions and disputed successions. In 1386 it united with rapidly expanding Lithuania, and the Polish-Lithuanian state became the largest political unit in Europe. It was also, very possibly, the worst governed. Under the Lithuanian warrior-prince Jagiello (1377–1434), who converted from paganism to Catholicism when he accepted the Polish crown, the dual state humbled the Teutonic Knights at the decisive battle of Tannenberg (1410). But even under Jagiello, Poland-Lithuania had no real central government; its nobles would cooperate with their ruler only against the hated Germans, and even then only momentarily. Stretching all the way from the Black Sea to the Baltic, incorporating many of the former lands of the Teutonic Order and most of the

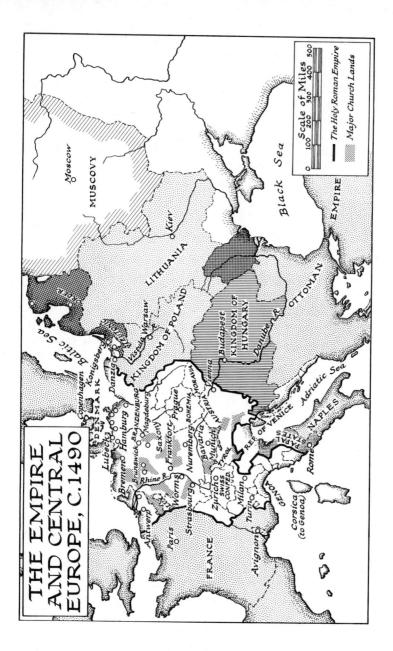

THE EMPIRE AND CENTRAL EUROPE, C.1490

old state of Kievan Russia, Poland-Lithuania lacked the skilled administrators and political institutions necessary to govern its vast territories. Its nobles were virtually all-powerful, and its peasantry was slipping toward serfdom. Its political impotence guaranteed that no strong state would emerge between Germany and Russia during Europe's early modern centuries.

Russia had acquired its religion from Constantinople rather than from the West, and Byzantine civilization was a potent factor in the development of Russian culture. This development was set back for a time by the Mongols, who had swept westward out of Asia between 1237 and 1242, crossing Russia and penetrating momentarily into the heart of Central Europe. The Mongols had quickly withdrawn from most of Europe, but they remained in Russia for about 240 years, allowing local autonomy to the Russian Christian princes but ruthlessly enforcing the collection of tribute.

During the centuries of Mongol domination, the Muscovite principality managed not only to survive but to expand and flourish. The Christian "Grand Princes" of Moscow extended their influence in northern Russia by collaborating with their Mongol khans and winning the support of the Orthodox Church. They were appointed sole collectors of the Mongol tribute, and on occasion they helped the Mongols crush the rebellions of other Russian princes. Moscow became the headquarters of Russian Orthodox Christianity, and when the Turks took Constantinople in 1453, Moscow, the "Third Rome," claimed spiritual sovereignty over the Orthodox Slavic world.

At first the Muscovite princes strengthened their positon with the full backing of the Mongol khans. But toward the end of the fourteenth century Moscow began taking the lead in anti-Mongol resistance. At last, in 1480, Ivan III, the Great, Grand Prince of Moscow and Czar of the Russians, repudiated Mongol authority altogether and abolished the tribute.

The Muscovite princes enjoyed a certain measure of popular support in their struggle against the Mongols and in their battles against the Roman Catholic Lithuanians, but their rule was autocratic to a degree worthy of Byzantine emperors and Mongol khans. Nascent republicanism in city-states such as Novgorod was crushed with the expansion of Muscovite authority. The grand princes were despots, inspired politically by Central Asia rather than by the West. Their state had no local or national assemblies and no articulate middle class. Russia was eventually to acquire the material and organizational attributes of a great power, but the centuries during which it had been isolated from the rest of Europe could not be made up overnight.

The Ottoman Empire

The great outside threat to Eastern Europe came from the southeast, where the Ottoman Turks pressed into the Balkans from Asia Minor. These Altaic nomads, propelled from their Central Asian homeland by the Mongols, came into Asia Minor first as mercenaries, then as conquerors. Adopting the Islamic faith, the Ottomans subjected the greater part of Asia Minor to their rule and intermarried with the local population. In 1354, bypassing the diminutive Byzantine Empire, they invaded Europe. During the latter half of the fourteenth century, they crushed Serbia and Bulgaria and extended their dominion

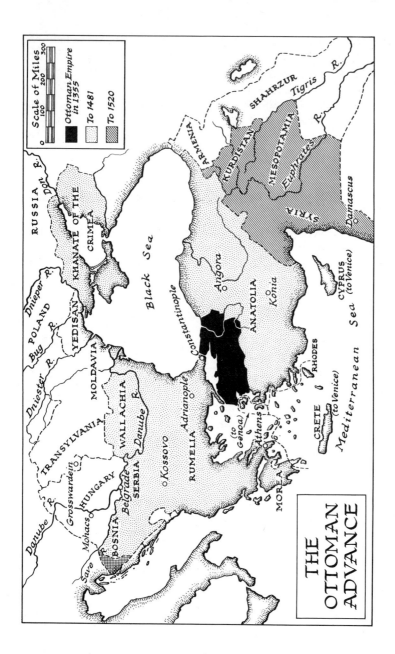

over most of the Balkan Peninsula. And in 1444, at the decisive battle of Varna, they decimated an anti-Turkish crusading army and consolidated their hold on southeastern Europe. After the great Ottoman victory at Varna, the storming of Constantinople in 1453 was little more than a postscript. Yet all Europe recognized that the sultan Mohammed II, in conquering the unconquerable city, had ended an era.

The Ottoman Empire endured until the twentieth century; as the Republic of Turkey it endures still. Like the Muscovite princes, the Ottoman sultans were autocrats. Slaves served in their administration and fought in their armies alongside mounted noblemen of the Ottoman landed aristocracy. And while the sultans were living in splendor on the Golden Horn, overlooking the Bosporus, their government was insulating southeastern Europe from the civilization of the West.

CHRONOLOGY OF LATE-MEDIEVAL EASTERN EUROPE

1237–1242:	Mongols invade Eastern Europe
1354:	Ottoman Turks invade Balkans
1377–1434:	Jagiello rules Lithuania
1386:	Union of Poland and Lithuania under Jagiello
1410:	Poland-Lithuania defeats Teutonic Knights at Tannenberg
1444:	Ottomans defeat Christians at Varna
1453:	Ottomans conquer Constantinople
1480:	Czar Ivan III the Great discontinues Mongol tribute

Chapter 16

ℭ

Economic
and Cultural
Change

Towns and Commerce

The shift from boom to depression came gradually and unevenly to Western Europe. As early as the mid-thirteenth century prosperity was starting to ebb. And from the early fourteenth century through much of the fifteenth, a number of related trends—shrinking population, contracting markets, an end to the long process of land reclamation, and a creeping mood of pessimism and retrenchment—resulted in a general economic slump and a deepening of social antagonisms.

These trends were far from universal. They were less marked in northern Italy than elsewhere; and various localities north of the Alps, profiting from favorable commercial situations or technological advances, became more prosperous than before. At a time when many English towns were declining, Coventry and certain others grew wealthy from the rise of woolen-cloth production. The Flemish town of Bruges remained throughout most of the late Middle Ages a bustling center of commerce on the northern seas. Florence, with its large textile industry and its international banking, was to become the focal point of Italian Renaissance culture. In Florence and elsewhere, enterprising individuals and families grew wealthy from the profits of international commerce and banking. The Bardi, Peruzzi, and Medici were the great Floren-

ℭ

tine banking families, and they had their counterparts north of the Alps in such figures as Jacques Coeur of Bourges, financier of the fifteenth-century French monarchy, and the Fuggers of Augsburg, bankers for the Holy Roman emperors. But such great financiers as these were exceedingly insecure in the turbulent years of the late Middle Ages. The Bardi and Peruzzi houses collapsed in the mid-fourteenth century, and Jacques Coeur was ruined by his royal debtor, King Charles VII. Some fortunes continued to grow, but the total assets of late-medieval bankers fell considerably below those of their thirteenth-century predecessors.

Even before the coming of the Black Death in the mid-fourteenth century, Europe's population appears to have been leveling off and perhaps beginning to decline. The growing shortage of good land, and a long-range shift to a colder, rainier climate, brought adverse agrarian conditions that discouraged large families and depressed the birth rate. But although the fundamental trends of demographic and economic decline were not initiated by the plague, they were enormously aggravated by it. Carried by fleas that infested black rats, the bubonic plague entered Europe along trade routes from the East and spread with terrifying speed. The death toll cannot be determined with any precision. The best estimate would be about a third of Europe's population. In many crowded towns the mortality rate exceeded fifty percent, whereas isolated rural areas tended to suffer much less. Consequently, the most enterprising and best trained Europeans were hit hardest. Few urban families could have been spared altogether.

Survivors were subjected to periodic revisitations of the plague. Indeed, Europeans for the next three centuries experienced recurring outbreaks of the dread disease. Fourteenth-century medical science was at a loss to explain the process of infection, while lack of sanitation in the towns encouraged its spread. Some fled, some gave way to religious frenzy or debauchery, and some remained faithfully at their posts, hoping for divine protection. An inhabitant of Siena provides this description:

66 Father abandoned child; wife, husband; one brother, another. For this illness seemed to strike through the breath and the sight. And so they died. And nobody could be found to bury the dead for money or for friendship . . . . And in many places in Siena huge pits were dug and piled deep with great heaps of the dead. . . . And I buried my five children with my own hands and many others did likewise. And there were many corpses about the city who were so sparsely covered with earth that dogs dragged them out and devoured their bodies. **99**

At papal Avignon great religious processions were organized:

66 Among them many of both sexes were barefoot; some were in sack cloth, some covered with ashes, wailing as they walked, tearing their hair, and lashing themselves with whips until they were bloody. **99**

Europe survived the catastrophe; the economies of town and countryside recovered, though incompletely. But the memory lingered, and death remained close at hand.

The troubled conditions of the late-medieval countryside prompted a heavier migration into the towns than ever before. But many of the newcomers, unable to find jobs, drifted into the growing mass of the urban unemployed. The gap between wealth and poverty widened as privileged classes did everything they could to close their ranks. Guilds guarded their monopolies, and heredity became the chief avenue to the status of guild master. In their grim efforts to retain their share of declining markets, guilds struggled with one another, with the district nobility, and with the increasingly desperate urban proletariat, its class consciousness growing as its upward mobility diminished.

Many of the Italian cities, as we have seen, evolved in the late Middle Ages from oligarchic republics to despotisms. Florence, for example, ravaged by the Black Death, terrorized by a proletarian rebellion in 1378, and impoverished by decades of inconclusive warfare, passed in 1434 into the control of the Medici banking family. Over a century before, Milan had fallen under the domination of the ambitious Visconti family, which gave way in 1450 to still another dynasty of despots—the Sforzas. In general, the rich mercantile familes retained their privileged economic status in the face of lower-class pressure by sharing their political authority with great magnates or kings or, in Italy, by abdicating it to despots.

The depressed conditions and general unpredictability of the era impelled merchants to experiment in new areas of enterprise and to increase the efficiency of their operations. A proliferation of economic records in the late Middle Ages reflects the anxiety of urban and rural elites to obtain a stricter accounting of their receipts and expenses. As times grew hard, business procedures, of necessity, became more rigorous and sophisticated.

The Landed Nobility and Peasantry

The rural nobility of Western Europe, like the urban upper class, managed to survive the socio-economic turmoil of the late Middle Ages. With some exceptions, they clung to their extensive lands and preserved much of their wealth. Some responded to declining grain prices by leasing their demesne lands to peasants and converting customary peasant services to money rents. Others retained their demesnes and converted them to the production of more profitable luxury goods such as wool, meat, wine, and beer (barley and hops).

The spectacular population drop resulting from the Black Death relieved the press of population on arable land, leaving the plague's peasant survivors better off economically than they had been for several generations. The plague-induced labor shortage resulted, at least for a time, in a dramatic rise in the wages of landless workers. And peasants could obtain lands at lower rents than before. Some enterprising peasants, profiting from the decline of land values, accumulated numerous estates, hired laborers to farm them, and prospered considerably in the process.

But the plague had adverse economic effects as well: it produced commercial shocks and disruptions; it encouraged violent price fluctuations; it diminished the numbers of consumers, particularly townspeople who had, throughout the High Middle Ages, constituted an ever-growing market for agrarian products. And while in some regions the labor shortage prompted lords to free their serfs, so as to induce them not to seek better opportunities elsewhere, lords in Germany and portions of France enforced the demesne labor services of their serfs more strictly than ever.

The privileged classes responded to the rising wage levels of the post-plague decades by attempting to hold down wages artificially, either by collective conspiracy or through legislation. In England, for example, the Statutes of Laborers of 1351 and thereafter were aimed at freezing wages in the wake of the plague. Such measures enjoyed little success, but they did create among the peasantry a deep sense of grievance that contributed to the abortive English Peasants' Revolt of 1381. This confused and bloody uprising was merely one of a considerable number that terrorized late-medieval Europe. Like the Jacquerie rebellion in France, and like many similar peasant insurrections of the period, it bore witness to a society in which classes struggled bitterly for their share of a declining wealth.

In Eastern Europe the peasant's lot was worse than in the West, for the late-medieval eastern nobility was everywhere reducing its peasantry to serfdom. In East and West alike, the landed aristocracy jealously guarded its privileges against peasantry and monarchy, and for a time, all across Europe, the high-medieval trend toward stronger royal government reversed itself. With the exception of Russia, Eastern monarchies made no real progress against the great landholders, but by the later fifteenth century, Western monarchies were beginning to curb their independence. The new Tudor monarchy in England tended to favor the mercantile class, but in Spain and France the nobility was rewarded for its political submissiveness by economic favoritism and privileged positions in the royal administration, the army, and the church.

Thus, the Western nobles were evolving from war lords into silk-clad courtiers. The traditional role of mounted knight in the feudal host was a thing of the past, for monarchs were now manning their armies with mercenaries, and footsoldiers were winning most of the battles. Moreover, the increasing use of gunpowder was making knightly armor and knightly castles highly vulnerable. But while the feudal knight was vanishing from European armies, he was becoming ever more prominent in art, literature, and court ceremonial. The fifteenth century was an age of shining armor, fairy-tale castles, coats of arms, and extravagant tournaments. Knighthood, driven from the battlefield, took refuge in fantasy, and an age of ruthless political cynicism saw the full flowering of a romantic code of chivalric ethics. Behind this fanciful facade, the landed aristocracy remained entrenched in its privileged position atop the social order.

Economic Recovery

The consolidation of royal authority in late-fifteenth-century Western Europe coincided with a general economic upturn following a long recession. Europe's population in 1500 was probably lower than in 1300, but it was increasing again. Commerce was quickening and towns were growing. Technological progress had never ceased, and now water-driven fulling mills were increasing wool production, while water-driven pumps were draining mines. With advances in mining technology, Europe was increasing its supply of silver and the various metals essential to its rising industries: iron, copper, alum, and tin. The development of artillery and movable-type printing depended not merely on the inventive idea but also on many generations of progress in the metallurgical arts. And advances in ship design and navigation lay behind the Atlantic voyages that would soon bring a torrent of wealth into Western Europe. By 1500 the long economic crisis had passed. Europe had entered on an era of economic growth and world expansion that would far outstrip her earlier surge in the High Middle Ages.

Growth and Decay

Printing and gunpowder were the two most spectacular technological innovations of the late Middle Ages. Gunpowder came first, and by the fifteenth century it was being used with some effect in the Hundred Years' War, the Turkish conquests and, indeed, most of the military engagements of Europe. Printing from movable type was developed midway through the fifteenth century, and although its effect on European culture was immense, the full impact was not felt until after 1500. Even among the "new men" of the Italian Renaissance, printed books were regarded as vulgar imitations of handwritten originals. This fact should warn us against viewing late-medieval Europe—and even Renaissance Italy—exclusively in terms of new beginnings. There was, to be sure, a strong sense of the new and "modern" among many creative Europeans of the period, but there was also a perpetuation of medieval ways, styles, and habits of thought. Often one encounters a sense of loss over the fading of medieval ideals and institutions, a conviction that civilization was declining. The Renaissance humanist Aeneas Sylvius—later Pope Pius II (d. 1464)— could look at the Turkish threat and the strife among Christian states and conclude that nothing good was in prospect. The generation living after 1500, aware of the voyages of exploration and of the growing prosperity and political consolidation, might well be more hopeful of the future, but between 1300 and 1500 a gloom hung over much of Europe.

Beneath the gloom one finds a sense of nervous unrest, a violent emotionalism that gives dramatic intensity to late-medieval works of art. The thirteenth-century ideal of balanced serenity lost its relevance in this new age of crisis and recession. The practice of self-flagellation acquired wide popularity, and the Dance of Death became a favorite artistic theme. In an era of depression, plague, and violence, the confidence and order of high-medieval civilization could not endure.

The breakdown expressed itself in a hundred ways—in the intensifying conflict between class and class, in the architectural shift from organic unity to flamboyant decoration, in the divorce between knightly function and chivalric fantasy, in the evolution from Christian commonwealth to territorial states, and in the disintegration of St. Thomas Aquinas' fusion of faith and reason. The medieval search for a rational cosmic order had reached its climax in Aquinas' hierarchical ordering and reconciliation of matter and spirit, body and soul, logic and revelation. The abandonment of the search is nowhere more evident than in the attacks of fourteenth-century philosophers on the Thomist system.

Late-Medieval Thought

St. Thomas's *Summa Theologica*, like the high-Gothic cathedral, unifies religious aspiration and logical order on the basis of an omnipotent God who is both loving and rational. The fourteenth-century attack on this reconciliation was founded on two related propositions: (1) To ascribe rationality to God is to limit his omnipotence by the finite rules of human logic; thus, the Thomist God of reason gave way to a God of will, and the high-medieval notion of a logical divine order was eroded. (2) Human reason, therefore, can tell us nothing of God; logic and Christian belief inhabit two separate, sealed worlds.

The first steps toward this concept of a willful, incomprehensible God were taken by the Oxford Franciscan, Duns Scotus (d. 1308), who produced a detailed critique of St. Thomas's theory of knowledge. Duns Scotus did not reject the possibility of elucidating revealed truth through reason, but he was more cautious in his use of logic than Aquinas had been. Whereas St. Thomas is called "The Angelic Doctor," Duns Scotus is called "The Subtle Doctor," and the extreme complexity of his thought prompted people in subsequent generations to describe anyone who bothered to follow Duns' arguments as a "dunce." The sobriquet is unfair, for Duns Scotus is an important and original figure in the development of late scholasticism. Yet one is tempted to draw a parallel between the intricacies of his intellectual system and the decorative elaborations of late-Gothic churches. A Christian rationalist of the most thoroughgoing kind, he nevertheless made the first move toward dismantling the Thomist synthesis and withdrawing reason from the realm of theology.

Another Oxford Franciscan, William of Ockham (d. 1349), attacked the

Thomist synthesis on all fronts. Ockham argued that God and Christian doctrine, utterly undemonstrable, must be accepted on faith alone, and that human reason must be limited to the realm of observable phenomena. In this unpredictable world of an unfathomable Creator, one can reason only about things that one can see or directly experience. Ockham's radical empiricism ruled out all metaphysical speculations, all rational arguments from an observable diversity of things to an underlying unity of things. And out of this great divorce of reason and faith came two characteristic expressions of late-medieval thought: the scientific manipulation of material facts, and pietistic mysticism untouched by logic. In Ockham and many of his followers, one finds empiricism and mysticism side by side. For since the two worlds never touched, they were in no way contradictory. An intelligent Christian could keep one foot in each of them.

The Ockhamist philosophy served as an appropriate foundation for both late-medieval mysticism and late-medieval science. Some mystics, indeed, regarded themselves as empiricists. For the empiricist is a person who accepts only those things that he experiences, and the mystic, abandoning the effort to *understand* God, strove to *experience* him. Science, on the other hand, was now freed of its theological underpinnings and could proceed on its own. Nicholas Oresme, a teacher at the University of Paris in the fourteenth century, attacked the Aristotelian theory of motion and proposed a rotating earth as a possible explanation for the apparent daily movement of the sun and stars across the sky. Oresme's theories probably owed more to thirteenth-century scientists such as Robert Grosseteste than to Ockham, but his willingness to tinker with traditional explanations of the physical structure of God's universe is characteristic of an age in which scientific speculation was being severed from revealed truth.

Many late-medieval philosophers rejected Ockham's criticism and remained Thomists. But owing to the very comprehensiveness of Aquinas' achievement, his successors were reduced to detailed elaboration or minor repair work. Faced with a choice between the tedious niggling of late Thomism and the drastic limitations imposed by Ockham on the scope of philosophical inquiry, many of Europe's finest minds shunned philosophy altogether for the more exciting fields of science, mathematics, and classical learning. When the philosopher John Gerson (d. 1429), chancellor of the University of Paris, spoke out in his lectures against "vain curiosity in the matter of faith," the collapse of the faith-reason synthesis was all but complete.

The fifteenth century witnessed a revival of Platonism and Neoplatonism, in Renaissance Italy and in the north as well. The two leading philosophers of the Italian Renaissance, Marsilio Ficino (d.1499) and Pico della Mirandola (d. 1494), were both Platonists. They were able to draw from an extensive body of Plato's writings that had been unknown to the high-medieval West, yet neither Ficino nor Pico was a first-echelon figure in the history of Western thought. Neither possessed the acumen of the best high-medieval philosophers, and neither approached the profundity of their great contemporary north of the Alps, Nicholas of Cusa (d. 1464).

Educated by the mystical Brethren of the Common Life, Nicholas of Cusa became first a conciliarist and later an ardent papist. He agreed, up to a point, with Ockham's view that human reason is limited to the disconnected phenomena of the physical universe. But he insisted that the contradictions and diversity of the material world were reconciled and unified in an unknowable God. Nicholas of Cusa regarded God as beyond rational apprehension—approachable only through a mystical process that he termed "learned ignorance." Like Aquinas, he believed in an underlying universal order, but like Ockham he denied that any such order could be grasped by human reason. Yet his concept of an unknowable God was derived from a tradition far older than Ockhamism. It was rooted in the late-Roman Neoplatonism of the pagan Plotinus* and his Christian followers, a tradition that had run as an undercurrent through the entire Middle Ages. Like the older Neoplatonists, Nicholas of Cusa conceived of the universe as a ceaseless creative unfolding of the infinite God. But going far beyond his Neoplatonic predecessors, he reasoned that a universe emanating from an infinite deity cannot be limited by human concepts of space and time. In short, God's created universe was potentially infinite. And since a universe without bounds is a universe without a physical center, Nicholas of Cusa concluded that neither the earth nor the sun occupied any special position in it. The earth was not at the center, nor was it stationary, since in an infinite universe position and motion are entirely relative. God was at the center, Christ was at the center, but only in the sense of metaphysical priority, not in the sense of physical location.

In his emphasis on mysticism and the limitation of human reason, Nicholas of Cusa was in tune with his age. In his synthetic vision of an ordered cosmos he echoed the thirteenth century. And in his bold conception of an infinite universe he anticipated modern philosophy and astronomy.

Arts and Letters

The change from high-medieval order to late-medieval diversity is clearly evident in the field of art. The high-Gothic balance between upward aspiration and harmonic proportion—between the vertical and horizontal—was shifting in the cathedrals of the later thirteenth century toward an ever-greater emphasis on verticality. Formerly, elaborate capitals and horizontal decorative lines had balanced the soaring piers and pointed arches of the Gothic cathedrals, creating a sense of tense equilibrium between heaven and earth. But during the late Middle Ages, capitals disappeared and horizontal lines became discontinuous, leaving little to relieve the dramatic upward thrust

*See pp. 6-7.

from floor to vaulting. Late medieval churches achieved a fluid, uncompromising verticality, a sense of heavenly aspiration that bordered on the mystical.

By about the mid-thirteenth century, the basic structural potentialities of the Gothic style had been fully exploited. Windows were as large as they could possibly be, vaultings could be raised no higher without structural disaster, and flying buttresses were used with maximum efficiency. The fundamental Gothic idea of a skeletal stone framework with walls of colored glass had been embodied in churches of incomparable nobility and beauty. During the late Middle Ages, buildings changed in appearance as tastes changed, but the

High Gothic interior: Nave of Amiens Cathedral, begun 1220, showing the capitals and decorated stringcourse.

originality of post-thirteenth-century Gothic architects was inhibited by their devotion to a style that had already achieved complete structural development. Accordingly, the innovations of late-Gothic architecture consisted chiefly of new and more elaborate decoration, with the result that a number of late-medieval churches are, to some modern tastes, overdecorated sculptural jungles.

Unrestrained verticality and unrestrained decorative elaboration were the architectural hallmarks of the age, and both reflected a shift away from rational unity and balance. Like Ockham's universe, the fourteenth- and fifteenth-century church became a fascinating miscellany of separate elements.

Late Gothic interior: Choir of Saint-Etienne at Beauvais, 1506–c.1550, showing the absence of capitals, inconspicuous and interrupted string-course, and elaborate vaulting.

Thus the "flamboyant Gothic" style emerged in late-medieval France, while English churches were evolving from the "decorated Gothic" of the fourteenth century to the "perpendicular Gothic" of the fifteenth and sixteenth, with its lacelike fan vaulting, its sculptural profusion, and its sweeping vertical lines. In the course of the sixteenth century, Gothic architecture, having reached its decorative as well as its structural limits, gave way throughout northern Europe to the classical Greco-Roman style that had been revived and developed in fifteenth-century Italy and flowed north with the spread of Renaissance humanism.

Flamboyant Gothic exterior: Saint-Maclou, Rouen (1437–1517).

Perpendicular Gothic interior: Chapel of Henry VII, Westminster Abbey,
London: early sixteenth century.

Sculpture and painting, like architecture and thought, evolved during the
late Middle Ages toward multiformity. The serene, idealized humanism of
thirteenth-century sculpture gave way to heightened emotionalism and an emphasis on individual peculiarities. Painting north of the Alps reached its
apogee in the mirrorlike realism of the Flemish school. Painters such as Jan van
Eyck (d. 1440), pioneering in the use of oil paints, excelled in reproducing the
natural world with a devotion to detail that was all but photographic. Critics
of the style have observed that detail seems to compromise the unity of the

High Gothic sculpture: *Le Beau Dieu,*
west portal of Amiens Cathedral
(thirteenth century).

Late medieval sculpture: *Three Mourners* from the tomb of Philip the
Bold of Burgundy, by Claus Sluter and Claus de Werve (early fifteenth
century).

total composition, but in a world viewed through Ockham's eyes, such is to be
expected. It was Italy, again, that developed a new style of painting and
sculpture, based on the classical canon of naturalism subordinated to a unifying idea. And the Italian Renaissance style of painting, like Renaissance architecture, streamed northward in the sixteenth century to bring a new vision
to trans-Alpine artists.

The Madonna of the Chancellor Rolin, by Jan van Eyck (Flemish School, *c.* 1432).

The decay of high-medieval forms of expression is vividly demonstrated in the late-medieval romance, which had once served as a vital literary form but now became sentimentalized, formalized, and drained of inspiration. Much of the popular literature of late-medieval Europe is beyond redemption, and writers could achieve vitality only by turning from warmed-over chivalry to graphic realism. Geoffrey Chaucer (d. 1400), in his *Canterbury Tales,* combines rare psychological insight with a descriptive skill worthy of the Flemish painters or the late-Gothic stone carvers. Chaucer describes one of his Canterbury pilgrims, a corrupt friar, in these words:

Highly beloved and intimate was he
With country folk wherever he might be,
And worthy city women with possessions;
For he was qualified to hear confessions,
Or so he said, with more than priestly scope;
He had a special license from the pope.
Sweetly he heard his penitents at shrift
With pleasant absolution, for a gift.

And François Villon (d. 1463), a brawling Parisian vagabond, expressed in his poems an anguished, sometimes brutal realism that captures the late-medieval mood of insecurity and plague:

Death makes one shudder and turn pale,
Pinches his nose, distends his veins,
Swells out his throat, his members fail,
Tendons and nerves grow hard with strains.

To Villon, writing in a society of sharp class distinctions, death was the great democrat:

I know this well, that rich and poor,
Fools, sages, laymen, friars in cowl,
Large-hearted lords and each mean boor,
Little and great and fair and foul,
Ladies in lace, who smile or scowl,
From whatsoever stock they stem,
Hatted or hooded, prone to prowl,
Death seizes every one of them.

Italian Renaissance Classicism

These northern moods and movements stood in sharp contrast to the growing, self-confident classicism of Renaissance Italy. Here the late-medieval economic depression was less severe and less prolonged; Italian merchants continued their domination of Mediterranean trade and extended their commercial activities into the Black Sea. Although endemic interurban warfare made conditions just as insecure as in the North, the civic spirit of the independent north-Italian communes encouraged innovation and novel forms of expression. Italy had never been entirely at ease with Gothic architecture, and the triumphs of high-medieval culture were more characteristically French than Italian. England and France had enjoyed relative peace during much of the thirteenth century, whereas Italy had been battered by papal-imperial wars. Italy, in short, had less reason to be nostalgic about its high-medieval past, and the coming of the Renaissance was not so much the advent of a new epoch in European history as a reassertion of Italian culture over French. By the time Renaissance ideas were significantly affecting trans-Alpine Europe, Renaissance Italy was already in sharp decline.

In an age of French arms and French culture, such as the thirteenth century had been, Italians could return in memory to the days when Rome ruled the world. Roman monuments and Roman sculpture were all around them, and when, in the fourteenth and fifteenth centuries, they abandoned the

Sistine Madonna, by Raphael (High Renaissance: early sixteenth century).

Gothic style and the intellectual habits of Paris theologians, it was to their indigenous classical heritage that they turned for inspiration. In sculpture, the calm spiritual nobility of stone saints gave way to a classical emphasis on the human body. The slender young Virgins of the High Middle Ages turned voluptuous. Architects, abandoning the Gothic spire and pointed arch, created buildings with domes and round arches and elegant classical facades. Scholars abandoned the logic of Aristotle and St. Thomas for the delights of Greco-Roman belles lettres. And painters, with few actual classical models to follow, pioneered in techniques of linear and atmospheric perspective and imposed a classical unity upon their lifelike figures and landscapes.

(left) *The Golden Virgin*, from the south portal of Amiens Cathedral (thirteenth century).

(right) *David*, by Michelangelo (High Renaissance, Florence: completed 1504).

Venus, by Titian (Renaissance, Venetian School, sixteenth century).

Interior of S. Andrea at Mantua, by Alberti (Renaissance: fifteenth century).

The Italian Renaissance, while rebelling against the Middle Ages, retained much that was medieval. In 1492, while a worldly Borgia was acceding to the papacy and Columbus was discovering America, high-Renaissance Florence was passing under the influence of the austere Christian revivalist, Savonarola. Renaissance humanism was always an elitist phenomenon, restricted to urban nobilities and favored artists and leaving the Italian masses unchanged. Yet for all that, the Renaissance style represents a profound shift from the forms and assumptions of the Middle Ages. St. Thomas and his contemporaries had studied the Greek philosophers, but Renaissance humanists looked back on classical antiquity with a fresh perspective, seeing not a collection of ideas that might be used but a total culture that deserved to be revered and revived. It was this vision that underlay the new art and the new classical learning of early modern Europe.

The Genesis of Modern Europe

Historians of the past have probably overemphasized the impact of the Renaissance on the development of modern civilization. The Renaissance contributed much to art and classical studies; its scholars brought the same intellectual precision to the fields of history and philology that their medieval predecessors had applied to theology and law. The Renaissance contributed much to the evolution of diplomatic techniques but little to constitutional development. Renaissance humanists were essentially scholars of the "humanities" and were no more interested in science than, say, a modern professor of English literature or Latin. Modern science grew out of the medieval universities. And modern legislatures—even if they meet in domed, round-arched buildings—are outgrowths of medieval representative assemblies.

In the Europe of 1500, Italian Renaissance ideas were beginning to move across the Alps. But the promise of the future did not depend on the Renaissance alone. All across Europe commerce was thriving again and the population was growing. New non-Renaissance inventions—gunpowder, the three-masted caravel, the water pump, the printing press—were changing the ways people lived. The papacy had degenerated into a local principality, but England, France, and Spain had achieved stable, centralized governments, and were on the road toward nationhood. European ships had reached America and India, and the first cargo direct from the Orient had arrived in Portugal. The late-medieval era of crisis and retrenchment was clearly at an end, and the world lay open.

SUGGESTED READINGS

The asterisk indicates a paperback edition.

GENERAL WORKS

Two good comprehensive accounts of the period are WALLACE K. FERGUSON, *Europe in Transition: 1300–1520* (1962), and DENYS HAY, *Europe in the Fourteenth and Fifteenth Centuries* (1966).

For somewhat shorter and lighter treatments, all in paperback, see MARGARET ASTON, *The Fifteenth Century* (1968); JERAH JOHNSON and WILLIAM PERCY, *The Age of Recovery: The Fifteenth Century* (1970); ROBERT E. LERNER, *The Age of Adversity: The Fourteenth Century* (1968); and PHILIP LEE RALPH, *The Renaissance in Perspective* (1973).

CHRISTIANITY AND THE CHURCH

J.M.CLARK, *The Great German Mystics* (1949). A perceptive study of Meister Eckhart and two of his followers, John Tauler and Henry Suso.

*NORMAN COHN, *The Pursuit of the Millennium* (1957). A penetrating work on radical heresy.

E.F. JACOB, *Essays in the Conciliar Epoch* (1953). A group of stimulating scholarly analyses.

*G. MOLLAT, *The Popes at Avignon: 1305–1378* (1965). A reprint of an older account, still valuable.

*BRIAN TIERNEY, *Foundations of the Conciliar Theory* (1955). An illuminating work on the medieval canonists' contributions to conciliarism.

*RUSSELL'S *History of Medieval Christianity*, cited earlier, covers this period as well as earlier ones.

THE LATE-MEDIEVAL STATE

Several books noted in previous bibliographies include this era:

OSTROGORSKY, *History of the Byzantine State;* HITTI, *History of the Arabs;* BARRACLOUGH, *Origins of Modern Germany;* LOPEZ, *Birth of Europe;* and HOLLISTER, *Making of England*

The appropriate volumes in the Oxford History of England are MAY McKISACK, *The Fourteenth Century* (1959); and E.F. JACOB, *The Fifteenth Century* (1961).

GENE A. BRUCKER. *Renaissance Florence* (1969). A valuable study that makes clear the political and social tensions in a major Renaissance city.

JOHN FENNELL, *The Emergence of Moscow: 1304–1359* (1968). An important, well-researched study; not light reading.

DAVID HERLIHY, *Pisa in the Early Renaissance* (1958). Another thoughtful, well-documented account of urban politics and society.

*GEORGE HOLMES, *The Later Middle Ages: 1272–1485* (1966). A history of late-medieval England, less comprehensive and more readable than the Oxford History volumes.

M.H. KEEN, *England in the Later Middle Ages* (1973). A detailed history stressing the impact of war on the society, economy, and political order.

P.S. LEWIS, *Later Medieval France: The Polity* (1968). Not a political narrative, but a highly original study of government and social structure.

J.H. MARIEJOL, *The Spain of Ferdinand and Isabella* (1961). Written originally in French in the nineteenth century, this valuable work has been edited and updated by B. Keen.

GARRETT MATTINGLY, *Renaissance Diplomacy* (1955). A thoughtful and original investigation of Italian diplomatic representation and dynastic politics.

*EDOUARD PERROY, *The Hundred Years' War* (1965). A reprint of an older, comprehensive account, particularly illuminating on the history of late-medieval France.

*FERDINAND SCHEVILL, *Siena: The History of a Medieval Commune* (1964, first published 1909). A detailed, well-written classic with a new introduction by William M. Bowsky.

*RICHARD VAUGHAN, *Valois Burgundy* (1975). A short version, for students and general readers, a four-volume history of late-medieval Burgundy.

*DANIEL WALEY, *The Italian City Republics* (1969). A lucid, well-illustrated discussion of the social and political milieu of the city-states.

ECONOMIC AND SOCIAL HISTORY

*T.S.R. BOASE, *Death in the Middle Ages* (1972). A splendidly illustrated study of death and its effects on medieval culture with emphasis on late-medieval society.

*R.H. HILTON, ED., *Peasants, Knights, and Heretics: Studies in Medieval English Social History* (1976). Fifteen innovative articles on aspects of English social and economic history in the High and late Middle Ages; not for beginners.

*HARRY A. MISKIMIN, *The Economy of Early Renaissance Europe, 1300–1460* (1969). A brief, lucid, economically sophisticated account covering all of late-medieval Western Europe.

*HENRI PIRENNE, *Early Democracies in the Low Countries* (1963). A reprint of a provocative older classic examining urban politics, institutions, and class struggles.

*RAYMOND DE ROOVER, *The Rise and Decline of the Medici Bank: 1397–1494* (1963). An authoritative study that elucidates the policies and methods of this great financial institution in the context of both Florentine local politics and the fifteenth-century economy.

*SYLVIA L. THRUPP, *The Merchant Class of Medieval London* (1948). A pioneering contribution to English social and economic history in the fourteenth and fifteenth centuries.

*PHILIP ZIEGLER, *The Black Death* (1969). A well-written summary addressed to the non-specialist reader.

Three books noted in previous bibliographies and useful here are:

BAUTIER, *Economic Development of Medieval Europe;* LOPEZ, *The Commerical Revolution of the Middle Ages;* and WHITE, *Medieval Technology and Social Change.*

INTELLECTUAL AND CULTURAL HISTORY

Again, several previously-cited books extend into the late Middle Ages:

GRANT, *Physical Science in the Middle Ages;* HENDERSON, *Gothic;* KNOWLES, *Evolution of Medieval Thought;* STODDARD, *Monastery and Cathedral in France;* and ULLMANN, *A History of Political Thought: The Middle Ages.*

The important problem of changing historical interpretations of the Italian Renaissance can be approached through two excellent paperbacks: WALLACE K. FERGUSON, *The Renaissance in Historical Thought* (1948); and DENYS HAY, *The Renaissance Debate* (1965).

JOSEPH CALMETTE, *The Golden Age of Burgundy* (1963). A splendid exploration of Burgundian politics and culture.

*JOHAN HUIZINGA, *The Waning of the Middle Ages* (1924). Concentrating on France and the Netherlands, this masterpiece of cultural history captures superbly the late-medieval mood.

*P.O. KRISTELLER, *Renaissance Thought* (1955). A brief, lucid interpretation, particularly interesting on the meaning of Renaissance humanism.

*GORDON LEFF, *The Dissolution of the Medieval Outlook* (1976). A brief, thoughtful essay on the gradual but far-reaching changes in the intellectual outlook that occurred in fourteenth-century Europe.

*GORDON LEFF, *Medieval Thought: St. Augustine to Ockham* (1958). A survey of metaphysical thought throughout the medieval period, particularly good on Ockham.

ERWIN PANOFSKY, *Early Netherlandish Painting: Its Origins and Character* (2 vols. 1953). A brilliant work of interpretation.

*J.H. PLUMB, ED., *Renaissance Profiles* (1965). Nine biographical sketches, each by a different scholar, on such Renaissance figures as Petrarch, Lorenzo de Medici, Leonardo da Vinci, and Pius II.

SOURCES

*RAYMOND B. BLAKNEY, ED., *Meister Eckhart; A Modern Translation.*

*JEAN FROISSART, *Chronicles.* Several editions. A contemporary bourgeois writer (d. 1410) treats the Hundred Years' War as a chivalric romance.

The Imitation of Christ, attributed to THOMAS À KEMPIS. Many editions.

*WILLIAM LANGLAND, *Piers the Ploughman*, tr. J.F. GOODRIDGE. A profound allegorical poem of fourteenth-century England.

Two good anthologies of contemporary literature, both in paperback, are, T. MORRISON. ED., *The Portable Chaucer* (1949); and J.B. ROSS and M.M. McLAUGHLIN, *The Portable Renaissance Reader* (1953).

ILLUSTRATION CREDITS

Alinari/Art Reference Bureau (pp. 8, 29, 32, 149, 150, 172, 320 top right: Accademia, Florence, 320 bottom: Uffizi, 321); Anderson/Art Reference Bureau (p. 31); Art Reference Bureau (p. 33); Bayerische Staatsbibliothek München Clm 4452 fol. 24ʳ (p. 107); Bibliothèque Nationale, Paris (p. 250); British Museum (p. 49); Cleveland Museum of Art (p. 316 bottom: 40.128 Purchase from the J. H. Wade Fund, Bequest of Leonard C. Hanna, Jr.); J. Combier (p. 117: Model after drawing by Professor K. J. Conant); Dresden Museum (p. 319); French Embassy Press and Information Division (p. 248); Historical Pictures Service, Chicago (p. 235); Louvre: Cliche des Musées Nationaux (p. 317); Marburg/Art Reference Bureau (pp. 30, 62, 79, 241, 242, 243 bottom, 244 top and bottom, 245 top and bottom, 247, 249, 314, 315, 316 top, 320 top left); Ann Münchow, Aachen, Germany (p. 73); New York Public Library (p. 252); Palais Synodale, Sens, France (p. 251); Pierpont Morgan Library (p. 66 left: 399f. 8v, and right: 399f. 10v); Sandak, Inc. (pp. 312, 313: Courtesy of Professor Whitney S. Stoddard).

Index

Egypt, 14, 25, 27, 34, 45, 54, 55, 59, 60, 154, 156, 174
Einhard, 73, 77, 78, 81
Eleanor of Aquitaine, Queen, 138, 206, 212
Empire, Angevin, 207, 212, 222, 223, 290
 Byzantine, 13–14, 26–29, 34, 36, 37, 43, 50, 51, 54, 56, 59, 64, 71, 77, 91, 112, 151
 Carolingian, 64–65, 67–85, 86, 91, 102, 110
 Holy Roman, 15, 77–78, 106, 148, 178–179, 183, 184, 195–196, 226, 287, 297
 Latin, 155
 Roman, 5, 6, 8, 13, 15, 17, 19, 25
Empiricism, 273, 310
England, Anglo-Saxon, 22, 69, 77, 99, 202, 203
 Celtic-Christian culture in, 43–44, 69
 high-medieval, 206–220, 237–238, 289–292
 invasions of, 91, 92, 95, 99, 100, 201
 late-medieval, 283, 284
 Norman monarchy of, 201–202, 203
Enqueteurs, 226
Epic, 231–233
Erasmus, 285
Essenes, 44
Estates General, 227, 292–293
Estonia, 157
Ethelbert of Kent, King, 48
Ethelred "the Unready", King, 99, 100
Etymologies (Isidore of Seville), 41, 93
Euclid, 270, 274
Evesham, battle of, 217
Exchequer, 205, 207, 218, 219
Excommunication, 184–185, 189, 192, 196, 198, 213

Fable, 238–239
Fabliaux, 238
Fairs, 129
Famine, 67, 142–143
Farming, see Agriculture
Fatima, 55
Fatimids, 55, 59
Fealty, 102
Ferdinand, King, 295
Feudalism, 103
 decline of, 134, 306–307
 development of, 46–47, 101–104, 105, 118
 English, 203, 204, 207–208, 213
 French, 100–104, 227
 German, 106, 186, 187, 195
 Norman, 148–149
Feudal law, 102–103, 139
Feudal obligations, 101–103, 116, 204

Ficino, Marsilio, 310–311
Finance, see Banking; Economic conditions
Finland, 94
Flanders, 104, 114, 127, 220, 226, 290, 296
Fleury, abbey of, 81
Florence, 127, 197, 298, 304, 306
Fourth Lateran Council, 192, 193
France, 88–89, 90, 94, 101–103, 152
 Capetians, 204, 220–228
 Carolingians, 64–85, 86–89, 100
 Frankland, 64, 67, 68, 69, 70, 72, 87–88, 91, 92, 204, 209
 High Middle Ages, 223, 226, 236–237
 Late Middle Ages, 283, 284
 relations with Catholic Church, 22, 43, 47, 167, 173, 179, 186, 197, 198–200
Francis, St., 170, 171–176, 180, 234, 261, 272
Franciscans, Order of Friars Minor, 126, 169, 171–176, 189, 192, 285
Franconia, 105
Frankfurt, Synod of, 80
Frankish Church, 68–72, 79–80, 80–81
Franks, 16, 22, 37, 42–43, 50, 56, 65, 72, 94
Frederick II, Emperor, 156, 191, 193–195, 196, 197
Frederick Barbarossa, Emperor, 154, 187–191, 194, 211
Friars, 255
Friars Minor, 173, 174
Friars Preachers, 169
Frisians, 69, 72
Frontiers, Byzantine, 34–35
 Carolingian, 75–76
 Crusades, 144
 Eastern, 104–105, 106
 internal, 144, 157
 pressure on, 15, 16, 19
Fuggers (Augsburg), 305
Fulda, monastery of, 70, 73, 81, 83
Fyrd, 203

Galahad, 237
Galen, 61, 256
Gascony, 220. 290
Gaul, 19, 20, 22, 41, 42–43, 56, 68, 90
Genoa, 112, 127
Gerbert of Aurillac (Pope Sylvester II), 109, 260, 273, 274
German Church, 184, 193, 194
Germania, (Tacitus), 16
Germanic culture, 16–18, 64, 137
Germanic law, 17–18, 32, 219, 257
Germanic tribes, 6, 15–21, 22, 25–56

in late Middle Ages, 317–318
Norse, 94
Renaissance, 318
see also Latin literature; Vernacular
    literature
Lithuania, 157, 299
Lives of the Twelve Caesars (Suetonius), 73
Lollards, 286
Lombard, Peter, 266–267
Lombard League, 189, 196
Lombards, 34, 43, 47, 71, 72, 75, 110, 112,
    183
Lombardy, 109, 187, 188, 189, 197
London, 92, 97, 129–131
London Bridge, 129
Longbow, 135
Lords, House of, 289–290
Lorraine, 89, 105
Lorris, 127
Lothar I, Emperor, 87–89, 105
Louis VI, king of France, 127, 222
Louis VII, king of France, 222
Louis VIII, king of France, 223–224
Louis IX, St., King of France, 128, 156, 197,
    224–226, 254
Louis XI, king of France, 294
Louis the Blind, King, 89
Louis the Child, King, 89, 105
Louis the German, King, 87–88
Louis the Pious, Emperor, 82, 85, 87
Louis the Stammerer, King, 89
Love, courtly, 138, 233, 237
Lucy of Chester, Countess, 139
Luther, Martin, 282, 288
Lyons, Council of, 196
Lyric poetry, 232–236

Madeiras, 296
Magna Carta, 214–215, 216, 220, 256
Magyars, see Invasions, Hungarian
Mainz, 69
    archbishop of, 297
Majorca, 295
Manfred, 197
Manor, 113, 115–116
Manzikert, battle of, 37, 151
Marcel, Etienne, 292
Marriage, 138–139, 141, 161
Marsiluis of Padua, 289
Martel, Charles, 56, 68, 69, 70, 84, 87, 101, 144
Martin V, Pope, 287, 288
Martin of Tours, St., 40, 81
Mary, St., 137–138

"Mary Church" (Anchen), 78, 79
Mathematics, 61, 109
Matilda, Empress (wife of Geoffrey
    Plantagenet), 130, 206
"Mayor" of Carolingian Household, 68
Mecca, 52–53, 54
Medici, house of, 304–305, 306
Medicine, 61, 254, 256
Medina, 53, 54, 55
Melfi, Treaty of, 147
Mendicantism, 169–176
Mercia, 96
Merovingians, 43, 56, 67, 70, 72
Mesopotamia, 52
Middle classes, 15, 127
Middle Kingdom, 89, 105
Milan, 9, 13, 113, 127, 183, 187, 188, 197, 298,
    306
Military, see Army
Milvian Bridge, battle of, 7
Minerva, 6
Mining, 30
Minnesingers, 237–238
Minuscule, Carolingian, 82
Missi dominici, 5
Missionaries, 60, 296
    Arian, 8
    Benedictine, 50, 65, 68–69, 77
    Byzantine, 35–36
    Carolingian, 68–69
    Celtic-Christian, 44, 47–48, 69
    Dominican, 170
    Franciscan, 173
Moderate realism, Aristotle, 264, 272
Moissac, 244, 245
Monarchy, Capetian, 290
    Carolingian, 67–85 100
    English, 96–97, 99, 198, 201–220, 203, 204,
        206, 291–292, 284
    French, 96, 100, 104, 154, 168, 187, 197, 198,
        202, 212, 220–222, 284, 293
    German, 96, 105, 107–108, 154, 185, 196
    Papal, 179, 185, 186, 199
    Scandinavian, 94–95, 99
    Spanish, 295
Monasticism, Benedictine, 45–46, 65, 116–117
    Carolingian, 81
    Celtic, 44–45
    early, 10, 44–45
    high-medieval, 162–166, 178, 179, 181
Mongolia, 36, 59–60, 301
Monophysitism, 27–28, 31, 54
Monotheism, 7, 52–53

St. Andrea, 321
Saint-Denis, monastery of, 72, 83, 222, 246, 250
Sainte-Foy, church of, 241, 243
Saint-Maclou, 314
St. Mark's, Venice, 29
St. Vitale, Ravenna, 29, 30, 32
Saladin, 154
Salerno, 110, 112, 148, 185
  University of, 256
Salians, 109, 185, 187
Sancta Sophia, Cathedral of, 29, 31–32, 33, 181
Sant' Apollinare Nuovo, Ravenna, 29
Saracens, see Islam
Savonarola, 321
Saxons, 16, 19, 22, 75–77, 105
Saxony, 85, 91, 184, 187
  duke of, 157, 297
Scandinavia, 36, 46, 56, 58, 91, 92, 95, 299
Schism, 287, 288
Scholasticism, 61, 260, 309
Schools, cathedral, 163, 253
  monastic, 80, 81, 83, 253
  parish, 116. See also Education
Science, 109, 145, 268, 273–275, 310, 322
Scientific method, 274
Scotland, 44, 91, 220
Sculpture, 245, 248, 316, 319
Scutage, 134, 207
Seine, 93
Sens, Cathedral of, 251
Serbia, 301
Serfs, 104, 115, 116, 140. See also Peasant life
Sforza, house of, 306
Sheriffs, 202–203, 205, 209, 218
Shi'ism, 55, 60
Shires, 202
Siberia, 67
Sic et Non (Abelard), 266
Sicilian Vespers, War of, 197
Sicily, 60, 147–150, 152, 191, 193–194, 195, 197, 295
Siena, 197
Siger of Brabant, 262
Simeon Stylites, St., 45
Simony, 179, 180, 183
Slaves, 6, 7, 14, 40, 58, 59, 67, 115, 132, 137, 140
Slavs, 34, 35, 65, 75, 299
Social conditions, early, Carolingian, 84–85
  Germanic, 40–41
  high-medieval, 126–141

Roman, 14–15
Scandinavian, 94–95
Soissons, 72
"Song of Brother Sun" (St. Francis), 174, 239
Song of Roland, 75, 231, 233
Southern Italy, 77, 147–150, 191
Spain, 19, 22, 34, 42, 43, 52, 56, 59, 75, 81, 90, 109, 112, 144–146, 157, 167, 173, 231, 237, 284, 295–297
Spanish March, 75, 145
Speculum Majus, (Vincent of Beauvais), 268
Spiritual Franciscans, 175, 286
"Statute on the Burning of Heretics," 286
Statutes of Laborers, 307
Stephen of Blois, King, 206, 207
Stigmata, 175
Studium Generale, 253–254
Stupor Mundi, see Frederick II, Emperor
Succession, Carolingian, 67–68, 87–89
  English, 99–100, 203, 206, 212
  German, 185, 193, 196, 197, 297
  Merovingian, 43
  Papal, 287
Suetonius, 72
Sufism, 60
Suger, Abbot, 222, 246, 250
Summa Theologica (St. Thomas Aquinas), 270–272, 309
Summas, 269
Sutri, Synod of, 181
Swabia, 105, 187, 188
Swedes, 91, 94
Syllogism, 260
Sylvester II, Pope, 109
Syria, 25, 27, 34, 35, 52, 54, 55, 59, 60, 152, 153, 154

Tacitus, 16
Tallage, 132
Tancred de Hauteville, 146–147
Tannenberg, battle of, 299
Tartary, 170
Taxation, 116
  Byzantine, 25, 26
  Carolingian, 85, 102, 111
  ecclesiastical, 91, 198, 199, 286–87, 288
  English, 198, 204, 205, 207, 213, 214, 215, 220
  French, 198, 199, 227, 293
  German, 187, 196
  high-medieval, 141, 143
  Islamic, 59, 60
  Roman Imperial, 14, 15, 40–41